AYURVEDIC COOKING
FOR WESTERNERS:

Familiar Western Food Prepared With Ayurvedic Principles

Other Lotus Press books by Amadea Morningstar

The Ayurvedic Cookbook
A Personalized Guide to Good Nutrition and Health,
with Urmila Desai

Breathe Free
Nutritional and Herbal Care for Your Respiratory System,
with Daniel Gagnon

Lotus Press
Twin Lakes, Wisconsin

AYURVEDIC COOKING FOR WESTERNERS:

*Familiar Western Food Prepared
With Ayurvedic Principles*

by Amadea Morningstar

Illustrations by Robin Noren

Lotus Press
Twin Lakes, Wisconsin

DISCLAIMER

This book is not intended to treat, diagnose or prescribe. The information contained herein is in no way to be considered as a substitute for your own inner guidance, or consultation with a duly licensed health care professional.

Permission to reprint "Dream Cookies" from *The Allergy Self-Help Cookbook,* © 1984 by Marjorie Hurt Jones is kindly granted by Rodale Press, Inc; Emmaus, PA 18098.

Permission to reprint "Ama-Reducing Dal", "Santa Fe Pinto Beans", the table on tastes, and revised versions of Discovering Your Constitution and Enlarged Food Guidelines for Basic Constitutional Types from *The Ayurvedic Cookbook,* © 1990 by Amadea Morningstar and Urmila Desai is kindly granted by the co-authors and Lotus Press, Silver Lake, WI 53170.

Permission to reprint quotes from Verna Williamson and Florencio Siquiera de Cravalho at the 1993 Bioneers Seeds of Change Conference in San Francisco is kindly granted by Seeds of Change, Santa Fe, New Mexico 87506-5700.

Parts of the introduction first appeared as an article on Ayurvedic cooking in *Yoga International*, July/August 1994.

A portion of the proceeds from this book support food relief, reforestation and local and global regeneration projects.

Text and illustrations copyright by Amadea Morningstar a.k.a. Robin Noren

Cover art, interior and cover design and additional illustrations: Jan Salerno

Page composition: Paul Bond, Art & Soul Design

First Edition, 1995

Printed in the United States of America

Library of Congress Cataloging-in-Publication-Data
Morningstar, Amadea, 1952 -
      Ayurvedic Cooking for Westerners: Familiar western food prepared with Ayurvedic principles / by Amadea Morningstar
      includes bibliographical references.
      ISBN 0-914955-14-4   94-79592
                                          CIP

Published by:
      Lotus Press, P.O. Box 325, Twin Lakes, Wisconsin 53181

Printed on recycled paper.

Dedication

To my mother and stepfather, Margie S. Noren and Ward Shepard
with much love and thanks

In loving memory of my father Robert B. Noren

and

to Ayurveda
with much thanks

ACKNOWLEDGEMENTS

I would very much like to thank:
All the friends who ate
All the clients and students who questioned
Nirankar Agarwal
LaVon Alt
Neem Karoli Baba
Elders Thomas and Fermina Banyacya, Sr., and David Monongye
Ivy and Lenny Blank
Paul Bond
Gordon Bruen, the Wise and Wonderful
Iza Bruen-Morningstar the Great
Dolores Chiappone
Jim, Dahlia, Anasha, and Rosalinda Cummings
Yogi Amrit and Urmila Desai
The Devas and Spirits of Nature
Everyone at Desert Montessori
Evie
David Frawley & Margo Gal
Roberto Gallegos and Lucy Moore
Concha Garcia
Liz Halford and Paul Botell
Michele the Blessed, and the Herling clan
Margie, Stephen and Ian Hughes
Sunil & Shalmali Joshi (and Siddha)
S. K. Kamlesh
Matthew Kelly
Santosh and Doris Krinsky
Vasant and Usha Lad
Greg Lonewolf
Deborah Madison
Missy, Laura, Pat, Rosie and the gang
The McBrides
All the Norens and Schmidts
Shamaan Ochaum
Joanne Rijmes the Marvelous
Melanie Sachs
Jan Salerno
Everyone at the Santa Fe Public Library
Bob Schrei and Donna Thomson
Morrnah Simeona and Stanley Hew Len
Spiderwoman Theater
David Stark
Robert Svoboda
Mary Ann Szydlowski
Rebekah, Ignacio and Selina Trujillo
Zenia Victor and Gaylon Duke
Angela Werneke
KinTree Whitecloud
The Wilkes, the Hankletanks, the LaVails, Bill and Julia et. al.
Rebecca Wood

TABLE OF CONTENTS

A List of Tables

FOREWORD

I review cookbooks for several different magazines and so there's a continuous flow of new cookbooks across my desk. Many of the books are quickly recycled. The best are read and garner space in my office library to be used as reference or for an occasional recipe. There's one cookbook, however, on my kitchen shelf at an easy reach to the right of my range. Amadea Morningstar and Urmila Desai's *The Ayurvedic Cookbook* is close at hand. Its smudges and dog ears attest to steady use during the past several years. Now, having read Amadea's *Ayurvedic Cooking For Westerners*, I'm making space for one more in-the-kitchen book.

I'm interested in books that further individual and global health. I'm put off by nouvelle cuisine that flaunts new for the sake of being new—or bizarre for the sake of being bizarre. Despite any media blitzkrieg, I've no time for shoddy fads or con jobs. In terms of my digestion, I will pass on synthetic fats, bioengineered tomatoes and/or any other highly refined, manipulated, desecrated ersatz food. Instead, thank you, I subscribe to the theme underlying countless natural food cookbooks. Simple, unadulterated foods afford greater nourishment.

Ayurveda takes this obvious, bedrock truth one profound step further. It ups the game with a whole new paradigm. Apply Ayurvedic principles to the selection and preparation of basic food stuffs and they become medicinal to our whole being. This truth is hot. Pharmaceutical companies, beware. Your match, in the form of this modest book, is the ring.

This East Indian holistic approach provides a radically different mind-set than our Western "magic bullet" approach. Sure, the thought of any magic solutions to our problems is seductive. However, taking vitamin C to prevent a cold, or radiation to combat a cancer does not ameliorate the impact of a lousy diet and lifestyle. The real magic lies in right relationship.

What excites me about *Ayurvedic Cooking For Westerners* is that it bridges East and West. Amadea Morningstar melds her years of western clinical nutritional training with the wisdom of Ayurveda to provide the contemporary westerner with a system that enhances total health through our familiar daily foods. It's that simple. Ayurveda provides a 5,000 year old, time-tested system that succors body, mind, and spirit. By bringing harmony and balance, it is preventive medicine.

Fortunately this preventive medicine is in the form of comforting dishes like Savory Vegetable Pot Pie and Carrot Cake. My guests, my adolescent children and even their friends ask for seconds of this kind of medicine.

There are hungry times and social times when we welcome food as the gift it is without judging its quality. Indeed, much of the world's population hasn't the luxury of making food quality choices. For many of our meals, however, we can discern.

The more we bring to this discernment, the greater our potential gain. This is true of any relationship be it with food or another person. With Ayuveda we have an opportunity to learn how food's subtle properties affect constitution. This enables us to more fully celebrate food and more fully receive it as a gift from our mother earth.

To get started, take 5 minutes to determine your constitutional type (see page 283). Next, at your own pace experiment with the recipes and note how you feel after eating a dish balanced for your particular health. Bringing this awareness to your cooking may very well become one of the most important self-help tools you'll ever give yourself.

There are parts of Ayurveda with which I wrestle, for some of it flies in the face of my culinary proclivity such as the nixing of ferments and use of tropical and semi-tropical fruits for cooks in a temperate region. However, given the scope of the book, these concerns are small. Thankfully, the author's undogmatic approach encourages and supports me to go at my own pace and glean my own truths.

Possibly Ayurveda's most relevant truth for westerners is its emphasis on freshly prepared foods. I've not found this so clearly expressed in any other traditional cuisine. If you happen to suffer from low energy, mental confusion, illness or depression then go without fast food, junk food, leftovers, restaurant meals, and canned or frozen foods.

For readers looking merely for vegetarian recipes, *Ayurvedic Cooking For Westerners* is an effective book for it contains excellent and workable recipes. But like a many layered cake, it offers much more. Let's briefly look at the layers.

It is an easy introduction to Ayurveda. Applying Ayurvedic principles to your diet enables you to literally embody and integrate the principles, and it provides a useful philosophy for understanding other people and the natural realm.

Thanks to the symbols at the top right of each recipe, this book is also a helpful seasonal guide. Hedonist that I am, seasonal foods are fresher and therefore more flavorful. Additionally, seasonal foods are more apt to be regional foods and eating locally strengthens the local economy. As we all dwell in a specific time and environment, I find that favoring seasonal and local foods supports our ability to be present to this specific time and environment.

Ayurvedic Cooking For Westerners is a godsend to people suffering from food allergies and/or degenerative illnesses. In the words of Hippocrates, the father of medicine, "Let food be your medicine, let medicine be your food." Cooking Ayurvedically and with Amadea's input for specific conditions (see appendixes) enables this fine tuning of foods to ones individual constitution and therefore the return— or maintenance of—good health.

A last reason why *Ayurvedic Cooking For Westerners* holds together so harmoniously is the author's generous gift of herself. I've had the fortune of breaking bread with Amadea, and attest that the book aptly mirrors her gentle being and geocentric wisdom. As a reader, you will feel comfortable and at home in Amadea's earthy and healthy kitchen. Step right in.

Rebecca Wood

Author of *Quinoa the Super Grain*, and
Whole Foods Encyclopedia:
A Shoppers Guide

AN INTRODUCTION

I have been exploring and cooking with Ayurveda, the "science of life", for the last eleven years. I was first drawn to this ancient system of healing in 1983, as a Western nutritionist seeking a deeper sense of how foods heal. I was excited by Ayurveda's emphasis on the therapeutic importance of food, and its systemized approach to different foods for different people. Ayurveda's way of approaching each person as a unique individual with unique conditions slowly turned around how I practiced nutrition, some 240 degrees. In my twenty years in practice, I had been drawn especially to therapeutic nutrition, food and healing, so Ayurveda attracted me quite naturally.

Cooking plays a prominent part in this five-thousand-year-old East Indian system, which makes use of other diverse therapies such as yoga, meditation, astrology, and gem healing. Because food and digestion are so important in Ayurveda, foods which are fresh, light, tasty and easy to digest are considered essential both to daily life and to any of the healing regimes one might undertake.

An Ayurvedic diet makes generous use of a full spectrum of fresh vegetables, fruits, grains, legumes, and milk. It plays with herbs and spices the way a painter would with the colors on her or his palette. These herbs and spices, often common kitchen items like fresh ginger, cardamom, cinnamon, cumin, coriander, or fennel, are used to support agni, the digestive fire within us.

As Ayurveda becomes more popular in this country, more and more people want to cook in an Ayurvedic way. And yet there have been limited resources available to learn how to do this. This was a large impetus for creating this book. I wanted to help people be able to create healing meals for themselves, with familiar healthy foods. Often the words "Ayurvedic cooking" evoke (if they evoke anything at all!) the aroma of delicate vegetable curries, gentle kichadis, hot chappatis, light basmati rice. And these are in fact the cornerstones of traditional Ayurvedic cooking from India. But Ayurvedic cuisine can encompass a wide variety of other sorts of vegetarian dishes, so long as they are fresh, easy to digest, not fermented, and prepared with loving care. In fact, one of the principles of Ayurveda is to make use of the plants, herbs and foods of one's own region. Making a healing Ayurvedic meal is likely to be a lot easier than you might have imagined. And it can include many of your old favorites from childhood, properly prepared.

In Ayurveda, food is considered to affect the mind as well as the body. By understanding how to prepare foods best suited to our minds and bodies, we can utilize nutrition as a deeper source of healing. Our diets are largely under our own control, often more than we realize: no one else can eat for us. This can be profoundly empowering, when we realize "what a healing tool we have in our own pots", as my friend Chandrakant once said.

Once the concepts of cooking fresh, light vegetarian meals in an Ayurvedic way are grasped practically, the speed with which you can heal and balance can be tremendously encouraging. Ayurveda recognizes that there are different causes for conditions: genetic, congenital, metabolic, and so forth. Depending on the cause, diet will provide a striking difference in some conditions and in others may only offer relief from certain symptoms. Yet given the help I have seen it give to individuals in widely varying circumstances in my two decades of practice, I would urge you to try it.

It is my hope that you will begin to understand the simple beauty of Ayurvedic cooking, and be able to apply it readily in your own life. May you have a growing confidence in creating your own Ayurvedic meals. In time, you may even find yourself choosing an "Ayurvedic" meal out at a Japanese or Mexican restaurant, say, as your grasp of how to eat in an Ayurvedic way becomes more and more clear. For those of you who have developed an appreciation for East Indian cuisine, my desire is that this book offer a bridge between culinary traditions, and broaden an understanding of the principles of Ayurveda here in the West. There are many people who understand Ayurveda and Ayurvedic cooking better than I do; numerous issues remain to be explored. May this cookbook serve as a springboard for others, diving deeper and ranging wider.

Ayurveda is an earth-based medicine, with its foundations in nature. This is a very different way of looking at healing than we Westerners are used to. To give an example from another earth-based healing system: Westerners often imagine that native "weather makers" control the weather, ordering it to rain here or there, say. Nothing could be further from the truth. There is not a control or power relationship here; weather people do not <u>make</u> the forces of nature do their bidding in a particular way. Rather it is a friendly and co-operative process. Weather people work with friends. These friends are non-human nature energies or nature spirits or whatever you would like to call them. Because they are long-time friends, they respond to the requests of the weather person, who honors their independence. It is not a hierarchical or one-up kind of relationship. It is several beings working together.

In Western medicine the approach is to "make" our bodies well, with pills, shots, radiation, and so forth. But when you are truly working in an Ayurvedic way, this is not what you are doing. You're befriending your body, your vehicle, so that it and you can co-exist more smoothly. Neither bodies or nature spirits like to be pushed around. Perhaps you are involved in an Ayurvedic approach already, perhaps not. In any case, before you pop that Ayurvedic herbal preparation in your mouth, or brew up your next soup, think again. What is your intention here? What are you doing, how are you working with yourself?

Healing and balance inevitably bring up deeper issues of how Ayurveda and food relate to the planet and her health at this time. This is a profound concern for me, and so I have included thoughts and information about the Earth and her beings in boxes throughout the text. It is my deep hope that these questions and searchings will resonate in some way with your own, as we all live in this increasingly fragile world together. In its deepest aspects, Ayurveda is the science of how to live in harmony both with our bodies and our planet. In reality, they are not two, but one.

Something the Dalai Lama wrote last year in his foreword to *Tibet: Reflections from the Wheel of Life* touched a deep chord in me. He said, "Like the lotus which thrives in mud, the potential for realization grows in the rich soil of our everyday lives." Cooking, cleaning, breathing, how we respond to one another, are all part of this soil.

This work is a kind of coming out for me: a daring to go deeper, and a hoping that this book connects with kindred spirits wherever it is needed. Thank you for joining me.

Amadea Morningstar
Santa Fe, New Mexico
April, 1994

PART ONE

UNDERSTANDING AYURVEDIC COOKING

It is important to understand that Ayurveda is a healing science. How you eat is considered a major therapeutic tool, one of the most important things you can do to help yourself from an Ayurvedic perspective.

In Ayurvedic cooking, *first* you want to regularize absorption, assimilation and elimination. This is the most important offering an Ayurvedic cook can make: sharing foods which are easy to digest. As the Ayurvedic "eater", your first aim is to be able to take in what you are eating well and easily.

Next you work (with an Ayurvedic practitioner, traditionally) to correct any imbalances that need righting (your *vikruti*). Then, you can choose foods best suited to your physical constitution (your *prakruti, Vata, Pitta, Kapha*). But, as Dr. Sunil Joshi, an internationally recognized Ayurvedic physician, once told me most kindly and emphatically, first attend to appetite, digestion and elimination. Then work to balance the finer points of constitution.

To do this, the first step is to eat a primarily *sattvic* (pure, fresh) diet, avoiding *rajasic* (fiery) and *tamasic* (spoiled) foods in the main. *Sattvic* foods are fresh and light and help clear the mind. For more information about *sattva, rajas* and *tamas,* see p. 10.

So most importantly, you begin to eat foods which are fresher and purer. This means, too, foods free of additives, preservatives and pesticides as much as possible. Once you feel you are getting the hang of this much of the dance, you can begin to consider some of the subtler points of Ayurvedic food dynamics. Ayurveda appreciates food from a number of perspectives. A food's taste (*rasa*) is important, whether it is sweet, sour, salty, bitter, astringent, or pungent. Each of these six tastes has different effects on the body. And food has varying impacts on the body, from the time you first taste it (*rasa*), to the time it enters your stomach (*virya*), to the time it has been absorbed (*vipak*). Each of these dynamics is considered when an Ayurvedic physician suggests a particular food. Will it relax you, will it stimulate you, will it warm you or sooth you? All of these questions are important.

In the ideal therapeutic setup, an individual working with an Ayurvedic way of eating gets to eat foods which are soothing to both the mind and body. (Contrast this with the many parts of our world, where an individual is lucky if s/he gets to eat at all.) And contrast this with the food which is typically available and advertised here in America. The vast majority of foods available to us on this planet are *sattvic* with sweet *vipak*. These are also the preferred foods from an Ayurvedic standpoint (see Table 5 p. 24). However, we are often and repeatedly given—or choose—foods in an American diet which are neither *sattvic* nor easy on the digestion: hard cheeses, ice cream, tomato-based foods being familiar examples.

We have acquired such a taste for these that it can take a good amount of persever-
ance to steer our boats in other directions. And this is a large part of what I wish to
offer here, relatively easy ways to begin to direct your habits and "vehicles" toward
healthy shores.

A BIT OF ORIENTATION

I begin with a discussion of the five elements, key to the practice of Ayurvedic
cooking. We then explore food and mind in the form of *sattva*, *rajas* and *tamas*,
a beginning point in Ayurvedic cuisine. There is then an explanation of food and
some of its effects on digestion, including post-digestive effect. I finish this introduction to Ayurvedic cooking with a brief section on constitution. There are a
number of fine books about Ayurvedic constitution, and it seemed unnecessary
to repeat them here. **Playing with Food** follows, which are all the recipes, which
I do hope you'll enjoy, both as a cook and an "eater".

In the Appendices, a lot of information lurks. If you've heard about Ayurvedic
constitution, *prakruti,* and are curious about beginning to understand what constitutional type you might be, there is info and a questionnaire to assess yourself
in Appendix I. If you know your constitutional type, but aren't clear about the kinds
of foods best suited to your constitution, there's a lot of information about that in
Appendix II. Tridoshic, *Vata*-calming, *Pitta*-calming, and *Kapha*-calming menus
can be found in Appendix IV.

In traditional Ayurvedic medicine, allergies comprise little if any of the attention.
Ayurveda was developed some four to five thousand years ago, in a world much
different than ours today. We were not producing chemicals by the ton then, or
setting off radioactive weapons for "practice". These actions have had a damaging
effect on beings, including human beings. I have seen ancient Ayurvedic approaches be of a great deal of help here, in strengthening immune systems and
assisting the gut in functioning more effectively. (Though it is no substitute for
working together as communities to stop the destructive processes in our midsts.)
In my own life and practice a number of years ago, I began to use modern rotation
diets in conjunction with Ayurveda, for people with food and/or environmental
sensitivities. In extreme cases rotation diets can be particularly useful, so I include
information in Appendix V for people who want to work with them. I also spent
time developing these vegetarian rotation meals, because even the excellent
books about allergies that I know of offer little, if anything, for vegetarians with
allergies. I need to say, though, that simply cleaning up one's diet and working
with a good Ayurvedic physician can do much to help milder allergies, and a
rotation diet may prove unnecessary in such cases. Entries like,*ROTATION DAY

1 DISH, related to this system of help for allergies. There is more information in Appendix V for those who are interested.

In struggling with my own food and mold sensitivities, I had moved back a number of years ago into occasional meals of chicken or fish simply to keep some kind of nutritional equilibrium inside. I am grateful to Dr. Sunil Joshi of Nagpur for many perspectives, including help in discovering ways to effectively heal Candida in a vegetarian way. A summary of this Ayurvedic approach to Candida can be found on page 233. I want to thank Dr. Shalmali Joshi for her clear and grounded review of this material on Candida for accuracy. (Any errors are, of course, my own.)

Polarity Therapy is a rising new healing practice in the West, based on ancient concepts from Ayurvedic and Chinese medicine. I was fortunate to be able to teach in a Polarity Therapy program this last year, and was struck by the many similarities between Polarity and Ayurveda. Many of the recipes in this cookbook are appropriate for a Polarity program. I have included a little bit of information about this healing science in Appendix VI, with lists of recipes you can use in a Polarity program. **POLARITY PURIFYING DIET DISH or **POLARITY HEALTH BUILDING DISH at the end of recipes, lets you know they make good Polarity dishes, as well as Ayurvedic ones.

Ultimately, though, food needs to taste good. In fact, this is a chief Ayurvedic premise! So, bon appetit!

THE FIVE ELEMENTS *(PANCHA MAHABHUTAS)*

At the core of Ayurveda is the five elements, *pancha mahabhutas*. Our bodies are made of the five elements, and we dissolve back through the five elements as we die. The five elements make up our food, our shelter, our clothing. Each of the five elements underlies the course of our health and healing. The elements are an important key to understanding how Ayurveda is structured, for they are the underpinnings of taste, constitution and all physical function. Some readers may wonder what the five elements have to do with their health and bodies. While I have said that we and our bodies are a part of nature, that is not the viewpoint with which many of us have been raised. It can be a challenge to release the old ideas of separateness encouraged by Western culture. We respond to the same laws of the elements as every one and every thing else, whether we are aware of it or not.

For example, say you are out on a camping trip; you've built a fire. The fire gets a little too big and hot. To calm it down, you can use either water or earth to bring it back to the size you need. If you want to put out the fire entirely, you use a lot of earth or water to douse it. You are applying basic laws of the elements here. The same laws operate within your own body. If your fire inside gets too big, out of balance, heat and pain result, in the form of ulcers, inflammation or fever. To calm this raging fire, you need more sweet earthy foods or fluids. If you take too much of these, you may douse your digestive fire entirely, and need to begin again to build it up. These are the kinds of issues with which Ayurvedic medicine works.

So what are all of the five elements? Ether *(akash)*, air *(vayu)*, fire *(tejas)*, water *(ap)*, and earth *(prithvi)*. Ether *(akash)* is the element which allows all other elements to manifest. It relates to space, the void, the ever expanding universe. In Samkhya philosophy it is said that ether arises directly out of the unmanifested reality through the soundless sound of *aum*. It was the first element to manifest, the element which then manifested as all the other elements. Space provides the room for everything to happen. Ether manifests within our bodies as our "spaces", bladder, lungs, stomach, even the spaces within our cells. Without space we lack the room to function in this realm. And so it is a basic beginning for all manifestation: we need a "parking spot" within this dimension in which to land. In the indigenous traditions of this continent, the Four Directions and the Above and the Below are honored. In this honoring, space, the void, the Ether element, is described. Ether plays a part in bitter taste, and in the constitutional type *Vata*. (No, *Vata* and "space case" are not identical! Just sometimes.)

The second element, air *(vayu)*, moves like the wind, quick, restless, constantly changing. And like our minds, quick, restless, constantly changing. Never stopping, never pausing, always moving. Like ether it is cool, light, dry. "Air is Ether in action," as Dr. Vasant Lad has said. From an Ayurvedic perspective, air underlies all bodily functions, because it is what moves substances and processes. It is intimately involved with the functions of the mind, the nervous system, the gut. It activates the senses (through the nervous system) and initiates most biological transformations. Indigenous peoples of North America call wind the gossip, because it is always moving around, spreading everyone's news, if you take the time to stop and listen. Like wind, air is the messenger, in all parts of the body. It is in fact the messenger for all five elements, and between all five elements. If the air element is impaired for some reason in our bodies, stoppages, blockages, miscommunications can occur. If it is overpowerful, we may be on the run all the time—our minds, our mouths, or our guts. The air element is present in the three tastes: pungent, bitter and astringent. And it plays a strong role in *Vata* constitution. Sometimes you may encounter individuals (or institutions) that are fond of the drama of high wind. When the wind is blowing hard, everything looks dramatic, exciting. As the wind calms down, so does the environment around it, becoming more peaceful. Not everyone enjoys this serenity. Some prefer the excitement and tension of a high wind state. Some people even attempt to fan the air element, making a big commotion over small things. This can increase excitement, but also fear and anxiety. Television operates in this style a great deal, in the way it covers events and issues.

The third element, fire *(tejas)*, is a transformative energy. It can turn raw vegetables into a soup, or grain into a dessert. In Ayurveda, it is the force behind our ability to digest food, in the form of digestive fire, *agni*. With the right amount of fire present in our bodies, in balance to all the other elements, we digest smoothly and well. Too little, things sit there in the gut. Too much, foods can charge through too quickly or with inflammatory reactions. Fire warms us. It can preserve or destroy us. Fire is much honored in Ayurveda for its creative action, this ability to make a relatively inedible raw grain into an easily assimilated dish. Fire is what brings the light to our eyes, the brightness to our minds, the warmth to our bellies. Sunlight is the fire of our solar system, the sustainer of our worlds. Fire plays a part in three tastes: sour, salty and pungent. It is intimately connected with the constitutional type *Pitta*. Fire has the capacity to stimulate—or burn out—the growth potential of seeds. For example, after a fire, a meadow may sprout wildflowers unseen in twenty years. These long-dormant species were stimulated to grow by the heat of the fire. On the other hand, that blackened unpopped kernel of popcorn at the bottom of your snack bowl will never birth a new ear of corn, no matter how you plant it and tend it. Similarly, in the face of emergency conditions, the body can respond with fever, to burn out the seeds of disease and infection.

Water *(ap)* flows. This fourth element, water, is a tremendous part of our globe, in terms of how much space it occupies on the earth's surface. Like the planet we live on, our bodies contain large amounts of water, in the form of many varying fluids with widely differing functions. Blood, saliva, lymph, digestive juices, these are all manifestations of water. When water is pure, life moves smoothly and with joy. When water is less than pure, immunity suffers, blood can become weak, kidneys struggle—and so can we. When there is too much water, we can be swept away, swollen, or worn down. When there is too little, our tissues can become desiccated or old before their time. Water is a nurturing force, one which supports growth. The presence of water is seen in processes with a unit-by-unit increase, a steady growth. It is also a powerful cleanser. When it is in harmony with all the other elements, it produces rain, dew, a healthy amount of humidity. Water flows; it needs to flow. Water is also like a mirror. It can reflect back to us what we need to see, about ourselves and others. Water is strongly present in the tastes sweet and salty. It manifests in the constitutional type *Kapha*, and also in the *prakruti Pitta*. After deep rains, long-hidden seeds can sprout. This can be advantageous or a problem, depending on the types of seeds. Similarly in Ayurveda we consider what kinds of seeds we are nurturing. We want to water the seeds of health, not disease.

The fifth element, earth *(prithvi)*, is a grounding force in our lives. It is the ground on which we live, the homes in which we dwell, the soil in which we grow. Earth is solid, heavy, not quick to move. It provides foundations for our creations. It is the solid substance of who we are, the nitty gritty bones and teeth and skin of it. When earth is in short supply in our bodies, it is easy to wander. When earth element is excessive, it can become easy to get stuck, or repeat the same programs and routines over and over again. Change does not come readily to earth. It needs the assistance of air, fire and water to make its moves. An earthquake has decades in its making. Earth element shows up in the tastes sweet, sour and astringent. And in the constitutional type *Kapha*. Food in general has a lot of the earth element in it. So if we overeat, take in too much earth, we are likely to increase our mass, and/or douse our digestive fire. (Think of the unseemly flatulence you have probably never experienced after an overly ambitious potluck or buffet.) Each of the elements needs to be used in proper balance in our bodies for healthy living.

While we take each element one at a time for understanding's sake, in reality they work together in the creation of the natural world. There is dust in the wind. Rain is not made through the forces of water alone, but in conjunction with air and earth as well. Likewise, when I say, for example, that fire is an important part of *Pitta* constitution, I mean that it has a predominant or strong part. All of the elements can be found in someone of *Pitta* constitution, not just fire. The five elements *(Pancha Mahabhutas)* make up a whole.

Dr. Sunil Joshi, in a recent series of lectures about Ayurveda and *Pancha Karma* in Santa Fe, gave a good example of how all five elements are involved in the process of growth. Imagine a seed, small and hard. You plant it in the earth. As *akash*, ether, enters into it, initiating its growth process, the seed begins to expand in all directions with moisture from the earth. This expansion in all directions is the nature of *akash*, ether. Then *vayu*, air, shows up in the process, as the emerging sprout begins to change direction and move in one direction. Air begins to limit the expression of ether. And with air comes change, and movement in a single direction. As *tejas*, fire, enters into the equation, the outer covering of the seed breaks open. To do this, a pH change must take place, the seed must become more acidic and its temperature must rise. Acidity and warmth are both properties of the fire element. Then the tiny seedling, as it breaks through the earth, adds mass and volume, unit by unit, as it incorporates more fluid. This unit by unit increase and incorporation of fluid are both qualities of the water element, *ap. Prithvi*, the earth element, is seen as the plant matures into a full tree, with deeply entrenched roots and strong solid bark. You can see this same sequence of events in any natural process. In Ayurveda the five elements are the main elements with which one works, and their sequence never changes. Everything is created by the *Pancha Mahabhutas*.

TABLE 1

THE ELEMENTS	TASTES	CONSTITUTION	SENSES*
Ether	bitter	*Vata*	hearing
Air	bitter astringent pungent	*Vata*	touch
Fire	pungent sour salty	*Pitta*	sight
Water	salty sweet	*Kapha* *Pitta*	taste
Earth	sweet sour astringent	*Kapha*	smell

* *Note: A good discussion of the elements and the senses can be found in* Ayurveda: The Science of Self-Healing, *by Dr. Vasant Lad (Lotus Press, 1984).*

FOOD AND MIND:

SATTVA, RAJAS AND TAMAS

Ayurveda embraces the whole person, soul, mind and body. Each of these is understood to impact the others. Practically, when cooking with Ayurveda, the cook considers the meal's impact on the mind as well as the body. The assumption is that with a clear mind and a healthy body, one can more easily fulfill one's soul purposes as well. In these days when much of the mass culture's media seems designed to confuse rather than enlighten, to stupefy or stultify us rather than motivate us to true service, our own efforts to keep ourselves clear and lively are especially important. The demands of life in the late twentieth century are crazy-making enough without us making ourselves worse!

My roots thus exposed, I'd like to talk a little bit about how Ayurveda approaches food. As mind is considered the builder, let us look at mind first. As Dr. Sunil Joshi has said, "Mind has three properties, *sattva, raja and tama*. All three properties are contained in every mind, not just one. Anything in this world has to have all these properties to have existence in the world . . .*Sattva* gives us curiosity, the ability to think, the desire to wake up. *Raja* gives us the urge to re-organize, to work, to push, to manifest. *Tama* gives us the desire to rest, to stop. We must stop somewhere!" In the manifestation of any project, we need *sattva* to design the plan, *raja* to re-organize and initiate its physical manifestation, and *tama* to complete it, to not continue building forever. In cooking, when *sattva* is manifesting, you plan the meal, open the windows, clean out your house, and light the candles in preparation for your guests. With *raja* you cook the meal, make the final preparations and set the table. With *tama* you say, "Enough! I'm done cooking! Let's sit and eat!"

In Ayurveda, foods are also used to support and bring out these three qualities of mind. Foods which support *sattva* are called *sattvic* foods; those which draw out *raja, rajasic* foods; and those which increase *tama, tamasic* foods.

Foods to help the mind become clear and stay focussed are highly valued. Such foods are *sattvic* in nature, or truth inspiring. *Sattvic* foods include most fresh vegetables, most fresh fruits, most freshly prepared grains, a good number of beans, milk, sweet cream, freshly made yogurt, mother's milk, ghee and butter in moderation, most nuts, seeds,and cold-pressed oils, and a good number of natural sweeteners. This is not to say that anyone following this diet will become instantly incorruptible, but if your intention is to get clear and stay clear, these foods will help. They calm the mind and help to establish a middle path through the confusing array of dietary possibilities available to us. A detailed list of *sattvic* foods follows in Table 2.

Eating in a *sattvic* way has a definite impact on each constitutional type. Enhancing *sattva* in *Vata* tends to support a calmer more peaceful mind and body. In *Pitta*, it makes it easier to manage impatience and irritability, again, enhancing calm and peace. In *Kapha*, a sattvic diet supports lightness and flexibility, as well as strengthening *Kapha's* innate quietness of mind.

Energetically, *rajasic* foods stimulate more fire, outward motion, creativity, aggression, passion. They are good foods for stirring up trouble or spurring on the dragons within. Traditionally in Ayurveda they were recommended for warriors before battle. A bit of these could be helpful if you were about to do battle with a tradition-entrenched bureaucrat, for example, to save an ancient forest. However, if your main intention is to stay calm and stick with the most cogent points,persuading through depth, integrity and sheer persistence, the *sattvic* foods will serve you best. *Rajasic* foods can enliven your tongue but will sometimes leave your brain behind! They include most fermented foods, including yogurt or kefir which has not been freshly made, garlic, peppers of all kinds, eggs, cheeses, white sugar, most sweeteners, some beans, avocado, salt, radishes, citrus, peanut, fructose, and other foods listed in Table 2.

Before you race to your refrigerator to toss out all that offending upstart sort of food, let me intercede. A bit of these foods can be used in meals with little ill effect and good enhancement of flavor. A couple of cloves of garlic per person per week, for example, would not be considered overboard at all by most Ayurvedic physicians. Avocados can be an excellent warming and grounding food, in the appropriate circumstances. If, however, you live on coffee, green chili, ketchup, or sugar, you may want to look again at how you eat. It is possible your "contentious factor" is high.

Speaking of contention, let us move on to that third category of Ayurvedic foods with a major impact on mind, the *tamasic* foods. *Tamasic* foods are those which increase inner darkness and confusion. They are good for numbing us out, depressing us, slowing us down, and enhancing inertia. "Couch potato" mentality is one apt example of a *tamasic* state (not to insult the noble and *sattvic* potato). *Tamasic* foods include most fast foods, fried foods, frozen foods, microwaved foods, processed foods, leftover night foods, alcohol, drugs, chemicals, onions, mushrooms, lard, meat, fish, and poultry. Again, before you attack your friend eating that mushroom omelet (or yourself), relax. Take a deep breath. There are degrees to this *adhidaivic* (*sattvic-rajasic-tamasic*) topic. Steamed mushrooms are likely to have a much milder effect on mental function than, say, a frozen steak which has been fried, rechilled, microwaved, then washed down with a hearty Manhattan cocktail.

And before you start taking yourself to task for that last frozen meal you fixed, again, slow down. This is information. It is okay to use it for your own benefit, you do not have to use it against yourself. (As I write this, my 4-year-old daughter has developed a deep-seated passion for frozen tofu pups, and turkey dogs, hardly my idea of exemplary.) Any urges you have for fresh food, let yourself notice and act on. And if you find your freezer section having less and less in it, you can know you're on the right track to a healthier lifestyle.

This is fine said on a full and happy belly. But what about when you're desperate to couch potato out with couch potato foods? Not the end of the world. Trust yourself and make your choices. It's like you're in a painting class and you've just gotten a recommendation from your painting instructor. Say they've said, if you put more red in this painting you're doing, it would bring out its depth. Great, you might consider putting some more red in this work. It doesn't mean you need to paint the whole painting red. There can be contrasts, plays of light. There need to be! Not every single item of your diet needs to be *sattvic*, unless you want it to be so. If the bulk of your choices are *sattvic*, that's great.

If you take a look at our culture at present, you can see that as a people we are eating tremendous amounts of *rajasic* and *tamasic* foods: ketchup, burgers, french fries, frozen dinners, processed yogurt, and so forth. We eat very little fresh food any more. From an Ayurvedic perspective, there is a connection between how we are eating and how we are acting, our levels of violence, crime and depression as a people.

In closing, in speaking to you as an individual, I'm someone who has taken comfort in categories. Categories can be helpful, they let us know where we stand in some realms. But sometimes rather than helping us get safe inside, they bedevil us, drive us to draw boxes around life experiences that are better left unboxed. These particular categories of *sattva*, *rajas* and *tamas* are core, essential, in most approaches to Ayurvedic cooking. But they are only categories. Let them be your friends rather than your masters.

TABLE 2: SATTVIC, RAJASIC AND TAMASIC FOODS

SATTCIC FOODS

Aduki beans
Alfalfa sprouts
Almonds
Amaranth
Apple
Apricot pits
Apricot
Artichoke
Arugula (in moderation)
Asparagus
Banana, ripe
Barley
Basmati rice
Bean sprouts of all kinds
Bee pollen
Beets
Black beans
Black-eyed peas
Blackberries
Blueberries
Brazil nuts
Broad beans

Broccoli
Brussels sprouts
Buckwheat
Butter
Buttermilk, fresh
Cabbage, green
Cabbage, red
Cantaloupe
Carob
Carrots
Cashew nuts
Cauliflower
Celery
Chard
Cherry, sour
Cherry, sweet
Chestnuts
Chinese yams
Coconut, ripe
Coconut, unripe
Collards
Corn, fresh

Cornmeal
Cranberries
Cream, sweet
Cucumber
Dates, fresh
Dewberries
Endive
Escarole
Fava beans
Fenugreek sprouts
Fig, fresh
Fig, dried
Filberts
Flowers, edible, if sweet taste
Fruit juices, freshly made*
Ghee in moderation
Grapefruit
Grapes
Green beans
Green peas
Hickory nuts
Honey, raw

Honeydew melon
Jerusalem artichoke
Kale
Kohlrabi
Lentils, black
Lentils, tan
Lettuce
Lima beans in moderation
Loganberries
Macadamia nuts
Mango, ripe
Maple syrup
Milk, fresh, raw, pure
Millet
Mother's milk
Mung dal, split
Mung beans, whole
Mustard greens
Navy beans in moderation
Nectarines
Oats
Okra

TABLE 2 CONTINUED

SATTVIC FOODS (cont.)

Oranges, sweet	Potato, all colors	Soy beans	Turnip
Papaya	Prunes	Soy milk, freshly prepared	Walnuts, English
Parsnip	Pumpkin	Spinach	Walnuts, black
Peaches	Quinoa	Strawberries	Watercress
Pecans	Raisins	Sugar cane, raw	Watermelon
Pine nuts	Raspberries	Summer squash	Wheat
Pineapple, sweet	Rice	Sunflower seeds	Wild rice
Pinto beans	Rutabaga	Sweet potatoes	Winter squash
Plum, sour	Sesame seeds, hulled	Tangerines, sweet	Yams
Plum, sweet	Sesame seeds, unhulled	Teff	Yogurt, fresh
Pomegranate	Sorghum	Tepary beans	Zucchini

RAJASIC FOODS

Any canned, sweetened fruit	Dates, dried	Garbanzo beans	Lentils, red
Avocado	Egg, yolk	Garlic	Lime
Brewer's yeast	Egg, white	Green peas, dried, in excess	Malt syrup
Buttermilk, not freshly made	Egg, whole	Guava	Mango, unripe
Cheeses, hard, salted	Eggplant	Ice cream	Molasses
Cheeses, hard, unsalted	Fermented foods of all kinds	Jaggery	Olives, black
Chile	Flowers, edible, pungent in taste	Kefir, not freshly made	Olives, green
Cottage cheese	Fructose	Kidney beans	Peanut oil
Date sugar	Fruit juices, bottled	Lemon	Peanuts

TABLE 2 CONTINUED

RAJASIC FOODS (cont.)

Peppers	Rhubarb	Soy milk, boxed or bottled	Tomates
Pickles	Rice bran syrup	Sugar, refined	Vinegar
Pistachios, salted	Ricotta cheese	Sugar, white	Yogurt, not freshly made
Pumpkin seeds	Salt of all kinds	Sugar, brown	
Radishes	Sour cream	Sugar cane juice	

TAMASIC FOODS

Alcohol	Frozen foods	Microwaved foods	Rabbit
Beef	Fruit juices, frozen	Milk, homogenized	Shallots
Chicken	Goat	Milk, pasteurized	Shellfish
Drugs	Ice cream	Milk, powdered	Texturized vegetable protein
Fast foods	Lamb	Mushrooms of all kinds	Turkey
Fish, saltwater	Lard	Onion, raw	Venison
Fish, freshwater	Leeks	Onion, cooked	
Fowl	Leftovers	Onion, green	
Fried foods	Margarine	Pork	

A DISCLAIMER!

Please know that these specific food categorizations can be, and are, disputed. There is a healthy amount of disagreement even amongst the Ayurvedic classics on the exact properties of one food or another. Some will say garlic is tamasic, another that onion is rajasic. The main intention here is to begin to give you an idea of these concepts, with concrete examples. Some of the examples may arouse argument in the alert or opinionated.

FOOD AND DIGESTION:

RASA, VIRYA AND VIPAK

RASA

Taste is an important way to assess food in Ayurvedic practice. Ayurveda considers six tastes or *rasas*. These include sweet, sour, salty, bitter, astringent, and pungent. *Rasa* is how food first tastes to us in our mouths; it is experienced directly through our perception.

Each of the tastes has different qualities, which affect our bodies differently. Sweet taste *(madhura rasa)* is cool, moist and heavy, and enhances those qualities inside us. If you tend to be hot and dry inside, sweet can be a welcome counterpoint. Some foods with a sweet taste are honey, maple syrup, apples, milk. A little bit of sweet taste is often used in Ayurveda to calm and sooth a condition, or to act as a medium for bitter medicinal herbs. Sweet taste is pleasing, softening, relaxing. It calms *Vata* and *Pitta* and in excess increases *Kapha*.

Sour taste *(amla rasa)* is hot, wet and heavy in its action in the body. One thing this means is that sour foods can increase heat or moisture inside the body. Specifically, sour taste will increase salivation and appetite. In excess, sour foods might aggravate an ulcer (hot) or a case of water retention (wet). Sour foods include pickles, citrus fruits, tomatoes, and yogurt. Sour foods are not recommended a great deal in Ayurveda, and yet when they are, it is often to calm a situation of excess air. For example, fresh yogurt or buttermilk might be recommended for a light bony person with a fair amount of gas. Sour taste soothes *Vata* and in excess imbalances *Pitta* and *Kapha*.

Salty taste *(lavana rasa)* is heating, moist and heavy as well, with a fairly strong tendency to cause us to hold on to water. Some salty foods are sea vegetables, salt itself and anything heavily salted. Moderate amounts of salt are used in Ayurveda to stimulate digestive fire and provide some grounding, particularly for *Vata dosha*. It calms *Vata* and in excess aggravates *Kapha* and *Pitta*.

Bitter taste *(tikta rasa)* is cold, light, dry. Few foods are exclusively bitter, which is perhaps fortunate, because this taste is said to dominate all the others! Usually bitter taste occurs in small amounts and is more often found in medicinal herbs than foodstuffs. It has a pronounced action on the body. Dark leafy greens, the herb gentian and Swedish stomach bitters are three examples of foods with a fair amount of bitter in them. Bitter foods are used to lighten and cool the body. In moderate amounts, bitter taste promotes appetite and is used to clear the palate. In excess it can produce drying of the mouth and other tissues. It soothes *Pitta* and *Kapha* and aggravates *Vata*.

Astringent taste *(kashaya rasa)* is also cool, light and dry, but with milder effects than bitter. Foods with noticeable astringency include pomegranates, persimmons and blackberries. Astringent foods are valued for their medicinal qualities, and their abilities to calm the constitutional types *Pitta* and *Kapha*. Astringent foods promote clarity; in excess they can create pain or stiffness and aggravate *Vata*.

Pungent taste *(katu rasa)* is hot, light and drying in action. Some pungent foods include chile, onion and garlic. Pungency is applied in small amounts to stimulate salivation and *agni* (digestive fire) and to burn out an undesired parasite or germ. An excess aggravates *Pitta* and can cause headache and/or inflammation. Pungent taste helps dry out moist *Kapha*. A little pungency is fine for *Vata*, but an excess can irritate or desiccate this *dosha*.

In Ayurveda it is often said, "eat as much bitter and astringent taste as you like; have sweet and salty taste in smaller amounts; and sour and pungent foods in the least amounts." You can see how sometimes this might be meant as a bit of a joke, because most of the bitter and astringent foods we would not naturally eat by the gallon! And yet it is also serious, reflecting the trust Ayurvedic practitioners have in the body's innate wisdom. If you are craving astringent or bitter foods, you are likely to be needing them. Sweet and salty foods are easy to eat a bit too much of, and so Ayurveda reminds us to watch this. Sour and pungent foods include many which can inflame or irritate the gut; and so from an Ayurvedic view, the lesser, the better.

If you were to compare the tastes to different locales or climes, sweet taste might be like a trip to a cool lake on a hot day, while sour taste would be rather like a tropical jungle. You could think of the Gulf of Mexico off the coast of Florida when you imagine salty taste's action on the body. And bitter taste acts much like the winds at the North Pole! Astringent taste is more like a cool autumn breeze than a biting winter gale, while pungent taste behaves like the winds of the Sahara at high noon. See next page for a summary of the dynamics of taste.

TABLE 3: *RASA*

TASTES	ELEMENTS	QUALITIES	IN MODERATION BALANCES	IN EXCESS AGGRAVATE
Sweet	earth & water	heavy, moist, cool	*Vata & Pitta*	*Kapha*
Sour	earth & fire	warm, moist, heavy	*Vata*	*Pitta & Kapha*
Salty	water & fire	heavy, moist, warm	*Vata*	*Pitta & Kapha*
Pungent	fire & air	hot, light, dry	*Kapha*	*Pitta & Vata*
Bitter	air & ether	cold, light, dry	*Kapha & Pitta*	*Vata*
Astringent	air & earth	cool, light, dry	*Pitta & Kapha*	*Vata*

Excerpted with permission from The Ayurvedic Cookbook: A Personalized Guide to Good Nutrition and Health, *by Amadea Morningstar with Urmila Desai (Lotus Press, 1990).*

VIRYA

Besides the immediate response of how a food tastes to us in our mouths, its *rasa*, there is also the action it has soon after in our digestive tracts, its *virya*. *Virya* is usually expressed in terms of temperature, i.e., hot *(ushna)* or cold *(sita)*. *Virya* is discovered both through direct perception (whether we experience a food as hot or cooling to our guts) and also by inference (by observing its action on the body). Foods with warming *viryas* usually stimulate digestion, while those with cooling *viryas* slow it down. Pungent, sour and salty tasting foods generally have warm *viryas*. Sour fresh yogurt can really help some people's guts move along, eliminate, more effectively. Or in Chinese medicine, sour umeboshi paste is much valued for its ability to enhance digestion. Sweet, bitter and astringent foods usually have a cooling *virya*, meaning they can at times slow the gut down a bit. Think of a time when you tried to put a sweet dessert on top of an already ample meal, and it just sat there like a sodden lump. In moments like these, the pungency and warmth of a small cup of fresh ginger tea can be appreciated.

Virya acts on the body from its first point of contact, when we first put it in our mouths or on our skins, until it is excreted from the body. According to Professor P. V. Sharma in *Introduction to Dravaguna (Indian Pharmacology)*, *virya* is of primary importance in evaluating the action of medicinal herbs and drugs; it is the first thing to consider. *Rasa* (taste), on the other hand, is weighed more heavily in assessing the action of foods on the body. So if you are wondering how a food might behave inside you, look first at its taste. If you are questioning the impact of a particular herb, consider first its *virya*, whether its action will heat you up or cool you down.

VIPAK

So there is *rasa*, the immediate taste of a food in the mouth; *virya*, the food's action as it moves through the digestive tract; and then there is *vipak*, the post-digestive effect of a food. When an Ayurvedic physician is contemplating what foods to recommend to you after feeling your pulses, s/he takes both taste and post-digestive effect into account a good deal. Both are important. The post-digestive effect is how the food impacts your body once it has been completely absorbed and assimilated, and not before.

Usually Ayurvedic physicians work with three *vipaks*: sweet, sour and pungent. These are the three *vipaks* used in *Charak*, the classic Ayurvedic medical text. There are variations in opinion here, though. *Susruta*, another key reference in Ayurvedic medical training, uses only two *vipaks* and does not recognize sour *vipak*, for example. And to further invigorate things, some *vaidyas* work with five *vipaks*, corresponding to the five great elements, and others use six *vipaks*, each one corresponding to each of the six tastes. But most *vaidyas* you might meet are likely to use the system of *Charak*, and so we will too.

Most foods have a sweet *vipak (madhura vipaka)*, which is considered beneficial and calming to the system. Foods with a sweet or salty taste will usually have a sweet *vipak*. Sweet *vipak* calms and builds the whole body, and so is often recommended in practice. Wheat and rice are two examples of foods with sweet *vipak*. Sweet *vipak* calms *Vata* and *Pitta*, and increases *Kapha*. (Normally mild excesses are simply excreted in the urine and feces. It would be unwise for *Kapha* to avoid foods with a sweet *vipak* as they are stabilizing and strengthening. Usually the thing to do here for *Kapha* is just to eat smaller portions of these foods than someone of another constitution.) Sweet *vipak* is laxative and diuretic and good for putting weight on skinny bones. Foods with a sweet *vipak* are valued in Ayurvedic fertility treatments as they increase semen production.

A few foods have a sour *vipak (amla vipaka)*. These are generally foods with an originally sour taste, like sour mango, buttermilk or sour cream. (An extended list of foods and *vipak* follows in Table 5.) They can be heating and irritating to the system in large quantities. Anyone who has had a duodenal ulcer can probably attest to the disturbing effect of tomato or lime juice, foods with a sour *vipak*, on their gut. Foods with a sour *vipak* especially increase *Pitta* and used in excess over time can decrease fertility.

And some foods possess a pungent *vipak (katu vipaka)*. Usually foods with a pungent, bitter or astringent taste have a pungent *vipak*, though other foods will have this *vipaka* as well. These foods are heating and drying, especially in the colon. They can be helpful in balancing someone whose constitution is cool and moist, like *Kapha's*, and are used in small amounts for this purpose in healthy people. But for the person with an inflamed colon, colitis say, large amounts of these foods would be counterproductive, even painful. Some examples of foods with pungent *vipak* are hard cheeses, pickles and chilies. Pungent *vipak* increases *Vata dosha*. In excess it is constipating and can inhibit urination.

Vipak, the post-digestive effect of a food, is discovered only through inference, how it ultimately affects the body. This can be confusing or seem intangible compared to *rasa* or *virya*, both which can be felt or tasted directly. And yet *vipak* has a definite affect on the body over time. To clarify, Professor Sharma gives a good comparison of the differences between *rasa* and *vipak* in his fine introduction to Indian pharmacology. *Rasa* is a taste sensation, while *vipak* is a state of metabolic transformation. With *rasa*, there is an immediate response or reaction to the taste, while with *vipak* the response is delayed. *Rasa* exerts a local effect and its impact is limited to the digestive system. *Vipak's* effect is systemic and takes place after the food has been completely metabolized. *Rasa* elicits an immediate psychological response, such as pleasure, relaxation and happiness or disgust and dismay. *Vipak* has a delayed response of a feeling of well-being or discomfort. If we are eating foods suited for us over a period of weeks or months, we will have a progressive feeling of satisfaction and well-being that simply increases over time. This is *vipak*. An immediate response to a tasty food, like, "Ah! what a nice dessert!": that is *rasa*. *Rasa* can be directly experienced through taste; *vipak* can only be inferred through its effects after it has been digested. For a summary of *rasa*, *virya* and *vipak*, see Table 4 on the following page.

TABLE 4

TASTE *RASA*	DIGESTIVE EFFECT *VIRYA*	POST-DIGESTIVE EFFECT *VIPAK*
Sweet	cooling	Sweet
Sour	heating	sour
Salty	heating	sweet
Pungent	heating	pungent
Bitter	cooling	pungent
Astringent	cooling	pungent

For a more in-depth discussion of the tastes and how they relate to constitution, see The Ayurvedic Cookbook, *Morningstar with Desai (Lotus Press, 1990). For good coverage about the tastes and their interactions with food qualities, see* Cooking for Life, *Linda Banchek (Harmony Books, © 1989).*

PRABHAU

You may notice I've used the words "most", "often" and "usually" a lot in the preceding sections. This is because in plants and foods, as in people, there are exceptions to the rule. Such cases are called *prabhau,* or the specific potency of a given herb or food, rather than anything you might generalize about it based on *rasa, virya* and *vipak.* For example, onion has a pungent taste. Based on general rules, you would expect it to have a warming *virya.* But it doesn't. It has a cooling *virya* (one of the reasons it can give a *Vata* tummy trouble).

As Professor P. V. Sharma explains, two herbs may have similar *rasa, virya* and *vipak* and yet have different physiological actions in the body. This specificity of their chemical make up, and the uniqueness of the areas on which they act, is the nature of their *prabhau.* For example: both rice and barley have sweet *rasa,* cool *virya* and sweet *vipak.* Yet barley has strong diuretic properties and rice does not. This is barley's *prabhau. Prabhau* is discovered first through direct experience, rather than through any kind of theorizing. As Professor Sharma says, it is not "unthinkable" *(acintya)*, rather "unthought of" *(acintita)*. *Prabhau* is always open to investigation, and as we explore, we understand better why a food or herb behaves in the way it does.*

INTEGRATING CONCEPTS

So how to begin to integrate all these ideas and categories? One at a time is one way. For example: white sugar. While white sugar has a sweet *vipak*, which is considered favorable usually, it also is *rajasic* with a heating *virya*. This means that in the long-run it is disturbing to the mind (*rajasic*) and heating to the gut (heating *virya*). It has such a strong effect that it is rarely, if ever, used by many Ayurvedic practitioners. (Some practitioners do take advantage of sugar's sweet *rasa* and sweet *vipak*, both cooling, to calm *Pitta* in specific short-term conditions. Again, sugar would not be used here on a regular basis.) Sweeteners which are *sattvic* (calming to the mind) and sweet in *vipak* (friendly to the gut), like honey or maple syrup, would be recommended much more often.

For another example: ice cream. Ice cream, being frozen, would be considered *tamasic*, slowing to the mind, a heavy influence. While it has a sweet initial taste (*rasa*), its *vipak*, post-digestive effect, is sour. Contrary to anything encouraging I might have implied about ice cream in *The Ayurvedic Cookbook*, both the sugar in ice cream and its sour post-digestive effect can create fermentation and heat

---

*****Footnote:** *There is yet another way to assess for* vipak, *based on botanical structure. While taste is often used to estimate* vipak, *sometimes taste can be subtle. We can also look for clues in how plants grow. Rice and wheat, for example, have a compact, upward movement of growth, indicative of sweet* vipak. *Corn and amaranth both grow with a spike formation, more indicative of pungent* vipak. *(Both corn and amaranth have a predominantly sweet* vipak, *as listed in Table 5. However, they will be more pungent than either wheat or rice.) Strong color and odor also can indicate more fire present, with probable pungent* vipak. *Think of bright orange nasturtium flowers with their hot taste. Thorns will often be associated with bitter and astringent taste and pungent* vipak. *One example of this would be the olive tree and green olives. A more scattered, open pattern of leaf growth is often associated with astringent, bitter or pungent taste, and pungent* vipak. *Think of how mustard greens grow (pungent* vipak) *compared to compact cabbage (sweet* vipak). *Tough and rough bark also often occur concomitant with astringent taste. Clearly there can be many exceptions to these rules, and I need more understanding of how different parts (roots, flowers, stems) may behave differently. Yet this is a potential way to begin evaluating plants unfamiliar to Ayurveda. (Reference: conversation with Dr. Sunil Joshi, 1994)*

in the body, especially in the colon.

For a more encouraging example. Let's take peaches. Peaches: *sattvic*, calming to the mind, fresh, balancing. Peaches: sweet *vipak*, soothing to the digestion. Now if you were to freeze that peach, its dynamics change. It becomes more *tamasic*. Or if you were to can that peach, it would become a little *rajasic*, because it is sitting, having a chance for minute amounts of fermentation to occur over time. But if you just eat that peach fresh and whole and unadorned, you have a great *sattvic* sweet thing.

You can also integrate these ideas in food groups or clumps. Most spicy foods, like chile, peppers and garlic are *rajasic*. They also have a pungent *vipak*, meaning they are heating from start to finish. These foods would be used rarely or in small quantities in Ayurveda, unlike, probably, your last meal at your local East Indian restaurant. Meals at Indian restaurants are likely to be tasty but quite spicy. Ayurvedic cooking is a lot milder than that. It is tasty, to stimulate appetite and digestion, but not fiery, as it cares for the gut as well as the palate.

Some foods which are *rajasic* with a sweet *vipak* are used for specific purposes. For example, protein-rich, *rajasic* garbanzos would be considered a good way to start a day in which you are faced with hard physical labor. (See KHALA CHANA AND POTATOES, p. 47. for one savory way to do this.) Another food with a sweet *vipak* and a *rajasic* nature is dried dates. It would be surprising to see either garbanzos or dates served daily at an Ayurvedically-aware meditation retreat. Energetically, this would be counterproductive, as both inflame the mind and get physical energies wanting to manifest. And yet you could see why dates have been regarded as aphrodisiacs in Ayurveda, can't you?

As I understand it, food can move from the *sattvic* to the *rajasic* category if eaten in excess. This is especially true of beans. Most beans in moderation promote *sattva*. Yet if eaten in excess, they can ferment in the gut, bringing out *rajas*, especially in a person of *Vata* constitution. Think, if you can, of a *Vata* friend, how irritable and upset, touchy, they can get, if their gut is not happy. This is one reason why you will see some beans listed sometimes as *sattvic*, sometimes as *rajasic*. The same can be true of dried food. A little dried food, well re-hydrated, can be *sattvic*. An excess can create gas and irritation in the gut, having a more *rajasic* effect.

The following table on *vipak* is a beginning. This information is not readily available and not infrequently disputed. That is to say, I include it to get us Westerners thinking about and working with *vipak*. I have attempted to include foods about which I am reasonably certain. I have not included many foods common to the West about which there is not yet agreement or adequate evaluation.

TABLE 5: *VIPAK*: THE POST DIGESTIVE EFFECT OF FOODS

Foods with a sweet *vipak*, i.e., those which are calming, grounding, lubricating, and add or help maintain mass. In moderation, they are generally non-irritating to the gut:

aduki beans	carob	green peas, fresh	oats	sesame oil
alfalfa sprouts	cashews	hickory nuts	olive oil	soy oil
almond oil	celery	honeydew melon	olives, black	soy beans
almonds	cherries, sweet	honey	oranges	strawberries
amaranth	coconut	Jerusalem artichokes	papaya	sugar, brown
apple	coconut oil	kidney beans	parsnips	sugar, white
apricot	corn, fresh	lemon	peach	sugar cane, raw
apricot oil	corn, blue, dried	lentils, red	peanut oil	summer squash of all kinds
apricot pits	corn, yellow, dried	lentils, black	peanuts	sunflower oil
artichokes	corn oil	lentils, tan	pecans	sunflower seeds
asparagus	cream, sweet, fresh	lettuce, especially head	pine nuts	sweet potatoes
avocado	cucumber	lima beans	pineapple, sweet	tangerines
avocado oil	date sugar	macadamia nuts	pinto beans	tepary beans
barley	dates, dried	mango, sweet ripe	pistachios	walnuts
beets	fava beans	maple syrup	plum, sweet	watermelon
black beans	figs, dried	milk, raw, fresh	pomegranate	wheat
black-eyed peas	figs, fresh	millet	potatoes	wild rice
Brazil nuts	filberts	molasses	pumpkin	winter squash of all kinds
broad beans	fructose	mother's milk	quinoa	yams
buckwheat	ghee	mung beans	raisins	zucchini
butter, unsalted	grapes	mushrooms	rice of all kinds	
cabbage	green beans	navy beans	rye	
cantaloupe	green peas, dried	nectarine	sea salt	

TABLE 5 CONTINUED

Foods with a sour *vipak*, i.e., those which stay sour after metabolism. They are lubricating and humidifying, and can cause irritation or fermentation in the gut with excessive or extended use:

banana	cottage cheese	ice cream	plum, sour	yogurt, not freshly made
butter, salted	grapefruit	kefir	ricotta cheese	yogurt, freshly made
buttermilk	green grapes	lime	sour cream	
cherries, sour	guava	mango, sour unripe	tomato	

Foods with a pungent *vipak*, i.e., those which have a drying and lightening effect after metabolism. They can cause inflammation or excess heat in the gut with extended or excessive use:

arugula	chard	fowl	onion	sesame seeds, hulled
bell peppers	cheeses, soft, salted	garlic	onion, green	sesame seeds, unhulled
broccoli	cheeses, hard	leek	pickles	spinach
carrot	chili peppers	meat	pumpkin seeds	turnip greens
castor oil	eggs	mustard greens	radish	white mustard oil
cauliflower	fenugreek	okra	rhubarb	
celery	fish	olives, green	safflower oil	

THE *DOSHAS* AND CONSTITUTIONAL TYPES

Of the five great elements, there are two that do not change readily and three which are changing constantly, cyclically. Space or the ether element changes very little and with tremendous effort. Likewise, earth, the earth element, alters with great infrequency on its own. Air, fire and water, however, are constantly changing. This can be seen, as Dr. Sunil Joshi points out, in the daily weather forecasts on TV. Every few hours we get reports on the changes in air, in the form of winds, clouds, tornados, hurricanes, and so forth. We hear about fire in the form of temperature changes and forecasts. And water is a point of constant focus, in the shape of rain, snow and humidity. In Ayurveda it is said that you always have the wind, the sun and the moon, or air, fire and water. They are constant features of our macrocosm, and also of our microcosm, in the form of the three *doshas*.

The three *doshas* are biological substances which move within our bodies, our own inner equivalents of air, fire and water. Western physiology offers no real counterparts for these, and yet they are a key part of Ayurvedic practice.

Vata, the *dosha* most closely aligned to the air element (and ether), is found especially in the hollow structures within the body, like the colon, bladder and uterus. It is present in all functions of motion and transmission, such as nerve impulses and sense perception. *Pitta* is the *dosha* related to the fire element (and to an extent, water). It works with rapid transformations. It is seen in our digestive secretions, especially those which are highly acidic, like stomach's hydrochloric acid, or strongly colored, like the bile from our livers. *Kapha* is the *dosha* related to the water element (and earth). It provides moisture, lubrication, mass. It moisturizes the air as we breathe it in to our lungs, and our food as we chew it in our mouths. It keeps our membranes lubricated and functional. Where there are whitish excretions, *Kapha* is likely to be present.

All three *doshas* function within all of us to keep us healthy and alive. The extreme flexibility of air, fire and water serve to help us biologically respond to the constantly changing conditions of our lives. They help to mediate between our essential physiological tissues, what Ayurveda calls the *dhatus* (plasma, blood, muscle, fat, bone, bone marrow and nerve, and reproductive tissue) and the biological materials we no longer need, our wastes *(malas)* (sweat, urine and feces). At conception, the balance of *doshas* present in our parents at this moment contributes to our lifelong constitution.

In Ayurvedic theory and practice, each individual is born with a particular constitution or *prakruti*. This constitution influences how we look, how our bodies metabolize, and often how we respond mentally and emotionally to conditions in our lives. There has been excellent coverage of constitution written elsewhere, so I will be addressing it briefly here. For more information, see Deepak Chopra's *Perfect Health*, Robert Svoboda's *Prakruti: Your Ayurvedic Constitution*, and *The Ayurvedic Cookbook* by Morningstar and Desai.

Constitution is based upon the elements predominating at your birth. Of the five elements, some people have more fire in their constitutions, some more air, some more earth or water. If you were born with air and ether predominant in your make-up, your Ayurvedic constitution is *Vata*. If you had more fire and water prominent at that time, you are working more with *Pitta* constitution. And if earth and water hold the greatest sway in your constitutional make-up, you are working primarily with *Kapha*. Or you could be a combination of two or more types, for example, *Vata-Pitta*, *Pitta-Kapha*, or even *Vata-Pitta-Kapha*.*

While constitution is most accurately assessed through reading the pulses by a trained Ayurvedic physician, there are many physical, mental and emotional traits that can give some indication of your constitutional make-up. For example, *Vatas* often tend to be thin, wiry, a bit restless or anxious, with quick minds. *Vatas* frequently like to nibble, rather than sit down to a big meal. Not all people of *Vata* constitution will look and act this way, but if you think of someone you know like this, there is a good chance they have more *Vata* in their constitution. *Pittas* are often more forceful. They like to take the lead and are more likely to get angry than scared as their first emotional response in a stressful situation. Generally they will have fairly well-proportioned medium-boned frames, often with many moles, or fair or reddish skin (relative to their racial group). When they are hungry, they are bears! *Kaphas* are often more solid in build and frame, and slower to come to decisions. They take their time, and are not easily shifted in their choices. A little food goes a long way in *Kaphas*. Many *Kapha* individuals find exercise the best way to keep their weights in reasonable realms. In the face of stress, *Kapha's* first response is often to hole up. So while *Vatas* can get scared, and *Pittas* mad, *Kaphas* can numb out. Now obviously we don't always respond in the same ways emotionally. Some things scare us, some conditions anger us, some paralyze us. But in general we will have an emotional style that coincides with our constitutional type. If you're curious to begin to assess your constitution, there is a questionnaire in the back of the book, in Appendix I, to quiz yourself.

---

* A frequent question is, is there an astrological correspondence between one's constitution and the natal horoscope? In my experience over the last eleven years, I see a closer correspondence between the constitution and the rising sign than with the sun sign. So, for example, it is not unusual for someone with Taurus (earth sign) rising to have some Kapha in their constitution. But not always. David Frawley has a good discussion of some of the factors that enter into this in The Astrology of Seers: A Comprehensive Guide to Vedic Astrology.

If, in taking the questionnaire, you find yourself choosing primarily one column or category, you may be simply that one constitutional type. Or if you pick two columns fairly equally, you could have a *"dual dosha"*, or constitution made up of two types. Both situations are fairly common. It is less often that someone is equally balanced between all three *doshas, Vata-Pitta-Kapha*, and yet this also can occur. If you find yourself deliberating between two choices, your constitution is best reflected by the answer which has been true for you most of your life. For example, say most of your life you've worked well with routine, but lately you've been chomping at the bit and hating any kind of regimentation. If most of your other choices on the questionnaire are also in the *Kapha* column, like ample build, heavy bone structure, and so forth, you could assume that you're probably *Kapha* in constitution, and that air is needing some balancing now (the restless showing up in the *Vata* column being an indicator). Maybe you need to make some big changes, mentally.

If you're eating fairly cleanly (or maybe even if you're not!) you may begin to notice that certain foods agree with you more than others. One of the beauties of Ayurvedic nutrition is its ability to respond to the individual and her or his needs. Because of the different balance of the five elements in each person and in each food, some foods combine better with certain bodies than others. For example, people with a lot of air in their constitution (*Vata*) need a balance of foods with less air and more grounding. "Airy" foods like popcorn or apples, from an Ayurvedic perspective, aggravate or increase an already airy type, causing excess air. One possible outcome: gas. Fiery *Pitta* bodies thrive on food which is more cooling and soothing. If you add fire to an already hot system, steam can result! Literally. You may know a hot-headed friend who breaks out in a sweat when they eat spicy food. This is a situation of too much fire in a fiery person. Similarly, earthy *Kapha* types need lighter crispier foods to balance that earth and water. Heavy breads, cakes, gooey sweets weigh these folks down.

In terms of taste, foods with a sweet, sour or salty taste are most beneficial for *Vata*. Foods with a sweet, bitter or astringent taste help *Pitta* most. Pungent, bitter and astringent foods support *Kapha* most effectively.

Warm moist foods help ground cool airy *Vata*, while cool soothing foods balance *Pitta*. Lighter foods, soups and salads, balance *Kapha*. So what kinds of foods are these? There are many examples beneficial for each type in the recipes which follow. Each recipe is coded,"-" meaning calms or helps the given constitution,"+" meaning aggravates it,"0" meaning a neutral effect on that dosha. Basically, in Ayurveda, certain foods, due to their elemental makeup, tastes and texture, have been found to be most balancing for each type. There are extended discussions about all of this in *The Ayurvedic Cookbook* if you find yourself interested. And there are detailed lists of foods in Appendix II for each constitution, to be able to create your own choices.

THE ATTRIBUTES OF FOOD AND THEIR INFLUENCES ON THE *DOSHAS*

Each food substance has different properties, textures, qualities. In Sanskrit these attributes of a substance are called *gunas*. Foods with qualities or *gunas* which are similar to the characteristics of our constitutional type tend to increase or aggravate it, especially in excess. Those with opposite qualities to a dosha tend to decrease it, or when used in moderation, balance it. So for example, *Vata dosha* tends to be light and dry. A food like popcorn is also light and dry. Eating too much popcorn can aggravate a person of *Vata* constitution, resulting in excess air: bloating or gas. Eating a food with opposite qualities to those of *Vata* can help calm this *dosha*, say, having a small bowl of rice pudding, which is warm, moist and a little heavy.

Ayurveda works with twenty attributes, ten pairs of opposites. The following table provides an introductory summary to the attributes and their influence on the *doshas*.

TABLE 6: THE ATTRIBUTES (GUNAS) AND THEIR INFLUENCE ON THE DOSHAS

Attribute (Guna):	Influence on Doshas in moderation, calms:	In excess, aggravates:	Examples of the Attribute and Other Information:
1) Heavy (guru)	Vata & Pitta	Kapha	figs, dates
2) Light (laghu)	Kapha	Vata & Pitta	basmati (in action), popcorn (in texture)
3) Cold (sita)	Pitta	Vata & Kapha	icy drinks, decreased agni
4) Hot (ushna)	Vata & Kapha	Pitta	warm foods, increased agni
5) Oily (snigda)	Vata	Pitta & Kapha	fish, sesame, moistening in action
6) Dry (ruksha)	Kapha & Pitta	Vata	barley (in action), crackers (in texture)
7) Slow (manda)	Vata & Pitta	Kapha	cottage cheese (in action)
8) Sharp (tikshna)	Kapha	Vata & Pitta	hot peppers
9) Static (sthira)	Vata & Pitta	Kapha	a daily ritual, or letting food stand a bit
10) Mobile (chala)	Kapha	Vata & Pitta	a laxative, or a ride on a subway
11) Soft (mrudu)	Vata	Pitta & Kapha	pudding
12) Hard (kathina)	Pitta	Vata	calcium tablets
13) Clear (vishada)	Kapha	Vata & Pitta	cleansing in action
14) Cloudy (avila or picchile)	Vata & Pitta	Kapha	composed of the water element
15) Slimy (slakshna)	Vata	Pitta & Kapha	cooked okra
16) Rough (khara)	Pitta & Kapha	Vata	granola
17) Subtle (sukshma)	Kapha	Vata & Pitta	increases emotions (its action), alcohol (one example)
18) Gross (sthula)	Vata & Pitta	Kapha	sweet cakes
19) Dense (sandra)	Vata & Pitta	Kapha	butter
20) Liquid (drava)	Vata	Kapha & Pitta	fresh warm milk, or a long hot bath

TO SUMMARIZE: TABLE 7:
HOW TO EAT IN AN AYURVEDIC WAY:

a step-by-step guide

1. Start cleaning up your diet: lighten up on the chemicals, fast foods, fried, fermented, and frozen foods.

2. Get familiar with the difference between *sattvic, rajas*ic and *tamasic* foods, and begin to include more *sattvic* dishes in your food choices. (See pages 10 through 16 for more information.)

3. Take some time to eat, relax, and let yourself digest good food.

4. With the help of an Ayurvedic practitioner, begin to use foods which will address current imbalances (*vikruti*). (See p. 357 for more information about *vikruti*.)

5. As you let your diet evolve toward one which supports your whole system, you will tend to get clearer in your thoughts and actions. This in turn allows you to fine tune your eating. At this point you can more specifically support and strengthen your personal constitution (*prakruti*). (See p. 27 for more information about *prakruti*.)

6. Relax, don't try to be "perfect" or develop the perfect diet, your diet will keep changing with you. Just keep eating in this healthier way, in the ways you've found that work for you, changing as you need to.

7. Let all this positive accumulated energy work in some great way for you, others, the planet.*

*(Don't let me slow you down here. Any time is a good time to serve, you don't have to be in perfect physical shape to do it!)

PART TWO

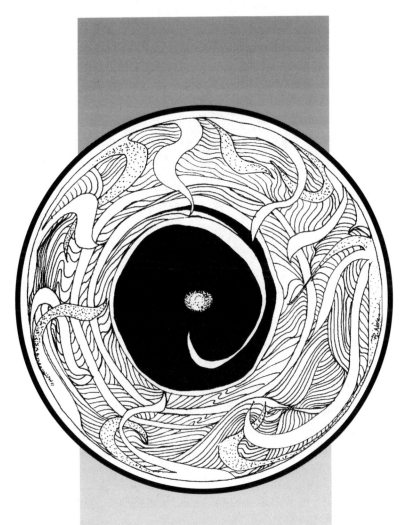

Breakfast

KEY

"–" means calms or helps the given constitution;

"+" means aggravates or increases it;

"0" means neutral effect.

 * ROTATION DIET can be helpful for people with food
   sensitivities, see p. 323.

**POLARITY DISH refers to recipes supporting Polarity Therapy
work, see p. 342.

✿ = Spring

✳ = Summer

⧉ = Fall

❄ = Winter

FRESH FRUIT BOWL

Preparation time: 20 minutes

SATTVIC, 0 Vata, - Pitta, 0 Kapha

Serves: 4

Wash and prepare:

    1 cup each:

        cantaloupe

        honeydew melon

        peaches

        blueberries

        cherries (optional)

Slice the melon, then cut the rind off and cut into pieces. Slice, then cut up the peaches. Use the blueberries and cherries whole. Spoon into a pretty bowl. Serve!

*ROTATION DAY 2 DISH

**POLARITY PURIFYING DIET DISH

Comments: To create a *sattvic*, fresh fruit bowl tailor-made for your constitution, simply combine any fruit from the list of foods calming for your type (see Appendix II, Revised Food Guidelines for Basic Constitutional Types), skipping the few fruits which are *rajasic* like unripe mango, guava, grapefruit, lime, lemon (a squeeze is fine), rhubarb.

For example:

A *VATA*-CALMING FRUIT BOWL

Apricots, bananas, berries, grapes, and cherries could be one.

SATTVIC, - Vata, 0 Pitta, 0 Kapha

or

Ripe mango, papaya, peaches, and strawberries

SATTVIC, - Vata, 0 Pitta, 0 Kapha

A *PITTA*-CALMING FRUIT BOWL

Sweet apple slices, apricots, berries, and pears

SATTVIC, + Vata, - Pitta, - Kapha

or

Plums, pomegranates, sweet purple grapes, and pale green honeydew

SATTVIC, + Vata, - Pitta, - Kapha

A *KAPHA*-CALMING FRUIT BOWL

Apples, cherries, pears, and strawberries
SATTVIC, + Vata, - Pitta, - Kapha

Pomegranate, blackberries, peaches, and blueberries
SATTVIC, 0 Vata, - Pitta, - Kapha

**All of the above fruit bowls are POLARITY PURIFYING DISHES.

A TRIDOSHIC FRUIT BOWL

(*Tridoshic* means balancing for all three constitutional types.)

Raspberries and blackberries with ripe sliced mango
SATTVIC, - Vata, - Pitta, - Kapha

or

Sweet cherries, blueberries and sweet apricot halves
SATTVIC, - Vata, - Pitta, - Kapha

**Both *TRIDOSHIC* FRUIT BOWLS are POLARITY PURIFYING DISHES

Eating healthfully clearly can be fun. Check out what produce is available in your area; support your local farmers' market and balance your doshas at the same time! If you have a few extra dollars, pick up an extra bag of fruit for the nearest shelter or food relief project and drop it off on your way home. From an Ayurvedic standpoint, sharing your loving strengthens your heart and immunity. It's a win-win way to go.

So what else is to eat for breakfast on an Ayurvedic program? Just about any cereal imaginable, from familiar belly-warming oatmeal to exotic teff. Check them out:

TASTY OATMEAL

Preparation time: 15 minutes
SATTVIC, - Vata, - Pitta, moderately + Kapha

Serves: 2
✿ ⟨ ❄

In a medium saucepan, bring to a boil:

> **2 - 3 c. pure water**
> **1/4 tsp. salt**
> **1/4 c. raisins**

Stir in:

> **2/3 c. rolled oats, organic preferred**
> **1 tsp. cinnamon**
> **1/4 tsp. ground cardamom***
> **or 1/4 tsp. nutmeg***

Let the cereal come to a bubbling boil again. Reduce heat to low, cover and let cook until good and mushy. Serve with honey or maple syrup.

**POLARITY HEALTH BUILDING DISH
*ROTATION DAY 1 DISH. If you are on a strict rotation, skip these spices with an asterisk next to them, and sweeten with barley malt.

Variation: ROLLED BARLEY: For a dish more calming to *Kapha*, substitute rolled barley for the oats and use the greater amount of water. Cook until soft, 20 minutes or more. Serve with raw honey.
SATTVIC, + Vata, - Pitta, - Kapha

**POLARITY HEALTH BUILDING DISH
*ROTATION DAY 1 DISH. If you are on a strict rotation, skip the spices with an asterisk next to them, and sweeten with barley malt.

ABOUT WASTING FOOD AND HAVING PLENTY FOR EVERYONE

    An intrinsic part of Ayurvedic cooking practice is the admonition not to waste food. And yet, paradoxically, among Indian cooks, it is very important to always have plenty of fresh food for everyone. Achieving both is a sadhana in itself! How you address these dual aims will be uniquely your own creation. Sharing, feeding others, making sure that any excess food goes back to the earth, either as food for animals or food for the compost pile, all of these are ways to cook Ayurvedically.

CREAM OF RYE (R)

Preparation time: 5-10 minutes
SATTVIC, + Vata, + Pitta, - Kapha

Serves: 2

Bring to a boil in a saucepan:

2 c. pure water
1/8 tsp. salt
2 Tbsps. dried fruit: raisins or dried apples are good

Stir into the boiling water;

2/3 c. Cream of Rye (R)
1/4 tsp. ground cardamom

Reduce heat to medium. Cook uncovered for about 3 minutes. Then cover, and let sit for a minute or two. Serve with raw honey or a little barley malt, if you like.

*ROTATION DAY 1 Variation: If you are on a strict allergy rotation diet (see Appendix V), substitute cinnamon for cardamom, and use barley malt or any of the sweeteners listed for DAY 1.

**POLARITY HEALTH BUILDING DISH

HOT BEARMUSH!

Preparation time: 5 minutes
SATTVIC, - Vata, - Pitta, + Kapha

Serves: 2

In a small covered saucepan, bring to a boil:

3 - 4 c. water

Stir in:

1 c. dry bearmush
Pinch of salt

Bring back to a boil, turn off heat, cover and let sit for 2 - 3 minutes. Nice with butter and barley malt.

*ROTATION DAY 1 DISH. If you are following a strict rotation diet, sweeten with barley malt, malt, jaggery, molasses, sorghum, or Sucanat. If you are not following this allergy program, sweeten with any Ayurvedic sweetener you like. (see About Sweetners, p. 264)

**POLARITY HEALTH BUILDING DISH

Comments: Bearmush is a ground wheat, sold in bulk in many natural groceries. It is basically the health food equivalent of Cream of Wheat, yes?

HOT QUINOA

Preparation time: 30 minutes
SATTVIC, 0 Vata, 0 Pitta, - Kapha

Serves: 4

❀ ☙ ❄

Put in a fine-mesh colander or strainer:

1 c. dry quinoa

Rinse it well. This is an important step in this South American grain's preparation; you are washing off the saponins which can otherwise disturb your tummy. Put the well-washed quinoa in a saucepan with:

2 1/2 c. pure water
2 Tbsps. dried apricots or peaches, chopped (optional)

and bring to a boil. Cover and cook over low heat until all the water is absorbed into the grain and it is tender, 20 - 30 minutes. Good with a little maple syrup.

*ROTATION DAY 2 DISH **POLARITY HEALTH BUILDING DISH

Variation: HOT AMARANTH: Amaranth can be substituted in equal measure for the quinoa. Cooking time is about the same. Again, nice with maple syrup.

SATTVIC, - Vata, mildly + Pitta, - Kapha

*ROTATION DAY 2 DISH **POLARITY HEALTH BUILDING DISH

True Confessions: To be totally honest, maybe 1 in 4 folks of my acquaintance is fond of amaranth, me among them. To find out if you are in this select few, perhaps you'll just have to try it.

ABOUT TEFF

Teff is a tiny grain native to the highlands of Ethiopia. A member of the grass family (like most grains), it counts buffalo grass and the ubiquitous Bermuda grass among its relations. It is a remarkably rich source of calcium for a grain, one very large bowl of teff (100 grams) having as much calcium as 2/3 cup of milk. It also has generous amounts of iron, zinc and copper. And it tastes very good. Like any unfamiliar grain, its flavor may seem odd at first. I've found that introducing it in a sweet form, like Banana Spice Cake, generally makes for a good beginning for folks. It is 12% protein by weight, high for a grain.

It comes in several colors, one a white teff and the other a pretty dark chocolate brown. I've cooked with the brown, which has a slightly sweet, nutty flavor. Teff works well in quick breads, pancakes and desserts. In Ethiopia it is used to make a tasty flat bread called injera. Teff is definitely sattvic, and its effect on the doshas (constitutions) is still to be explored further. I got my introduction to teff from the fine cook and writer Rebecca Wood. Most of this information on teff comes from her forthcoming extensive book on grains. See recipe next page.

KIDS' CREAM OF MILLET

Preparation time: 35 minutes, 90% of it unattended
SATTVIC, 0 Vata, + Pitta, 0 Kapha

Serves: 4

In a small saucepan, place:

> **1 c. dry millet**
> **2 1/2 c. water**
> **1/2 tsp. salt**

Bring to a boil. Cover and reduce heat to low, cook until done, about 30 minutes. Just before serving, blend together in a blender:

> **2 tsps. raw almond butter**
> **1 ripe banana**
> **1 Tbsp. maple syrup**
> **4 Tbsps. water**

Slowly blend in the cooked millet at a low speed, with extra hot water if necessary to get the texture you like. Serve. Makes 4 1/2 cup servings.

*ROTATION DAY 2 DISH

**POLARITY HEALTH BUILDING DISH

Comments: Start this when you first get up, let yourself gallop around doing all those pre-school or pre-work or animal tending things, then come back and blend up the last step when you're ready to eat. Good day to you!

HOT TEFF

Preparation time: 15 minutes or less
SATTVIC. I am not yet certain of its effects on the doshas.

Serves: 2

Measure into a saucepan:

> **3/4 c. whole grain teff flour**

Roast it over low heat on a burner until it begins to smell wonderful and aromatic, 2 - 3 minutes or so. Stir in with a fork until smooth:

> **2 c. water**
> **1/8 tsp. salt**

Bring to a boil over high heat, then reduce heat to low, and add:

> **1/8 tsp. nutmeg (optional)**

Cover the pot, and simmer for about five minutes, stirring occasionally. Good with honey or maple syrup and milk.

*ROTATION DAY 3 DISH **POLARITY HEALTH BUILDING DISH

ABOUT DAIRY

There are many references in the Ayurvedic classics to the virtues of milk and its nourishing and therapeutic properties. These were recorded literally thousands of years ago, before the advent of pasteurization, homogenization, ultra-pasteurization, radiation, bovine growth hormone, dioxin, sulfa drugs, and pesticides, none of which are recommended in an Ayurvedic diet. It may be that wide-spread dairy intolerances may often be intolerances to what is in the milk and what has been done to it, as much as to the milk itself. If you can obtain fresh pure raw milk or buttermilk or yogurt which has been produced the same day you are using it, then dairy, especially milk, is still recommended. If you cannot, it is best avoided, sadly, or used very occasionally. For example, in our town we are fortunate enough to have one certified dairy which delivers fresh raw milk in glass bottles to a local grocery four days a week. In many places in the United States, this is no longer the case.

If you are able to get fresh milk, you can bring it to a boil immediately before use, usually with a slice of fresh ginger root per cup to increase digestive fire and enhance elimination. Let the milk boil for a good 20 to 30 seconds. The milk needs to be used the same day. Pasteurization originally came into being as a way to eliminate disease organisms, particularly bacteria. Conscientious boiling at home can also eliminate these, and makes a product easier on the digestive tract. (Drinking cold, unboiled raw milk runs you the risk of bacterial infection, plus it is harder to digest than the pre-boiled warm raw milk.) If a recipe calls for cold milk, raw milk can be boiled and cooled prior to preparation.

Since only half-gallons are available from our dairy, I'll make a milk-rich dessert (like tapioca) or an entree like Light Basil Pasta Sauce and have friends over. Any excess I donate to our animals. A far cry from milking your own cow, eh?

Processed hard and soft cheeses, commercial yogurt, ultra-pasteurized whip cream, cream cheese, sour cream and so forth may be tasty, but sadly they are generally not helpful for health on any regular basis. Fresh yogurt can be made at home with boiled raw milk, and yogurt cheese (paneer) or homemade ricotta can also be used on occasion. (See Glossary for how-tos on paneer and ricotta). These tend to be more sour and heavier than milk, and so are recommended for occasional rather than regular use.

A BREAKFAST RICE

Preparation time: 25 minutes
SATTVIC*

Serves: 1

✿ ✳ 🍵 ❄

Make up:

PLAIN *BASMATI* RICE, p. 205

Take 3/4 cup of the cooked rice and warm it in a small saucepan with:

1/2 c. milk (cow, goat, soy or nut)
1/4 tsp. ground coriander
1/8 tsp. ground cardamom
1 tsp. ghee (optional, beneficial)

Bring all ingredients to a boil, then reduce heat to low and simmer for 5 minutes or less. Serve whole or blended to a smooth texture, whichever you like. Good with a little maple syrup or honey.

* - *Vata*, - *Pitta*, + *Kapha* (with cow's milk)
* + *Vata*, - *Pitta*, 0 *Kapha* (with goat's milk)
* 0 *Vata*, - *Pitta*, 0 *Kapha* (with soy milk)
* - *Vata*, 0 *Pitta*, + *Kapha* (with nut milk)

Variation: For a DAY 3 ROTATION DISH, use plain *basmati* rice, soy or hazelnut milk, coriander and/or nutmeg, and raw honey or brown rice syrup. Skip the ghee and cardamom.

SATTVIC, 0 *Vata*, - *Pitta*, 0 *Kapha* (with soy milk)
SATTVIC, - *Vata*, 0 *Pitta*, + *Kapha* (with nut milk)

RICE ALMOND BREAKFAST CEREAL

Preparation time: 10 minutes
SATTVIC, - *Vata*, mildly + *Pitta*, moderately + *Kapha*

Serves: 2

✿ 🍵 ❄

In a blender, grind:

2/3 c. uncooked Texmati or white *basmati* rice

Then grind:

2/3 c. raw almonds (preferably soaked overnight)

You may need to do about three short pulse-sort of blends to get them each ground finely enough. Set aside for a moment. Bring to a boil:

3 c. pure water
Pinch of salt

When the water is boiling, stir the ground rice and almonds into it with a fork. Reduce heat to medium-low and continue cooking uncovered until done, about five minutes. Good with a dab of ghee and some maple syrup.

Comments: This is a good breakfast for those days when you feel like you need something which will keep you going steadily, but which is not too heavy.

Variation: MILLET ALMOND BREAKFAST CEREAL

Prepare same as above, but use dry millet instead of the rice. Use additional water if you like a creamier consistency.

SATTVIC, + Vata, + Pitta, - Kapha

*ROTATION DAY 2 DISH

**POLARITY HEALTH BUILDING DISH

Variation: RICE HAZELNUT BREAKFAST CEREAL

Prepare same as above, but use hazelnuts rather than almonds.

SATTVIC, - Vata, mildly + Pitta, + Kapha

*ROTATION DAY 3 DISH

**POLARITY HEALTH BUILDING DISH

ABOUT GHEE AND HONEY

In differing amounts, ghee and honey are used therapeutically in a number of ways. For example, to increase weight, you use more ghee than honey; to increase digestive fire, you use "twice as much honey as ghee". Linda Banchek, in Cooking for Life, *has a good discussion of this. She points out that traditionally, these two* sattvic *foods are never given in equal proportions, as they can aggravate skin conditions. To apply this practically, consider A SIMPLE BREAKFAST RICE, p. 44. If you are needing to increase your agni, you might have this cereal with 2 teaspoons of honey and a teaspoon of ghee. If you are more interested in putting on weight, you would mix in a tablespoon of ghee and a teaspoon of honey. You would avoid using equal amounts of both. To see results, you would need to use these proportions on a consistent basis, rather than occasionally or sporadically. For more information about the healing properties of ghee, see p. 122.*

HOT BLUE CORNMEAL WITH RAISINS

Preparation time: 15 minutes

Serves: 4

SATTVIC, + Vata, 0 Pitta, - Kapha

Before you get your saucepan anywhere near the heat, stir together in it:

1 c. dry blue cornmeal

3 - 4 c. cold water

This is important, else you are likely to be stuck with lumps of the most unappealing variety. If you stir it with a fork beforehand, you are creating the ground for a silky smooth cereal of deep satisfaction. Then stir in:

1/2 tsp. salt

1/4 c. raisins*

Bring the blue cornmeal to a boil over medium-high heat. Reduce heat to low and cook until done, stirring periodically with a fork to keep it smooth. Serve hot with ghee or butter, and/or maple syrup.

* Omit the raisins for a ROTATION DAY 4 DISH

**POLARITY HEALTH BUILDING DISH

Comments: Blue cornmeal is reputed to be a little less heating than her yellow sister.

ABOUT SOUPS FOR BREAKFAST

While it is an alien concept to some, hot soups can make a great break-fast in cooler weather. This is especially true for **Kaphas,** *who can feel dragged down by the concentrated cereals. You can make up your favorites from your own repertoire, or get ideas from the soup section here in* Ayurvedic Cooking for Westerners, *or play with the healthy dried one-serving soups on the market.*

The same folks who find themselves gravitating toward soups in fall might want to experiment with the lighter fresh fruit breakfasts in warm weather.

KHALA CHANA AND POTATOES

Preparation time: with a pressure cooker, about 1 hour, or a little less;
in an open pot, 3 - 4 hours

Serves: 2 - 4

Moderately RAJASIC (the khala chana), + Vata, - Pitta, - Kapha

Rinse and soak overnight:
>   1 c. dry *khala chana* (or dry garbanzos or chickpeas)

Place them in a stainless steel pressure cooker with:
>   5 c. water
>   1/8 tsp. hing
>   1 Tbsp. sesame oil

Bring them to pressure and cook 30 - 40 minutes or until tender. While they are cooking, you can wash and cube:
>   2 c. raw new potatoes, in 1/2" cubes. It is not necessary to peel them.

When the beans are cooked, reduce pressure by running cold water over the closed pot. Open the pot, add the potatoes and put back on medium heat to cook with the *khala chana*. Cook until the potatoes are done, about 15 minutes.
In a small skillet, warm:
>   1 Tbsp. sesame oil

Stir in:
>   1 tsp. cumin seeds
>   1/2 tsp. turmeric
>   1 tsp. salt

Let them brown for a minute or two. Add in:
>   1 1/2 tsps. ground coriander
>   1/8 tsp. cayenne (optional)
>   1 tsp. fresh lemon juice

and stir the whole spice mixture into the *khala chana* and potatoes once they have completed cooking. Garnish with:
>   3 Tbsps. fresh cilantro leaves, finely chopped

Traditionally these would be served like small tacos, with the *khala chana* and potatoes spooned into:
>   6 whole wheat *chappatis* or tortillas

Fold over and serve. Or the *khala chana* can be served alone like a thick stew.

Comments: *KHALA CHANA* AND POTATOES, p. 47, is one of my favorite breakfasts from anywhere, and it is included for entirely sentimental reasons. I can still remember the first time it was served to me, on a chilly October morning in the mountains of Uttar Pradesh in north India, the cook fire blowing in our faces and a lemon-colored sun just beginning to peer out from above the gray clouds. I thought I was in heaven. So this one is dedicated to all the East Indians who have joined us in the U. S., and all the East Indians who have been so kind to us Westerners in our travels to your home. Blessings to you, and much thanks!

The first time I found this recipe here in the States, I almost ate the whole pot alone! I hadn't realized just how much I'd missed it.

TASTY SCRAMBLED TOFU

Preparation time: 10 minutes   Serves: 3 - 4
Moderately RAJASIC, 0 Vata, 0 Pitta, mildly + Kapha   ✿ ✳ ⚘ ❄

Warm in a large skillet:
> 1 Tbsp. ghee
> 1 Tbsp. extra-virgin olive oil

Saute in the ghee until tender but not brown:
> 1 small fresh onion, chopped (with its greens if you have them)
> or 2 green onions, chopped (about 1 Tbsp.)
> 1 small clove garlic, minced
> 1-2 tsps. fresh sage leaves, finely chopped

Mash with a fork, directly into the saute in the skillet:
> 1 cube (16 oz.) fresh tofu

Saute until thoroughly warm. Right before serving, mash well into the tofu:
> 1 heaping Tbsp. yellow miso

Add:
> **Salt and freshly ground black pepper to taste**

Variation: For a dish more balancing to *Kapha*, omit the ghee and use a maximum of 1 Tbsp. of olive oil. Stir frequently. Use a scant tablespoon of miso, even less if you like. Stir 1 tablespoon of water into the tofu just before serving. This is just as tasty, but lower in fat content.

Moderately RAJASIC, mildly + Vata, - Pitta, 0 Kapha

Comments: This is a good alternative to hot cereals. And it is quick! If you have some fresh arugula and parsley available, a small handful of arugula leaves, finely chopped, and a tablespoon of chopped parsley are nice stirred in just before serving.

BREAKFAST TACOS

Preparation time: 10 minutes   Serves: 2
RAJASIC*   ❧ ✳ ൠ ❄

This is a quick easy meal from the Southwest. You will need two skillets for this. Put one iron skillet or griddle on to heat on medium-high. Beat:

4 fresh non-fertile eggs
or make up 1 batch of TASTY SCRAMBLED TOFU

The eggs go in the second skillet at medium heat with:

1 tsp. ghee

Pour the eggs (or tofu) in this medium heat pan and scramble them. While they are cooking, put a dab of ghee in the first hot skillet and quickly warm:

4 corn or whole wheat tortillas

just a few seconds on each side. They should be soft, not crispy. Spoon a tablespoon or two of scrambled egg or scrambled tofu into the hot tortilla, fold over. Make up 3 more tortillas in like fashion. Serve immediately. Very good with FRESH CILANTRO SALSA, p. 218.

*With eggs and corn tortillas: *RAJASIC, - Vata, + Pitta, moderately + Kapha*
*With eggs and whole wheat tortillas: *RAJASIC,- Vata, moderately + Pitta, + Kapha*
*With SCRAMBLED TOFU and corn tortillas: *Mildly RAJASIC, mildly + Vata, mildly + Pitta, - Kapha*
*With SCRAMBLED TOFU and whole wheat tortillas: *Mildly RAJASIC, 0 Vata, 0 Pitta, mildly + Kapha*
*With scrambled eggs and corn tortillas and sesame oil in place of the ghee, this is a ROTATION DAY 4 DISH. You can saute a little onion or garlic in the oil before scrambling the eggs in this for a different flavor.

ABOUT MISO

Miso, fermented soybean paste, is a food unfamiliar to most East Indians. And because it is fermented, it is assumed to be rajasic. So it is recommended that it be eaten only occasionally, if at all. And yet I would ask that this position be reconsidered.

We live in the mountains of northern New Mexico, an area high in both man-made and natural radioactive elements. In the winter, I find myself serving miso more often. It is warming, rich in protein and B vitamins (and salt!). It also possesses the natural binding agent zybicolin, which is effective in detoxifying and clearing radiation from the body. A beneficial amount of miso by Japanese standards would be 1/2 - 1 teaspoon per day.

Miso is a food not known in traditional Ayurvedic food practice. Yet due to the reality of widespread low-level radioactive waste around the globe, it could become a valued part of Ayurvedic practice. This remains to be seen.

SCRAMBLED EGGS AND VEGGIES

Preparation time: 5 - 7 minutes   Serves: 3
RAJASIC,- Vata, + Pitta, moderately + Kapha (fine for occasional use)   ✿ ✳ ⅋ ❄

In a medium mixing bowl, beat:
> **4 fresh non-fertile eggs (if available)**

In a heavy skillet, warm:
> **1 Tbsp. ghee or olive oil**

Put in the skillet to saute:
> **1 Tbsp. onion, finely chopped (optional)**
> **1/2 tsp. dry thyme**

When the onion is tender and translucent, add:
> **1/2 - 1 medium zucchini (depending on how much you like veggies in the morning), cut in 1/4" cubes or julienne strips**

Saute for a minute or two. Pour in the beaten eggs and stir. Cook until done. Nice served with scones or fresh melon slices, if your *agni* (digestive fire) is good.

For special brunches, see: CILANTRO QUICHE, p. 126 and POTATO FRITTATA, p. 127.

ABOUT EGGS

Eggs are hot, heavy, and rajasic. Eating many of them brings out your warrior more than your inner mediator. They are a good source of inexpensive balanced protein. Ayurvedic physicians vary in their outlook on them. Some say fine, occasionally no problem. Others, especially those honoring traditional Hindu practices, will not use them. As in all matters, it is ultimately up to you. There are a number of good egg substitutes, including Egg Replacer and cooked ground flax seeds, which can be used pretty readily in most baking and some cooking.

The yolk of the egg is the hottest, heaviest part of this food. Consequently, warm Pitta needs to take it easy on foods rich in egg yolk. An occasional egg white, more cooling, dry and light, can often be tolerated by Pitta. Food with egg yolks are also hard on Kapha, being rich and heavy. Both egg yolk and egg white are rajasic in action, and both have a post-digestive effect which is pungent. This is to say, if you have an inflamed condition, any part of the egg, used in excess, can aggravate this heat. Vatas and Kaphas can usually handle 2 - 3 eggs per week without difficulty, especially in baked items, souffles, and such. Fried and hard-boiled are the hardest forms in which to try to digest an egg.

BASIC PANCAKE BATTER

Preparation time: about 30 minutes
SATTVIC*

Makes 10 3" cakes

Beat in a blender:
> 1/2 ripe banana
> 1 egg
> 1 Tbsp. sunflower oil
> 1 Tbsp. (or less) maple syrup
> 1 1/2 c. fresh boiled raw milk (or soy milk)
> 1/2 tsp. cinnamon
> 1/8 tsp. nutmeg

Mix together in a measuring cup, then blend in:
> 1 1/4 - 1 1/3 c. whole wheat flour (or barley flour)
> 1/4 tsp. salt
> 1 tsp. baking powder (a scant tsp. at high altitude)

Stir the batter with a rubber spatula if you need,to get the flour off the sides of the blender. Heat a couple of skillets on medium-high heat, either lightly oiled or non-stick, and pour the batter into them in the appropriate puddles. When the first side begins to bubble and underside is golden brown, flip the cakes. Serve hot, with ghee and maple syrup.

*With milk, whole wheat, and lightly oiled pan, *SATTVIC, - Vata, - Pitta, + Kapha*

*With soy milk, barley flour, and non-stick pan, *SATTVIC, 0 Vata, - Pitta, - Kapha*

Comments: There are many variations which can be made on these. Perhaps our most memorable were BLUEBERRY PANCAKES made with tiny wild "blubes" gathered by our resourceful kids and intrepid male consorts up in the California Sierras last autumn. Scatter a few fresh berries (one cup per batch of batter) into each pancake after you've poured it onto the griddle or skillet. Flip as usual. Blueberries, raspberries, thin-sliced fresh peaches, or pecans all are good here.

Variations: Rotation Day 1: Skip the banana and nutmeg; use Egg Replacer instead of the egg; 1 Tbsp. ghee, melted butter or walnut oil for the oil; 1 Tbsp. barley malt, sorghum or Sucanat for the sweetener; 1 1/2 c. milk; 1/2 tsp cinnamon; 1 1/3 c. whole wheat flour; 1/4 tsp. salt; 1 tsp. baking powder (corn-free). Prepare as usual.

SATTVIC, - Vata, - Pitta, + Kapha

*ROTATION DAY 1 DISH

BASIC PANCAKE BATTER (Continued)

Another Rotation Day 1: Exactly the same as the first, but use 1 1/3 c. barley or oat flour in place of the whole wheat.

SATTVIC, 0 Vata, - Pitta, 0 Kapha (for barley flour)

SATTVIC, 0 Vata, 0 Pitta, 0 Kapha (for oat flour)

*ROTATION DAY 1 DISH

*ROTATION DAY 2 DISH: See BANANA PEACH MUFFINS, p. 174, as pancake batter.

Rotation Day 4: BUCKWHEAT CAKES: Mix together: 1 egg; 1 Tbsp. cold-pressed sesame oil; skip sweetener or use 1 Tbsp. date sugar or fructose; 1 Tbsp. raw sesame tahini; 1 1/3 c. water; 1 1/3 c. buckwheat flour; 1/4 tsp. salt; 1 tsp. baking powder. Prepare as usual.

SATTVIC, 0 Vata, mildly + Pitta, - Kapha

*ROTATION DAY 4 DISH

Rotation Day 4: CORN CAKES: Same as above, but with 1 1/3 c. blue cornmeal in place of the flour.

SATTVIC, 0 Vata (with maple syrup), O Pitta (with maple syrup), - Kapha (with raw honey)

*ROTATION DAY 4 DISH

See also CREPES, p. 54 and APPLE CAKES, below.

APPLE CAKES

Preparation time: 45 minutes
SATTVIC, 0 Vata, - Pitta, + Kapha

Makes 16 cakes

✿ ✳ 🐚 ❄

In a largish mixing bowl, mash:
> **1 ripe banana**

Beat in:
> **2 eggs**

Then add:
> **2 Tbsps. sunflower oil**
> **2 Tbsps. maple syrup**
> **1 c. fresh boiled raw milk**

Stir well. Mix together:
> **2 c. whole wheat or barley flour**
> **1 Tbsp. baking powder (2 1/2 tsps. if high altitude)**
> **1 tsp. salt**

Wash and grate:
> **2 c. grated apple (about 2 apples)**

Add to the batter the apple and:
> **2 tsps. cinnamon**
> **1/4 tsp. nutmeg**

Stir in the dry ingredients. Spoon onto a lightly oiled griddle or non-stick skillet and cook over medium heat until bubbles begin to appear; then flip. (I usually cook most pancakes over medium-high heat, so this is a cooler temperature than most. The fruit needs the extra time to cook.) Cook until golden brown; serve with maple syrup and/or blueberries.

Variations: Soy milk can be substituted for the cow's milk. With barley flour, this is the most calming arrangement for *Kapha*. The sweetener and oil can be reduced to 1 table-spoon each.

SATTVIC, 0 Vata, - Pitta, mildly + Kapha

Ripe pears can be used in place of the apples.

SATTVIC, 0 Vata, - Pitta, + Kapha

ABOUT AIR TRAVEL

Travelling by air is hard on Vata *dosha, as you might expect. You are travelling through* Vata's *own element, air, hurdling through space at a rapid rate, with some definite changes in altitude as you go. Consequently all constitutional types are wise to tend to their* Vata *dosha when they fly. Food-wise this means choosing warm drinks, or certainly those without ice or carbonation, while in flight. A liter of pure plain water to carry with you can be helpful. It is beneficial to have* Vata-*calming meals before and after your flight as well. You can choose soups or stews or any* Vata-*pacifying foods rather than salads, popcorn, frozen food, or icy or bubbly drinks. In-terestingly, a modern day folk remedy for jet lag includes garlic capsules, taken at the rate of 2, three times per day, for the three days before, day of, and one day after a trip (especially useful if the flight is a long one). Garlic is specifically calming to* Vata, *though* rajasic *or* tamasic *in action. Its literally ground-ing effect can be helpful here. Oil massage, especially to the feet, and a hot bath are also good afterward for minimizing effects of this modern transport.*

CREPES

Preparation time: 30 - 40 minutes
RAJASIC, mildly + Vata, + Pitta, 0 Kapha

Makes 12 5" crepes

✿ ✳ 🐾 ❄

Blend in a blender:
3 eggs

Add and blend on low for 2 - 3 minutes:
1 c. fresh boiled raw milk or soy milk
1/2 c. water
1/8 tsp. salt
1 c. buckwheat flour

Let the batter sit for 15 minutes. Pour 1/4 c. of batter into a pan lightly oiled with:
sesame oil

Tilt the pan with a circular motion so that the crepe covers it well and roundly. Let brown on one side, about one minute, and flip. Put each finished crepe in a 250° F. oven to warm while you make up the rest. Serve with fruit-sweetened raspberry or strawberry jam and a drizzle of maple syrup, or whatever filling you like.

*ROTATION DAY 4 DISH. If you are following a rotation diet, the crepes can be served with MANGO SAUCE, p. 211.

Variation: You can substitute whole wheat flour for the buckwheat. Serve both variations at a holiday brunch.
RAJASIC, - Vata, + Pitta, + Kapha

Comments: If you're in a bit of a hurry, you can skip letting the batter sit. It holds together best with the resting though, so you hazard losing a third to harder-to-flip pieces. You can also substitute Egg Replacer for up to half the eggs.

Crepe Fillings: Applesauce, Yummy Apple Butter, Hot Apricot Sauce, Sweet Potato Soup, Vegetarian Stroganoff, or **Punjabi Greens** are all options, depending on what sort of meal you have in mind.

Scones: see LIZ'S SCONES, p. 171 in BREADS.

CINNAMON ROLLS

Preparation time: an hour or more
SATTVIC, 0 Vata, - Pitta, + Kapha

Makes 6 rolls.

❀ ☙ ❄

Prepare:
One batch of LIZ'S SCONES, p. 171, with the optional sweetener

Divide the dough into six pieces and pat them into rectangular shapes about 1/2 inch high, 1 1/2 inches wide and 6 inches long.

Scatter over them:
1/2 c. raisins
1/2 c. raw walnuts or pecans, chopped

Then sprinkle over them:
1 Tbsp. cinnamon

Roll them up and set them upright on a lightly oiled baking pan. Chill for 1/2 hour or more.

Preheat oven to 400° F. Before putting the rolls in to bake, gently drizzle over the six:
6 Tbsps. real maple syrup (about a tablespoon per roll)

Bake until lightly browned, about 15 minutes. Very scrumptious.

Variation: For a ROTATION DAY 1, substitute barley malt for the maple syrup.

Where is the sacred space in your life? Is it in quiet moments alone, with your family or friends, in community? Is it in boisterous celebrations in temples, churches, forests, deserts, mountains? Perhaps you find it in every breath.

Where is the time and space which nurtures that yearning inside? For the sacred nourishes us, as people of all races and religions and times have known. In Ayurveda, sacred time and space help build ojas, our energy cushion and reserve. Sacred space is essential in our healing, living, dying.

APPLE DELIGHT SCONE

Preparation time: 1 hour
SATTVIC*

Serves: 6 - 8

Prepare:

A double batch of LIZ'S SCONES, p. 171, with the optional sweetener

Divide the dough into 2 equal parts. Lightly oil, then flour, 2 cookie sheets or baking pans. Pat each of the balls of dough lightly and gently into a 1 1/2" - 2" high round on a baking sheet. Chill for 30 minutes or more. Preheat oven to 400° F.

While the dough is chilling, grate:
2 organic apples

Mix the apples with:
1/2 c. Sucanat or apple concentrate
1 Tbsp. cinnamon
1/4 c. raisins (optional)**

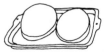  

Spread the grated apple filling evenly on one round scone. Place the other round on top of it. Bake for 20 minutes or until lightly brown on top. Serve in wedges, warm or cool.

*ROTATION DAY 1 DISH

* *mildly + Vata, - Pitta, + Kapha* (with whole wheat flour)

* *moderately + Vata, - Pitta, moderately + Kapha* (with barley flour)

** Raisins increase *Vata*, and are best avoided for them in this dish.

Variation: PEACH SCONE: Prepare the scone as above. Thin-slice:
2 c. peaches or nectarines

Mix with:
1/2 c. Sucanat, apple concentrate or maple syrup
1 tsp. ground cardamom

Bake as above.

SATTVIC, 0 Vata, - Pitta, + Kapha

Comment: PEACH SCONE, APPLE DELIGHT SCONE and CINNAMON ROLLS are rich, dessert-grade offerings. So while they are made without yeast, they are heavy and sweet enough that they are best avoided on a Candida-free diet.

ABOUT FOOD AND CONSTITUTION

A lot of focus has been put on food and constitution in these early days of Ayurveda in the United States. I would like to suggest that we relax and not fuss so much over this as we have in this first decade or so of getting to know Ayurveda. If you are eating a sattvic *diet, you can usually make effective adaptations for your particular constitution without shunning a food entirely.*

For example, say you are a guest at a Kapha *household, staying for a few days with friends. One morning, instead of the usual warm rice cereal, they serve you a hot cream of rye dish. Rye is warming, light and dry, good for* Kapha, *not so balancing for* Vata *and* Pitta. *As a* Vata, *do you skip breakfast and hope for better selections at lunch? I hope not! Just put extra ghee and a little sweetener on this, and you will be fine. If you were a* Pitta, *you could cool the qualities of the cereal down a bit by choosing maple syrup as your sweetener, which your hosts have graciously offered you. Both* Vata *and* Pitta *could sooth themselves with some warm fresh milk or chai to accompany their meal (if available).*

On the other hand, say you are a Vata *and you get into eating cream of rye every morning for breakfast at home. It's really delicious; you like that cardamom flavoring in the recipe. For a while all is fine, but then you notice that you're getting a little constipated, perhaps your lips are also getting cracked or dry, another indication of dryness in the colon. On a regular basis, it is more beneficial for you to use a warm moist cereal balancing to your* dosha, *like rice or wheat or oats. Everything in moderation in Ayurveda. Your body will let you know if you're less than moderate!*

If, on the third hand (this must be Lakshmi we're talking about, ah?) if you know that even a little potato gives you gas or those strawberries will create hives, don't push it. Trust your experience and pass up this food.

The food lists for constitutional types (in Appendix II) are offered as information to test out in your own body. Try them out for yourself; see what foods best suit you. Begin to develop your own experience and understanding of this science of self-healing.

Lunch

KEY

"–" means calms or helps the given constitution;

"+" means aggravates or increases it;

"0" means neutral effect.

 * ROTATION DIET can be helpful for people with food
   sensitivities, see p. 323

**POLARITY DISH refers to recipes supporting Polarity Therapy
   work, see p. 342

✿ = Spring

✳ = Summer

🜂 = Fall

❋ = Winter

Traditionally in Ayurveda, the mid-day meal is the largest. Digestion is at its peak at this time and best able to handle a variety of foods. However, in our country, less time is scheduled for lunch and more for dinner. Bowing to the realities of most people's days, I list here quick, light, easy to prepare dishes and their effects on the *doshas*, for lunch. Keep in mind that traditionally these would be more likely to be served at the end of the day, rather than in the middle. When I say quick and easy, I mean 25 minutes or less, start to finish.

ABOUT COOKING WITH CLIMATE

Ayurveda views us as the microcosm within the greater macrocosm, which includes our climate and where we live. We can use cooking as a way to adapt ourselves more comfortably to our surroundings. In a cool dry climate like the one in which I live, more liquids and oils are used in cooking to balance the high Vata *conditions which easily develop here. More oil is recommended for external use as well, as oil massage to the tender tissues which can dry out readily in the high mountain desert. Extra water inside the home is also balancing, such as a small fish pond or a tiny recycling fountain.*

In a hot wet humid climate like Louisiana or Florida, more drying measures need to be made. A little less oil, and more cornbread, and red beans, and rice. Larger salads help with the balancing and less sour food can be used (which holds in moisture).

In a cool damp climate like the Pacific Northwest, we are looking to both warm ourselves up and dry ourselves out. Warm slightly spicy food, with generous amounts of fresh ginger, is good. Extra indoor light in the form of full spectrum bulbs adds the fire needed to stimulate our systems. Saunas can be helpful or dry-brush massage, therapeutics usually reserved for a sluggish Kapha.

We still need to assess first our individual conditions and needs. A Pitta *in Seattle is wise to eat fewer spicy foods than a* Kapha *in the same city. But that same* Pitta *person is likely to be able to handle more pungent foods at home in the Northwest, than if he or she were to visit hot Tucson or steamy Miami.*

People living in urban areas are often first impacted by the energy created by the city and its inhabitants, and secondarily by the climate (except when it hits extremes, like July in New York City or January in Chicago). There is a general need in most metropolitan areas to calm Vata *and* Pitta. *This can be done with any of the light, soothing, easy to digest recipes offered here. Oil massage and* pranayama *are also beneficial for deeper balancing.*

TABLE 8: QUICK, EASY LUNCH DISHES

Fresh Baby Zuke Salad	- Vata	- Pitta	0 Kapha
Zucchini Salad	0 Vata	0 Pitta	0 Kapha
Summer Squash Salad	0 Vata	- Pitta	- Kapha
Bright Sunchoke Salad	0 Vata	0 Pitta	- Kapha
Fresh Spinach-Cucumber Salad	0 Vata	0 Pitta	0 Kapha
Fresh Chinese Cabbage Slaw	+ Vata	- Pitta	- Kapha
Fresh Grated Carrots	- Vata	0 Pitta	- Kapha
Carrot Raisin Salad	- Vata	0 Pitta	0 Kapha
Stuffed Avocado with Black	moderately	mildly	mildly
Beans and Cilantro	+ Vata	+ Pitta	+ Kapha
Pasta Salad, wheat	- Vata	- Pitta	+ Kapha
Pasta Salad, corn	0 Vata	slighty + Pitta	- Kapha
Sprouted Mung Salad	0 Vata	- Pitta	— Kapha
Jicama Tangerine Salad	- Vata	0 Pitta	0 Kapha
Cream of Broccoli Soup	0 Vata	0 Pitta	0 Kapha
Luciano's Zucchini Soup	- Vata	- Pitta	0 Kapha
Quick Black Bean Soup	+ Vata	0 Pitta	0 Kapha
Sprouted Mung Soup	0 Vata	- Pitta	0 Kapha
Lebanese Chickpeas	+ Vata	- Pitta	- Kapha
Hummus and Crackers	+ Vata	0 Pitta	0 Kapha
Quick Bean Dip with Tortillas	0 Vata	- Pitta	- Kapha
Creamed Spinach over Toast	0 Vata	0 Pitta	- Kapha
Almond Ginger Sauce over Vegs	- Vata	+ Pitta	+ Kapha
Bean Threads with Snow Peas	- Vata	0 Pitta	0 Kapha
Soba Noodles with Garlic and Vegetables	0 Vata	slightly + Pitta	0 Kapha
Simple Adukis	0 Vata	- Pitta	- Kapha
Cashew Cream Cauliflower	moderately + Vata	0 Pitta	0 Kapha
Brand "Z" Tofu, Generic with vegetables and Basmati or Kasha and Leeks	0 Vata	0 Pitta	0 Kapha
Pasta with Light Basil Sauce	- Vata	- Pitta	0 Kapha
Pasta with Pesto Sauce	- Vata	+ Pitta	+ Kapha
Pasta with Creamy Oregano Sauce	- Vata	- Pitta	0 Kapha
Pasta Primavera	- Vata	0 Pitta	- Kapha
Simplest Pasta	- Vata	0 Pitta	- Kapha

TABLE 9: LUNCHEON DISHES TO MAKE AHEAD OF TIME

Quinoa-Cilantro Salad	0 Vata	- Pitta	- Kapha
"Salad Bar Supreme"	0 Vata	- Pitta	- Kapha
Sweet Potato Salad	- Vata	0 Pitta	+ Kapha
Potato Salad, Light	moderately + Vata	0 Pitta	- Kapha
Fresh Carrot Aspic	- Vata	+ Pitta	- Kapha
Raspberry Kiwi Jelled Salad	0 Vata	- Pitta	0 Kapha
Strawberry Pineapple Jelled Salad	- Vata	- Pitta	+ Kapha
Light Cucumber Gazpacho	- Vata	- Pitta	0 Kapha
Hearty Vegetable Soup	0 Vata	- Pitta	- Kapha
Sweet Potato Soup	- Vata	- Pitta	+ Kapha
Very Basic Beet Borscht	- Vata	+ Pitta	- Kapha
Poor Woman's Creamy Asparagus Soup	- Vata	- Pitta	- Kapha
Split Pea Soup	0 Vata	- Pitta	- Kapha
Split Mung Soup	- Vata	- Pitta	mildly + Kapha
Quinoa-Asparagus Pilaf	- Vata	- Pitta	- Kapha
A Kichadi	- Vata	- Pitta	- Kapha
Ama-Reducing Dal	- Vata	- Pitta	- Kapha
Cilantro Quiche	- Vata	0 Pitta	0 Kapha
Nice Burger	0 Vata	0 Pitta	0 Kapha
Paneer and Scones	- Vata	- Pitta	+ Kapha
Tahini, Scones and Honey	- Vata	0 Pitta	+ Kapha
Blue Corn Bread and Santa Fe Pinto Beans	+ Vata	0 Pitta	- Kapha
Almond Butter and Fruit-Sweetened Jam on Irish Soda Bread	- Vata	0 Pitta	+ Kapha
Nori Rolls and Dipping Sauce	- Vata	- Pitta	0 Kapha

Salads

KEY

"–" means calms or helps the given constitution;

"+" means aggravates or increases it;

"0" means neutral effect.

 * ROTATION DIET can be helpful for people with food
   sensitivities, see p. 323.

**POLARITY DISH refers to recipes supporting Polarity Therapy
work, see p. 342.

✿ = Spring

✳ = Summer

୧ᴥ = Fall

❄ = Winter

RAINBOW SUMMER SALAD

Preparation time: 20 minutes
SATTVIC, 0 Vata, - Pitta, - Kapha

Serves: 4

Combine:

> 1 c. endive leaves, finely chopped
> 2 c. small tender lettuce leaves, finely chopped or broken up
> 8 mâche rosettes
> 2 tsps. fresh peppermint, finely chopped
> 1/4 c. (or less) arugula leaves and flowers
> 8 basil leaves, finely chopped
> 1 small yellow summer squash, thinly sliced, julienne
> 1 small carrot, grated
> 6 spinach leaves, finely chopped

Dress with:
TARRAGON PARSLEY SALAD DRESSING, p. 87.

Garnish with:

> fresh blue borage flowers, orange nasturtiums and toasted sunflower seeds (all optional but fun!).

**POLARITY PURIFYING DIET DISH

Comments: This is obviously a gardener's kind of salad, and gives some idea of how you might play with your own garden to create colorful light treats. Have fun with your own combinations. A home garden, even in the form of a tiny window box, can offer variety and freshness no supermarket can.

ZUCCHINI SALAD

Preparation time: 15 minutes
SATTVIC, 0 Vata, 0 Pitta, 0 Kapha

Serves: 3 - 4

Wash and prepare:

> 2 medium zucchinis, thin sliced
> 1 Tbsp. leeks, thin sliced
> 2 Tbsps. Italian parsley, finely chopped

Put the zucchini and the leek in a steamer to steam for about 2 minutes. (The zucchini can also be used raw if you like.) Put in a medium serving bowl; add the Italian parsley and toss with CREAMY PESTO DRESSING, p. 87.

**POLARITY PURIFYING DIET DISH

FRESH BABY ZUKE SALAD

Preparation time: 10 minutes   Serves: 2
SATTVIC, - Vata, - Pitta, 0 Kapha

Wash:

> **2 - 3 fresh baby zucchinis**
> **1 cucumber, peeled if not organic**
> **6 - 12 young comfrey leaves or 1/2 bunch fresh spinach, washed**

Slice the zucchinis lengthwise (ILLUS) and then crosswise
in very thin half-moon shapes. Peel the cucumber and cut
it in similar fashion. (If it is larger, quarter, then slice it.)
Finely chop the comfrey or spinach greens.

In a small heavy skillet, roast over low heat:

> **1/4 c. raw pumpkin seeds**

Toast until they begin to pop, about 1 - 3 minutes.
Toss the seeds in a pretty bowl with all the vegetables.
Drizzle directly over them:

> **1 Tbsp. olive oil**
> **1 1/2 tsps. fresh lemon or lime juice***

Toss and serve.

**POLARITY PURIFYING DIET DISH

*Variation: If you are following a strict rotation diet, omit the lemon or lime and use 1/4
tsp. vitamin C powder and 1 tsp. cool water instead. Unorthodox, and certainly not traditional, but helpful in a pinch, if your allergies are extreme.

*A DAY 2 ROTATION DISH

SUMMER SQUASH SALAD

Preparation time: 10 minutes (includes preparing dressing)　　　　Serves: 4

SATTVIC, 0 Vata, - Pitta, - Kapha　　　　

Wash and thin-slice:
> **4 small very fresh squash, either yellow crookneck or scallopini**

Steam:
> **1/2 c. fresh peas, shelled, raw ***

Stir into the squash. Marinade in:
> **TARRAGON PARSLEY SALAD DRESSING, p. 87.**

Serve. Nice light refreshing salad.

**POLARITY PURIFYING DIET DISH

NOTE: Raw peas are fine for *Pitta* and *Kapha*; some *Vatas* find them a little hard to digest. In this case, they can be steamed, covered, in a small pot for a minute or two.

WHAT'S FRESH?

As my esteemed copy editor and old friend Margie Hughes asked me, "What do you mean by fresh? Does this mean buying or picking veggies or fruit every day or does it refer to cooking it fresh each day? That is, could one buy broccoli on Tuesday and use half of it in a stir-fry that night, then store the rest of it (raw) in the fridge and put that in another dish on Thursday?" Sure. What is most important here is the transformative effect of fire, cooking. Once a food has been cooked, it is open to much more rapid processes of breakdown and fermentation. So it is recommended that you eat a cooked dish (or a cut-up marinated raw dish) the same day you prepare them.

Fresh whole raw fruit can be stored at room temperature whenever appropriate; most vegetables can be stored whole in the refrigerator for a few days.

For the freshest food, getting produce fresh-picked daily from your garden or another's is, of course, ideal. It will have the most vitality as well as nutrients. (Like many cooks, this quest for freshness has spurred my interest in gardening, especially Ayurvedic gardening.) If you were to rank them, fresh-picked is best; fresh pre-picked produce comes next; and raw produce which has sat whole in cold storage after that. All of these would be considered "fresh", though, compared to a dish which was cooked one day and served the next. This last is not fresh, from an Ayurvedic perspective.

BRIGHT SUNCHOKE SALAD

Preparation time: 10 minutes   Serves: 2 - 3
SATTVIC (amount of garlic used is minimal), 0 Vata, 0 Pitta, - Kapha ✿ ✳ 🐌 ❄

Wash very well:
12 large sunchokes (Jerusalem artichokes), raw

They definitely have a tendency to accumulate dirt behind their ears, so to speak. Grate them into a bowl, leaving their peels on.

Stir in:
1 clove garlic, minced

Toss with:
TARRAGON PARSLEY DRESSING, p. 87

and serve immediately.

**POLARITY PURIFYING DIET DISH

Comment: It is the flavor that is bright here, not the color!

FRESH SPINACH-CUCUMBER SALAD

Preparation time: 15 minutes   Serves: 3
SATTVIC*   ✿ ✳ 🐌 ❄

Wash well and dry:
2 c. fresh spinach

Wash and peel:
1/2 cucumber

Cut it lengthwise (ILLUS) and then thin-slice it into half moons.
Arrange the spinach on salad plates with the cucumber slices on top.

Serve with:
ALMOND-CUCUMBER DRESSING, p. 88
or TARRAGON HONEY MUSTARD DRESSING, p. 88
And toasted chopped almonds on top

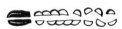

* *0 Vata, 0 Pitta, + Kapha (with Almond-Cucumber Dressing)*
* *0 Vata, 0 Pitta, 0 Kapha (with Tarragon Honey Mustard Dressing)*

Comments: To make this more calming for *Kapha*, use a larger amount of fresh spinach. You can also dilute the Almond-Cucumber Dressing with water, or use less of it.

FRESH CHINESE CABBAGE SLAW

Preparation time: 10 - 15 minutes, including dressing
SATTVIC, + Vata, - Pitta, - Kapha

Serves: 4

♣ ✳ 🫖 ❄

Wash and chop into 1/2" slices across the ribs:
1/2 head fresh Chinese cabbage, about 2 c.

Set aside. Make up:
ORANGE - SESAME DRESSING, p. 89

Pour about half the dressing over the chopped Chinese cabbage, tossing well. The rest of the dressing can be reserved for another use.

*A ROTATION DAY 4 DISH

**POLARITY PURIFYING DIET DISH

Comments: This makes a nice mild, easier-to-digest slaw than most, popular with kids.

CARROT RAISIN SALAD

Preparation time: 15 minutes
SATTVIC, -Vata, 0 Pitta, 0 Kapha

Serves: 2 - 3

♣ ✳ ❄

Put in a cup and cover with hot water:
2 Tbsps. raisins, organic preferred

Let them soak 10 minutes at least. This helps plump them up and makes them easier to digest. Wash well and grate:
2 medium carrots

Whisk together:
1 Tbsp. fresh lemon juice
1/2 tsp. raw honey

Then whisk in:
2 Tbsps. cold-pressed olive oil

Drain the raisins and add them to the carrots in a mixing bowl. Pour the dressing over the salad. Stir well.

**POLARITY PURIFYING DIET DISH

ANTIPASTO CARROTS

Preparation time: 30 minutes, plus an hour to cool   Serves: 4
SATTVIC,- Vata, 0 Pitta, - Kapha*   ✿ ✳ ꙮ ❄

Bring to a boil in a medium saucepan:
>   **1/2 tsp. salt**
>   **1/2 tsp. Sucanat or fructose**
>   **4 c. water**

Wash and julienne slice:
>   **4 medium organic carrots (about 4 cups)**

Toss them into the boiling water and blanch, covered for about 3 minutes. Drain and put them in a bowl which can be easily covered (Tupperware works well). Combine:
>   **1 1/2 Tbsps. fresh lemon juice**
>   **3 Tbsps. olive oil**
>   **1 small clove garlic, minced (can be omitted)***
>   **2 tsps. fresh spearmint, chopped**
>   **1/2 tsp. fresh rosemary, finely chopped**
>   **Salt and pepper to taste (can be omitted)**

Pour the dressing over the carrots and stir or shake well. Marinade in the refrigerator until the flavors have mingled. Serve.

*SATTVIC, - Vata, - Pitta, 0 Kapha, if garlic is omitted

Comments: This is an old Sicilian recipe shared by my friend Dolores Chiappone. The original uses red wine vinegar rather than lemon juice.

Variation:

FRESH GRATED CARROTS WITH SPEARMINT AND LIME

Preparation time: 10 minutes   Serves: 4
SATTVIC, - Vata, 0 Pitta, - Kapha   ✿ ✳ ꙮ ❄

Wash and grate into a medium bowl:
>   **4 medium carrots, organic are tastiest**

Wash and finely chop:
>   **1 tsp. fresh spearmint**

Stir it into the carrots. Drizzle over the carrots and mint:
>   **1 Tbsp. cold-pressed extra-virgin olive oil**
>   **1 1/2 tsps. fresh lime juice (or lemon)**

Stir well.

** POLARITY PURIFYING DIET DISH

FRESH VEGETABLES

So how do you get the freshest vegetables? Fresh vegetables have a great deal more vital energy, prana, *than frozen or canned ones. And this vital energy can be shared with you. One delightful book that can get you started growing your own fresh salad greens year-round is Eliot Coleman's* The New Organic Grower's Four-Season Harvest. *Coleman uses simple, practical, ecologically sound ways to protect vegetables in even the coldest weather, without elaborate greenhouses or piped in heat. With a four-season harvest, you are not trying to eat asparagus in October or tomatoes in January. You eat with the rhythm of the seasons. And each season has its own greens to enjoy: lettuce and spinach in spring, early summer and fall, New Zealand spinach and orach in high summer, arugula, mache and miner's lettuce as the weather gets very cold. Sprouts can be grown year-round if you like. (See ABOUT SPROUTING, p. 104)*

SWEET POTATO SALAD

Preparation time: 30-45 minutes   Serves: 4
SATTVIC, - Vata, 0 Pitta, + Kapha   ✿ ✳ ⋙ ❄

Boil whole or cut in several pieces:
>   **4 c. sweet potatoes (2 large)**

Whisk together in a small mixing bowl:
>   **1 Tbsp. fresh ginger root, finely grated**
>   **1/2 tsp. organic lemon peel, finely grated**
>   **1/4 c. fresh lemon juice (1 1/2 lemons)**
>   **1 1/2 tsps. raw honey**
>   **2-3 Tbsps. sesame oil**
>   **Salt to taste**

When the potatoes are tender enough for a fork to go into them easily, drain off the water (I often save it for future use in soup stock), and peel the potatoes. The peels will come off easily using your fingers or a small knife. Cube the sweet potatoes into 1/2 inch pieces. Put them in a serving bowl and toss well with the dressing. Serve warm or cool.

**POLARITY PURIFYING DIET DISH

Comments: This beta-carotene rich salad is especially strengthening for the lungs.

STUFFED AVOCADO WITH BLACK BEAN AND CILANTRO

Preparation time: 10 minutes

Serves: 2-4

RAJASIC (due to the avocado), moderately + Vata, mildly + Pitta and Kapha

In a medium saucepan, place:

1 c. water
1 steamer
1 Tbsp. red onion, finely chopped, in the steamer

Steam the onion over the water for 2- 5 minutes.
Remove it from the steamer and mix it together with:

1 c. cooked black beans, unsalted
1/2 c. organic celery, finely chopped
1/2 - 3/4 tsp. salt (omit if beans are salted)
1/4 c. fresh lemon juice
1/3 c. fresh cilantro, chopped
Pinch of cayenne

Spoon into:

1 or 2 avocados, halved

Serves 2 for entree or 4 for appetizer.

**POLARITY HEALTH BUILDING DISH

POTATO SALAD, LIGHT

Preparation time: 40 minutes

Serves: 4

SATTVIC, moderately + Vata, 0 Pitta, - Kapha

Scrub and pare the eyes from:

6 medium red potatoes

Cover with boiling water in a deep, medium saucepan and cook uncovered over medium heat until soft, about 30 minutes. While the potatoes are cooking, make up:

1 recipe of TARRAGON HONEY MUSTARD DRESSING, p. 88

and steam:

1 c. fresh peas

Let cool. Finely chop:

>**2 stalks celery**
>**1/4 c. parsley**

Set aside.

When the potatoes are done, drain them (the cooking liquid makes a good potential soup stock) and let them cool. Cube or slice them as is your inclination. Put them in a large mixing bowl with the rest of the ingredients and mix well. Serve.

WILD RICE SALAD

Preparation time: 1 1/2 hours, most of it unattended
SATTVIC, - Vata, 0 Pitta, 0 Kapha

Serves: 4

Wash:

>**1 c. uncooked wild rice or 1/2 c. wild rice and 1/2 c. brown** *basmati*

Bring it to a boil in a medium saucepan with:

>**3 1/2 c. vegetable stock***
>**1 tsp. salt or less**

Reduce heat to medium-low, cover and cook until done, about an hour. When the rice is close to being done, come back into the kitchen and wash and chop:

>**1 small yellow crookneck squash, sliced**
>**1 very small sweet red bell pepper, finely diced**

When the wild rice is tender and easy to chew, add the vegetables to the pot of rice. Cover and cook on low heat for another 10 minutes. Drain the rice if necessary (most or all of the water should have been absorbed into it) and stir in:

>**1/4 c. raw pine nuts**
>**1 - 6 Tbsps. Creamy Garlic Salad Dressing (p, 86), depending on your taste**
>**1/8 tsp. cayenne**

Serve hot or cool.

**POLARITY HEALTH BUILDING DISH

*If I do not have a good vegetable stock on hand, I put **1 whole washed uncooked carrot, broken into about 3 pieces, and 3 small dried Shiitaake mushrooms** in the pot to cook with the wild rice. Some kind of stock or vegetable is needed in this recipe to give it its finest flavor. A person following a strict *sattvic* diet could skip the mushrooms.

QUINOA CILANTRO SALAD: see p. 202, under Whole Grain Side Dishes

WHY AVOID MEAT?

There's plenty of reasons. Foremost among them is that our American habit of eating and raising cattle is consuming huge amounts of habitat (and food) from other species planet-wide. The United States is the leading importer of beef, and the leading exporter of the fast-food burger lifestyle. Raising cattle takes lots of land. Such land is more vulnerable to erosion and compaction. And cows' nitrogenous wastes are contaminating many water supplies.

Cows create a demand for protein-rich feed, and water. As much as half of an area's grain and oilseed reserves end up fed to cattle, routinely, in countries across the planet. This meat is then shipped to us gluttons "up north". As Francis Moore Lappé pointed out more than two decades ago in Diet for a Small Planet, *this disgustingly routine inequity can be encapsulated in the following: imagine seating yourself in a restaurant in front of an 8 ounce prime rib. Then see, with you, 45 - 50 people sitting with empty bowls. This is the "feed cost" of that one steak, 45 - 50 cups of whole cooked grain.*

And once you dive into that steak or burger, what happens inside you? Meat is getting more dangerous with regards to personal health. For example, one new strain of bacteria in hamburger, E. coli 0157:H7, has become so deadly that in 1994 a joint panel of scientists, meat industry representatives and government officials recommended to the U.S. Department of Agriculture that most ground beef be irradiated before sale.

Their view was that this cobalt radiation was the only way to kill the lethal microbes in ground meat and guarantee its safety for consumers. (The bacteria under scrutiny was the same one which infected 700 people in the Pacific Northwest in 1993.) That meat has become so putrid that the only way to sterilize it is to radiate it, is pretty appalling.

It also indicates the depths to which the meat-producing industry at large has sunk, in terms of raising healthy animals and offering clean produce. A factor which does not seem to be under consideration is the long-term possibilities of creating even more deadly and resistant strains of bacteria through radiation-induced mutations.

While the consumption of meat has long been associated with a greater likelihood of getting colon cancer, heart disease, osteoporosis, and other diseases, some grisly new twists are unfortunately appearing in the picture. "Mad cow disease" is epidemic in England. Here in the United States we refer to "downer cows" as those that fall down and can't get back up, for a variety of reasons. The vast majority of downer cows in this country are slaughtered and their meat is sent out, either for human consumption or to be rendered into animal feeds. These high-protein animal feeds are then fed back to other animals, including cows.

Why Avoid Meat? (continued)

There is serious concern in England that this process of feeding cows to other cows is spreading BSE, bovine spongiform encephalopathy. BSE is a degenerative brain disease which causes animals first to get unsteady on their feet, then to go mad and die. At this point there is no known cure for the disease and it is invariably fatal. Even more disturbing, the disease seems to be able to infect other mammals.

For example, in Britain, it is thought that the affected cows originally contracted the disease by eating feeds made of rendered sheep. (Goats and sheep can carry a transmissible spongiform brain disease known as scrapie.) And at least one British dairy farmer whose herd was infected with BSE has since died of Creutzfeldt-Jakob disease, a human form of "spongy brain" disease. Alarm in England is high. More than two thousand public schools in the U.K. no longer serve beef to children. In the spring of 1993, 885 British cows were dying of the disease each week, up from 675 cows weekly the previous year. According to the U.S. government, BSE is not a concern in America. And yet given our feeding practices it would appear that this disease or others could easily spread here.

So you don't eat beef and haven't in years. What about other animal flesh foods? Again, animals have fallen prey to human practices, both in terms of filth in production and planetary contaminants. Because they eat high on the food chain, many animals concentrate commonly circulating toxins like PCBs (polychlorinated biphenols) and mercury in their tissues. Fish larger than salmon, such as swordfish and tuna, can have dangerously high levels of mercury. Fish in the Great Lakes have accumulated PCBs to the point that the official recommendation has been to eat them no more than once per week, and not at all if you are pregnant.

Salmon, an extraordinarily nutritious food rich in calcium, protein and essential fatty acids, is being fished to extinction in many areas. Do you want to contribute to this specie's demise? Chicken, because of sloppy production methods, run you the risk of anti-biotic resistant salmonella infection. And hogs show rising levels of sulfa drug residues in their tissues over the last ten years. Turkeys have the lowest levels of pesticide and chemical residues at present. If you raise your own animals and care for them well, or have another reliable source of organic produce, this can be an option.

And yet if you are working with an Ayurvedic physician, the chances are high, at least in this decade, that she or he is a vegetarian. And most Ayurvedic doctors trained in India are most familiar with vegetarian regimes. They know best how these diets interact with the practices they recommend, and the herbal preparations they may suggest. They are aware that meat is a heavy food, and that it often causes internal fermentation in the gut. And they are likely to be able to work with you more easily if you are on a diet familiar to them. At the same time this must be a diet agreeable to you!

Why Avoid Meat? (continued)

So if you are continuing to eat meat and yet are interested in cutting it back or out, you might want to try the Ayurvedic practice of "1/4, 1/4, 1/4": gauge your current animal flesh consumption, and cut yourself back by 25% of that amount. When this level feels comfortable to you, reduce your consumption of meat by another quarter, and so on. Let yourself stabilize at each level before reducing any further.

Some people have found that they genuinely seem to need more protein and are hesitant to give up meat for this reason. Kids and pregnant women often crave animal products, and as a nutritionist I tend to support this, recommending the cleanest, freshest, purest produce possible. A traditional Ayurvedic cook would likely disagree with me on this point. On the other hand, in my experience, I have often seen other adults who felt that they needed animal flesh in their diets. Not infrequently this need arises from problems with inefficient digestion and absorption, which can be substantially improved on an Ayurvedic program. If you sense this description could apply to you, my recommendation would be to find an Ayurvedic physician you trust, describe your situation, and see what they recommend. Often Ayurvedic digestive preparations can be given to help you access the protein and other nutrients in a vegetarian diet more readily than you have in the past. And you may be surprised in your overall improvements in health and vitality.

Many Americans have cut back on animal flesh consumption a lot in the last few decades, and save meat, poultry or fish for those special occasions eating out in restaurants.

To be a miserably wet blanket, I have to say that it is a rare establishment that serves chicken or meat which is clean or organic. (Argh. How can I be so practical, so unfeeling?)

What about vitamin B-12? If you are eating fresh milk and eggs, you are getting this nutrient. If you are a strict vegan (eating no animal products at all), the algae Spirulina is a good source of this B vitamin. If none of these agrees with you, you might need an occasional B-12 supplement. However, if you have taken animal foods in the past, it is good to know that the liver normally stores enough B-12 within it to cover our needs for six to seven years. (I often used to see vegans in my nutrition practice at this critical time, about seven years into their choice of diet. After years of feeling good, they would report feeling gradually tired, cranky, off-balance. Often working extra B-12 sources into their regimes, with goodly amounts of other vitamin B-rich and mineral-rich foods, helped a good deal.) One concern I have is for the child who has been raised as a vegan, or who has chosen on their own this eating style. Since he or she has built up no stores of this vitamin, a regular source of B-12 is needed in their diet, such as a Spirulina-enhanced smoothie. Some parents and kids may even find themselves adding back in fresh eggs or milk to meet this need.

Ultimately, of course, whether or not you eat meat is up to you.

PASTA SALAD

Preparation time: 20 minutes

Serves: 4

SATTVIC*

❁ ✳ ೞ

Cook:

> **2 c. whole grain rotini pasta, wheat or corn**

As the pasta is cooking, you can wash, chop, or grate:

> **1 c. fresh grated vegetables: carrot, jicama, summer squash (all work well)**
>
> **1 c. fresh chopped vegetables: a tomato, some snow peas, a thin sliced zucchini, mizuna, and/or parsley are good**

Steam for 1 - 2 minutes in a stainless steel steamer in a saucepan with an inch or so of water:

> **1/4 onion, finely chopped (optional)**
>
> **1 clove garlic, minced (optional)**

If you like (say you are calming *Vata*, air) you can put the thin-sliced zucchini or snow peas or shelled peas to steam with the onion and garlic for those couple of minutes. It is not necessary to do this for *Pitta* or *Kapha*, yet it makes the dish easier to digest for *Vata*.

Drain the pasta when it is done, and run cool water over it.

Mix:

> **1/2 c. ORANGE-SESAME DRESSING, p. 89**

with:

> **1 Tbsp. raw sesame tahini**

Put the pasta and all the vegetables into a serving bowl. Sprinkle over them the dressing and:

> **1 tsp. fresh dill seeds**
>
> **Salt to taste**
>
> **1 Tbsp. chopped walnuts**

Stir well and serve.

*With wheat rotini: SATTVIC, - Vata, - Pitta, + Kapha

*With corn rotini: SATTVIC, 0 Vata, slightly + Pitta, - Kapha

**POLARITY HEALTH BUILDING DISH

Variation: For a DAY 4 ROTATION dish, use corn rotini, DAY 4 vegetable choices such as watercress, arugula, asparagus,and/or shallots, omit the dill, and substitute pistachio nuts for the walnuts. See p. 323 for more information about rotation diets.

SATTVIC, 0 Vata, + Pitta, 0 Kapha

**POLARITY HEALTH BUILDING DISH

FAVORITE ITALIAN BEAN SALAD

Preparation time: 1 hour   Serves: 6
SATTVIC, + Vata, - Pitta, - Kapha   ✿ ✳ ೩

Bring to pressure in a stainless steel pressure cooker:
>   1/2 c. dry kidney beans
>   1/2 c. dry navy beans
>   4 1/2 c. stock, see VEGETABLE SOUP STOCK, p. 113
>   1 bay leaf
>   Pinch of hing or epazote
>   1 whole small onion (optional)
>   1/2 tsp. whole coriander seeds
>   5 - 6 black peppercorns
>   1 Tbsp. olive or sesame oil

Cook until the beans are done, about 30 minutes at pressure. While the beans are cooking, wash and prepare:
>   1 c. fresh broccoli, finely chopped
>   2 medium carrots, thin-sliced in half-moons or quarters
>   1/4 - 1/2 c. fresh raw greens: mustard or kale
>   1 - 3 c. zucchini, chopped
>   1 Tbsp. fresh chives or red onion, finely chopped (optional)

In a large saucepan or skillet, warm:
>   1 Tbsp. extra-virgin olive oil

Saute the vegetables in the oil on medium low, not more than 5 minutes. When the beans are done, drain them, and toss them in with the vegetables. Add:
>   2 Tbsps. fresh Italian parsley, finely chopped
>   2 tsps. fresh basil, chopped or 1 tsp. dried
>   1 tsp. fresh or dried oregano, chopped
>   1/4 tsp. ground black pepper
>   1/2 tsp. salt
>   2 Tbsps. fresh lemon juice
>   1 - 2 Tbsps. extra-virgin olive oil

Toss. Serve warm or cool.

Comments: For an all-out supper, this is good with a simple pasta with olive oil, and an arugula-tomato salad. For a lighter meal, it is nice by itself with a few crackers and ghee. The lavish amounts of black pepper, basil and oregano are all designed to help support *agni*, so that it is easier for your body to digest the beans.

Variations: If you steam the veggies rather than saute them, this is a POLARITY HEALTH BUILDING DISH. Add the olive oil at the end, uncooked.

SPROUTED MUNG SALAD: If you are looking for something more neutral for *Vata*, try **2 cups of sprouted mung beans** in place of the kidney and navy beans. Skip the pressure cooking and simply add the sprouted beans in the last minute of sauteing the vegetables. Cover and steam for about a minute, then add the rest of the herbs, lemon and oil as before. This is calming for *Pitta* and *Kapha* as well.

SATTVIC, 0 Vata,- - Pitta,- - Kapha

**POLARITY PURIFYING DIET DISH

Total preparation time for this last variation: 10 - 15 minutes

---

JICAMA-TANGERINE SALAD

Preparation time: 15 minutes   Serves: 4
SATTVIC, - Vata, 0 Pitta, 0 Kapha   ✳ ૨ล

Prepare the dressing by mixing together:
> **Juice of 2 lemons (about 1/3 c.)**
> **2 tsp. raw honey**
> **1 tsp. ground coriander**
> **2 Tbsps. sesame or sunflower oil**

Peel and slice very thinly:
> **2 c. jicama**

Peel and section:
> **2 c. sweet tangerines**

Toss about 1/2 cup of the dressing with the jicama and tangerine. Put in a pretty serving bowl and garnish with:
> **2 Tbsps. fresh cilantro leaves, finely chopped**
> **Salt to taste (optional)**

Serve.

**POLARITY PURIFYING DIET DISH, omit salt

Comments: To make this even more calming for *Kapha* and *Pitta*, use more jicama in proportion to the tangerines. This is an old Mexican favorite; light and tasty. If the tangerines are sour, the salad will still be helpful for *Vata*; but the sourness aggravates *Pitta* and *Kapha*, and so should be avoided for them.

FRESH CARROT ASPIC

Preparation time: 20 minutes, plus 1/2 hour to chill   Serves: 4
SATTVIC, - Vata, 0 Pitta, - Kapha

In a skillet, toast uncovered over low heat until lightly brown:
    2 Tbsps. raw sunflower seeds

stirring occasionally. This can take about 5 minutes. Remove from heat.

Wash and prepare:
    1 1/2 c. raw carrot (about 2 medium carrots), freshly grated
    2 Tbsps. raw celery, finely chopped
    1 Tbsp. fresh parsley, finely chopped
Stir together in a small saucepan:
    1 c. water
    2 tsps. agar agar

Bring to a boil, then reduce heat to low and simmer for 5 minutes. Remove from heat and stir in:
    1/4 c. fresh lemon juice
    2 tsps. raw honey

Add the vegetables, sunflower seeds and:
    1 tsp. dried tarragon
    1/8 tsp. ground cumin
    1/2 c. fresh carrot juice

Mix well. Lightly wet a mold or stainless steel bowl and pour in the aspic. Chill until set, about 30 minutes.

*ROTATION DAY 3 DISH

**POLARITY PURIFYING DIET DISH

Variation: Finely chopped raw walnuts can be used in place of the sunflower seeds.

SATTVIC, - Vata, mildly + Pitta, 0 Kapha

**POLARITY PURIFYING DIET DISH

Comments: This averages over 12,000 i.u. of beta-carotene per serving. This is great for immunity, strengthens the liver, and serves as a cancer-preventive.

RASPBERRY KIWI JELLED SALAD

Preparation time: 15 - 20 minutes, 1 hour to cool   Serves: 4 - 6
SATTVIC, 0 Vata, - Pitta, 0 Kapha   ✳

Bring to a boil in a small saucepan:
   3 c. fruit-sweetened raspberry nectar (Knudsen's works well)

Pour the juice into a blender, then add:
   1 Tbsp. Universal pectin (Pomona's works well)
   1 Tbsp. Calcium solution (comes with pectin)

Blend for a full minute. Pour into a stainless steel bowl or mold and stir in:
   3 fresh peaches, peeled and sliced
   2 fresh kiwis, peeled and sliced

Chill until set, about 30 minutes or more.

**POLARITY PURIFYING DIET DISH

ABOUT CHOOSING PINEAPPLES

It is best not to figure you are having a pineapple dish until you have a marvelous fragrant pineapple in hand. In other words, do not plan to have the next dish with pineapple sight unseen, for you may not find a pineapple worth using. (Like avocados north of the border, there may be none ripe and delectable about.)

If you are wandering through the produce section of your market and suddenly are hit by a wonderful pineapple aroma, head that way. If the fruit is firm and not overly soft and smells quite good, your prospects are promising. Try one other test: pull a leaf from the center or top of the pineapple. If it comes out easily, this pineapple is ready to be eaten. If it passes all tests but this one, you can figure a few days at home ripening should do it.)

To ripen a pineapple evenly, store it upside down. As the bottom of the pineapple begins to ripen and become fragrant, the sugars below it in the upper part will also develop more evenly and quickly than if you store it on its bottom. Under no circumstance bother to make any fresh pineapple recipe here without a good sweet pineapple; your results will be only as good as the fruit itself.

Pineapples are usually eaten on an occasional, rather than regular, basis in Ayurveda, due to their acidity. This acidity can be heating, which is to be avoided if there is any inflammation already present in the system.

STRAWBERRY PINEAPPLE JELLED SALAD

Preparation time: 20 minutes, plus 1/2 hour to chill   Serves: 4-6
SATTVIC, - Vata, - Pitta, mildly + Kapha with pineapple juice

Stir together in a small saucepan:

1 Tbsp. agar agar
1 c. fresh pineapple juice (or apple can be used)*

Bring to a boil, then reduce heat and simmer for five minutes. When the agar agar has dissolved into the juice, remove the pan from the heat.

Wash and prepare:

1 c. fresh strawberries
1 c. fresh sweet pineapple, peeled and chopped, leaving the strawberries whole or halved as you like, and the pineapple in whatever size chunk you prefer.

Stir the fruit into the agar agar solution. Spoon into a mold or bowl, or into individual serving cups. Chill until set, 30 minutes or more.

*ROTATION DAY 3 DISH, if pineapple is used.

**SATTVIC, mildly + Vata, - Pitta, 0 Kapha if apple juice is used*

**POLARITY PURIFYING DIET DISH, with either juice.

Comments: A garnish of fresh mint leaves is good.

ABOUT SALAD BARS

A fresh salad bar can be a win-win situation for all constitutions, if you choose wisely. Vata folks can hold with foods easier to digest for them, like avocado, a little greens, a nice creamy or oil and lemony dressing, some nuts or seeds, steamed veggies. Pittas and Kaphas can go for more of the beans, plenty of greens, whatever veggies they like, perhaps a baked potato on the side. Trust your knowledge of what your own body can handle, when faced with an alluring buffet or potluck. Remembering this wisdom is sometimes less than easy, but always appreciated by your body!

SALAD BAR SUPREME

Preparation time: 10 - 45 minutes, depending on what you serve   Serves: 6 - 8

SATTVIC, 0 Vata, - Pitta, - Kapha*

Put out any of the following which appeal to you:

> 4 - 8 c. washed fresh salad greens
> Spinach, arugula or radicchio
> Avocados, diced, in a bowl
> Sprouts, in bowls
> A few cherry tomatoes
> 1 c. cooked beans: sprouted mung, kidney, lima, whatever you choose
> Toasted sunflower seeds or pumpkin seeds
> Pine nuts
> Cauliflower or broccoli florets (lightly steamed)
> Fresh peas
> Coarsely ground black pepper
> 2 or 3 freshly made salad dressings: Tarragon Parsley, Creamy Garlic, or
> Orange Sesame dressing are all flavorful choices.

Just wash what needs to be washed and/or chopped and put your selections out in attractive bowls with serving spoons. If anyone you are serving has some excess air (*Vata*) in their makeup, quickly steaming the cauliflower, broccoli or peas for a couple of minutes, would be appreciated.

Make up any salad dressings that you need, enlisting willing help from your company if you've got it.

If you want to splurge a bit, you can make a special salad dish or two, like the ANTIPASTO CARROTS, FAVORITE ITALIAN BEAN SALAD, or WILD RICE SALAD. But if you're in a scramble, let yourself relax and keep it simple.

**POLARITY HEALTH BUILDING DISH

BASIC LEMON AND OLIVE OIL DRESSING

Preparation time: 5-10 minutes   Makes 1 cup
SATTVIC, 0 Vata, 0 Pitta, 0 Kapha (if eaten with salad greens) *   ✿ ✳ 🐌 ❄

Whisk together in a small bowl with a fork:

> 1/3 c. fresh squeezed lemon juice (about 2 lemons)
> 1/3 - 1/2 c. extra-virgin olive oil
> 1 tsp. raw honey (optional)
> Salt and pepper to taste

SATTVIC, - Vata, + Pitta, + Kapha (if eaten alone, which is unlikely!)

**POLARITY PURIFYING DIET DISH

Variation: Add one small clove of minced garlic.

SATTVIC WITH SOME RAJASIC QUALITY, 0 Vata, + Pitta, 0 Kapha (with salad greens)

**POLARITY PURIFYING DIET DISH

Comments: This is the basic duo I keep around the kitchen at all times, a few organic lemons and some extra-virgin olive oil. It is then easy to whisk in some fresh or dried herbs, like tarragon, rosemary, sage, parsley, or oregano to make a dressing which makes "more of a statement", as my honey Gord would say.

CREAMY GARLIC SALAD DRESSING

Preparation time: 10 minutes   Serves: 4
RAJASIC, 0 Vata, + Pitta, 0 Kapha (with salad)   ✿ 🐌 ❄

Stir together:

> 1 1/2 Tbsps. sesame tahini
> 1 1/2 Tbsps. fresh lemon juice
> 1 - 2 cloves of garlic, minced
> 2 - 4 Tbsps. water
> 2 -3 tsps. toasted sesame oil
> 1/8 tsp. freshly ground black pepper*

Serve. This is quite good over a simple salad of butter crunch lettuce, spinach and avocado chunks.

*ROTATION DAY 4 DRESSING, skip the pepper if you are following a strict rotation.

**POLARITY PURIFYING DIET DISH, if you skip the toasted sesame oil.

TARRAGON PARSLEY SALAD DRESSING

Preparation time: 10 minutes   Serves: 6
SATTVIC, 0 Vata, 0 Pitta, 0 Kapha (with salad)

Whisk together in a small bowl, adding the oil last:
> **1/4 c. fresh lemon or lime juice**
> **1/2 tsp. salt**
> **1/4 tsp. freshly ground black pepper**
> **1 tsp. fresh tarragon, finely chopped**
> **1 tsp. fresh parsley, finely chopped**
> **1/2 c. cold-pressed extra-virgin olive oil - sesame or sunflower also work fine**

Or blend in a blender. Makes 3/4 cup of salad dressing. Can be used immediately or stored in the refrigerator until ready.

**POLARITY PURIFYING DIET DISH, omit the salt

Variation: This recipe can easily be used to make A DAY 3 ROTATION dressing. Substitute 1/4 c. rice vinegar for the lemon or juice, and use sunflower oil.

RAJASIC, 0 Vata, 0 Pitta, 0 Kapha (with salad)
**POLARITY HEALTH BUILDING DISH

Variation: Another simple tarragon dressing can be made with 1/2 tsp. dried tarragon in place of the fresh. The salt, pepper and parsley can be omitted if you like in this version.

SATTVIC, 0 Vata, 0 Pitta, 0 Kapha
**POLARITY PURIFYING DIET DISH, without the salt

CREAMY PESTO DRESSING

Preparation time: 10 minutes   Makes about 1 1/4 cups
SATTVIC, 0 Vata, 0 Pitta, 0 Kapha (with salad)

Grind until fine in a blender:
> **1/4 c. raw walnuts or pine nuts**

Add and blend together with the nuts until smooth:
> **1 c. fresh basil leaves, chopped**
> **1 small clove garlic**
> **1/4 c. fresh lemon juice**
> **1/4 c. extra-virgin olive oil**
> **1/4 - 3/8 c. water**

Serve.

**POLARITY HEALTH BUILDING DISH

RICH ALMOND-CUCUMBER DRESSING

Preparation time: 15 minutes   Serves: 3
SATTVIC, 0 Vata, 0 Pitta, mildly + Kapha (with salad)   ✳ ૨⚫

In a small heavy skillet, toast until lightly browned, about 3 - 4 minutes on medium-low heat:
   1/2 c. blanched almonds

Let them cool. Set aside 1/4 c. to be used as garnish with the dressing. Grind the other 1/4 c. in the blender into a fine powder. Add to the ground almonds in the blender:
   2 Tbsps - 1/4 c. extra virgin olive oil (depending on your taste)
   1/4 c. fresh lemon juice
   1/2 medium cucumber, peeled and sliced
   1/4 tsp. salt
   1 - 2 Tbsps. water

Blend until smooth. Best if used immediately. Very good over FRESH SPINACH-CUCUMBER SALAD, p. 70.

Variation: A clove of steamed garlic can be added to the blend.

A LITTLE RAJASIC, 0 Vata, mildly + Pitta, mildly + Kapha (with salad)

*ROTATION DAY 2 Variation: Prepare as in the basic recipe above, omitting the lemon juice. Instead, use 1/4 cup water (total) and 1/4 tsp. corn-free vitamin C crystals. The idea of using vitamin C in place of lemon or vinegar in a salad dressing comes from Marjorie H. Jones in her book, *The Allergy Self-Help Cookbook*. Vitamin C is certainly not traditionally Ayurvedic, and yet it can be a helpful substitute for those individuals who are currently reacting to citrus or vinegar.

TARRAGON HONEY MUSTARD DRESSING

Preparation time: 10 minutes   Serves: 6
SATTVIC, 0 Vata, 0 Pitta, 0 Kapha (with salad)   ❁ ✳ ૨⚫ ❆

Blend together in a blender:
   1 tsp. dried tarragon or 1 Tbsp. fresh
   1/4 c. fresh lemon juice
   1/4 - 1/2 tsp. salt
   1/4 tsp. freshly ground black pepper
   1 clove garlic, minced
   1/8 tsp. dry mustard
   2 tsps. raw honey
   1/2 c. olive oil - sunflower can also be used

Serve.

Comments: One of our favorites.

ORANGE-SESAME DRESSING

Preparation time: 10 minutes   Makes about 1 cup
SATTVIC, - Vata, 0 Pitta, 0 Kapha (with salad)   ❀ ✳ 🐌 ❄

Mix together in a pint-sized jar or bowl:
>   **Juice of 1/2 orange**
>   **Juice of 1/2 lemon**
>   **1 tsp. orange zest (plain old ORGANIC orange peel, grated)**
>   **1/8 tsp. fresh rosemary, finely chopped (optional)***
>   **1 tsp. fructose or date sugar**
>   **Salt to taste**

Whisk in:
>   **1/3- 1/2 c. cold-pressed sesame oil**

Serve. This makes a mild, slightly sweet dressing.

*Skip rosemary if using a strict rotation diet. This is a ROTATION DAY 4 DISH.

**POLARITY PURIFYING DIET DISH

Variation: 1 teaspoon of honey can be substituted for the sweetener, and sunflower oil for the sesame.

SATTVIC, 0 Vata, 0 Pitta, 0 Kapha

**POLARITY PURIFYING DIET DISH

ABOUT VEGETARIAN EQUANIMITY

*To take up the subject of meat-eaters for a moment. This life is an oppor-
tunity to respect and honor all beings, including those who might disagree
with us. Ayurveda, as it is practiced today, is a vegetarian pursuit. Most
Ayurvedic physicians of my acquaintance have been vegetarian from birth.
Meat as it is prepared today ferments in many bodies and slows down
many Ayurvedic healing processes. You are likely to get better faster on an
Ayurvedic program eating a vegetarian regime. However, Ayurveda as it
was practiced in ancient times was not a vegetarian healing art. Many diverse sorts of animals were recommended in the Ayurvedic texts for specific
medicinal purposes. And some people today do genuinely better with some
animal flesh in their diets, the Dalai Lama being perhaps the most famous example. There are also many places in the world today where it is more economi-
cally and practically feasible for a person to eat a chicken or egg they have
grown themselves in their backyard, than to subsist entirely on acres of beans.*

*So this is a very basic plea for tolerance. Having worked with many
people and many diets, I have never found that making someone wrong for
what they ate was helpful either for them or me. This is not to condone the
many miserable practices occurring on the planet at this time. It is a request
that you, as the reader, use your knowledge with as much equanimity,
humor and balance as you can muster.*

Soups

KEY

"–" means calms or helps the given constitution;

"+" means aggravates or increases it;

"0" means neutral effect.

 * ROTATION DIET can be helpful for people with food
   sensitivities, see p. 323.

**POLARITY DISH refers to recipes supporting Polarity Therapy
   work, see p. 342.

✿   = Spring

✳   = Summer

𖤣   = Fall

❄   = Winter

LIGHT CUCUMBER GAZPACHO

Preparation time: 30 minutes, plus cooling time   Makes 3 - 4 cups
SATTVIC, - Vata, - Pitta, 0 Kapha (with extra cayenne for Kapha)   ✳

Set a stainless steel steamer in a small saucepan of water; bring to a boil. Wash and slice:
>   **1 fresh leek**

Put it in the steamer with:
>   **1 clove garlic, minced**

Cover and steam for 5 minutes, to calm some of their pungency. Remove from heat when done.

Wash, peel and seed:
>   **3 smallish cucumbers**

and chop them in largish pieces.

Wash and finely chop:
>   **1/2 c. fresh Italian parsley**

Put the cucumber, parsley, leek, and garlic in the blender and blend until smooth with:
>   **Juice of 1 lemon**
>   **1 c. vegetable stock, cooled**
>   **1/4 c. olive oil**
>   **1/2 tsp. salt**
>   **1/8 tsp. cayenne or less, as desired**
>   **1/8 tsp. black pepper, ground**

This will take about 20 - 30 seconds. Adjust for taste with the salt and peppers. Chill just enough to serve cool.

**POLARITY PURIFYING DIET DISH

HONORING THE ELEMENTS

Whether we acknowledge it or not, we become connected with the planet with every bite of food we eat. Without the earth's energy and co-operation, no food would come to us. A number of years ago I was shocked into realization of this. We had moved out to the country when our daughter was born, and we had had many problems with water in our rural home. There was a growing feeling of anger from somewhere on our land, which even I could feel. As I began a dialogue with the land through paintings and dreams, I realized that the Water Element was very angry at us. We had put in a well and taken her water with no thought of thanks or permission. As we continued to take without regard for her, her rage grew. To someone raised in the Western scientific view as I was, this can sound fantastic. And yet it was our reality, a reality easily seen from an Ayurvedic or indigenous point of view.

As Verna Williamson, former Governor of Isleta Pueblo here in New Mexico said recently, "The environmental issue is a very spiritual one, and it takes a recognition of water and all those natural resources that are really spirits. Indian people recognize that, and so when those spirits are wounded or soiled,* then it's very much of a degradation of that particular spirit. We're all paying for it, and so it's very important that we recognize the power of these spirits. We have no control over them. They are very powerful and if we're not real careful how we treat them, we may be seeing some very serious end to us, because the spirits can only put up with so much, and we have to be very careful that we work with them. They are very real—Indian people recognize that, and I think that after a long time of being underground, especially the Pueblos, with our religion and many of our sacred beliefs, Pueblo people are finally becoming more open about it and beginning to share it a little bit more because we're finding that it is very important that the world recognizes the spirituality of it all."

(quoted with permission from Seeds of Change 1994 Catalog, from the 1993 Bioneers Seeds of Change Conference in San Francisco, Seeds of Change, P. O. Box 15700, Santa Fe, N.M. 87506-5700)

*Author's note: Verna Williamson is talking here about the radioactive and human wastes being dumped in the Rio Grande, the river which nurtures her community.

CREAM OF BROCCOLI SOUP

Preparation time: 10 minutes   Serves: 2 (Makes 3 cups)
SATTVIC, 0 Vata, 0 Pitta, 0 Kapha   ✿ ✳ 🐚 ❄

In a medium saucepan, place a stainless steel steamer and:
> **1 c. pure water**

Bring to a boil. Wash and coarsely chop:
> **1 small head of broccoli, about 1 1/2 - 2 c. chopped including about 2/3 of the stalk in your preparation.**

Wash and slice in rounds:
> **1 Tbsp. leek greens (optional)**

When the water is boiling, put the broccoli and leek in the steamer and cover. Steam for 3 - 5 minutes at most, until the broccoli is bright green.

Grind together, dry, in the blender until they are a fine powder:
> **2 Tbsps. raw walnut or cashew pieces***
> **1/2 tsp. salt**

Pour in the steamed vegetables and their steaming water. Blend until smooth.

Serve with:
> **freshly ground white pepper**

* For a ROTATION DAY 4 DISH, use cashews.

**POLARITY HEALTH BUILDING DISH

Comments: This is a very satisfying and quick lunch, served with a couple of hot corn tortillas or BLUE CORN MUFFINS, p. 178.

HEARTY VEGETABLE SOUP

Preparation time: about 1 hour   Serves: 4
SATTVIC, 0 Vata, - Pitta, - Kapha

❀ 🐦 ❄

Wash and put in a large soup pot:
> **1/2 c. uncooked barley**

Add:
> **8 - 10 c. pure water**
> **1 tsp. crumbled bay leaf (2-3 whole)**
> **1 tsp. salt**
> **1 - 2 Tbsps. extra-virgin olive oil (omit if desired for *Kapha*)**

Bring the pot to a boil over high heat, then reduce to medium. As it simmers, add:
> **2 organic carrots, with tops**

Put the carrot tops in whole, then dice the carrots. If you cannot find organic carrots, do not use the tops. Add:
> **2 stalks celery, finely chopped**
> **1 c. (or more) fresh parsley, finely chopped**
> **2 Tbsps. onion, chopped (optional)**
> **1 clove garlic, unpeeled**
> **3 c. potatoes or turnips (as fresh as possible), diced**

Let the soup cook covered over medium heat for 50 minutes or so. Remove the carrot tops. Stir in:
> **1 small bunch fresh spinach, washed and chopped**
> **1 tsp. dried chervil (optional)**
> **1/2 tsp. dried thyme**
> **Freshly ground black pepper to taste**

Let the soup simmer another 5 minutes. Serve with ghee, especially for *Vata*.

**POLARITY HEALTH BUILDING DISH

Comments: If you have fresh new potatoes, this dish is lifted from pedestrian to scrumptious. One of our favorites on cold wet days.

Variation: ROTATION DAY 1 DISH: Begin as above with the barley, water, bay leaves, and salt. Bring to a boil with: 6 sun-dried tomatoes and 4 - 6 dried Shiitaake mushrooms. Add the diced potatoes, but omit the other vegetables. Let the soup cook for about 50 minutes. Then stir in: 1 - 1 1/2 tsps. dried rosemary, 1/2 tsp. dried marjoram, 1/8 tsp. cayenne (optional). If you like, you can put these in an herb pouch to let their flavors simmer into the soup without scattering the tougher rosemary leaves throughout the soup. Let the soup simmer for another 5 minutes. Stir in 1 - 2 Tbsps. ghee and serve.

SOME RAJAS AND TAMAS, 0 Vata, 0 Pitta, - Kapha

MINESTRONE SOUP

Preparation time: 1 1/2 hours, from scratch   Serves: 4-6
SATTVIC, 0 Vata, 0 Pitta, - Kapha   ✿ 🦡 ❄

Bring to pressure in a stainless steel pressure cooker:

2/3 c. dry beans: navy, whole mung & chickpea are good
8 c. pure water
Pinch of hing or epazote (optional, aids digestion)
1 bay leaf

Cook until done, about 30 minutes. Or you can use 2 cups of pre-cooked beans in their liquid plus 6 cups of water.

Wash and chop:

2 potatoes, cubed
1 carrot, diced
3 inches of leek, chopped
2 stalks of celery, finely chopped
1 c. fresh green vegetables: zucchini, peas or string beans

Once the beans are done, add the vegetables to the bean pot with:

1 c. Rose Petal Tomato Sauce, p. 160
1/2 c. white basmati rice, dry, washed
1 tsp. salt
2 tsps. dried sweet basil
1/2 tsp. dried thyme

Let the soup simmer until tender, about 45 minutes. Add extra water if needed for the broth. Serve hot with:

freshly ground pepper

ABOUT OIL MASSAGE

Oil massage is one of the best ways to calm Vata. A little sesame oil rubbed into the feet and legs, before bedtime, on a regular basis is all that is needed. Or coconut oil can be especially calming.

IVY'S SOUP ORIENTALE

Preparation time: 30 - 40 minutes   Serves: 4
SATTVIC, - Vata, 0 Pitta, 0 Kapha   ❁ ✳ ☙ ❄

In a large soup pot, warm:
4 Tbsps. ghee or sunflower oil

Add:
2 inches of fresh ginger root, peeled and grated
4 - 6 cloves of garlic, minced (omit or reduce if *Pitta* is high)
1 - 2 bunches scallions (green onions), thinly sliced (optional)
(Reserve about 1/2 c. of chopped scallions for garnish later.)

Stir-fry these for a minute or two. Add:
3 - 4 c. assorted vegetables, chopped

(In keeping with an oriental style, choose vegetables like: pak choy, Chinese cabbage (Napa, savoy), snow peas, turnip, mung bean sprouts, mustard greens. Add a few of these vegetables to our usual ones like carrot, celery, onion, asparagus, zucchini, cauliflower. Avoid green peppers and eggplant.)

Add the harder vegetables first, and add the faster cooking ones like snow peas, mung bean sprouts and asparagus near the finish. Add:
6 - 8 c. water
1 tsp. freshly ground black pepper
Approximately 1/3 of an 8 oz. package of noodles: udon, soba, or pasta

Bring to a boil. Simmer until the veggies and noodles are tender, stirring occasionally. Turn off heat. Drizzle with:
1 tsp. toasted sesame oil

Stir in:
4 Tbsps. Bragg's Liquid Aminos, or to taste

Garnish with scallions and:
1 bunch of fresh watercress, whole or chopped

Variation: 1/3 cup uncooked rice or yellow dal may be substituted for the noodles.

Variation: For a ROTATION DAY 4 DISH, use sunflower oil, 100% buckwheat soba noodles or corn spaghetti, and any vegetables listed for Day 4. Skip the ginger, black pepper and Bragg's Liquid Aminos if you are following a strict Day 4.

Comments: This is a great, quick meal, which comes from Ivy Blank, co-director of Ayurveda at Spirit Rest, Pagosa Springs, CO. Ivy is an outstanding Ayurvedic cook; she teaches Ayurvedic cooking classes throughout the United States. She would usually serve this soup in big bowls as a main dish, with extra ghee stirred in for *Vata* just before serving.

SWEET POTATO SOUP

Preparation time: 1 hour, most of it unattended   Serves: 4
SATTVIC, - Vata, - Pitta, + Kapha   ✿ ☙ ❄

Scrub:
3 large sweet potatoes

Put them in a large pot with enough boiling water to cover them. Add:
1 inch fresh ginger root, peeled and sliced

Bring the sweet potatoes and ginger to a boil, then reduce heat to medium and cook until the potatoes are soft, about 35 - 40 minutes.

In a small saucepan, bring to a boil:
1 1/2 c. soy milk or fresh raw cow's milk

Reserve 1 1/2 cups of cooking water from the sweet potatoes (the rest of the water makes good soup stock). Blend this cooking water, the hot milk, the cooked sweet potato and ginger in a blender with:
1/4 tsp. freshly ground allspice
1 Tbsp. maple syrup (optional)
Salt to taste

Add more milk or water as desired to reach a creamy consistency. Puree the finished soup until satiny smooth. Serve hot with fresh greens and a quick bread.

**POLARITY HEALTH BUILDING DISH

Variation: YAM SOUP If you can obtain true yams rather than sweet potatoes (not easy to do in the United States), this dish can be adapted for A DAY 2 ROTATION. Use yams instead of sweet potatoes, skip the milk, substituting all hot cooking water instead. Use spice and sweetener as above.

SATTVIC, - Vata, - Pitta, moderately + Kapha

*ROTATION DAY 2 DISH

**POLARITY PURIFYING DIET DISH

Variation: Prepare as above, omitting the ginger and using plain soy milk. Blend the soup with 1/4 tsp. mace or nutmeg, 1 Tbsp. raw honey (optional) and salt to taste.

SATTVIC, - Vata, - Pitta, moderately + Kapha

*ROTATION DAY 3 DISH

**POLARITY HEALTH BUILDING DISH

OUR BODIES AND THEIR MESSAGES

Sometimes it may look to us as if our bodies have betrayed us, when they break down or don't perform in the ways we'd like. More often I think it is a long-standing breakdown in communication which has occurred. If a good friend or spouse were to come to us and say, "Hey, look, this isn't working, I feel uncomfortable about how things are going here," we would listen, hopefully. And yet when the body communicates something like this, we often miss or ignore it, partly because it uses a different language than the one we know.

The chronic sinus congestion, sore feet, aching lower back are all saying, "Hey! Please pay attention, something is not comfortable here, what can we do together to improve it?" Often our response to these physical signals is to ignore them and hope that they will go away. And sometimes they do. But you can imagine what would happen if you treated a partner or friend this way all the time. The body is no different. The frustration, fatigue and imbalance build up inside and often get worse when left unaddressed.

While Ayurveda frequently can help in serious cases, its shining strength is in prevention. If we are willing to befriend our bodies and take their messages seriously, Ayurveda has many tools to help in recovering health and balance. It is up to us to listen to what is going on in our bodies, our own direct link with nature. At first the messages may be subtle ones, but later the body may have to resort to "shouts" to get our attention. How open is your communication with your body?

POOR WOMAN'S CREAMY ASPARAGUS SOUP

Preparation time: 1 1/2 hrs, most of it unattended   Serves: 4
SATTVIC , - Vata, - Pitta, - Kapha   ✿ ✳ ☙

Braise together in a heavy-bottomed skillet for a couple of minutes:
>   **1 small onion, finely chopped (1 - 2 Tbsps.)**
>   **2 cloves of garlic, minced**
>   **Ends (not tips) from 1 lb. of asparagus* (about 2 cups)**
>   **1 - 2 Tbsps. olive oil**

Add:
>   **4 c. water**

Cover and simmer for about an hour.

Grind into a fine powder in a blender:
>   **1/2 c. raw sunflower seeds, hulled**

Gradually pour the broth and vegetables into the blender with the ground seeds, blending a little at a time. Blend well. Put the soup through a food mill or a coarse stainless steel strainer, stirring it through the mesh with a wooden spoon.

Add:
>   **1 tsp. salt**
>   **Freshly ground black pepper to taste**
>   **1/4 tsp. ground nutmeg, fresh if you have it**

Serve. Good warm or cool.

Comments: This is a pleasantly light soup that I make when I've used asparagus tops in another dish, like QUINOA ASPARAGUS PILAF, p. 118 or THAI STIR-FRY, p. 142. If you are looking for something more substantial, you can add 2 cups of steamed asparagus in 1" pieces, or milk in place of some of the water.

Variation: turn this into A DAY 4 ROTATION DISH, substitute sesame oil for the olive oil and 1/2 c. ground cashews for the sunflower seeds. Omit pepper and nutmeg and use 1/16 tsp. saffron instead.

Sattvic, - Vata, 0 Pitta, 0 Kapha

SOPA DE ELOTE (FRESH CORN SOUP)

Preparation time: 30 minutes with stock   Serves: 4
SATTVIC*

Husk and cut from its ears with a sharp paring knife:
4 ears fresh sweet corn, raw

Cutting it into a bowl can help keep it from flying about. Wash and chop:
5 green onions, finely chopped
1/2 bunch fresh cilantro, finely chopped (about 1/2 c.)

Set aside the chopped green onion tops with the cilantro to be used as garnish. The chopped white onion bottoms will be used in a moment in the soup.

Warm in a 4 quart saucepan over medium-low heat:
1 Tbsp. extra-virgin olive oil or ghee

Stir the chopped white bottoms of the green onions into the oil. Stir for a minute, then stir in:
1 Tbsp. barley or whole wheat flour

Heat for a couple of minutes on low heat. Pour in:
1 - 2 c. vegetable stock, I use VEGETARIAN SOUP STOCK II, p. 113

and bring heat to medium-high. Once the stock is hot, add the fresh corn and cook about 5 minutes. Stir in, a little at a time, until you have the consistency you like:
2 - 3 c. fresh milk or soy milk

Bring the soup to a boil. Add:
2 *chiles poblanos* **or 1/4 - 1/2 tsp. ground red chili, preferably poblano**
1 tsp. freshly ground coriander seeds, or 2 tsps. commercially ground

Reduce heat to simmer and let cook for another 10 - 15 minutes. Garnish with chopped onion greens and cilantro. Serve.

SATTVIC, 0 Vata, - Pitta, slightly + Kapha (with cow's milk)

SATTVIC, mildly + Vata, - Pitta, - Kapha (with soy milk)

Comments: This is a delicious and satisfying soup. Traditionally this would be served with *queso fresco* (Mexican cheese) and sometimes strips of *chiles poblanos*. If your digestion is strong and you have no troubles with mold or fermentation, you might add a little of these occasionally. However, it is tasty without them, too.

VERY BASIC BEET BORSCHT

Preparation time: about 50 minutes, most of it unattended   Serves: 2

SATTVIC, - Vata, mildly + Pitta, - Kapha   ❧ ❄

Bring to a boil in a large saucepan:
4 c. water

Wash well and slice, reserving any greens if they are fresh:
3 medium beets

Put them in the water to boil with:
1 quarter-sized piece of peeled ginger root

Cover and let simmer over medium heat for about 45 minutes. Pour contents of the soup pot into a blender and puree until smooth.

Blend in:
1 Tbsp. extra-virgin olive oil
Salt and freshly ground black pepper to taste*

Serve.

*ROTATION DAY 2 DISH, omit pepper if you are on a strict rotation.

**POLARITY PURIFYING DIET DISH, omit the salt

ABOUT COOKING GEAR

Gear for Ayurvedic cooking need not be fancy or expensive. Stainless steel pots, pans and serving ware, in the size or sizes you need, are overwhelmingly preferred. Heatproof glass enamel or ironware can also be used. Aluminum ware of any kind, light, heavy or alloyed, is not recommended, as it is considered damaging to the immune, digestive and nervous systems. Toss out that old aluminum rice pot and pull out a stainless steel soup pot for your next meal! Indian groceries are often a good source for durable stainless steel plates.

ABOUT SPROUTING

Younger Ayurvedic physicians of my acquaintance are recommending sprouting as a vital part of Ayurvedic cooking. If you have never sprouted beans before, it is likely to be easier than you have imagined. While beans sprout at different rates, their natural inclination is to sprout, since they are seeds.

To sprout mung beans, soak a cup or less of whole mung beans, (or about 1/3 cup for a single person) in several cups of pure water overnight. (Whole mung beans can be purchased in bulk in natural foods groceries and Asian markets.) In the morning, drain the water from the beans. Draining them into a wire-mesh strainer or colander works well. This soaking water can be used in cooking if you like. Rinse the beans in the colander with fresh water, then put them, drained, into a covered dish at room temperature. A casserole dish or a bowl covered with a plate are fine, so long as they do not let in light. You want to protect these seeds from the sun until they sprout, as if they were in the earth. Rinse the seeds in the strainer once or twice a day. They are ready to use in soups and other recipes once they have begun to sprout, about two to three days into the process. You can use as many as you like and leave the rest to keep growing, still rinsing once or twice a day.

In this way, you can have an easily assimilated source of fresh proteinaceous sprouts from one batch of whole mung beans, using a handful or so a day for as long as a week. Other beans, peas and lentils can be done in the same way. Some sprout more easily than others, and some need to be rinsed more often than mung, up to three times per day.

If you find yourself wanting to play with smaller seeds, like alfalfa, the simple mesh sprouting tops sold in health food stores, which fit on Mason jars, work well. Just remember to keep your seeds in the dark until they begin to sprout.

Sprouting significantly enhances digestibility of legumes and other seeds. It increases their content of vitamins C and B complex. It can also cut cooking time for legumes in half.

Ironically, the ancient texts advised against using sprouted grain, since sprouting was associated with a bag of grain going "bad", i.e.,getting wet, sprouting spontaneously, then getting moldy. (This can happen. You want to keep your sprouts fresh and well-rinsed.) Intentional sprouting is a different matter and is being used more and more to enhance nutritional value of foods in Ayurveda.

LUCIANO'S ZUCCHINI SOUP

Preparation time: 15 - 20 minutes   Serves: 2 - 4
SATTVIC,- Vata, - Pitta, 0 Kapha   ✹ ۿ

Wash:
>   **2 medium zucchini**

With a spoon, carefully scoop out ALL the seeds, every last one of them. Cube the zucchini.

Chop:
>   **1/2 small onion**

Put both the zucchini and onion in an iron skillet on medium heat with:
>   **1 Tbsp. extra-virgin olive oil**

Stir, coating the vegetables with oil. Add:
>   **1/4 c. water**

Cover. Cook until tender, about 5 minutes. Blend the vegetables until smooth in a blender; add:
>   **Salt and pepper to taste**

Serve.

Comments: While making this soup for the first time, my partner and I had one of those moments that can strain a relationship, or at least an evening. While I adored the color, taste and texture of this soup, Gord had the audacity to label it "green slime" upon first viewing. The tacky barbarian then proceeded to gobble down two large bowls. Decide for yourself!

CALABACITAS STEW: see Side Dishes, p. 199.

See also: AMA-REDUCING DAL, p. 120.

SPROUTED MUNG SOUP

Preparation time: 15 minutes, plus 3 days to sprout the beans   Serves: 4
SATTVIC, 0 Vata, - Pitta, 0 Kapha   ✿ ✳ ⚬ ❄

In a heavy saucepan cook until thoroughly soft:
>   1 1/2 c. **fresh sprouted mung beans**
>   3 c. **water**
>   A pinch of **epazote or hing**
>   1 - 1 1/2" **fresh ginger root, finely chopped**

This takes 10 - 15 minutes with the sprouted beans. Pour this hot cooked mixture into the blender with:
>   1/2 c. **fresh cilantro, finely chopped**
>   1 tsp. **ground cumin**
>   1/2 tsp. **salt**
>   2 - 4 Tbsps. **extra-virgin olive oil (the lesser amount for *Kapha*, the greater for *Vata*.)**

Blend well. Serve hot.

**POLARITY PURIFYING DIET DISH

SPLIT MUNG SOUP

Preparation time: 1 hour   Serves: 4
SATTVIC, - Vata, - Pitta, mildly + Kapha   ✿ ✳ ⚬ ❄

In a heavy saucepan cook until thoroughly soft:
>   1 c. **dry split mung beans**
>   6 c. **or more water**
>   A pinch of **epazote or hing**
>   1 - 1 1/2" **fresh ginger root, finely chopped**

This could take up to an hour with the split mung, 5 - 10 minutes with the sprouted beans. Pour this hot cooked mixture into the blender with:
>   1/2 c. **fresh cilantro, finely chopped**
>   1 1/2 tsps. **ground cumin**
>   1/2 - 1 tsp. **salt**
>   3 Tbsps. **cold-pressed olive oil**

Blend well. Serve hot.

**POLARITY HEALTH BUILDING DISH

Comments: I first started making these soups when my dad was doing *Pancha Karma* here in New Mexico. The oil can be increased if needed, for therapeutic purposes, with no damage to the soup's flavor.

EQUINOX SOUP

Preparation time: 45 minutes   Serves: 4
SATTVIC, mildly + Vata, - Pitta, - Kapha*   ੨ও

Wash:
> 1 c. dried black mitla beans

Place them in a pressure cooker with:
> 6 c. water
> 1 large bay leaf

Bring to pressure over medium-high heat. Reduce heat to medium and cook until tender, about 30 minutes. While the beans are cooking, wash and chop:
> 1/2 medium onion, chopped
> 2 small cloves of garlic, minced
> 3 small fresh carrots, thin sliced
> 1/2 c. fresh purple string beans, in 1" slices
> 1/2 bunch fresh mustard greens (or other greens), chopped

In a large soup kettle, warm:
> 2 Tbsps. cold-pressed olive oil

Saute the onion and garlic in the oil for a minute or two, then add the fresh vegetables and stir until tender, about 5 - 10 minutes. When the beans are cooked, pour the beans and their cooking liquid into the veggies and simmer together for 5 - 15 minutes. Just before serving add:
> 1 bunch (about 1 c.) fresh arugula, chopped (optional)
> Freshly ground black pepper to taste
> 1 tsp. salt

Serve hot. The contrast of shining black beans, bright orange carrots and deep greens is most pleasurable to the eye.

*Vata should add a tablespoon of oil to the pot when first cooking the beans, for best results.

Variation: POLARITY VERSION: Simmer the veggies directly into the cooked beans rather than saute them beforehand. Follow the recipe as above. Add the oil (optional) just before serving, with the salt, arugula and pepper. Preparation time: 1 hour. Good on its own, or served with PLAIN BASMATI RICE.

SATTVIC, mildly + Vata, - Pitta , - Kapha
**POLARITY HEALTH BUILDING DISH

Comments: Before you drive yourself wild trying to find black mitlas, know that they are hard, maybe impossible, to find in your standard market. They are a wonderful smoky-tasting bean grown in the Southwest and around Oaxaca, Mexico (where they can occasionally be found in cloth sacks in the *mercado*). They are not to be confused with black turtle beans, which look quite similar but which are a different legume entirely. The easiest way I know to get black mitlas is to grow them. Seed for black mitlas, and Louisiana Purple Pod Pole Bean, a beautiful purple string bean I use in this dish, can often be obtained in the spring as a member of Seed Savers Exchange, 3076 North Winn Road, Decorah, Iowa 52101, a hardy organization which saves many rare seeds from around the world, most especially from the Americas. These folks do great work.

MILD-MANNERED GREEN CHILI STEW

Preparation time: 1 hour or a little more   Serves: 4

SATTVIC WITH RAJASIC LEANINGS, + Vata, 0 Pitta, - Kapha   ✿ 🍵 ❄

Wash and put in a large soup pot:
> 1/2 c. uncooked brown basmati rice
> 1/2 c. uncooked lima beans

with:
> 8 - 10 c, pure water on high heat.

Chop:
> 2 Tbsps. onion

Wash and cube:
> 2 c. new potatoes

Add these to the pot with:
> 1 medium tomato, finely chopped
> 2 dried long green New Mexico chilies
> 1 c. greens: spinach, baby kale, chopped
> 1 tsp. dried oregano
> 1/8 tsp. thyme
> 1 clove garlic, unpeeled for *Pitta*, otherwise minced

Reduce heat to medium and let stew until the beans and potatoes are tender.
> **Salt and pepper to taste**

**POLARITY HEALTH BUILDING DISH

Comments: Okay, let's be honest. Where I come from here in northern New Mexico, this would not even be considered a green chili stew. Heretical or foolish, perhaps. A nice mild soup, sure. Good flavor, yes. But green chili stew? No. Add 10 more fresh green chilies, roast them, peel them, simmer the stew well with 6 more cloves of garlic and 3 large onions, and you begin to be in the ballpark. Plus no green chili stew I know of puts something green in (as in vegetable) besides the green chili. But enter this traditional New Mexican Rajasic Park only if you are a *Kapha*. Tis rough on all others, all this hot stuff.

   To make this a little less aggravating for *Vata*, you can soak the lima beans over night and serve the stew with a dollop of ghee or a dash of olive oil. Still it would somewhat imbalance *Vata* (moderately + *Vata*).

SOOTHING SOUP

Preparation time: 1 hour   Serves: 4
SATTVIC, 0 Vata, 0 Pitta, 0 Kapha   ✿ ❋ ໕ ❄

Bring to a boil in a soup pot:
   1/4 c. whole dried peas
   1/2 c. sprouted mung beans
   1 c. long grain brown rice
   1/8 tsp. epazote or hing
   1 - 2 Tbsps. sesame oil
   1 inch fresh ginger root, finely chopped
   2 small cloves garlic, minced
   8 c. pure water

Reduce heat to medium-low and cook uncovered for about 50 minutes, adding extra water
if needed. Stir in:
   1 c. fresh chopped Italian parsley
   1/2 c. zucchini, sliced
   1/2 tsp. dried oregano
   2 tsps. dried basil

Cook until the vegetable is tender. Serve with ghee.

ABOUT COOKING

*Skilled Ayurvedic cook Usha Lad recommends that whenever you can,
let your uncovered pot simmer out its excess* vayu, *air, into the air around
it. Slow cooking helps excess* vayu *escape from foods, as Melanie Sachs
aptly points out in* Ayurvedic Beauty Care. *This is especially helpful when
you are cooking airy foods, like legumes, and for airy types, like* Vata. *It also
supports easier digestion with less excess "wind" for all types. At the same time,
tastes have a greater chance to mingle and integrate as they simmer.*

*Often I have recommended pressure cooking, as a quicker, energy-sav-
ing approach to cooking slow items. Pressure cooking can be helpful for
stimulating slow-moving earth,* Kapha, *in positive ways. When pressure
cooking, leave the pressure cap off the cooker until the
first burst of steam comes through. Then put the cap
on. This will also help disperse excess* vayu. *And yet,
slower cooking methods calm air more. (From the
Western point of view there is the trade-off of some
water-soluble vitamins lost in the steam.)*

QUICK BLACK BEAN SOUP

Preparation time: 15 minutes   Serves: 3 - 4
SATTVIC BORDERING ON RAJASIC (so much lemon),   ✿ 🐾 ❄
+ Vata, 0 Pitta, 0 Kapha

Bring to a boil in a medium saucepan:
> **1 1/2 c. cooked black beans**
> **1 1/2 c. pure water**
> **2 Tbsps. onion, finely chopped**

Reduce to simmer, cook uncovered. (This helps release some of the extra *vayu*, air, in the beans.) After about 10 minutes of heating, stir in:
> **1 small clove garlic, minced (optional)**
> **1/8 tsp. cumin seeds**
> **1/2 tsp. salt**

Just before serving, stir in:
> **1 small tomato, chopped**
> **1/3 c. fresh lemon juice**
> **1 Tbsp. extra-virgin olive oil**

Garnish with:
> **Fresh cilantro leaves, chopped (optional)**

**POLARITY HEALTH BUILDING DISH

Comments: Good with avocado tacos. The Black Bean Ful in *Sundays at Moosewood Restaurant* were the beginnings of the inspiration for this dish.

SPLIT PEA SOUP

Preparation time: 1 1/2 hours, most of it unattended   Serves: 3 - 4
SATTVIC, 0 Vata, - Pitta, - Kapha   ✿ 🐾 ❄

Bring to a boil in a medium saucepan:
> **1 c. dry split peas**
> **6 - 8 c. water (or more as needed)**
> **1 large carrot, sliced in rounds**
> **1" fresh ginger root, peeled and *finely* minced**
> **1/2 tsp. whole cumin seeds**
> **1/2 tsp. turmeric**

Reduce heat to medium and cook uncovered until tender, an hour or more. Add more water as needed. When good and soupy, add:

> 1 tsp. salt
> Freshly ground black pepper to taste

**POLARITY HEALTH BUILDING DISH

Comments: This is an unorthodox, but quite flavorful and digestible, version of your standard pea soup. Good with BUTTERFLY BISCUITS, p. 170 and a light salad.

MY FAVORITE CAJUN GUMBO: See Entrees, p. 119.

GUMBO STOCK

Preparation time: 1/2 hour or more   Makes 2 quarts
SATTVIC, - Vata, - Pitta, - Kapha   ✿ ✳ 🍃 ❄

Bring to a boil in a large soap pot:

> 3 qts. water
> 1 small onion, whole
> 3 stalks celery
> 2 bay leaves
> 1/2 tsp. dry thyme leaves
> 1 tsp. salt
> 2 c. additional vegetables, could be carrots, spinach, parsley (not cabbage family!)
> 1 clove of garlic, unpeeled

Cover, reduce heat and let simmer for a half hour or more. The longer you let it cook, the tastier it will be. When it is done, remove the vegetables and bay leaves (they make a good donation to the compost pile), and the stock is ready to be used.

**POLARITY HEALTH BUILDING DISH

ABOUT STOVES

I remember waking at dawn one morning in my room on the thirty-sixth floor of the government-sponsored high rise hotel in New Delhi and peering out toward the earth. There, far below, people had already started making their cooking fires for the morning's chai and grain, in the shadows thrown by the skyscraper's West wall. The walls of their abodes were made of cardboard boxes, and to be honest I wasn't sure what the fuel for their fires was. But the smoke from the cooking rose up toward me, a testimony to the many ways we humans heat food.

In this country, you've generally got a choice between gas stoves and electric stoves, with an occasional barbecue thrown in for flavor. If you are on a limited budget, a single electric hot plate serves fine. For the environmentally sensitive, electric ranges are preferable to gas ones, as the latter are notorious for their noxious by-products and leakages. However, as many good cooks know, a gas stove is a lot more fun to cook on, as it responds quickly to temperature controls in a way no electric can. And gas stoves are generally more economical, from an energy consumption point of view. If you choose to cook on a gas range, it is important that it have proper ventilation (a hood and fan). I am amazed at how many gas stoves I see in this country with no fans or hoods at all. If you have a gas stove, it also needs to be in a room well-closed off from everyone's sleeping quarters. If you are dealing with a family with chronic respiratory problems, gas leaks are a possible cause.

For truly clean, low-cost, energy efficient cooking, solar stoves are spreading across the globe. They can be the low-tech equivalent of the crock pot: put your stew in, in the morning, and pop it out hours later. More information about solar cookers, including instructions on how to make your own solar box cooker, can be obtained from Solar Box Cookers International, 1724 Eleventh Street, Sacramento, California, U.S.A. 95814.

VEGETARIAN SOUP STOCK

Preparation time: 30 minutes or more   Makes 6 cups
SATTVIC, 0 Vata, - Pitta, - Kapha

Bring to a boil in a soup pot:
> 8 c. pure water
> 2 celery stalks
> 1 small leek
> 1 medium tomato (optional)
> 1 tsp. salt
> 1 sweet potato

Cover, reduce heat and simmer for one half hour or more. Remove any remains of vegetables. It is then ready to use in any recipe.

**POLARITY HEALTH BUILDING DISH

VEGETARIAN SOUP STOCK II

Preparation time: 45 minutes or more   Makes 2 quarts
SATTVIC, 0 Vata, 0 Pitta, - Kapha

Bring to a boil in a large soup pot:
> 1 ear of corn
> 1 small onion
> 1 clove garlic, unpeeled
> 1 large carrot
> 1 bay leaf
> 1/2 tsp. cumin seeds
> 1 tsp. salt
> 2 potatoes (optional)
> 2 stalks of celery (optional)
> 10 c. water

Reduce heat to medium-low and let simmer, covered, until savory. This is the basic soup stock for SOPA DE ELOTE, p. 102.

**POLARITY HEALTH BUILDING DISH

Comments: If you're starting with a prepared vegetarian stock, simply add 1/2 tsp. cumin to it for a stock roughly comparable to the one above.

ABOUT COOKING WITH THE WEATHER

Changes in the weather ask us to shift, adjust. Our bodies (the microcosm) are moving within a greater macrocosm, the environment. Often when there is a sudden shift in weather, like an unexpected snowstorm in late spring, the body will manifest signs of adjusting to this change. You might notice sudden congestion, fatigue, headache, or flu-like symptoms (if you don't, that's fine too). Your doshas *are responding to the shift in balance, seeking health. No need to panic. Think back about how you've been eating and living, look at the changes, and adjust yourself accordingly. In the example just given,* Kapha *is predominant: cold wet weather, congestion, heaviness. You can tend to your Kapha right now more than you usually would by eating lighter, drier, warm fresh foods. I find the Polarity Purifying Diet (see Appendix VI) helpful at times like these.*

Likewise, if a sudden hot dry spell, or chilly windy weather arises, you can respond accordingly, with support for your Pitta *and* Vata *doshas respectively. These changes in weather are likely to elicit a more pronounced response from your body if they come at the change of seasons, as they often do. It's a chance to create a deeper balance, which you can make if you like.*

To get a little more specific, I use more cooling cilantro, saffron and mint in hot weather. You can use more fresh pungent ginger to warm you up in cold weather. When the weather is damp, I select more drying foods, like barley, quinoa and amaranth. When it is dry I'll go for more lubricating substances, like ghee or extra oil. What you use will vary with your own tastes and constitution.

Entrees

KEY

"–" means calms or helps the given constitution;

"+" means aggravates or increases it;

"0" means neutral effect.

 * ROTATION DIET can be helpful for people with food
   sensitivities, see p. 323.

**POLARITY DISH refers to recipes supporting Polarity Therapy
   work, see p. 342.

✿ = Spring

☀ = Summer

ॐ = Fall

❄ = Winter

PAELLA

Preparation time: 50 minutes   Serves: 4
SATTVIC, - Vata, 0 Pitta, 0 Kapha   ✿ ✳ ⟪⟫ ❄

Wash:

> 1 c. uncooked brown *basmati* rice

Bring it to a boil with:

> 1/2 tsp. salt
> 2 1/2 c. pure water

Cover and reduce heat to low. Cook until done, about 45 minutes. Wash and prepare:

> 1 c. broccoli in florets
> 2 Roma tomatoes, cubed (can be omitted)
> 1 Tbsp. red bell pepper, finely chopped (optional)
> 1 c. fresh peas, shelled
> 2 Tbsps. fresh parsley, finely chopped

When the rice is about 20 minutes from being done, you can start sauteing. Having the rice hot and the vegetables just completed in their cooking gives the freshest appearance to the paella. Warm in a large skillet on medium-low heat:

> 1 Tbsp. ghee
> 1 Tbsp. cold-pressed extra-virgin olive oil

Add:

> 1/8 tsp. whole cumin seeds
> 1 large clove garlic, minced

Let them saute for a couple of minutes. Then add the vegetables: broccoli first, then tomatoes, bell pepper, peas. (Put up the heat to medium-high for a few minutes after you first add the broccoli so it gets seared a bit, then reduce it back to medium-low.) Make sure all the veggies are well-coated with herbs and oil. Cook them covered until tender and then turn off heat. When the rice is ready, stir it into the vegetables, adding the parsley and:

> 1/32 tsp. saffron
> 1/8 tsp. cayenne (or less)

Serve.

Quick Variation: White *basmati* rice can be used in place of brown, which cuts about 30 minutes off the prep time, for a total of 20 minutes to mealtime. I'll toss in 2 tablespoons of raw cashew pieces and/or a little fresh arugula sometimes to cook with the veggies, for a different touch.

SATTVIC, - Vata, 0 Pitta, 0 Kapha

QUINOA - ASPARAGUS PILAF

Preparation time: 20 minutes

SATTVIC, - Vata, - Pitta, - Kapha

Serves: 4 - 6

♣ ✳ ᦥ

Rinse well:

> 1 c. dry quinoa

This is important, as it has a natural soapy residue which can disturb some people's digestion. Bring the quinoa to a boil in a small saucepan with:

> 2 c. water
> 1/2 tsp. salt

Reduce heat to low, cover, and cook until done, about 15 minutes. Wash and chop:

> 1/2 - 1 lb. asparagus, in 1" pieces
> 1 large carrot, in half moons
> 1 Tbsp. fresh rosemary leaves, finely chopped or 1 tsp. dried
> 2 Tbsps. onion, finely chopped
> 1 tsp. fresh savory leaves, finely chopped or 1/2 tsp. dry (this is optional but tasty)

As the quinoa continues to cook, warm in a large iron skillet:

> 2 Tbsps. cold-pressed olive oil

Add the onion and rosemary and saute until the onion begins to get translucent. It's time to put in the carrot. Let it cook on medium heat in the skillet, covered, until tender, about 5 minutes. Add the asparagus, cover and cook another 2 - 3 minutes until it is tender yet still slightly crispy. When quinoa is done, toss it lightly into the vegetables in the skillet, using a fork to fluff it. Stir in the freshly chopped savory. Serve. Very good with SIMPLE ADUKIS, p. 135.

Variation: POLARITY VERSION: Cook the veggies, onion and rosemary with the quinoa. Add the olive oil and savory after the quinoa is done, fluffing it in with a fork. Easier on the liver than Version I above.

SATTVIC, - Vata, - Pitta, - Kapha

**POLARITY HEALTH BUILDING DISH

> "Love people. Serve people. Feed people."
>
> Neem Karoli Baba's chief recommendation for spiritual practice, when asked.

MY FAVORITE CAJUN GUMBO

Preparation time: 1 3/4 hours, if you make the stock from scratch.
Otherwise, less than an hour. Again, most of this is unattended.   Makes 12 cups
SATTVIC, 0 Vata, 0 Pitta, 0 Kapha   ✳ ☕ ❄

First make up:
> **Gumbo Stock, p. 111**

Then go on to prepare your burnt roue. Warm in a large heavy bottomed pot:
> **1 Tbsp. oil (olive, sesame, or sunflower are good)**

Stir in:
> **1 Tbsp. flour (whole wheat, barley, or quinoa work fine)**

Let the flour cook in the oil on medium-low heat until it is a butterscotch brown, stirring occasionally. When it turns that darkish brown, stir in:
> **1 small white onion, finely chopped**
> **1 large bell pepper, red, yellow or green, chopped**

Cook over medium heat until the onion and pepper are soft but not brown. Pour the stock liquid into your roue pot, tossing the stock vegetables into your compost bucket if you've got one. Add:
> **1 rib of celery, finely chopped**
> **3 fresh tomatoes, chopped**
> **30 fresh okra, sliced in 1/4" rounds**
> **1/3 c. uncooked *basmati* rice**

Cook until the vegetables and rice are well-mingled and soft, about 45 minutes on medium heat. Stir in:
> **1/2 tsp. dry thyme**
> **1/8 tsp. cayenne**
> **3 Tbsps. fresh parsley, finely chopped**
> **Salt to taste**

Serve in pre-warmed bowls with:
> **Gumbo filé to taste (ground sassafras leaves). This inexpensive condiment is often available in delis or fish markets) A pinch per bowl is tasty.**

Comments: Let yourself play with colors if you're in the mood here. If you have some golden tomatoes, try combining them with a red bell pepper and green okra, or vice versa. It's a pretty dish! This makes a scrumptious company dinner, served with hot BLUE CORN-BREAD or SWEET POTATO BISCUITS, a simple salad, and CREAMY GARLIC DRESSING. With VERY BERRY PIE for dessert? Or to go a lighter tack, let your guests rest and chat after dinner, and a bit later serve *Chai* and CANTALOUPE WITH FRESH RASPBERRIES.

Another very yummy soup which makes an excellent one-dish entree is IVY'S SOUP ORI-ENTALE, p. 98.

AMA-REDUCING *DAL*

Preparation time: 3 days to sprout the mung,
30 minutes to 1 hour to make the soup.   Serves: 5-6
*SATTVIC**

✿ ✳ ❧ ❄

In a pressure cooker, put:
>   **2 - 3 c. sprouted mung beans**
>   **3 - 4 c. water**

Bring to pressure and cook for about two minutes. Or cook the beans and water in a covered saucepan until soft. Blend the beans and cooking liquid in blender. Set aside. In a stainless steel soup pot, warm:
>   **1 1/2 Tbsps. ghee or olive oil**

Add:
>   **1 - 2 inches fresh ginger root (1 - 2 Tbsps.), peeled and chopped finely**
>   **1- 3 cloves of garlic, minced (omit if *Pitta* is high)**
>   **1/2 - 1 tsp. cumin seeds**
>   **1 tsp. coriander seeds**
>   **1/2 - 1 tsp. turmeric**
>   **1/2 tsp. freshly ground black pepper**
>   **2 - 3 bay leaves**
>   **1/8 tsp. each of fennel seeds, hing, cinnamon, and cardamom**

Toss until coated and their aromas emerge. Add to the spices and oil:
>   **2 - 3 c. chopped vegetables (broccoli, carrots, greens, sprouts, green beans, or asparagus work well)**

Toss until coated. Stir for two minutes, then add:
>   **4 - 6 c. additional water**

Mix well. Bring to a boil, then reduce heat and simmer covered until veggies are cooked. Add pureed mung beans to soup pot. Stir. Bring to a boil again. Reduce heat and let soup simmer for 5 minutes. Add more water if a thinner consistency is desired. Add:
>   **1/2 tsp. salt, or to taste**

Comments: This recipe comes from Ivy Blank, based on a dish made by Drs. Smita and Pankaj Naram of Bombay. It is specifically designed to reduce *ama* and rest the digestive tract during illness, convalescence or rejuvenation therapy. The mung beans are cooling by nature, yet are warmed by the addition of the ginger and the other warming spices. Amounts of the spices and the type of vegetables used can be adjusted to suit the individual. One stick of kombu can also be added to reduce gas and add trace minerals. This is an excellent one-dish meal which can be served a few times each week to rest the system, if you like.

NOTE: If you are using this dish during *Pancha Karma* therapy, increase the oil or ghee to 5 - 6 Tbsps. for best effects. Greater amounts of oleation are needed during this process.

* - *Vata,* - *Pitta,* - *Kapha (without garlic)*
* - *Vata,* + *Pitta,* - *Kapha (with garlic)*

(Reprinted with permission from *The Ayurvedic Cookbook,* Amadea Morningstar with Urmila Desai, Lotus Press, 1990.)

A *KICHADI*

Preparation time: about 45 minutes to one hour   Serves: 2 - 3
SATTVIC, - *Vata,* - *Pitta,* - *Kapha*   ✿ ✳ ᴥ ❄

Wash well:
>   1/2 c. *basmati* rice
>   1/2 c. sprouted mung beans

Put in a medium saucepan with:
>   4 c. pure water (or more)
>   1 tsp. - 2 Tbsps. grated fresh ginger root, the lesser amount with high *Pitta*
>   1 bay leaf
>   Pinch of hing or epazote
>   1/4 tsp. cumin seeds
>   1/2 - 1 tsp. coriander seeds
>   1 heaping tsp. dried oregano leaves

Bring to a boil, then reduce heat to medium. Cover and cook. Or cook uncovered, adding more water as needed. While the beans and rice are cooking, wash and chop:
>   2 carrots, diced
>   1 tender zucchini, diced
>   1/2 c. broccoli, chopped
>   2 Tbsps. parsley, chopped
>   1 clove garlic, minced (optional)

Add the diced carrot immediately to the cooking mung and rice. Put the zucchini, broccoli, parsley and garlic in after the *kichadi* has cooked for a half hour or so. When all the ingredients are tender and done, take the pot off the heat and add:
>   1 Tbsp. ghee or extra-virgin olive oil (optional)
>   Salt to taste

Stir. Can be served with:
>   fresh chopped cilantro leaves as a garnish on top.

**POLARITY HEALTH BUILDING DISH

Comments: *Kichadis* (pronounced ki-cha-ree, with a slight mix of "r" and "d" sounds) are the staple food of Ayurvedic healing, and can be used any time one feels like one. The "soupier" it is, the easier it is to digest. You can always add more water to get the consistency you need. It is relatively easy to adjust *kichadis* so that they are maximally soothing for a given *dosha*. For example, if you are especially working with *Vata*, use more water so that the *kichadi* is quite soupy, cook for a good hour or more, and garnish lavishly with ghee and freshly ground black pepper. For *Pitta*, reduce the ginger, ease up on the black pepper, and increase the coriander seeds and cilantro a bit. Again use the longer cooking time (it helps settle *Pitta*). For *Kapha*, use the maximum amount of ginger, generous amounts of black pepper, more of any of the spices that appeal to you, a slightly shorter cooking time (see what agrees with you) and a minimal amount of ghee or oil and salt.

If you find yourself enjoying this recipe, many variations can be found in *The Ayurvedic Cookbook* (Morningstar with Desai), or also, I bet, in your own creative mind and kitchen. *Kichadis* can be made first thing in the morning and taken for lunch or supper. They make an easy one-pot meal which is gentle on all *doshas*.

If, on the other hand, you have been faithfully eating *kichadis* night and day for months and are a bit "*kichadi*-ed out", you might want to take a break from this revered basic. Consider exploring some of the other Ayurvedic recipes offered here.

Variation: for Rotation Day 3: Wash the *basmati* and sprouted mung beans as given. Put them in a saucepan with the water, hing, cumin, coriander, 1/4 tsp. freshly ground black pepper, and 1 Tbsp. sunflower oil. Cook as before. For vegetables, use sliced carrot, cubed sweet potato, parsnip, and/or fresh peas. Skip the ghee or olive oil at the end, and garnish, if you like, with fresh chopped cilantro. Salt to taste.

SATTVIC, - Vata, - Pitta, - Kapha
*ROTATION DAY 3 DISH

ABOUT THERAPEUTIC USES OF GHEE

The cow is revered in India as a sacred being. Her milk and her butter, clarified as ghee, are like mother's milk in Ayurveda, absolutely essential for health and well-being. They must be pure to do this. Many Westerners are concerned that the use of ghee will increase their cholesterol or add unnecessary amounts of fat to their diet. Used within the context of an Ayurvedic lifestyle, this is quite unlikely to occur. Abused, it could.

To explain: Ghee, unlike butter, helps to stimulate the healthy flow of fluids throughout the body. Butter can congest; ghee removes blockages. No other substance stimulates the flow of bodily fluids as ghee does. Cold-pressed olive oil is specific for stimulating the flow of bile from the liver and gall bladder and thereby relieving congestion there. But ghee does this throughout the body.

About Therapeutic Uses of Ghee (continued)

At the same time, ghee strengthens ojas, *our vital energy cushion, which is at the root of our well-being and immunity. Through* ojas, *ghee nourishes* tejas *as well, the fire of our minds. In this way, intelligence, energy, confidence, understanding, and memory are enhanced.*

Ghee is a rejuvenative to Vata *and* Pitta *and in moderation strengthens* Kapha *as well. For directions on how to make ghee, see p. 206. These days it seems important to get butter which is organic as the chief ingredient for ghee, whenever possible. It is not necessary to refrigerate ghee; in fact if you do, it can slow its positive actions somewhat.*

There are many practical therapeutic ways to use ghee. Dr. Vasant Lad does an excellent job of describing many of them in Ayurveda: The Science of Self-Healing. *A dab of ghee can be put on a little finger and massaged gently into the nasal passages before bed and upon rising. This* nasya *clears the sinus passages, which also clears feelings and can improve eyesight. As a simple laxative, especially good for* Vata, *ghee can be taken at the rate of one to two teaspoons per cup of hot milk, again at bedtime. Taken with food, ghee stimulates* agni *(digestive fire) and all the other digestive juices and enzymes.*

Used externally as a medicated licorice root ghee or ghrita, *it is especially good for wound healing. In* Ayurveda: The Science of Self-Healing, *Dr. Lad describes how to make your own licorice and calamus root* ghritas. *There are many medicated ghees in Ayurvedic practice. For example, ghee is combined with a bitter herb like barberry to relieve* Pitta, *fever, and liver congestion. In combination with* shatavari, *it is used to enhance fertility. With the proper herbs, ghee can even be used to relieve colitis and gastric ulcers.*

It is important to understand that ghee is given and taken within the context of an Ayurvedic program. Usually the fortunate and wise person will do Pancha Karma *(the Ayurvedic cleansing programs) once or twice per year, at the change of seasons or whenever it is recommended. This, in conjunction with a healthy lifestyle, relaxed balanced eating, and attention to community and loved ones, supports balance, inner and outer. And yet this whole lifestyle is new to us to a certain extent, as Westerners. Adding a little fresh ghee to our rice, or* kichadi, *or steamed vegetables, or hot fresh milk, is likely to help us. Adding ghee to our frozen food entree is unlikely to do so (despite ghee's reputation for alleviating poison!). Making rich desserts daily with ghee is also unlikely to have the desired effect. We must use it with common sense and prudence, within its context. As always, this is up to us.*

NORI ROLLS

Preparation time: an hour or less　　　Makes 7 nori rolls, or 35 - 42 pieces

SATTVIC, - Vata, - Pitta, 0 Kapha

Make up one recipe of:
Plain *Basmati* Rice, p. 205

When it is finished cooking, remove from heat. Let it rest for ten minutes before you remove the cover. Mix together:
1 1/2 Tbsps. fresh lemon juice
2 Tbsps. brown rice syrup

When the rice has cooled, stir this mixture thoroughly into the rice with a fork, mashing the rice a bit as you do. Let the rice cool to room temperature. While it does, wash and cut into julienne strips:
2 carrots, 1 cucumber, 2 celery sticks, 1 avocado (optional) and
a 2-inch piece of fresh ginger root, peeled (optional)

Steam the carrot and ginger pieces for five minutes, leaving the other vegetables raw. The avocado can be cut chunkier than the rest. Toast in a small skillet:
1/2 c. raw sesame seeds

Set aside to cool. Open:
1 package sushi nori, 7 sheets

If they are not pre-toasted, toast them for a moment by putting them over an open flame for a second or two on each side. If you have a bamboo sushi mat, place a sheet of nori on that. Otherwise, it is quite possible to "wing it" by working on a wooden cutting board and doing all the rolling up with your hands.

IMPORTANT: put out a small bowl of:
cold salted water

This is to wet your hands, to keep the rice from sticking to them as you work. So, wet your hands and put several large tablespoonfuls of rice onto your sheet of nori. With moistened hands, pat the rice evenly into place, covering the whole nori about 1/4 - 3/8" thick, save the last inch or two farthest from you, which is left vacant. (ILLUS)

Arrange your vegetable fillings in 2 or 3 rows. (ILLUS) Sprinkle toasted sesame lightly over the entire surface. Then tuck the edge closest to you in (ILLUS) and keep rolling, with a lot of the same kind of motion you would use to roll up a sleeping bag or tent. When you come to the end of the rice, lightly moisten that last inch or two of bare nori, and roll on to it, letting the pressure of the roll and gentle pressure from your hand seal it.

With a sharp knife, cut the roll into 5 or 6 pieces. (ILLUS) Repeat for the rest of the sheets of nori. Arrange the sushi on a plate and serve with:
DIPPING SAUCE, p. 217

Despite the complexity of this nori roll making process, kids often enjoy making and eating these. Give them the space to make a few "logs" of their own.

Variation: For a ROTATION DAY 3 DISH, make up the plain basmati rice as usual. Mix together 1/4 tsp. tamarind concentrate and 2 Tbsps. raw honey. Stir this into the rice once it has cooled. For fillings, use Day 3 choices: carrots, celery, tofu, cilantro, and/or jicama; skip the ginger. Steam the carrot as described; leave the other vegetables raw. The tofu can be cut into match sticks and lightly sauteed in sunflower oil and Dr. Bragg's Liquid Aminos, before adding it to the roll. Skip the sesame seeds, otherwise prepare as described. Serve with ROTATION DAY 3 Dipping Sauce, p. 217.

STUFFED CABBAGE LEAVES

Preparation time: 50 minutes total   Serves: 4 - 6
SATTVIC, moderately + Vata, mildly + Pitta, - Kapha   ❄

Preheat oven to 300° F. Steam for about ten minutes:
1 small head of cabbage, red or green

Steam the leaves long enough that they are easy to handle but not falling apart. Set aside. Make up one recipe of:
KASHA AND LEEKS, p. 204

And make up one batch of:
CREAMY GREEN SAUCE, p. 214

Lightly oil a 9"x 13" baking pan, stainless steel or glass is good. Gently pull the cabbage leaves off the head, saving the best leaves for the rolls and using any smaller pieces to line the bottom of the baking dish. This will keep the stuffed ones from sticking.

Spoon one tablespoon of kasha and leek filling on to each cabbage leaf. Tuck in the ends and roll snugly along the rib. Line them into the baking dish and pour the creamy green sauce over them all. Bake uncovered for 20-25 minutes. Garnish with:
toasted sesame seeds

You can also scoop out the heart of the inner cabbage and fill it with kasha like a little nest, this is another pretty way to present this entree. If you use red cabbage, you will have the contrast of purple leaves and forest green sauce. Or you can have an all-green dish with the green cabbage.

*ROTATION DAY 4 DISH

CILANTRO QUICHE

Preparation time: 1 1/2 hours, most of it unattended   Makes 1 9" quiche
MODERATELY RAJASIC*   ✿ ✳ ﷼

Make and bake:
    1 9" baked pie crust, *KAPHA* CRUST, p. 258.

Lower oven heat to 350° F. once the crust is baked. In a small saucepan, warm:
    2 Tbsps. olive oil or ghee

Saute until tender but not brown:
    3 Tbsps. onion, finely chopped
    1 clove garlic, minced

With a fork, stir into the oil:
    1 Tbsp. whole wheat or barley flour

Slowly add:
    1/2 c. rice milk, soy milk, or fresh raw cow's milk

Cook over low heat until thickened, stirring frequently (about 5 minutes). Stir in:
    1/2 tsp. salt
    1/8 tsp. cayenne

In a blender, combine:
    2 non-fertile eggs, preferred*
    1/2 c. more of the milk
    1/2 lb. firm tofu
    1/2 tsp. fresh lemon juice
    1 c. fresh cilantro leaves, finely chopped and lightly packed

Fold the blended ingredients into the cream sauce, folding in at the same time:
    1 ripe avocado, diced (optional)

Pour into *KAPHA* CRUST and bake for 45 minutes at 350° F. or until knife comes out cleanly. Can be served hot or cold. It is especially good after it has cooled for a while.

* - *Vata*, 0 *Pitta*, 0 *Kapha* (when using soy or rice milk, no avocado)
* - *Vata*, mildly + *Pitta*, + *Kapha* (when using cow's milk and avocado)

*NOTE: In the absence of a rooster, a hen will continue to lay eggs. These nutritious non-fertile eggs are a natural part of her biological cycle and do not involve the taking of a life when consumed. For this reason, whenever I can get them, I choose non-fertile eggs.

POTATO FRITTATA

Preparation time: 30 minutes   Serves: 2- 4
RAJASIC, 0 Vata, mildly + Pitta, mildly + Kapha

Wash and cut up:
> **12 small new potatoes, quartered or diced**
> **1 Tbsp. onion, finely chopped**
> **1 tsp. fresh rosemary, finely chopped**

Saute the vegetables over medium heat in a 9 or 10 inch heavy skillet, with:
> **1 1/2 Tbsps. extra-virgin olive oil**

Stir occasionally. Cover and let cook for 10 -15 minutes. Beat together:
> **6 fresh non-fertile eggs**
> **Salt and pepper to taste**

Wash and chop:
> **1 Tbsp. fresh parsley, finely chopped**
> **1 c. fresh spinach, arugula or baby kale, chopped**

When the potatoes are tender, pour the eggs over them in the skillet. Stir in the greens and cover. Cook over low heat until the top of the eggs is firm. Put a plate over the skillet; turn the skillet over so that the frittata slides on to it. (ILLUS) Serve immediately.

Comments: This is a light entree. It needs a hearty muffin recipe to go with it, like GIN-GER-PEAR MUFFINS, p. 176 or MOCK BOSTON BROWN BREAD MUFFINS, p. 177.

When only 3% of Americans serve the rest of us as food producers, most of us must be pretty cut off from the realities of how our food gets grown. Obviously thousands of us are gardeners. But a lot of us are not connected at all, in this vital exchange with nature, with where our food is coming from. As I was collecting eggs this morning in the chicken coop, I marvelled at the way they magically appear, in the nest of straw, even in the cold. They come from the earth, not some carton! Remarkable.

SAVORY VEGETABLE POT PIE

Preparation time: 1 1/4 hours   Makes 1 9" pie
SATTVIC, - Vata, - Pitta, 0 Kapha*

Prepare the crust:
BARLEY OR WHOLE WHEAT PIE CRUST, p. 257

Chill for 30 minutes in the refrigerator, while you prepare the filling. Wash and chop:
> **3 c. raw, diced, peeled sweet potato (2 large)**
> **2 c. green beans, French cut (ILLUS)**
> **1 Tbsp. onion or leek, finely chopped**
> **2 Tbsps. celery, finely chopped**
> **1 1/2 Tbsps. fresh ginger root, peeled and grated**
> **or very finely chopped**

Saute the onion, celery and ginger in a large skillet with:
> **1 Tbsp. sesame oil**

Pour into the skillet:
> **1 1/2 c. soy milk or freshly boiled raw cow's milk (boil an extra 1/2 cup for use later in the recipe)**

Warm the filling over medium heat. Stir in the sweet potato, green beans and:
> **1/2 tsp. salt**
> **1/4 tsp. cinnamon**
> **1/2 tsp. curry powder**

Cover and let cook over medium heat for 20 - 30 minutes, or until the vegetables are tender. Finely chop:
> **2 Tbsps. raw blanched almonds**

Set aside to be used in the topping. Stir together in a cup:
> **1/2 c. more soy or cow's milk**
> **1 tsp. arrowroot (cornstarch or flour may be substituted)**

Wash and chop:
> **1 Tbsp. fresh parsley, finely chopped**

Preheat the oven to 350° F. When the pie crust has chilled, pat it out into a 9" pie pan. Prick 5 or 6 times, and set aside. Stir the milk, arrowroot and parsley into the veggies when they are done. Spoon the filling into the uncooked pie crust and sprinkle the top with the chopped almonds and:
> **1 Tbsp. raw sesame seeds**

Bake for about 20 to 30 minutes, or until done. Serve hot.

*This recipe is most neutral for *Kapha* with soy milk and barley flour, and most calming to *Vata* with cow's milk and whole wheat flour. *Pitta* is calmed by any of these.

ABOUT GARLIC AND ONIONS

Those tasty creatures. How much is too much? While garlic and onions are used liberally in commercial East Indian cooking, they are more sparsely consumed in Ayurvedic fare. Garlic is considered rajasic, *or sometimes* tamasic. *Onions are* tamasic, *and both aggravate* Pitta. *For a number of years I was pretty strait-laced about this pair, avoiding them at every opportunity. Then I began to notice that other good Ayurvedic cooks whom I respected, used them, in small quantities. (We also had a nice garlic crop that year, so the temptation to re-evaluate was high.) A reasonable rule of thumb for someone of* Pitta *constitution on a* sattvic *diet, who wants to have a little of these, would be about one good-sized onion per week and a clove or two of garlic (less if you want).* Kaphas *on a sattvic regime might have a similar amount of onion and 4 or more cloves of garlic without a problem (again, less if you like).*

Vatas *might have a little less onion, cooked, depending on how it agrees with them, and perhaps 2 or 3 cloves of garlic, if they want them. Heating garlic in oil enhances its medicinal properties. On the plus side, garlic can be a helpful rejuvenative, especially for* Vata.

I find myself using leeks more and more in place of onions, when they are available. They have a milder, sweeter taste and so disrupt Pitta *less than regular onions. Shallots are similar in their dynamics to leeks.*

Daily activities can also influence how much of these you choose. If you are doing quiet, light or contemplative work, you may find yourself using less than if you are doing competitive work or strenuous physical activities like construction, sports or waiting tables.

Consideration for children's tastes in the household can also drag (lead?) a cook in a more sattvic *direction!*

DORIE'S MOLÉ ENCHILADAS

Preparation time: 1 1/4 hours   Serves: 4 - 6 for 12 enchiladas
SATTVIC, - Vata, mildly + Pitta, + Kapha*

✿ 🦢 ❄

Molé Sauce (Makes 2 quarts sauce)

Saute over low heat until soft:
> **1 small onion, chopped**
> **2 cloves garlic, minced**

in:
> **2 Tbsps. sunflower oil**

Stir into the saute:
> **1 tsp. chile ancho (or ground red chile)**
> **1 tsp. cocoa**

While the chile is cooking, grind into a fine powder in a blender:
> **2/3 c. raw pumpkin seeds**

Stir the ground seeds into the saute, and continue to cook on low for another 10 - 15 minutes. Now it's time to add to the sauce:
> **2 Tbsps. sesame tahini**
> **1 corn tortilla, crumbled up with your hands**
> **1/4 tsp. cumin seeds**
> **1/8 tsp. cinnamon**
> **1/4 c. organic raisins**

Stir well. Yes, I agree, this is a most improbable list of ingredients. And it makes a very good sauce. Immediately pour in, a little at a time, stirring as you do:
> **About 8 c. boiling water**
> **1 tsp. Sucanat**

Let the sauce simmer for about an hour, stirring occasionally or frequently as is your wont. Serve hot over enchiladas, below.

Enchilada Filling

Steam:
> **3 medium zucchini and/or crookneck squash, diced**

Mix with:
> **1/2 c. raw pine nuts**
> **Salt to taste**

Let a skillet warm on high heat for a minute. One by one, heat:
> **12 corn tortillas, blue or yellow, on the skillet with: a drop of oil**

Toss a tortilla onto the hot skillet, flip it as soon as it is hot and soft, take off a couple of seconds later. If your tortillas are not heating up and softening, you need to let your skillet warm longer before adding the tortillas. If the tortillas are getting stiff, you are leaving them on to cook too long (or you have stale tortillas). Sometimes adding a drop of water to the top of a stiff tortilla, as you cook it, can help it soften up.

Put the hot tortilla on an individual serving plate. Spoon on to it a tablespoonful of the molé sauce, then a heaping tablespoon of the enchilada filling. Roll up the tortilla, do the same for one or two more tortillas, then spoon generous amounts of molé sauce over the enchiladas. Serve immediately. Do the same for the rest of your enchiladas. Enjoy!

*Kaphas can thin the sauce with more water to make it more soothing for them.

Comments: MASHED SWEET POTATOES, p. 192 makes another good, if improbable, enchilada filling here, with a light sprinkling of toasted sesame seeds on top. The molé sauce is also delicious over rice, steamed vegetables, or eggs. With much thanks to my friend Dolores Chiappone for this recipe.

ABOUT SALT

A little salt sparks digestive fire, agni, *in a good way. Small amounts of salt are used in some Ayurvedic medicinal herb combinations for digestion. Rock salt is most respected in Ayurveda for its ability to enhance agni, and is most often used in herbal formulations for this purpose. It can often be found in Indian groceries.*

Too much salt can ignite ulcers, blood pressure and other high-Pitta conditions. Canned foods frequently contain mind-boggling amounts of salt, as can fast foods and other foods eaten out in restaurants. This excess can subtly aggravate both Pitta and Kapha. Fresh food, properly prepared, can contain as little as 10% of the salt of their canned counterparts.

If you find yourself using a heavy hand with the salt shaker, you could be zinc deficient. Zinc is needed for taste acuity. When we can't taste as well, we often use more and more salt or spice to compensate. A nutritionist can be helpful here for evaluating zinc status, as it is a mineral you can get too much of, as well as too little.

NICE BURGER

Preparation time: 1 1/2 hours, most of it unattended   Makes 16 burgers
SATTVIC, mildly + Vata, 0 Pitta, 0 Kapha   ✿ ✳ ಜ ❄

In a medium saucepan, bring to a boil:
> 1 1/3 c. uncooked brown *basmati* rice
> 1/4 c. whole grain teff (optional)
> 3 c. water

Reduce heat to medium-low, cover and cook until almost done, about 40 minutes. Add:
> 1 c. sprouted mung beans

Cover and let cook a final 5 minutes. Set aside. Preheat oven to 350° F. Chop very finely:
> 1/3 c. tender leek greens
> 2 stalks celery

Finely grate:
> 1/2 c. carrot

And mince:
> 1 clove garlic

Stir all the vegetables together in a large mixing bowl with:
> 2 tsps. dried oregano
> 1 tsp. fresh sage, chopped
> 4 tsps. dried sweet basil
> 2/3 c. finely ground pumpkin seeds
> 2/3 c. finely ground almonds
> 2 - 4 Tbsps. finely chopped parsley
> 1 tsp. salt

When the grain and bean mixture is done, stir it thoroughly into the rest of the ingredients. Lightly oil 2 cookie sheets. Shape into patties and bake for 30 - 35 minutes. Or saute on a lightly oiled or non-stick pan, flipping when golden brown.

Comments: This is our favorite burger. It was originally inspired by a nice article by Bharti Kirchner about veggie burgers in the August 1993 issue of Vegetarian Times. Seattle chef Jim Watkins of Cafe Flora had a delectable sounding Vegetable-Nut Burger with Fennel Coulis, which got us to goofing with our own Ayurvedic version.

Variation: A DAY 2 BURGER: Prepare as above, combining: 2 c. cooked millet, 1/2 c. roasted and ground almonds, 1 c. grated raw zucchini, 1 Tbsp. extra-virgin olive oil, 3/4 tsp. salt, 1 tsp. turmeric. Shape into patties and bake at 350° F. for 30 minutes.

SATTVIC, + Vata, mildly + Pitta, 0 Kapha

Comments: This variation is a fairly bland burger, but edible. Specifically designed for the allergy rotation diet. For more information about rotation diets, see p. 323.

SANTA FE PINTO BEANS

Preparation time: with pressure cooker, 45 minutes
Without pressure cooker, 9 - 10 hours; can be made in crock pot   Serves: 6 - 8
SATTVIC, + Vata, - Pitta, - Kapha*   ✿ ✹ ☕ ❄

Sort and wash, soaking overnight if possible:
    1 1/2 c. dried pinto beans

Place the beans in a pressure cooker with:
    6 c. pure water
    1/4 - 1/2 medium onion, finely chopped (use the smaller amount for *Pitta***)**
    1 - 2 cloves garlic, minced (omit for *Pitta***)**
    1/2 - 2 tsps. chili powder (use the smaller amount for *Pitta***)**
    1 bay leaf
    1/2 tsp. dried oregano, or 2 tsps. fresh, chopped
    1/2 tsp. dried basil, or 2 tsps. fresh, chopped
    1/2 tsp. whole cumin seeds
    1/8 tsp hing or epazote
    1 piece kombu (optional)

Bring to pressure and cook at medium heat for 30 minutes or until tender. Or soak the beans at least 4 hours, rinsing half a dozen times to reduce the gas-producing raffinose in the outer coating of the bean. Place beans in large pot with fresh water and bring to a boil, cook two minutes. Drain beans, discarding the cooking water and add a fresh 6 cups water. Let sit two hours in this water. Add all the ingredients above and bring to a boil in a pot or crock pot uncovered. Cover and reduce heat to medium-low. Cook covered for 3 to 4 hours or until beans are quite soft.

Once beans are tender, by either method, stir in:
    1 tsp. coriander powder
    1 tsp. spearmint or yerba buena, fresh if possible
    Salt to taste, about 1 tsp.

Cook over medium heat for another 10 minutes. Stir, serve.

Comments: This dish is good with hot corn or wheat tortillas and ghee, or cornbread, and a fresh vegetable or salad. The salt should not be added until the end as it makes the beans tough. The hing or epazote, kombu and cumin substantially aid digestion of this dish for *Vata*. Spearmint or yerba buena with coriander assists digestion and cools the other herbs and spices for *Pitta*. Excellent for *Kapha*. One of my favorite "American" dishes. I am glad my friend Juan Morgan first taught me this way of fixing beans some twenty years ago.

* If well-soaked and served with ghee or oil, this is well-tolerated by *Vata* in small amounts. Rather than eating it with corn, *Vata* is likely to find it easier to eat with rice.

BAKED PINQUITO BEANS

Preparation time: 1 hour   Serves: 3 - 4

SATTVIC, + Vata, - Pitta, - Kapha   ✿ ✳ ⁊⁊ ❄

In a stainless steel pressure cooker, put:
>   1 c. dry pinquito beans*
>   1/2 medium onion, chopped
>   1 clove of garlic, minced
>   3/4 " fresh ginger root, peeled and finely grated or chopped
>   2 c. apple juice
>   2 c. water
>   1/4 tsp. red chile, Chimayo is good

Bring to pressure and cook until tender, 30 minutes or more. Let cool, and stir in:
>   1 Tbsp. raw honey
>   1 tsp. salt

Serve.

**POLARITY HEALTH BUILDING DISH

Comments: This makes a nice light baked bean entree. Navy beans can be used in place of pinquitos, if necessary. If you can get them, though, pinquitos are wonderful! Nichols Nursery sells pinquito seed (see Appendix VII), if you want to grow your own.

It is amazing what a difference there is between fresh dried beans and older dry beans. The first time I made this recipe, the pinquitos were straight from their dried pods and took a scant 20 minutes to cook. A year later I used beans from the same harvest in the same recipe, and they took almost an hour to get tender! With no difference in outward appearance.

Sprouting the beans before you cook them, no matter how old, makes them easier to digest, lighter and speeds cooking time. For more info, see ABOUT SPROUTING, p. 104. Fresher beans sprout more readily.

SIMPLE ADUKIS

Preparation time: 20 minutes with precooked beans, 1 hour without   Serves: 3 - 4
A LITTLE TAMASIC (with the mushrooms), 0 Vata, - Pitta, - Kapha   ❀ 🐚 ❄

If you can, soak overnight or sprout:
> **1 c. dry aduki beans**
> **(Or you can use 2 c. precooked aduki beans)**

To make the beans from scratch, put the dry adukis and all the ingredients below into a pressure cooker and bring to pressure:
> **6 dry Shiitaake mushrooms or 1 or 2 large fresh ones**
> **1/4 c. hijiki, dry**
> **1 Tbsp. cold-pressed sunflower oil**
> **6 - 8 c. water**
> **Salt and pepper to taste**

Cook for 30 minutes. When done, remove from heat, and stir in:
> **A few drops of toasted sesame oil (optional)**

Serve.

Variation: If you are working with pre-cooked beans, pour 1 c. of boiling water over the dried mushrooms and hijiki in an ovenproof bowl. Let sit for fifteen minutes. While these are soaking, put the adukis in a saucepan and heat up with the sunflower oil and salt and pepper, if needed. (They easily might not be needed, if the beans are already salted or spiced.) Once the mushrooms and sea veggies have plumped up enough to be chewable and tasty, add them to the adukis and simmer together over medium-low heat for 5 minutes or so. Add toasted sesame oil, stir, serve.

A LITTLE TAMASIC (with the mushrooms), 0 Vata, - Pitta, - Kapha

Variation: For a ROTATION DAY 3 DISH, omit the Shiitaake mushrooms and the toasted sesame oil.

SATTVIC, 0 Vata, - Pitta, - Kapha

Variation: POLARITY VERSION: Instead of putting the oil in with the beans while they are cooking, add it after they are done. This is easier on the liver, though sometimes less effective in preventing gas, especially for *Vata*.

A LITTLE TAMASIC, 0 Vata,- Pitta,- Kapha
**POLARITY HEALTH BUILDING DISH

Comments: This is a nice combo with QUINOA ASPARAGUS PILAF, p. 118. It also makes a good quick lunch on a fall or winter day. If you want an indisputably *sattvic* meal, skip the Shiitaakes.

WILD RICE SALAD: See Salads, p. 75. This makes a good entree, hot or cool.

PESTO PIZZA

Preparation time: 45 minutes - 1 hour
SATTVIC, - Vata, + Pitta, + Kapha

Serves: 2 - 3
✿ ✳ 🫖 ❄

Make up:
Pizza Crust, p. 138

While the crust is cooking, the sauce can be blended together:
Pesto Sauce, p. 156

Set aside and prepare:

Topping:

Wash and chop:
2 c. tender zucchini, thin-sliced in rounds
1/2 red bell pepper, thin sliced (optional)

When the crust is done, reduce oven heat to 350° F. Thinly spread the pesto sauce over the entire crust. Arrange the zucchini rounds and pepper slices on top. Put back in the oven to bake for another 15 - 20 minutes. Serve hot.

Comments: This is a very tasty dish.

ROSE PETAL PIZZA

Preparation time: 45 minutes - 1 hour
MILDLY RAJASIC, 0 *Vata*, moderately + *Pitta*, 0 *Kapha*

Serves: 2 - 3
🫖 ❄

Make up:
Pizza Crust, p. 138

While the crust is baking, the sauce can be made:

Rose Petal Sauce:

Wash and chop:
6 medium tomatoes, fresh
2 Tbsps. red onion, finely chopped (optional)

Put them in a saucepan with:
1 Tbsp. olive oil
1 clove garlic, minced

and let them cook down over medium heat into sauce. In Italy, a food mill would be used to strain the seeds out of the fresh tomatoes. If you have one and are so inclined, removing the seeds helps calm the tomatoes' action on *Vata*. I usually push away as many seeds as I can as I chop. The tomato sauce should be cooked down soon after the crust comes out of the oven.

Once the tomatoes have thickened, pour them into a blender with:

1 heaping Tbsp. organic rose petals, dried
1 Tbsp. (or more) fresh oregano, chopped, or 2 tsps. dried
1/4 tsp. dried marjoram
1/4 tsp. dried thyme
Salt and pepper to taste

Puree for a few seconds. Set aside.

Topping:

To prepare the topping, wash:

4 cherry tomatoes
1/2 red bell pepper
2 inches of leek, the white bulb

Thin-slice the cherry tomatoes into little rounds, the leek as well. Cut the bell pepper into long thin slices.

Dice:

1/2 ripe avocado (optional)

Pour the sauce onto the baked crust and spread it over the whole surface. It will cover it thinly. Arrange the topping in any way you like. This is a fun thing for kids to help with if they are available. Put the pizza back in the oven and bake at 425° F for 10 - 12 minutes. Makes one 12-inch round pizza.

Comments: This is a good, easy pizza, passed on to me by my mother and sister, Margie and Cindy Noren. It has a yeast-free crust, and can be used even on a strict yeast-free diet. The rose petals calm the otherwise heating and acidic qualities of the tomato a great deal. And it is another way for the person on an Ayurvedic program to play with pizza. Like Pesto Pizza, it can be made so as to be suitable for people sensitive to wheat and/or dairy. A fun way to eat at home!

Variation: ROTATION DAY 1: Use ROTATION DAY 1 Pizza Crust, p.   and 1/2 recipe of ROTATION DAY 1 Basic Rose Petal Tomato Sauce. For topping, use any of the following: cherry tomatoes, bell pepper, avocado, mushrooms, or any Day 1 vegetable.

MILDLY RAJASIC, 0 Vata, moderately + Pitta, 0 Kapha

PIZZA CRUST

Preparation time: 20 minutes
SATTVIC*

Makes one 12" crust

Preheat oven to 425° F. Combine in a mixing bowl:
2 c. barley or whole wheat flour
3/4 tsp. salt
1 tsp. aluminum-free baking powder

With a fork, stir in:
2/3 c. soy or freshly boiled raw cow's milk
1/4 c. sunflower oil

The mixture will begin to hold together in a ball. Turn the dough out onto a floured surface (like your clean kitchen counter) and knead it lightly a dozen times. Lightly oil a 12-inch round stainless steel pizza pan and press the dough into the pan, making an edge for the rim with your fingers. Put it in the oven to bake for 15 to 20 minutes.

* - *Vata*, - *Pitta*, + *Kapha* (with whole wheat flour and cow's milk)

* 0 *Vata*, - *Pitta*, - *Kapha* (with barley flour and soy milk)

Variation: ROTATION DAY 1 DISH: Use either flour, fresh cow's milk and walnut oil. Bake as usual.

ABOUT NIGHTSHADES

The "deadly nightshade" family, as it is called, includes tomatoes, potatoes, eggplant, sweet bell peppers, chili peppers, and tobacco. Ayurvedic cooking tends to shy away from the use of these foods on any kind of regular basis. When you see them, it is more for an occasional accent than for the bulk of a meal. Most night-shades tend to have a pungent or sour vipak *(with the exception of potato) and as a family they are aggravating to* Vata *and* Pitta *doshas. It would be beneficial to serve nightshade meals no more than once or twice a month (like My Favorite Cajun Gumbo, which is heavy on the okra and light on the tomato, or Potato Frittata or Rose Petal Pizza or Delish Tofu Spaghetti Sauce, for notorious examples). If you've got a pizza or tomato paste habit, that much of a limit could feel extreme to you. If you want to change your approach on this, you might try cutting back slowly on your tomatoes and peppers, until you reach a place agreeable both to your health and you.*

About Nightshades (continued)

In Ayurveda, this approach is the "1/4 - 1/4 - 1/4" one; cutting back one-quarter of what you are used to, until that feels comfortable and normal, then cutting back another quarter, and so on, until you are eating or drinking the right amount for you.

POLENTA

Preparation time: 45 minutes
Serves: 4, lightly

SATTVIC, + Vata, + Pitta, - Kapha

✿ ❧ ❄

In a large saucepan, bring to a boil:

5 c. water
1 tsp. salt

Lower heat to simmer, and slowly begin to pour in, 1/2 cup at a time:

1 1/2 c. polenta (coarsely ground cornmeal)*

A long-handled spoon really helps keep splattering to a minimum. Once you've added all the polenta, keep stirring. The polenta will begin to get thicker, then dry. Sprinkle in:

1 tsp. spearmint (optional)

Keep stirring! After 20 to 30 minutes of stirring (this is a dish Italian women used to make with their friends, talking as they made it in big pots over a central hearth), the polenta will be so thick that it comes away from the sides of the pot as you stir it with the spoon. Pour the polenta into a casserole dish or on to a wooden board. Shape it into a 2" high round mound. Wet hands and a light touch work best for this. Let sit for 10 - 15 minutes or until the polenta becomes fairly solid. Cut into 1" slices and serve with PESTO SAUCE, p. 156 or LIGHT BASIL SAUCE, p. 155 or BASIC ROSE PETAL TOMATO SAUCE, p. 160. The polenta can be reheated by placing it in a 350° F. oven for 15 minutes.

*ROTATION DAY 4 DISH, omit the mint

**POLARITY HEALTH BUILDING DISH

Comments: Polenta is sold in bulk at many natural groceries, or in Italian groceries. Regular cornmeal should not be used, it is too fine a grind to work here.

CASHEW CREAM CAULIFLOWER

Preparation time: 20 minutes   Serves: 4 - 6

SATTVIC, moderately + Vata, 0 Pitta, 0 Kapha   ❁ ✳ 🐚 ❄

Wash:
1 medium head fresh cauliflower

Put it on to steam, *whole*, in a saucepan with:
1 c. water

Cover and let cook over medium heat until soft, about 15 - 20 minutes. In a blender or food processor, grind finely:
1/2 tsp. ground coriander*
1/2 tsp. rock salt
1 c. raw cashews

When the cauliflower is done, pour 1/2 cup of its cooking water into the blender with the ground nuts and blend until smooth. More hot water can be added as needed, until you have the consistency you desire. Serve the cauliflower whole in a serving dish with the cashew cream poured over it. Cut into wedges to serve.

* ROTATION DAY 4 DISH. Omit coriander if following a strict rotation diet.

** POLARITY HEALTH BUILDING DISH

> There is an old Buddhist saying, "You can see the flags waving, but you don't see the wind." This is beginning to stimulate a deeper understanding of karma, as I understand it in my daily life. On a more physical level, this expression can also describe how Ayurveda relates to the workings of our bodies. We may not always know what it is that is "off", but we often suspect something is out of balance before it becomes clearly evident. Or perhaps for a graphic and simple example, if you eat too much of a Vata-imbalancing food, or a Vata-imbalancing combination, even if you do not realize which one(s), your body will let you know by waving its flag of flatulence, yes?

BEAN THREADS WITH SNOW PEAS

Preparation time: 15 minutes   Serves: 2 - 3
SATTVIC BORDERING ON RAJASIC, - Vata, 0 Pitta, 0 Kapha*   ✳ 🐌

In a medium saucepan or heatproof bowl, place:
     1 (3.75 oz.) package bean thread noodles (Saifun)

Pour enough boiling water over the noodles so that they are completely covered. Let soak for 10 - 15 minutes. While the bean threads are soaking, mix:
     2 Tbsps. miso*
     1 c. boiling water

Set aside. In a large skillet, warm:
     2 Tbsps. sunflower oil

Add:
     1-2 cloves garlic, minced*

and saute for a minute. Stir in:
     1/3 c. raw sunflower seeds

and let simmer on low heat for another couple of minutes. Wash:
     1 1/2 c. fresh snow peas (1/3 lb.)
     3 c. fresh bean sprouts (1/4 lb.)

and trim the ends off the snow peas. Stir the veggies into the oil. Cover and cook until done, 5 minutes or less on medium heat. Turn off the heat. Pour in the miso broth, then the bean threads. Stir as best you can, it will be unwieldy. Add:
     1/8 tsp. freshly ground black pepper

*The less miso and garlic you use, the more *sattvic* it is.

*For a strict ROTATION DAY 3 DISH, omit the garlic and be sure to use a bean and rice-based miso.

SATTVIC with some *rajasic* leanings, - *Vata, 0 Pitta, mildly + Kapha*

Comments: Good, light, quick dish. Unless your appetite is scant, you'll need another dish here, like STEAMED BROCCOLI AND GARLIC, p. 197 or steamed Swiss chard.

THAI STIR-FRY

Preparation time: 30 minutes   Serves: 3 - 4
SATTVIC, - Vata, 0 Pitta, - Kapha   ❀ ✳ ೩ ❅

Make up:
PLAIN BASMATI RICE, p. 205*

As it is cooking, wash and chop the vegetables:
1/2 lb. fresh asparagus, in 1-inch pieces
1 c. Chinese cabbage, thin-sliced
1 medium bunch fresh spinach, well-washed and chopped
1 c. fresh cilantro leaves, loosely packed, then minced
1/2 c. cucumber, peeled and julienne sliced
3 Tbsps. fresh ginger root, peeled and very thin-sliced (less if you like)
2 cloves garlic, minced

When the rice looks like it is close to being done, begin the stir-fry:

In a large skillet, warm:
2 Tbsps. sesame oil

With the temperature on high, add the garlic and the ginger and stir. About one minute later, stir in the asparagus, Chinese cabbage and spinach. Stir until the spinach begins to wilt a bit. Pour in:
3/4 c. coconut milk

and stir well. When the spinach is cooked, take the stir-fry off the heat and stir in the cilantro and cucumber. Serve hot over rice.

* **NOTE:** If you would like to be true to Thai custom, the rice you use would be long-grained Thai jasmine rice.

ABOUT LEFTOVERS

"What is a leftover?" I asked Dr. Sunil Joshi somewhat plaintively one day, of course hoping he would affirm whatever slovenly habits I had developed in this regard. "A leftover is a food which has been kept over night," he replied steadily, dashing all my hopes. He added, in response to my questioning look, "(Think about it. . .) a food sits overnight, in the time of cool and dark, it is a perfect time for slime and fermentation" (or something to that effect). "Food which has been prepared the same day, say in the morning and eaten by nightfall, that is fresh."

It has taken me a while to get used to this approach. As an American, I was so used to the "creative use of leftovers." And yet after eating in this fresher way for a while, I am surprised to find that food that has been sitting in the fridge for a day or more is now distinctly unappealing.

Practically, I would like to offer help to readers in shifting over to a fresher way of eating. The miles of freezer entrees in America testify to the multitudes of us who eat otherwise.

SOME WAYS TO EAT FRESHLY

1) Fix it yourself; begin by doing it when you can. When I'm at home for the day, I'll often make a one-dish meal to serve for both lunch and dinner. Also, getting in the practice of making smaller portions helps, so there are fewer leftovers by which to be tempted.

2) Live with (or hire) a "fresh" cook, appreciating them lavishly.

3) "Meal-pool": share meals with friends, passing around the responsibility for preparation.

4) Find a good deli in your neighborhood with at least some fresh, preservative-free dishes.

5) See if there's an Ayurvedic or vegetarian cook in your area who prepares fresh meals, for cash or barter.

6) Find a good local market or produce stand with fresh ready-to-eat food for part of your fare: avocados, mixed greens, peaches, apples, berries, whathaveyou.

7) Keep it simple and easy (check out LUNCH ideas, p. 62 for more clues).

SOBA NOODLES WITH GARLIC AND VEGETABLES

Preparation time: 20 - 25 minutes   Serves: 2 - 4
SATTVIC, 0 Vata, slightly + Pitta, 0 Kapha   ✿ 🍵 ❄

Put a large pot of water on to boil for the noodles. (Covering it will speed cooking time and save energy.) Chop in cross-wise slices:
> **1/2 medium onion**

Saute the onion over low heat until tender, not brown, with:
> **2 Tbsps. cold-pressed sesame oil**
> **1 large clove garlic, minced**

Wash and chop:
> **1 1/2 c. red cabbage, thin-sliced**
> **1 1/2 c. Chinese cabbage, thin-sliced**

Stir the red cabbage into the oil and cook covered over medium heat until almost done, about 6 - 8 minutes. Add the Chinese cabbage and:
> **1 tsp. sea salt**

Cover and cook for another 2 - 3 minutes. Remove from heat when done. Put into boil:
> **1 8 oz. package 100% buckwheat soba noodles**

following any instructions on the package for cooking. Usually.the cooking time is 10 minutes in boiling water. When the noodles are done, rinse them in cold water. Toss them with the sauteed vegetables in a large serving bowl. Garnish with:
> **1/2 c. ground toasted sesame seeds**
> **1/8 tsp. freshly ground white pepper (optional)***

* ROTATION DAY 4 DISH, omit the pepper if you are following a strict rotation.

MICHELE'S HOLIDAY BUTTERNUT

Preparation time: a leisurely 2 hours
SATTVIC, - Vata, 0 Pitta, moderately + Kapha*

Serves: 3 - 4

✿ 🐌 ❄

Preheat oven to 350° F. In a saucepan, bring to a boil:

1/2 c. mixture of wild rice and brown basmati rice
1 1/2 c. water

Reduce heat to low, cover and cook for 45 minutes, or until done. While the rice is cooking, wash:

a 3 - 4 lb. butternut squash

Slice it lengthwise and place in a 9"x 12" covered baking dish with:

about 1 c. water

Bake in the oven for 1 hour, or until tender straight through. When done, remove from oven and let cool a bit. Scoop out the seeds and gently spoon the squash out of the shell, leaving the shell intact (maintaining its integrity, as Michele would say). Reserve the squash in a bowl. Saute together until translucent:

1 Tbsp. sunflower or walnut oil
2 Tbsps. onion, chopped
2 hearty cloves of garlic, minced

Add:

3/4 lb. mushrooms, sliced (optional)
2 medium carrots, grated

Saute 3 more minutes. Add:

1 bunch fresh spinach, chopped

Saute for another minute, stirring occasionally. Mix the squash and cooked rice into the sauteing vegetables. Add:

1 Tbsp. dried dill weed
1/2 c. dried cranberries ("optional but yummy")
1/4 - 3/4 c. raw walnuts, chopped

Stir well. Place the mixture in the scooped out squash shell and bake in covered pan for 20 - 30 minutes more at 350° F. Serve hot, with the butternut presented whole. Good with a tossed salad and any of the oil and lemon dressings.

* Entirely *sattvic* without mushrooms; *tamasic* with them.

Comment: a delicious holiday dish that goes together easily.

MIDDLE EASTERN OLIVE CASSEROLE

Preparation time: 40 minutes   Serves: 3 - 4

Moderately RAJASIC (with the olives), 0 Vata, moderately + Pitta,
mildly + Kapha   ✿ 🐌 ❄

Rinse well:
> **1/4 c. dry quinoa**

Put it in a medium saucepan with:
> **3/4 c. dry millet, rinsed**
> **2 c. water**
> **1/2 tsp. salt**

Bring to a boil, reduce heat to low and cover. Cook until done, about 30 minutes. While the grain is cooking, chop finely and set aside:
> **1/4 lb. black olives (1/2 cup)**

Peel and chop finely:
> **1 tsp. fresh ginger root**
> **1 small onion***

In a large iron skillet, warm:
> **2 - 3 Tbsps. olive oil or ghee**

Toss the ginger and the onion in the oil and saute on medium heat until the onion is translucent. Stir in:
> **1 tsp. paprika***
> **1/4 tsp. ground cloves**

Stir the spices evenly into the onion mixture, and set aside until the grains have cooked. When the quinoa and millet are done, stir them into the onion and spices in the skillet, mixing well. Add the olives and:
> **Freshly ground black pepper* and salt to taste**

Serve!

*This is a ROTATION DAY 2 DISH. If you are following a strict rotation diet, omit these items which have an asterisk, and use olive oil rather than ghee.

ABOUT SOY PRODUCTS

Many highly processed soy foods have become popular in vegetarian cuisine. How do they look from an Ayurvedic perspective? Take soy milk. Just as with any milk, fresh is best. The Farm in Tennessee has pioneered many wild and wonderful uses of soy, and their cookbook (The Farm Vegetarian Cookbook, *1978) offers a good how-to recipe on soy milk, if you're so inclined. But what about the boxed or bottled soy milks? They can expand one's options enormously, especially for people who are dairy sensitive, used for simple things, like the occasional bowl of cold cereal or for baking. As far as I can ascertain, boxed soy milk is mildly* rajasic, *depending on the brand. It is moderately imbalancing to* Vata, *calming to* Pitta, *neutral or slightly increasing* Kapha. *If you can tolerate fresh cow's milk and it is available, it is a better option for* Vata *and* Pitta. *If you cannot, soy milk can help.*

Soy cheese offers few advantages over animal cheeses in terms of digestibility or health. Its main advantage, obviously, is that if you are sensitive to dairy products, you can get a cheese flavor without immediately getting ill. But in the long run, soy cheese is heavy, fatty and ama-*producing. If you use it, do not imagine that it is likely to help you clear out your system any more than regular cheese would. And for people who are sensitive to milk proteins, it offers no advantage at all, as the soy cheeses currently on the market in America (that I have found) all contain casein, milk protein. They are simply lactose-free, milk sugar free. This means they are a viable alternative for those who cannot digest lactose, but still a problem for those who cannot handle milk proteins.*

Soy ice creams, like cow's milk ice creams, are cold, heavy, and good for producing ama, *toxic waste, in the body. Both soy and cow ice creams have a potential secondary effect of inflaming the gut, as they are* rajasic *in nature. Again, if you are desperately craving ice cream and know that cow's milk products don't do well for you, soy is an alternative. But a cleansing alternative, from an Ayurvedic perspective? No. Just a different choice. The same would be true for most of the new soy products coming out on the market, such as soy sour cream, soy cream cheese, etc.*

Ghee, sesame butter or fresh cold-pressed oils would be considered stronger choices in a healing regime than a quality soy margarine. A small amount of a good soy margarine would be fine occasionally, but the aforementioned foods would be considered preferable.

About Soy Products (continued)

Soybeans themselves are cool and heavy in quality, which means that eaten simply baked or cooked, they can be a challenge to digest. They should never be eaten raw (as in sprouts), as the raw bean contains enzymes which specifically inhibit the human digestive process. (Whether an extended course of sprouting would inactivate or change these enzymes, I do not know.) Over centuries, people have learned to work with this problematic digestive quality in soybeans in order to benefit from the rich source of protein it offers. It has been fermented and processed in order to render it lighter and easier to consume. Some of these products, like tamari and miso, would generally be considered rajasic, inflaming to the mind, from an Ayurvedic perspective. They are recommended for occasional use. (For another discussion of miso, see p. 49) Tofu is not fermented, but curdled, with epsom salts, rather the way paneer is made from curdled milk with lemon or other coagulating agents. Fresh, it can be considered sattvic. Purchased in a package, it is most likely to be rajasic.

Freshly made soy yogurt (see glossary) is only mildly rajasic. If it sits, it becomes rajasic or tamasic.

Other soy foods, like tempeh, are considered tamasic, due to their abundant mold cultures, and are not well-regarded in Ayurveda. Texturized soy vegetable protein is considered tamasic as well, since it is extensively processed, dry, and a challenge to agni, digestive fire. It is a common ingredient in commercial veggie burgers and in hamburger extenders.

In polling Ayurvedic practitioners about soy in general, its reputation runs the gamut from wonderful to awful, depending on the authority. Take tofu. Some practitioners consider it light, easy to digest and sattvic. Many consider that it has some rajasic qualities. A few hold the opinion that it is tamasic or otherwise undigestible. As one Ayurvedic doc told me, "My mother told me never to touch the stuff (soy). It is food for donkeys and horses. Do you want to be a donkey?! Eat soy!" So you see the passion this small plant inspires (thereby leading me to think that perhaps it does have some rajas?) If you are sensitive to dairy and yet loth to use soy, Ayurveda recommends sesame milk, or nut milks (see Beverages), which can be easy to prepare.

It may take a while to differentiate the cultural and digestive impacts of soy. In the meanwhile, I'll continue to recommend occasional use of soy milk, tofu, miso, tamari, and cooked soybeans, and take it much easier on the more highly processed soy products.

STUFFED BUTTERNUT WITH OLIVES

Preparation time: 1 1/2 hours, most of it unattended

Serves: 4 - 6

MILDLY RAJASIC, 0 Vata, 0 Pitta, mildly + Kapha

♣ 🦪 ❄

Preheat oven to 350° F.

Wash and cut in half lengthwise:
1 butternut squash, 3 lbs. (or 3 1 lb. squashes)

Figure 1/2 pound of squash per person. Place the squash face side down in a baking sheet with about:
1 c. water

Put in the oven to bake until tender, about an hour. While it is baking, prepare:
MIDDLE EASTERN OLIVE CASSEROLE, p. 146

When the squash is done, take it out of the oven, and scoop out its seeds. Drain most of the water from the pan (makes fine soup stock) and place each squash face side up in the pan. Mound the casserole mixture evenly onto each squash half. Bake for 10 - 15 minutes at 350° F.

*ROTATION DAY 2 DISH

Comment: This makes a nice company dinner. I make the salad and salad dressing while the stuffed squash is warming in the oven for those last ten minutes or so.

WHAT ABOUT MUSHROOMS?

In traditional Ayurvedic cooking, mushrooms are not highly regarded, because they usually grow on decaying matter. For this reason they are categorized as a tamasic food. They would also be avoided in a strict mold-free or anti-Candida diet because they are a fungus. In other parts of the world, in particular China and Japan, mushrooms are used therapeutically. Shiitaake mushrooms especially are valued as a strengthener and tonifier for the immune system. Mushrooms are a rich source of the amino acid methionine, which provides an excellent complement to methionine-short beans or tofu. They enhance the total protein value of legume dishes. Mushrooms in general are low in calories, and rich in methionine and zinc. But you would not be likely to find them widely used in India.

VEGETARIAN STROGANOFF

Preparation time: 15 minutes, plus a 2 hour soak (or more)   Serves: 2 - 4
TAMASIC (so many mushrooms) - Vata, - Pitta, 0 Kapha   ✿ 🐌 ❄

Place in a medium-sized heatproof bowl:
  1 1/2 oz. dried Shiitaake mushrooms
  1/3 c. raw almonds, preferably blanched

Pour over them:
  2 c. boiling water

Cover with a lid or plate. Let them sit for a couple of hours until the mushrooms are good and plump. If you like, you can do this in the morning before work or school, and complete the dish just before dinner. When you're within a half-hour of dinner, spoon the mushrooms out of the liquid onto a cutting board and thin-slice them. Pour the almonds and the remaining soaking water (about a cup) into a blender. (You can peel the almonds now if you want them blanched, this does it.) Blend the nuts and water on low for a few seconds, then liquify them at high speed for about 20 seconds, into almond milk. Pour the almond milk back into the mixing bowl, stir in the sliced mushrooms and:
  1/8 tsp. freshly ground nutmeg
  1/8 tsp. freshly ground black pepper

Set aside. Rinse and drain well:
  1 lb. tofu, organic hard style preferred

Pat dry and cut into 3/4 " cubes. In a large iron skillet, warm:
  1 - 2 Tbsps. ghee

Add and saute until tender:
  1 Tbsp. finely chopped onion (optional)

Stir the tofu into the ghee and onion and warm over medium heat until hot. Pour in the almond milk and the mushrooms; continue heating a couple more minutes over medium heat until the whole mixture is thoroughly warm. Stir in:
  Salt to taste
  1/2 - 1 tsp. paprika

Comments: I include this dish because it is truly scrumptious, and a good vegetarian alternative for the person seeking to eat less meat. (Meat being more *tamasic* than mushrooms by a long shot.) It is a zinc-rich, protein-rich meal with little of the excess fat of traditional stroganoff. However, it is also one of the few dishes in here I would not recommend for someone with a serious Candida condition, because of the generous amount of mushrooms plus tofu. (For more about mushrooms, see the enclosed box on page 149.) Vegetarian Stroganoff is good over *basmati* rice, or your favorite pasta, and a fresh arugula, spinach or lettuce salad with TARRAGON PARSLEY SALAD DRESSING, p. 87.

See also CREAMED SPINACH SAUCE, p. 214, as an entree over whole grains.

BRAND "Z" TOFU, GENERIC

Preparation time: 10 minutes   Serves: 2 - 4
MILDLY RAJASIC, 0 Vata, 0 Pitta, 0 Kapha   ❁ ✳ ⋰ ❄

Thin-slice or cube in 1/2" pieces:
> **1 lb. tofu**

In a large skillet, warm:
> **2 tsps. sunflower oil**

Put in the tofu with:
> **About 2 Tbsps. Bragg's Liquid Aminos**

Heat over medium heat until the tofu is thoroughly warmed. Serve with PLAIN *BASMATI RICE*, P. 205 and a steamed vegetable.

*ROTATION DAY 3 DISH

Variations: The variations on this are endless, as any practiced vegetarian can attest. A tablespoon of grated fresh ginger and 1 minced clove of garlic, added to the oil just before the tofu, is tasty. Or you can toss in any vegetable you like, broccoli being a popular choice, despite our past president's predilections. If you add vegetables, allot a few more minutes for them to cook, covered, with the tofu.

ABOUT THE DANCE OF THE DOSHAS

The three biological doshas, Vata, Pitta *and* Kapha, *are constantly in motion throughout the body. This movement is a cyclical one, with each* dosha *arising and predominating in its own time. It then subsides, as the next dosha comes forward. This dance happens twice a day.* Kapha *predominates from sunrise to mid-morning, from about 6 a.m. to 10 a.m. This is when* Kapha *is most available, like a fish at the surface of the waters so to speak, and any excesses of the* dosha *are released, in the form of sputum (coughing, spitting, blowing one's nose). Then* Pitta *arises, being most accessible and available from mid-morning to mid-afternoon (from about 10 a.m. to 2 p.m.), in the heat of the day. This is when we can clear excess* Pitta *in urine and perspiration, and when we are likely to feel most hungry.* Vata *comes forward from mid-afternoon to dusk, from around 2 p.m. to 6 p.m. Then the cycle begins again, with* Kapha *strong from 6 p.m. to 10 p.m.,* Pitta *from 10 p.m. to 2 a.m. and* Vata *from 2 a.m. to 6 a.m., just before dawn.*

About the Dance of the Doshas (continued)

Many Ayurvedic routines are designed around this dance. It is important to understand that the three doshas *mediate between our essential body tissues and our bodily wastes. So, for example, the natural process in the body is to get waste moving (a* Vata *function) just before dawn, and release any excess, heaviness, in the bowel movement as* Kapha *time is just beginning. If we skip this step and race off to work or play without eliminating, waste begins to build up in the colon in the form of* ama, *obstructing some of the natural flow of the body's energy. We tend to have more energy when we're eliminating regularly. And the body fulfills its processes more smoothly. The* doshas *move back and forth between the essential tissues* (dhatus) *and the wastes* (malas). *The* doshas *nourish the essential tissues, bringing them energy and stability. If the way is blocked, as is happening in the example above, our tissues don't receive all of the nourishment from the daily dance of the* doshas *that they could. Energy is sent out in the wastes, say as unabsorbed nutrients in the feces.*

When the dance is going well, in rhythm, the doshas *arise in their time, nourish the tissues, release any excesses in the wastes, and dance on.* Kapha *strengthens and moistens the body in* Kapha *time,* Pitta *warms and digests and transforms in* Pitta *time,* Vata *performs essential movements and communications in* Vata *time. (Obviously all of the functions are happening in every micro-second. And yet there is this larger rhythm which superimposes itself on this picture.) Our bodies want to be healthy and they have great systems in place to be able to do so. We simply need to work with the rhythm which is already in place.*

Ayurvedic physicians often recommend taking a particular herb or food, or doing a specific process, at a particular time. This is why. Working with the doshas *in their own time will give the best results. I once saw a striking example of this. A* vaidya *recommended a certain herb to a woman. She had already been taking this herb, but he now recommended taking it at a different time. Within weeks, she began shedding weight she had long held. Only the timing had changed here.*

So Vata *and* Pitta *are recommended to have breakfast between 6 and 10 a.m., to stabilize themselves, avail themselves of* Kapha *in* Kapha *time. Predominantly* Kapha *constitutional types do best to skip eating at this time, and eat a light fresh meal a little later if they can, say fruit or soup at 10 or 11 a.m. Digestive fire is generally strong in* Pitta *time, in the middle of the day, so the biggest meal is usually recommended then. Then, a lighter meal (with respect for* Vata) *is taken at dusk. Eating large, late meals only increases* Kapha *or* ama.

Pastas

KEY

"–" means calms or helps the given constitution;

"+" means aggravates or increases it;

"0" means neutral effect.

 * ROTATION DIET can be helpful for people with food sensitivities, see p. 323.

**POLARITY DISH refers to recipes supporting Polarity Therapy work, see p. 342.

✿ = Spring

✹ = Summer

૱ = Fall

❄ = Winter

LIGHT BASIL SAUCE

Preparation time: 20 minutes or less   Serves: 2-3
SATTVIC, - Vata, - Pitta, moderately + Kapha   ❀ ✳ 🐚 ❄

Bring to a boil in a small saucepan over medium-high heat:
   2 c. fresh raw cow's milk or soy milk
   1 garlic clove, unpeeled*
   6 black peppercorns*

While the milk is warming, finely grind in a blender:
   1/2 c. raw walnuts

Wash and chop:
   1 bunch fresh basil leaves, finely chopped (at least 1 cup)

When the hot milk has come to a boil, take it off the heat and remove the clove of garlic, (if you are feeding someone with high *Pitta*, a lot of fire). If you are mainly serving people of *Kapha* or *Vata* constitution, the garlic can be peeled and left in. Pour the milk and pepper into the blender with the ground nuts. Add the chopped basil. Puree.

If you like, stir into the puree:
   2 Tbsps. fresh ghee (optional, omit for *Kapha*)
   Salt to taste

Serve over sea shell noodles or fettucini noodles in bowls, slightly swimming in sauce. Very good, very simple. Add steamed greens on the side and you have a meal.

*A DAY 1 ROTATION DISH, omit the black pepper and garlic.

Note: If you skip the ghee, use 1/4 c. walnuts, and soy milk rather than cow's milk, this is 0 (neutral to) *Kapha*, especially if served over a corn pasta.

Variation: You can add 1 - 2 cups of chopped broccoli or asparagus directly to the pot of cooking pasta for the last four minutes of cooking time for a flavorful and pretty touch.

Sometimes very simple acts are very powerful. Having a meal together, with family or friends, reaffirms a web of connection and co-operation, communion, sorely needed for our healing as a people.

PESTO SAUCE

Preparation time: 10 minutes   Makes two cups
SATTVIC BORDERING ON RAJASIC, - Vata, + Pitta, + Kapha

Steam in a steamer in a small saucepan for about five minutes:
   1 large clove garlic, unpeeled

Grind until finely powdered in a blender:
   1/2 c. pine nuts or walnuts

Add to the nuts in the blender:
   2 c. loosely packed fresh basil leaves, then chopped
   1 c. fresh Italian parsley, chopped
   1/8 c. extra-virgin olive oil
   2 tsps. miso
   3 Tbsps. raw sesame tahini
   1/2 cup water or a little more (enough to be able to blend the sauce smoothly)

and blend until the sauce is creamy smooth. Blend the garlic into the sauce, peeled and minced. Serve!

**POLARITY HEALTH BUILDING DISH

Comments: The original inspiration for this began with a recipe from Biba Caggiano's *Northern Italian Cooking* (HP Books, 1981), which I warmly recommend. While many of the recipes contain meat, her sense of Italian cooking is delightful, and the recipes are well illustrated with full color photographs.

BUTTER PECAN PASTA

Preparation time: 20 minutes   Serves: 3
*SATTVIC**

In a medium saucepan, melt:
   3 Tbsps. ghee or butter

Stir in:
   1 Tbsp. onion, finely chopped
   1/3 c. raw pecans, finely chopped

Let them saute for about five minutes. Add:
   1 tsp. crumbled dried sage
   1/2 tsp. fresh rosemary, chopped
   1 Tbsp. whole wheat flour

Mix well over low heat. Gradually stir in:

    1 c. fresh boiled raw milk or soy milk

and let thicken, stirring occasionally, for a few minutes. After the sauce has thickened, add:

    1 small clove garlic, minced
    1 small zucchini, in Julienne strips (about 1 cup)
    1/2 small red bell pepper, finely diced (about 1/4 c.)
    1/4 c. grated carrot
    1/2 c. watercress, finely chopped
    Salt and pepper to taste

Cook over medium-low heat for 5 minutes more. Serve over freshly cooked pasta.

* - *Vata, - Pitta, + Kapha (with cow's milk and wheat pasta)*

* + *Vata, 0 Pitta, 0 Kapha (with soy milk and corn pasta)*

Comments: We first had this as a special New Year's Eve supper, with a simple green salad. Nice!

See also: Vegetarian Stroganoff, p. 150

The energies of Nature are ready to speak to us, to work with us, if we will only listen. This extends from the energy of our bodies speaking through our pulses and other actions to the wild weed in the field, with unsuspected medicinal properties. Are we available for this communication? I become scared, as I realize that 99.5% of us with electricity have televisions, and that according to the A.C. Nielsen Company, 95% of Americans watch some TV each day. Research done at Australian National University found that television has two paradoxical effects: while it induces a more passive state of mind, it also trains the brain to become accustomed to much faster changes of sequences than those found in nature (information from Jerry Mander's In the Absence of the Sacred, see bibliography). We are being mentally trained to move at a pace much different than nature's. How many of us will have the patience to receive the communication which she offers? How many of us are willing to work with the elements and nature at this critical juncture? How many of us will be able to? How many of us are "nature illiterates"?

PASTA PRIMAVERA

Preparation time: 15 - 20 minutes   Serves: 2 - 4
SATTVIC, - Vata, 0 Pitta, + Kapha*   ❁ ✳ 🐌 ❄

Put a large pot of water on for your favorite pasta. Wash and prepare:
> **1 baby zucchini, thinly sliced**
> **2 baby yellow crookneck squash, thinly sliced**
> **2 Tbsps. red onion, thinly sliced**
> **1/2 - 1 cup fresh peas, shelled**

Blend together in a blender:
> **1 clove garlic**
> **1/3 c. extra-virgin olive oil**

(Now is a good time to put in your noodles, if the water is boiling.)
Warm the blended oil in a large skillet over medium heat. Add all the vegetables and simmer for 5 - 10 minutes or until tender but not limp. Stir in:
> **1 Tbsp. dried sage (or 2 Tbsps. fresh sage, finely chopped)**
> **Salt and pepper to taste**

Toss your sauteed veggies into your freshly cooked pasta and serve with:
> **Freshly grated parmesan (optional)**
> **or gomasio (ground, toasted sesame seeds with an optional pinch of salt)**

* For a *rajasic* dish, use 2 large cloves of garlic, and plenty of parmesan cheese.

Kapha Variation: Use corn spaghetti (available in most natural foods groceries) and steam the veggies instead of sautéing them. You can steam the garlic with the rest of the vegetables. If you like, add 1 Tbsp. extra-virgin olive oil to the pasta and veggies after you've taken them off the heat and tossed them together. Skip the parmesan; a little gomasio is fine if you would like it.

SATTVIC, 0 Vata, 0 Pitta, - Kapha
**POLARITY HEALTH BUILDING DISH

DAY 4 Variation: Similar to the *Kapha* Variation above, you would use corn pasta and whatever Day 4 vegetables you like: asparagus, watercress, broccoli, garlic, onion, cauliflower and/or arugula. Drizzle cold-pressed sesame oil over the pasta and veggies after you have stirred them together. Garnish with gomasio (optional).

SATTVIC, 0 Vata, 0 Pitta, - Kapha
**POLARITY HEALTH BUILDING DISH

Comments: This is a dish that is generally light enough for everyone, and it can easily be played with to suit individual constitutions. For example, if you are working with high *Pitta*, you can omit the onion entirely and use 1 small clove of garlic. Even as the recipe stands above, it is much more calming to *Pitta* than the standard tomato sauce. One of our favorite quick and easy suppers.

HOMEMADE EGG NOODLES

Preparation time: 45 minutes or less   Serves: 4
SLIGHTLY RAJASIC (the eggs), - Vata, 0 Pitta, + Kapha   🐌 ❄

I know, homemade egg noodles seem very fancy, perhaps daunting. But in reality they're fun and easy. The first time you try them, you might want to have extra time, to be able to goof off. If you enlist under-age helpers, they can use cookie cutters to make a few bunnies, stars, hearts, what have you. This is most popular in our house. My warm thanks to my friend Dorie Chiappone for introducing me to the world of homemade pasta!

In a good-sized mixing bowl with a fork, beat:
> **3 eggs**

Then beat in:
> **3 Tbsps. water**
> **(basically one egg and one tablespoon of water per voracious person, is the rule).**

Then stir in:
> **About 3 c. durum wheat semolina flour**
> **Pinch of salt**

Stir the flour in with a spoon or fork until it begins to get thick, then stiff. At this point, abandon the spoon and roll the dough out on to a floured board. MASH, PAT, ROLL, and CUT are the basic instructions. In other words, mash and knead the dough until it is difficult to pick up any more flour with it. Then pat it into a ball and flatten it a bit. Then get out your rolling pin and roll it as thin as you can get, half again as thin as your average pie crust at least. Once the dough is rolled out thinly, get a small sharp paring knife and cut it into 1/2" fettucini ribbons or whatever width you like. (ILLUS)

Put on a big pot of water, just as you would with any pasta, and bring it to a boil. Carefully lift your fresh pasta off its floured surface and into the boiling water. Cook until done, from 30 seconds to 1 or 2 minutes, stirring occasionally. (Fresh pasta cooks up considerably faster than her dried sister.) Serve with your favorite pasta sauce. One nice dinner combination is homemade egg noodles with fresh **Pesto Sauce**, p. 156, steamed zucchini, and **Crunchy Coconut Cookies**, p. 248.

Variation: This same recipe can be made with buckwheat flour.
SLIGHTLY RAJASIC, + Vata, moderately + Pitta, - Kapha
*A ROTATION DAY 4 DISH

Comments: Buckwheat Egg Noodles are a good option for those sensitive to wheat, as buckwheat belongs to an entirely different botanical family than wheat. It is also a nice option for *Kaphas* yearning for fresh pasta. Last but not least, this dish is a great economical choice if dinner guests arrive unexpectedly. All you need is a few eggs, some flour and a veggie sauce.

BASIC ROSE PETAL TOMATO SAUCE

Preparation time: 20 minutes   Makes 2 c. sauce
RAJASIC, + Vata, moderately + Pitta, 0 Kapha

Wash and chop, or put through a food mill:
12 fresh medium tomatoes (about 4 cups)

A food mill helps cull out the tomato seeds which can aggravate *Vata* a bit. Or you can simply leave as many seeds on the cutting board as you can. Simmer the tomatoes in a stainless steel saucepan with:
1/4 c. finely chopped onion
2 cloves garlic, minced
2 - 4 Tbsps. extra-virgin olive oil

Cook over medium heat uncovered until thick, about 15 minutes or so. Pour the thickened tomatoes in a blender with:
2 Tbsps. or more organic dried rose petals
4 tsps. fresh oregano, chopped or 2 tsps. dried oregano
1/2 tsp. dried thyme
2 Tbsps. fresh Italian parsley, finely chopped
Salt and pepper to taste
Up to 1/4 c. water (optional)

Puree well. Ready to serve.

Comments: So what's with rose petals? They're sweet, cooling and very soothing, and take the edge off tomato. *Rajasic* tomato, in general, is not often used in an Ayurvedic regime, as it is hot, sour and acidic, especially in its effect on the gut. Rose petals will not totally neutralize this effect, but they help. I first learned about this from Dr. Sunil Joshi, when I took my daughter to him for a consult. Iza's normal *Kapha-Pitta* constitution had climbed into the heat zones with her fondness for tomatoes. We now save organic rose petals from our garden (and from anyone else's who is willing!) for those times when we're cooking with tomato.

Variation: ROTATION DAY 1 SAUCE: Omit the onion, garlic and olive oil, and saute the tomatoes in walnut oil, with 1 bay leaf, plus the oregano and thyme. When the sauce is thick, put it in the blender and puree with the rose petals and 1/4 cup fresh chopped basil leaves. (Omit the parsley and pepper.) Thin with 2 - 4 Tbsps. warm water if you like. Salt to taste. Serve immediately.

CREAMY OREGANO PASTA SAUCE

Preparation time: 10 minutes or less
RAJASIC*

Serves: 3

❀ ✳ ༅ ❄

Blend in a blender until smooth:

> 1 1/2 c. freshly made ricotta or Creamy Non-Dairy "Ricotta" (see p. 164)
> 1/4 c. fresh Italian parsley, chopped
> 1 tsp. dried oregano
> 1 clove garlic, minced (optional)
> 1/4 c. or more water

Heat over low temperature, stirring often, until hot. Serve over your favorite pasta: bows, shells, fettucini noodles.

* - Vata, - Pitta, + Kapha (with ricotta)

* 0 Vata, 0 Pitta, slightly + Kapha (with non-dairy sub)

Comments: This makes a good simple meal served with BROCCOLI AND GARLIC, p. 197. The whole dinner can be prepared easily in a half hour.

ABOUT THE LONGEVITY OF SPICES

Fresh herbs need to be used immediately, while they still have a good strong bouquet to them. I personally value the aroma and taste of fresh herbs most, but I know that many cooks do not have them easily available year-round. Dried spices are best kept no more than a year, in a tightly sealed container. After that, they have lost most of their potency as well as their flavor.

DELISH TOFU SPAGHETTI SAUCE

Preparation time: 30 minutes

RAJASIC, 0 Vata, + Pitta, 0 Kapha

Serves: 3 - 4

Saute in a large skillet over low heat:

>   **2 Tbsps. extra-virgin olive oil**
>   **1 small onion, chopped (2 Tbsps.)**
>   **1 - 2 large cloves garlic, minced**

When they are tender but not brown, mash into them with a fork:

>   **1 cube (16 oz.) tofu**
>   **1/8 tsp. fennel seeds, crushed**
>   **1/4 tsp. red chili pepper**

Raise the heat to medium and cook long enough to warm, about five minutes. Add:

>   **2 - 3 fresh tomatoes, finely chopped**
>   **1 bunch fresh arugula, finely chopped (1/4 cup) (if available)**
>   **1 tsp. fresh thyme, finely chopped, 1/2 tsp. dried**
>   **2 tsps. fresh oregano, finely chopped, 1 tsp. dried**
>   **1/2 tsp. salt**
>   **1/8 tsp. freshly ground pepper**

Stir well. Raise heat to medium-high, cook 1 - 2 minutes. If you want to cook it longer, reduce heat to simmer until you are ready to serve. Just before serving stir in:

>   **1 Tbsp. dried organic rose petals**

Serve over freshly cooked spaghetti.

ABOUT PASTA

As any good cook knows, pasta is best prepared immediately before serving. You will get good results if you "treat it as if you were about to eat it plain," as Dolores Chiappone says. This means, after you have drained your pasta well, put it back in the pot and dash a bit of olive oil, salt and pepper on it. This keeps the texture of the pasta resilient, and provides a good base for any sauce.

For Asian pastas, see BEAN THREADS WITH SNOW PEAS, p. 141 and SOBA NOODLES WITH GARLIC AND VEGETABLES, p. 144.

SIMPLEST PASTA

Preparation time: 15 minutes max   Serves: 4
SATTVIC*

Make up:

> 3/4 lb. pasta

When it is done, drain it well, put it back in the pot and toss it with:

> 2 Tbsps. extra-virgin olive oil
> 1/2 c. fresh Italian parsley, finely chopped
> 1 clove garlic, minced (optional)
> 1 Tbsp. dried basil, or 1/4 c. finely chopped fresh
> Salt to taste
> Coarsely ground black pepper

Serve.

* - *Vata, 0 Pitta, + Kapha* (with a wheat pasta)

* - *Vata, 0 Pitta, 0 Kapha* (with a rice pasta)

* + *Vata, + Pitta, - Kapha* (with a corn pasta)

**In all cases, POLARITY HEALTH BUILDING DISH

QUICK MACARONI

Preparation time: 15 minutes   Serves: 4

Make up:

> 3/4 lb. macaroni, whole wheat or corn

While the pasta water is coming to a boil and the macaroni is cooking, prepare:

> Basic Cream Sauce, p. 164
> or Creamy Non-Dairy "Ricotta", p. 164

When the pasta is done, drain it, put it back in the pan and lightly oil it with:

> 1 - 2 tsps. ghee or extra-virgin olive oil

Stir the sauce into the macaroni and serve.

SATTVIC with Basic Cream Sauce

RAJASIC with Creamy Non-Dairy "Ricotta"

Corn pasta is most calming for *Kapha*, whole wheat best for *Vata* or *Pitta*

BASIC CREAM SAUCE

Preparation time: 10 - 15 minutes
SATTVIC*

Makes 1 1/2 cups

❀ ✳ ༀ ❄

Warm in a saucepan over low heat:
>   **2 Tbsps. ghee, butter or olive oil**

Stir in:
>   **1 1/2 Tbsps. flour, wholewheat or other whole grain (I like to use a wooden spoon; it makes it easy to rub the flour into the ghee.)**

Then gradually stir in, still over low heat:
>   **1 1/2 c. freshly boiled raw cow's milk, soy milk or nut milk**

Continue to heat over low, stirring occasionally, until the sauce thickens to a consistency you like. Season with:
>   **A dash of salt**

* - Vata, - Pitta, + Kapha (with whole wheat and cow's milk)
* 0 Vata, - Pitta, - Kapha (with barley flour and soy milk)
* - Vata, + Pitta, + Kapha (with nut milk)

Comments: This serves as a ROTATION DAY 1 DISH if you use any of the following: butter or ghee, whole wheat or barley flour, cow's milk, pecan milk or walnut milk.

CREAMY NON-DAIRY "RICOTTA"

Preparation time: 5 minutes
RAJASIC, 0 Vata, 0 Pitta, + Kapha

Makes 1 1/2 cups

❀ ✳ ༀ ❄

Blend together well in a blender:
>   **1/2 lb. tofu**
>   **1/2 c. hot water**
>   **1/4 c. raw sesame tahini**
>   **2 Tbsps. miso**
>   **Freshly ground black pepper to taste**

**POLARITY HEALTH BUILDING DISH

Comments: There are many possible variations on this. We will sometimes skip the tofu and instead use ground nuts, extra water and half the miso. Or we will cut back on the salty miso if other dishes being served are rather heavy, as saltiness and heaviness together provide challenges to the digestive tract.

TABLE 10: PASTAS AND CONSTITUTION

Say the word "pasta" and you're likely to think of the popular white flour variety. And yet there are many pastas made of other plant foods, each with their own unique effect on *Vata*, *Pitta* and *Kapha*. Here is a summary of some pastas available here in the U.S. and their effect on the *doshas*.

Effect on Dosha

Type of Pasta	Vata	Pitta	Kapha	Where to Find
Bean thread noodles	0 Vata	- Pitta	- Kapha	Asian markets, Asian section of supermarkets, natural groceries
Buckwheat soba noodles (100%)	+ Vata	+ Pitta	- Kapha	Japanese markets, macrobiotic or pasta section of natural groceries
Corn pastas	+ Vata	+ Pitta	- Kapha	Natural groceries, sometimes in bulk
Corn-quinoa pastas	- Vata	+ Pitta	- Kapha	Natural groceries, sometimes in bulk
Jerusalem artichoke pastas (with wheat)	- Vata	- Pitta	moderately + Kapha	Many supermarkets and natural groceries
Jinenjo (wild yam) pasta	- Vata	- Pitta	+ Kapha	Asian markets, macrobiotic or pasta section of natural groceries
Rice pastas	- Vata	- Pitta	moderately + Kapha	Allergy, specialty foods or pasta section, natural foods groceries; Asian markets
"Regular" (white flour) pasta	- Vata	- Pitta	+ + Kapha	Supermarkets, natural groceries
Spaghetti squash (used like pasta)	0 Vata	- Pitta	- Kapha	Produce sections
Spinach (with wheat)	- Vata	0 Pitta	+ Kapha	Pasta shops, supermarkets, natural groceries
Tomato (with wheat)	0 Vata	mildly + Pitta	+ Kapha	Pasta shops, supermarkets, natural groceries
Whole wheat pastas	- Vata	- Pitta	+ Kapha	Natural groceries

Breads

KEY

"–" means calms or helps the given constitution;

"+" means aggravates or increases it;

"0" means neutral effect.

 * ROTATION DIET can be helpful for people with food
   sensitivities, see p. 323.

**POLARITY DISH refers to recipes supporting Polarity Therapy
work, see p. 342.

❀ = Spring

✳ = Summer

🐌 = Fall

❄ = Winter

SWEET POTATO BISCUITS

Preparation time: 30 minutes   Makes 24 biscuits
*SATTVIC, - Vata, - Pitta, moderately + Kapha**

Combine:
>   2 c. barley or whole wheat flour
>   1 tsp. salt
>   1 Tbsp. baking powder
>   1/4 tsp. baking soda

Cut into the flour mixture until it is the consistency of coarse cornmeal:
>   1/4 c. butter or ghee

Peel and mash:
>   1 medium sweet potato, cooked **

Spoon it into a measuring cup. You should have a little less than 3/4 cup total mashed potato. Add to it:
>   Juice of 1 lemon or lime
>   About 1/4 c. soy or freshly boiled raw cow's milk

or enough milk to bring the volume up to 1 cup total. Stir together with a spoon or fork.

Mix the wet ingredients into the dry ones with your very clean hands, working quickly and lightly. Add extra flour if you need it. Cover the dough and chill it for about 15 minutes. Preheat oven to 450° F.

Butter 2 cookie sheets. Roll the dough out on one until it is about 1/2 inch thick. Cut into rounds, pumpkins, whatever you like, directly on the cookie sheet. (This minimizes the use of extra flour in the rolling process, which can make a biscuit tough. It is also easy for clean up.) Use the remaining dough for biscuits as well, lightly kneading it into a ball, then rolling it out again on the other buttered cookie sheet.Bake for about 12 minutes, or until lightly browned.

* a modest 1 1/2 tsps. butter per biscuit

Comment: Nice, easy, light. You can start this when you get home, go on to make the rest of dinner, say **Ivy's Soup Orientale**, and then put the biscuits in to bake just before you're ready to eat.

NOTE: If you have a raw sweet potato, but no inkling as to how to get it to the cooked stage: Put the sweet potato in a saucepan, cover with water, bring to a boil. Cook over medium heat until done, about 30 minutes. If you like sweet potato in your lunch, you might pop a few in at the same time for that. The cooking water also makes a nutritious beginning for a soup stock.

BUTTERFLY BISCUITS

Preparation time: an hour or more, most of it unattended *Makes 12 biscuits*
SATTVIC, - Vata, - Pitta, + Kapha   ✿ ✹ 🐦 ❄

Stir together in a mixing bowl:
> **1 c. whole wheat or barley flour**
> **1/2 tsp. salt**
> **1/8 tsp. baking soda**
> **1 1/2 tsps. baking powder**

Crumble into the dry ingredients with your hands, or a pastry blender:
> **3 Tbsps. ghee or butter, chilled**

Pour in:
> **3/8 c. fresh buttermilk**

and mix lightly with your hands. Knead for a minute, adding more flour if the dough is too moist or sticky. Put the dough back in the bowl, cover and chill in the refrigerator for 30 minutes or more. Preheat the oven to 450° F. Lightly oil a cookie sheet and roll the dough directly out on it, about 1/2 inch thick, or on a lightly floured board. The less flour you use, the more tender your biscuits will be. Cut into butterfly shapes with a cookie cutter, or whatever shape you like. Put in the oven and bake until golden brown, about 10 - 12 minutes. Serve immediately.

*ROTATION DAY 1 DISH

Comments: This recipe is based on one for Southern Buttermilk Biscuits from Camille Glenn's book, *The Heritage of Southern Cooking*. This cookbook has provided inspiration for me on many a chill and hungry night. (She advises us to roll our dough from the center outward for the most crisp and tender biscuits.) We call these whole grain buttermilk biscuits "butterfly biscuits" because that was the shape in which we first made them, and they felt light enough to fly away.

Variation: Equal parts of soy milk and fresh soy yogurt can be substituted for the buttermilk, i.e., 3 Tbsps. soy milk, 3 Tbsps. soy yogurt.

RAJASIC, 0 Vata, 0 Pitta, mildly + Kapha

Or fresh cow's milk and cow's yogurt can be used.

SATTVIC, - Vata, - Pitta, + Kapha

*ROTATION DAY 1 DISH

Variation: "Tahini milk" can be substituted for the buttermilk. In this case, omit the baking soda. Combine 1 Tbsp. sesame tahini with enough pure water to make 3/8 c. total. Proceed as usual.

SATTVIC, - Vata, mildly + Pitta, + Kapha

LIZ'S SCONES

Preparation time: 1 hour or more
SATTVIC, - Vata, - Pitta, + Kapha

Serves: 3 - 4

This comes from a dear heart, expert cook and English high-tea *afficianda*. She advises us Americans: "Imagine you are making pie crust. *This is like making pastry, not biscuits. Keep everything cool.*" The rewards are most satisfying.

Bring to a boil:
> 1/2 c. fresh raw milk
> 1 quarter-sized slice of fresh ginger root, peeled

Cover and put in the refrigerator to cool. Take a pause. Mix together in a medium-sized bowl:
> 2 c. whole wheat or barley flour
> 1 1/3 Tbsps. baking powder
> Pinch of salt

Work into the flour mixture with your fingers, until it is pea-sized or smaller:
> 1/2 c. COLD butter or ghee

Pour into the dough, again working it in with your hands:
> 1/2 c. COLD milk mixed with
> 2 Tbsps. apple concentrate (optional)

Depending on the humidity of the day, you may need a little more milk. You will have a very stiff dough. Flour a board, and pat the dough into a rough square 1 1/2 - 2" high. Cut the dough into 6 squares (ILLUS) and place on a floured cookie sheet. Brush the tops with milk, cover, and chill in the fridge for at least 1/2 hour. Preheat the oven to 400° F. Bake the scones for 15 - 20 minutes, until brown on top. You can cut them in half diagonally to serve for tea. Traditionally they are served with butter and jam.

*ROTATION DAY 1 DISH

Comments: You can add raisins, dates, or currants to these. They are good with soups and can be made up into little sandwiches. If you want to warm them up, they can be toasted, or put in the oven at 350° F for a few minutes.

Variation: You can use soy milk in place of cow's milk, in equal amounts.
With soy milk and barley flour: SATTVIC, - Vata, - Pitta, moderately + Kapha
With soy milk and whole wheat flour: SATTVIC, - Vata, - Pitta, + Kapha

Lower-Fat Variation: You can cut the butter or ghee in half, to 1/4 cup, for a version more gentle on the liver and arteries. In this case, be sure to add the optional sweetener.

The originator of this recipe, Liz Halford, is a woman of all trades. A lawyer in her native New Zealand, a social worker in London, and now a cook and food stylist here in the States, she also gives a mean tea-cup reading. I look forward to her first cookbook with pleasure.

REBEKAH'S TORTILLAS

Preparation time: an hour or less
SATTVIC, - Vata, - Pitta, + Kapha

Makes 12 (6") tortillas
✿ ✳ ৶ ❄

Sift:

3 c. stoneground whole wheat flour

Then mix it with a fork together in a large bowl with:

1/2 tsp. salt
1 tsp. aluminum-free baking powder (1/2 tsp. at high altitude)

With your hands, work into the flour mixture:

1/4 c. oil (half ghee and half sesame oil is good)

Then pour in:

1 c. hot water

Knead the liquid into the dough with your hands. Knead the dough about a dozen times, or until it holds together well. It will have a slightly springy feel. Divide the dough into a dozen balls, and let them rest in the mixing bowl covered with a towel for about twenty minutes.

Warm a heavy ungreased iron skillet on medium-high heat until it is quite hot. Roll each ball out on a clean unfloured surface until it is the size you want. (If you want larger tortillas, make eight balls rather than twelve.) The flour shouldn't be sticky. If it is, knead a little more flour into the dough. Put in the first tortilla, cook until it is lightly browned, then flip. You can wrap the finished tortilla in a clean towel, adding the rest as you make them. Traditionally, they would be served wrapped up in a fresh towel or cloth napkin in a covered tortilla basket. Good with SANTA FE PINTO BEANS or soup, or in TAHINI ROLL-UPS.

*For a ROTATION DAY 1 DISH, use all ghee as the "oil", and a corn-free baking powder.

Comment: This recipe comes from Rebekah Trujillo, a long-time professional baker of tortillas, quick breads and other delectable goodies. She advises, " It is better to have a dough that is too sticky, you can always add more flour. If you add extra water (after you have already mixed together the flour and water), your tortillas will be tough. Always add extra flour, not extra water." She has found wide variations in the amounts of ingredients, depending on the altitude at which she lives. In California, at sea-level, one teaspoon of baking powder is needed per batch to make the best tortillas. In the mountains of northern New Mexico, only one-half that is better. Whole wheat flour tortillas tend to need a little less baking powder than white flour ones. The amounts given above will give you a good whole wheat tortilla, easier to make than you might suspect. And quite tasty.

PECAN MUFFINS

Preparation time: 45 minutes

SATTVIC, 0 Vata, 0 Pitta, + Kapha

Makes 12 muffins

❀ ❧ ❄

Preheat oven to 375° F. Mix together in small bowl:

3 Tbsps. Sucanat

2 Tbsps. fresh buttermilk

1 tsp. baking soda

Set aside. In a medium mixing bowl, beat:

2 eggs (or egg replacer if you are using it)

then stir into the eggs:

3 Tbsps. sunflower oil or ghee

1 c. oat bran

1 c. fresh buttermilk

Stir the Sucanat mixture into the batter. Then add:

2 c. whole wheat flour

1/4 tsp. salt

1/2 tsp. cinnamon

Fold in:

1 c. chopped dried Medjool dates, lightly floured

1 c. chopped raw pecans

Spoon into a lightly oiled muffin tin. Bake for 25 - 30 minutes or until a toothpick inserted into the middle of a muffin comes out cleanly.

Variations: Egg Replacer can be used in place of the eggs; and soy milk in place of the buttermilk.

SATTVIC, mildly + Vata, - Pitta, mildly + Kapha

BANANA PEACH MUFFINS

Preparation time: 55 minutes

Makes 12 muffins

SATTVIC, - Vata, 0 Pitta, + Kapha

❀ ✳ ꙮ ❄

Preheat oven to 350° F. Soak in 1/2 c. hot water:
> **6 dried organic peaches (about 1/3 cup)**

In a mixing bowl, mash:
> **2 ripe bananas**

Stir into the bananas:
> **3 Tbsps. cold-pressed almond oil**
> **1/4 c. maple syrup**

Mix together:
> **1 1/4 c. whole wheat or barley flour**
> **1 1/2 tsps. baking powder**
> **1/2 tsp. salt**

Drain the peaches and finely chop them. Mix them into the wet ingredients. Mix the dry ingredients into the wet ones. Stir lightly and quickly. The batter is a thick one. Spoon into one lightly-oiled muffin tin. Bake for 25 minutes or until a toothpick inserted into the center of a muffin comes out cleanly.

Variation, Banana Apricot Muffins: use 9 dried apricots in place of the peaches.

Variation: DAY 2 ROTATION DISH: Substitute an equal amount of amaranth flour for the whole wheat or barley. Use 2 tsp. baking powder, or 1 3/4 tsps. at high altitude. Bake for 30 - 40 minutes or until done. (NOTE: This recipe can also be used as a Day 2 pancake.)

SATTVIC , - Vata, 0 Pitta, moderately + Kapha

ABOUT SOAKING

Soaking reduces excess dryness, calming the air element in foods and enhancing the water element. The added moisture supports the action of agni, digestive fire, on food, making foods easier for the body to break down. This beneficial Ayurvedic practice of soaking is used with beans, peas, nuts, some seeds, and dried fruits. Soaking is most often done overnight by simply covering the food with pure water and letting it sit, covered, until the morning.

GLUTEN-FREE PECAN MUFFINS

Preparation time: 45 minutes   Makes 12 muffins
SATTVIC*

Preheat oven to 375° F. Mix together in small bowl:
>   **3 Tbsps. rice bran syrup**
>   **1 tsp. baking soda**

Set aside. In a medium mixing bowl, beat:
>   **2 eggs (or egg replacer)**

then stir into the eggs:
>   **3 Tbsps. sunflower or sesame oil**
>   **1 c. rice bran**
>   **1 c. soy milk or fresh buttermilk**

Stir the rice syrup and soda into the batter. Then add:
>   **2 c. white rice flour**
>   **1/4 tsp. salt**
>   **1/2 tsp. cinnamon**

Fold in:
>   **1 c. chopped dried Medjool dates, lightly floured**
>   **1 c. chopped raw pecans**

Spoon into a lightly oiled muffin tin. Bake for 30 minutes or until a toothpick inserted into the middle of a muffin comes out cleanly.

* *0 Vata, 0 Pitta, + Kapha* (with buttermilk)

* *mildly + Vata, - Pitta, + Kapha* (with soy milk)

With every in breath, we open to the universe and all that it offers us.
With every out breath, we release the old and prepare to receive the new.

GINGER-PEAR MUFFINS

Preparation time: 40 minutes

SATTVIC, + Vata, - Pitta, 0 Kapha*

Makes 12 muffins

Preheat oven to 375° F. Wash and dice:

> **1 1/2 c. fresh pear, finely chopped (about 2 ripe pears)**

Mix together with:

> **2 tsps. fresh ginger root, peeled and finely grated**

Beat:

> **2 eggs**

and stir into them:

> **1/2 c. fresh yogurt or soy yogurt**
> **1/4 c. apple juice**
> **2 Tbsps. sunflower oil**
> **1/4 c. Sucanat**

Stir well into this wet mix:

> **1 tsp. baking soda**

Add the pears and ginger, then:

> **1 1/2 c. rice bran or oat bran**
> **1 c. rice flour or whole wheat pastry flour or oat flour**
> **1/4 tsp. salt**

Stir well. Spoon into oiled muffin tin; bake until done, about 25 minutes (a toothpick inserted in the center of a muffin will come out cleanly).

*This is for muffins with rice bran and rice flour, or oat bran and oat flour. *Vatas* could have a few of these to no serious effect if they were spread generously with ghee or butter.

* With whole wheat pastry flour, 0 Vata, - Pitta, + Kapha

Comments: The bran is an important ingredient in these in terms of texture and baking. If you decide to try to make these with all rice flour and no bran, you are likely to get rather pasty lumps, as the author did!

Our bodies are transformative temples for food. We offer food the gift of transformation every time we digest it. It is okay to notice this.

MOCK BOSTON BROWN BREAD (MUFFINS)

Preparation time: 45 minutes   Makes 10-12 muffins
SATTVIC, + Vata, 0 Pitta, - Kapha   ♣ 🦋 ❄

Mix together:
> 1/2 c. raisins or chopped Black Mission figs
> 1 1/2 c. soy milk
> 1/2 c. blackstrap molasses

Preheat oven to 350° F. Put a large pan of water on the bottom shelf of the oven for humidity. Mix together:
> 2/3 c. yellow cornmeal
> 2/3 c. rye flour
> 2/3 c. rice bran or oat bran
> 1 Tbsp. flax seeds (optional)
> 1 1/2 tsps. baking soda (1 tsp. at high altitude)
> 1/2 tsp. salt

Stir the wet ingredients into the dry ones. Very lightly oil a muffin tin and spoon the batter into the tin, 1/2 to 2/3 full for each muffin. Place on a shelf above the pan of water in the oven. Bake for 25 - 30 minutes or until done, when a toothpick inserted into the center of a muffin comes out cleanly.

**POLARITY HEALTH BUILDING DISH

Comments: Traditionally, Boston Brown Bread is made by steaming it in a coffee can for 3 or 4 hours. This version makes up a lot faster, and yet it is important to put the pan of water in the oven, to replicate the old "steaming" conditions. This also keeps this fat-free bread from becoming dry.

ABOUT CRISS-CROSS THINKING

I'm very leery of criss-cross thinking. By this I mean, say I've been saying, "If you want to clear your mind and heart, eating fresh vegetarian food can help." Personally, I've experienced this to be true. Yet some folks may be tempted to turn this around, criss-cross it, and conclude, "If you're not eating fresh vegetarian food, you must be a toad or dolt or unenlightened slob." Maybe so, maybe not. I don't know that vegetarians have any monopoly on greatness. And making judgements about people based on a lifestyle choice looks pretty dangerous to me. I'd rather not make judgements about people based on what they eat. There's a lot of room for variation here.

BLUE CORN BREAD

Preparation time: 30 - 35 minutes   Serves: 4
SATTVIC, 0 Vata, + Pitta, - Kapha*

❁ ✳ ☙ ❄

Preheat oven to 400° F. In a medium-sized bowl beat:

> **1 egg**

Stir into the beaten egg:

> **3 Tbsps. sesame oil or sesame tahini**
> **1 1/2 Tbsps. date sugar or fructose**
> **1 1/4 c. hot water**

Add:

> **1 c. blue cornmeal**
> **1/2 c. buckwheat flour**
> **3/4 tsp. salt**
> **1 1/2 tsps. baking powder**

Stir lightly. The batter is a thin one. Spoon into a well-greased 9"x 9" pan. Bake for 20 -25 minutes or until a toothpick inserted into the middle of the cornbread comes out cleanly.

* For this to be *0 Vata*, you need to serve this with goodly amounts of ghee. Otherwise, it can be too dry for this constitution.

*ROTATION DAY 4 DISH

Comments: This can range in color from blueberry blue to purple to steely gray, depending on your cornmeal. It's very good with ghee and fruit-sweetened strawberry jam. I use the sesame tahini rather than the oil when I want to add extra calcium, iron and protein. For a rotation day 4 meal, Blue Cornbread can be served with Cream of Broccoli Soup and a DAY 4 salad of steamed asparagus spears and watercress with Creamy Garlic Dressing.

IRISH SODA BREAD

Preparation time: 1 hour or a little more

Serves: 6-8

SATTVIC, - Vata, - Pitta, + Kapha

❀ ✳ ⚭ ❄

Preheat oven to 350F. Bring to a boil:

1 2/3 c. fresh raw milk

Let boil for about 20 seconds, then remove from heat and let cool to room temperature. Then combine the milk with:

1 1/2 Tbsps. fresh lemon juice

Let stand for 5 minutes.

Stir into the milk and lemon mixture:

1/2 tsp. baking soda

Let stand another 2 minutes. Mix together in a largish bowl:

3 1/4 c. whole wheat pastry flour

2 Tbsps. Sucanat or apple concentrate

1 Tbsp. baking powder (scant Tbsp. if at high altitude)

3/4 tsp. salt

Then stir into the dry ingredients:

1 c. dried currants

1 tsp. caraway seeds

Gradually pour the lemon-milk into the dry ingredients in their large mixing bowl. Gently transfer the dough to a floured surface and knead for about three minutes. Place the kneaded dough into an oiled 9" pie pan (a shallow iron skillet also works well) and bake until done, about 45 minutes. A clean toothpick inserted into the center should come out cleanly when the bread is done.

Variation: You can substitute soy milk for the milk, and barley flour for the whole wheat flour in identical amounts for a flavorful bread.

SATTVIC, mildly + Vata, - Pitta, - Kapha

Variation: You can substitute 1 3/4 c. fresh buttermilk for the milk and lemon for a ROTATION DAY 1 DISH. You need to skip the caraway and use Sucanat for a strict rotation.

A TAD RAJASIC, - Vata, 0 Pitta, + Kapha

Variation: You can substitute 1 tsp. cinnamon for the caraway seeds.

Comment: I got this recipe from my friend Liz Halford, of LIZ'S SCONES fame. A New Zealander, she got this "rule" via an American, who brought it back from Ireland.

TABLE 11: FLOURS IN BAKED GOODS:
THEIR EFFECTS ON CONSTITUTION

Type of Flour	Effect on:		
	Vata	Pitta	Kapha
Barley	+ Vata	- Pitta	- Kapha
Buckwheat	+ Vata	+ Pitta	- Kapha
Chickpea (garbanzo)	+ Vata	- Pitta	- Kapha
Corn, blue	+ Vata	mildly + Pitta	- Kapha
Corn, yellow	+ Vata	+ Pitta	- Kapha
Millet	+ Vata	+ Pitta	- Kapha
Oat, bran	+ Vata	0 Pitta	- Kapha
Oat, flour	0 Vata	0 Pitta	0 Kapha
Potato	+ Vata	0 Pitta	- Kapha
Rice, bran	+ Vata	- Pitta	0 Kapha
Rice flour, brown	- Vata	mildly + Pitta	moderately + Kapha
Rice flour, white	- Vata	- Pitta	+ Kapha
Rye	+ Vata	+ Pitta	- Kapha
Soy	+ Vata	- Pitta	moderately + Kapha
Tapioca	- Vata	- Pitta	0 Kapha
Urud	- Vata	+ Pitta	+ Kapha
Wheat, bran	+ Vata	- Pitta	moderately + Kapha
Wheat, whole wheat flour	- Vata	- Pitta	+ Kapha
Wheat, white flour	- Vata	- Pitta	++ Kapha

Note: *The following flours I have worked with for five years or less, and need more experience (or experienced advice) before I could say for certain their effects on the doshas. The guesses I would hazard are: amaranth flour, 0 Vata, 0 Pitta, - Kapha; quinoa flour, 0 Vata, mildly + Pitta, - Kapha; teff flour, really not sure yet. It appears to be warming and strengthening.*

Side Dishes

KEY

"–" means calms or helps the given constitution;

"+" means aggravates or increases it;

"0" means neutral effect.

 * ROTATION DIET can be helpful for people with food
   sensitivities, see p. 323.

**POLARITY DISH refers to recipes supporting Polarity Therapy
work, see p. 342.

✿ = Spring

✳ = Summer

⚘ = Fall

❄ = Winter

PUNJABI GREENS

Preparation time: 15 minutes or less
SATTVIC BORDERING ON RAJASIC,
0 Vata, slightly + Pitta, 0 Kapha

Serves: 4 - 6

✿ ✳ ⛄ ❄

Wash well and chop into one-inch slices or less:
2 small or 1 very large bunch of kale or other dark leafy green

Warm in a large skillet:
2 Tbsps. ghee or olive oil
1/2 - 1 tsp. whole cumin seeds
1 tsp. turmeric
1/8 tsp. hing or epazote

Add to the ghee and saute until soft:
3 Tbsps. onion (optional, can be omitted)
2 small cloves of garlic, minced

Add the washed greens and cover. Cook over medium-low heat until tender, about 8 minutes, stirring once or twice. The vegetables may or may not need any salt.

Variations: If you have access to a couple of large bunches of fresh arugula, it is divine in place of the kale. It cooks up fast, say in 2 - 3 minutes, so it is best to stay close to the stove after you've added it to the pot. (RAJASIC, 0 *Vata*, slightly + *Pitta*, 0 *Kapha*) Another delicious green in the springtime is fresh lambs quarters, harvested when they are under one foot tall. Washed well and chopped, this recipe is our favorite way to have them.

(*SATTVIC WITH SOME RAJAS, 0 Vata, - Pitta, 0 Kapha*)

GREEN BEANS WITH ROASTED ALMONDS

Preparation time: 10-15 minutes   Serves: 4
SATTVIC, 0 Vata, - Pitta, 0 Kapha   ✿ ✳ 🐚 ❄

Wash:

2 c. fresh green beans

Trim the ends and any strings as needed. Cut each bean diagonally in 2-inch pieces. Bring to a boil:

1 1/2 c. salted water

Immerse the beans in the boiling water, cover, and cook on medium heat until they are tender and still a beautiful green, 5 - 8 minutes. Drain. Mix in a serving bowl with:

1 Tbsp. ghee
1/4 c. roasted sliced blanched almonds, p. 225
Salt to taste

Serve.

Comments: With thanks to Liz for original ideas about what goes with what! A favorite tasty, easy side dish of our family.

DORIE'S SICILIAN SPINACH

Preparation time: 10 minutes or less   Serves: 4
RAJASIC, - Vata, + Pitta, - Kapha   ✿ ✳ 🐚 ❄

Wash well:

1 large bunch fresh spinach

Heat an iron skillet and warm in it for a moment or two:

1 Tbsp. extra-virgin olive oil

Saute in the oil:

4 - 5 cloves of garlic, minced

Put in the spinach, stirring over medium heat until cooked. Sprinkle on:

4 - 5 drops of red wine vinegar (lemon juice can be substituted)

Serve.

Comments: My friend Dorie, who has provided much of the inspiration for the Sicilian and Italian dishes here, was first served this dish at Palermo's, a great Sicilian restaurant on the East Coast.

If you are on a yeast-free program, lemon juice can be used in place of the vinegar.

GORD'S GREENS

Preparation time: under 10 minutes Serves: 4
RAJASIC, — Vata, + Pitta, mildly + Kapha

Wash and chop:
> **8 - 12 c. loosely packed arugula flowers and leaves**

Warm in a heavy skillet over medium heat:
> **3 Tbsps. sunflower oil**

Add:
> **4 cloves garlic, minced**

Brown the garlic lightly, for about a minute. Cut the heat to simmer and add:
> **2 tsps. ghee or butter**
> **1 leaf fresh sage, finely chopped**
> **2 - 3 inches fresh oregano, about 1 1/2 tsps., finely chopped**

Stir a couple of times. Add the arugula flowers and leaves. Cook them down until they are tender, about two minutes.

Add:
> **Salt, if needed (it often isn't).**

Comment: A delectable dish. If you want to cut the fat in half or more, it is definitely possible. Cut the oil to 1 1/2 tablespoons, and the ghee to 1 teaspoon. Stir a bit more often to ensure that the greens do not stick.

ROASTED ITALIAN VEGETABLES

Preparation time: about 40 minutes   Serves: 4
MILDLY RAJASIC, + Vata, + Pitta, 0 Kapha   ❄

Preheat the oven to 350° F. Wash and prepare:
> **8 cherry tomatoes, whole or halved**
> **1 large bell pepper, of pretty color, in one-inch wedges**
> **4 new potatoes, quartered and thin-sliced**
> **1 small eggplant, peeled, halved and sliced in 1/4" thick pieces**

Arrange the vegetables on a lightly oiled cookie sheet and drizzle over them:
> **1 - 2 Tbsps. of extra-virgin olive oil**

Crumble on top of the vegetables:
> **1 tsp. dried sweet basil**
> **1 tsp. dried oregano**

Cook uncovered in the oven for 30 minutes. Serve hot.

Comments: This is a tasty way to fix a variety of vegetables easily. Both of my friends Zenia and Dorie quietly urged me to try this for months, before I happily discovered the reason for their enthusiasm. *The Silver Palate Cookbook* has a yummy version with a good deal more salt.

Variation: For a ROTATION DAY 1 DISH, use walnut oil in place of the olive oil.

ROSEMARY POTATOES

Preparation time: 45 minutes, 30 of it unattended   Serves: 4 - 6
SATTVIC, 0 Vata, - Pitta, 0 Kapha

Bring to a boil in a large saucepan:
> **6 c. pure water or enough to cover the potatoes**

Wash:
> **6 medium red boiling potatoes**

and pare out any eyes. Put the potatoes in the boiling water (adding them after the water has come to a boil preserves vitamins, especially vitamin C) and cook uncovered until done, about 30 minutes. If you are in a hurry, you can cut them in halves or quarters and cut your time and energy use to about 20 minutes. Nutrients are best preserved if you cook them whole.

While the potatoes are cooking, chop:
> **1 Tbsp. fresh rosemary, or 3/4 - 1 1/2 tsps. dried, finely chopped**
> **1 Tbsp. fresh leek or 2 Tbsps. onion**

In a largish skillet or saucepan, saute the leek in:
> **3 Tbsps. olive oil**

Set aside until the potatoes are done. Then drain the 'tatoes, slice them with their peels on, and put them in the oiled pan with the leek. Stir and let cook over medium heat for 5 - 10 minutes. Add the chopped rosemary and:
> **1 tsp. salt**
> **1/4 tsp. freshly ground white or black pepper**

and cook until a tad crispy.

Comments: This is in fond memory of Grandma Dorothy and special times with the Bruen clan at Wright's Lake.

Variation: For a ROTATION DAY 1 DISH, skip the onion and use ghee or butter in place of the olive oil. It can also be made into patties like the following recipe.

SATTVIC, 0 Vata, - Pitta, 0 Kapha

Variation:

ROSEMARY POTATO PATTIES
Preparation time: 1 hour   Makes 12 (3") patties
SATTVIC, 0 Vata, - Pitta, 0 Kapha

Follow the recipe above until it comes time to take the potatoes out of their boiling water. Preheat your oven to 350° F. Drain the potatoes as above, then put them whole in with the leek and olive oil, as well as the rest of the ingredients. Mash everything together with a strong fork or potato masher, and form into patties. Place on an oiled cookie sheet and bake for 10 - 15 minutes.

Variation II:

Preparation time: 45 - 50 minutes   Makes 12 (3") patties
SATTVIC BORDERING ON RAJASIC, - Vata, 0 Pitta, slightly + Kapha

Make the patties as above, but add one beaten egg and 1/2 c. finely chopped Italian parsley. Nice, light, slightly richer dish.

FOR THE RECORD

Occasionally I meet someone who has read my work and who imagines that because I speak about this sane and beautiful science of healing called Ayurveda, that my life and personal health are equally sane and pristine. In reality, I'm a child of the latter half of the twentieth century, born in America, nurtured on Pop Tarts, meatballs and Kraft's Macaroni and Cheese. My teenage acne was treated with radiation (as best I can ascertain) and daily hormonal treatments, before I turned 16. I was fond of steak, when we had it, and even ate it leftover for breakfast, when there was some. My favorite snack after school in junior high and high school was to grab a spoon from the drawer, head for the middle cabinet, pull out the box of brown sugar, and eat it straight. This was a great pleasure. This is not to cast aspersion on my parents, who took great care of us, according to the standards of the day. My mother was a blessedly good cook who served well-balanced meals with plenty of veggies. (The six of us kids fought over who got the most spinach. It was an object of desire and competition.) I was a fairly typical middle-class American kid.

I do eat more cleanly now, and have for quite a while because I've noticed what a difference it makes in how I feel. I'd be surprised to see myself do most of those things again. And I share this because it is part of my history, what I'm responsible for now, some of which is still undoubtedly present in my "body record", my pulses and such. I imagine that almost every one of us at this point has a story of less than pure living, from mild periods of "self-sins", as Dr. Sunil Joshi puts it, to more extreme situations, like being down wind from a chemicals plant or downstream from a waste dump. Our individual experiences will differ in degree and impact tremendously from person to person, yet each of us is responsible now for ourselves and what we will do with our situations as they stand today.

ROASTED SWEET CORN

Preparation time: 20 minutes max, if you have a fire.
Figure an hour or two if you're making the fire from scratch.   Serves: 4 - 6
SATTVIC, 0 Vata (with plenty of ghee and salt), - Pitta,
- Kapha (easy on the salt and ghee)

You will need:
> **8 ears of sweet corn, unhusked, as fresh as possible (fresh-picked is great)**
> **A fire gone to charcoal**

Get the fire going, in an already established fire circle, or in a hibachi. (The latter is the method practiced by most of the street vendors of roasted corn in Mexico and Guatemala, and works well.) After much of your wood has caught fire, let it burn down to embers. This is when you put on your corn, still in the husks, right on the coals.

Line the corn on the coals with about an inch or more space between the ears. Turn every five minutes or so until they are done. When the husks are beginning to blacken and the kernels are tender, serve. Serve with ghee, butter and/or lemon.

* For a ROTATION DAY 4 DISH, serve with salt, lemon, and/or toasted sesame oil.

**POLARITY PURIFYING DIET DISH

STEAMED PARSNIPS

Preparation time: 20 minutes   Serves: 4
SATTVIC, - Vata, - Pitta, slightly + Kapha

Wash well:
> **4 medium-sized parsnips**

Cut them lengthwise in quarters (ILLUS), then crosswise in 1/2-inch sections. In a medium saucepan, put a steamer and:
> **Steaming water, about 1 1/2 cups**

When the water has come to a boil, put the parsnips in the steamer, cover, and let cook until sweet and tender, up to 20 minutes.

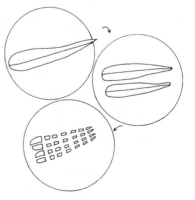

*ROTATION DAY 3 DISH

**POLARITY PURIFYING DIET DISH

PARSNIPS, CARROTS, AND PEAS

Preparation time: 20 - 25 minutes   Serves: 3 - 4
SATTVIC, - Vata, 0 Pitta, mildly + Kapha   ✿ 🐌 ❄

Wash and cut up:
> **3 - 4 parsnips, cubed (about 3 cups)**
> **2 large carrots, sliced (about 3 cups)**
> **1 c. fresh peas**

You might want to thank them for joining you in this culinary adventure, if you are so inclined. Warm in an iron skillet over medium heat:
> **1 - 2 Tbsps. cold-pressed sunflower oil**

Put in the parsnips and carrots. Cover and cook until tender and sweet smelling, about 15 minutes. Add the peas, cover again, and cook until done, a minute or two. Serve.

* ROTATION DAY 3 DISH

Variation: Wash and chop the vegetables as before. Warm one inch of water in the bottom of a saucepan with a steamer. Once the water is steaming, put the veggies in to steam, covering until done, about fifteen minutes. You can put the oil over them when they are done if you like, depending on your needs and inclinations.

Without oil, SATTVIC, 0 Vata, - Pitta, 0 Kapha
With oil, SATTVIC, - Vata, 0 Pitta, very mildly + Kapha
* ROTATION DAY 3 DISH
** POLARITY PURIFYING DIET DISH

ABOUT ROOT CELLARS

Traditionally, Ayurvedic nutrition minimizes the use of refrigerators, especially freezers. Ayurvedic physicians often state that the excess cold which permeates frozen and refrigerated food is hard on the body. And this cold inhibits agni, *digestive fire. Most of us are unlikely to give away our refrigerators. And yet how else to store fresh fruits and vegetables, say? One low-tech energy-sparing alternative is the old-fashioned root cellar, whose temperatures hover from just above freezing to 40° F. You can gather fresh vegetables there (like cabbage or Chinese cabbage) weeks or months after you've stored them. They will not have the* prana *(vital energy) they did when they began, but in most cases they will still have more* prana *than frozen or canned produce.*

Whether you are talking about a lovely north-facing pantry, a box in your basement, or a simple well-vented hole in the ground, you are likely to find help in Mike and Nancy Bubel's book, Root Cellaring *(Storey Communications, 1991).*

PLAIN SIMMERED CABBAGE

Preparation time: 15 minutes   Serves: 6
SATTVIC, + Vata, - Pitta, - Kapha   ✿ ❄

Bring to a boil in a medium saucepan:
> **2 c. pure water**

Wash and cut into one-inch wedges:
> **1 small head purple cabbage**

Put the cabbage into the water, cover, and reduce heat to low. Cook covered for 8-10 minutes. Serve plain, or with a little lemon juice or ghee.

*ROTATION DAY 4 DISH

**POLARITY PURIFYING DIET DISH

CHINESE CABBAGE WITH SHIITAAKE MUSHROOMS

Preparation time: 20 - 30 minutes   Serves: 4
TAMASIC (with the mushrooms), 0 Vata, - Pitta, - Kapha   ✿ ✳ 🍃 ❄

Boil:
> **1/2 c. water**

Pour it into a heatproof bowl with:
> **6 dried Shiitaake mushrooms**

Soak the mushrooms for 15 minutes or more. Drain the water into an iron skillet or wok. Slice the mushrooms in thin strips. Wash and slice:
> **3 c. Chinese cabbage**

Bring the water again to a boil, put in the mushrooms and the Chinese cabbage and:
> **1/2 tsp. salt**

Cover and cook on medium heat until done, about 5 - 10 minutes, stirring once or twice.

**POLARITY PURIFYING DIET DISH

SWEET POTATOES WITH APPLES

Preparation time: 2 hours, almost none of it attended   Serves: 4
SATTVIC, 0 Vata, - Pitta, moderately + Kapha

Preheat the oven to 350° F.

Wash well:
>   **3 medium sweet potatoes**
>   **3 medium apples, organic preferred**

Cube them into 1/2 - 1" pieces, leaving on the peels of both (unless you are especially interested in calming *Vata*, in which case removing the peels is beneficial. Otherwise the nutrients in the peel are strengthening.) Place the sweet potatoes and apples in a 6" x 11" baking dish. Mix together:
>   **1 1/2 c. organic apple juice**
>   **1 1/2 tsps. cinnamon**
>   **1 1/2 tsps. maple syrup (optional)**

Pour this sauce over the potatoes and apple. Cover and bake until soft, 1 - 1 1/2 hours. Very satisfying, fat-free.

**POLARITY HEALTH BUILDING DISH

MASHED SWEET POTATOES

Preparation time: 45 minutes   Serves: 4 - 6
SATTVIC, - Vata, - Pitta, moderately + Kapha*

Wash and boil:
>   **3 large sweet potatoes**

in:
>   **2 quarts water**

until soft, about 30 - 35 minutes. Drain (the cooking liquid makes the beginnings of a good soup stock) and peel the potatoes, with a paring knife. Or, if the peel is loose enough, it can sometimes be easily rubbed off with clean fingers.

Mash the potatoes in a large bowl with:
>   **1/4 tsp. salt**
>   **1/8 tsp. nutmeg**
>   **2 tsps. raw honey or rice bran syrup**

Whip with a fork for extra smoothness. Serve hot.

* While these two sweet potato recipes increase *Kapha* because of this vegetable's natural sweet, earthy quality, both of these non-fat versions are easier on *Kapha* than many richer holiday versions.)

*ROTATION DAY 3 DISH

**POLARITY HEALTH BUILDING DISH (If you skip the salt, this is a POLARITY PURIFY-ING DIET DISH.)

SIMMERED OKRA

Preparation time: 10 minutes   Serves: 2 - 4, depending on your enthusiasms
SATTVIC, - Vata, - Pitta, - Kapha

This is one of those foods you either like or you don't. On the plus side, it looks like beautiful green stars and is soothing and strengthening to the gut in the short-term. On the minus side, it's slimy, and has a pungent post-digestive effect. So see what your choice is. This is a very simple way to prepare this nutritious vegetable.

Bring to a boil in a small saucepan:
   3/4 c. water

Wash and cut in 1/4" rounds:
   1/2 lb. young fresh small okra

Toss it in the boiling water, cover and cook over medium-high heat until tender, about 5 to 8 minutes. Drain the water (into a soup stock or your compost is nice; it is loaded with nutrients).

Into the hot okra, toss:
   1 Tbsp. ghee or butter
   1 1/2 tsps. fresh dill leaves, finely chopped (optional)
   Salt and pepper to taste

In the American South, this is often served with a dash of lemon as well as the dill.

**POLARITY HEALTH BUILDING DISH

FAVORITE SNOW PEAS

Preparation time: 10 minutes or less   Serves: 4
SATTVIC, 0 Vata, - Pitta, 0 Kapha   ✳ ༀ

Wash and pat dry:
> **2 cups fresh snow peas**

Warm in a large skillet:
> **1 1/2 Tbsps. ghee**

Toss in the snow peas. Stir to coat well with ghee. Cover and cook over medium heat until beautifully green and tender, two to three minutes at most. Don't let them go to the olive drab stage; they are much tastier fresher.

Variation: Use sunflower oil in place of the ghee for a ROTATION DAY 3 DISH.

SATTVIC, 0 Vata, - Pitta, 0 Kapha

TABLE 12: STEAMED VEGETABLES

Steaming vegetables is a simple fat-free way to mingle fire and water in produce for easy-to-digest dishes. You can serve a wide variety of vegetables in this simple style. The steamed food will be even more balancing to *Vata* if you serve it with ghee after it is done, while *Kapha* benefits most by having it served without extra lubrication. *Pitta* can go either way, using a little ghee or not.

A stainless steel steamer can be obtained at most discount stores or stores specializing in cook wares, for a few dollars. To use your steamer, put it in a saucepan large enough to accommodate it and still be able to have the lid of the saucepan fit tightly. Add an inch or two of pure water and bring the water to a boil over high heat. In a few minutes, enough steam will be released from the water to begin to steam your vegetables. Lift the lid, put in your vegetables, whole or sliced depending on what you are fixing, and cover the pan tightly once more. Reduce heat to low and cook until tender. A guide to approximate cooking times for each vegetable and their effects on each *dosha* follows.

TABLE 12: STEAMED VEGETABLES (continued)

Vegetable	Time to Steam	Effect on Each Dosha		
Acorn squash, in one-inch wedges	20-30 minutes	- *Vata*	- *Pitta*	+ *Kapha*
Artichoke, whole	60 minutes	- *Vata*	- *Pitta*	0 *Kapha*
Asparagus, whole	8-15 minutes	- *Vata*	- *Pitta*	- *Kapha*
Beets, in 1/4" slices	15-20 minutes	- *Vata*	+ *Pitta*	- *Kapha*
Beet greens, chopped	5-10 minutes	moderately + *Vata*	+ *Pitta*	- *Kapha*
Bell pepper, in one-inch wedges	5 minutes	moderately + *Vata*	0 *Pitta*	- *Kapha*
Broccoli, stalks	5-12 minutes	moderately + *Vata*	- *Pitta*	- *Kapha*
Brussels sprouts, whole	10-20 minutes	+ *Vata*	- *Pitta*	- *Kapha*
Burdock root, chopped	20-30 minutes	+ *Vata*	- *Pitta*	- *Kapha*
Butternut squash, in one-inch wedges	20-30 minutes	- *Vata*	- *Pitta*	+ *Kapha*
Cabbage, quartered	10-15 minutes	+ *Vata*	- *Pitta*	- *Kapha*
Carrots, in 1/4" slices	10-15 minutes	- *Vata*	moderately + *Pitta*	- *Kapha*
Cauliflower, quartered	10-20 minutes	+ *Vata*	- *Pitta*	- *Kapha*
Celery, chopped	5 minutes	+ *Vata*	- *Pitta*	- *Kapha*
Chard, Swiss, chopped	3-6 minutes	moderately + *Vata*	0 *Pitta*	- *Kapha*
Collard greens, chopped	5-12 minutes	+ *Vata*	- *Pitta*	- *Kapha*
Corn on the cob, whole	7-10 minutes	moderately + *Vata*	- *Pitta*	- *Kapha*
Daikon radish, chopped	7-15 minutes	- *Vata*	moderately + *Pitta*	- *Kapha*
Dandelion greens, chopped	3-5 minutes	moderately + *Vata*	- *Pitta*	- *Kapha*
Fennel, in one-inch slices	5-8 minutes	- *Vata*	- *Pitta*	mildly + *Kapha*
Fenugreek greens	1-3 minutes	- *Vata*	+ *Pitta*	- *Kapha*
Garlic, minced	3-5 minutes	- *Vata* (in moderation)	+ *Pitta*	- *Kapha*
Green beans, in one-inch pieces	7-12 minutes	moderately + *Vata*	- *Pitta*	- *Kapha*

TABLE 12 (continued)

Fresh Vegetable	Time to Steam	Effect on Each Dosha		
Horseradish, grated	5-10 minutes	0 Vata	+ Pitta	- Kapha
Jerusalem artichokes, in 1/4" slices	10-12 minutes	moderately + Vata	- Pitta	- Kapha
Kale, chopped	4-8 minutes	moderately + Vata	- Pitta	- Kapha
Kohlrabi, in 1/4" slices	5-10 minutes	+ Vata	0 Pitta	- Kapha
Leeks, in 1/4" rounds	5-10 minutes	0 Vata	mildly + Pitta (in moderation)	- Kapha
Mung sprouts, whole	3-5 minutes	0 Vata	- Pitta	- Kapha
Mushrooms, whole	5-10 minutes	+ Vata	- Pitta	0 Kapha
Mustard greens, chopped	5-12 minutes	0 Vata	+ Pitta	- Kapha
Okra, in 1/2" rounds	5-8 minutes	- Vata	0 Pitta	- Kapha
Onion, chopped finely	3-5 minutes	0 Vata	+ Pitta	- Kapha
Parsnips, in 1/4" slices	7-10 minutes	- Vata	- Pitta	moderately + Kapha
Peas, shelled	5-8 minutes	moderately + Vata	- Pitta	- Kapha
Peas, snow	3-5 minutes	moderately + Vata	- Pitta	- Kapha
Potatoes, sweet, in 1/2" slices	5-10 minutes	- Vata	- Pitta	+ Kapha
Potatoes, white, red, purple, et. al., in 1/2" slices	5-12 minutes	+ Vata	0 Pitta	- Kapha
Pumpkin, in one-inch wedges	20-30 minutes	- Vata	moderately + Pitta	+ Kapha
Rutabaga, in 1/4" slices	5-7 minutes	- Vata	0 Pitta	+ Kapha
Spinach, chopped	3-5 minutes	moderately + Vata	moderately + Pitta	- Kapha
Squash, summer, in 1/4" slices	5-10 minutes	- Vata	- Pitta	0 Kapha
Tomato, whole (medium)	5-10 minutes	+ Vata	+ Pitta	mildly + Kapha
Turnips, in 1/4" slices	5-7 minutes	moderately + Vata	+ Pitta	- Kapha
Turnip greens, chopped	5-12 minutes	+ Vata	+ Pitta	- Kapha
Zucchini, in 1/4" slices	5-10 minutes	- Vata	- Pitta	0 Kapha

NOTE: Steamed vegetables can be even more balancing to Vata if they are served with ghee once they are done.

BROCCOLI AND GARLIC

Preparation time: 15 minutes   Serves: 4 - 6
SATTVIC, mildly + Vata, 0 Pitta, - Kapha

♣ ✳ 🍵 ❄

Put about an inch of water and a stainless steel steamer in the bottom of a large saucepan. Bring to a boil, covered, over high heat. Wash:

4 c. fresh broccoli, organic preferred

Discard about a third of the stalk (that is to say, compost it if at all possible) and thinly slice the rest up to the florets. Break these into small pieces. Arrange the broccoli, thin stalk pieces first, on the steamer, florets on top. Mince onto the broccoli from a garlic press:

1 clove garlic

Cover; reduce heat to medium and steam until a bright beautiful green, about five minutes. Stir and serve immediately.

*ROTATION DAY 4 DISH

**POLARITY PURIFYING DIET DISH

Comment: Putting a little ghee on this dish for *Vata* helps calm it to a neutral (0) effect.

**POLARITY HEALTH BUILDING DISH

BLACK-EYED PEAS

Preparation time: 1 1/2 hours   Serves: 4
SATTVIC, + Vata, 0 Pitta, 0 Kapha

♣ ✳ 🍵 ❄

Saute in a medium-sized saucepan:

2 Tbsps. ghee
3 Tbsps. red onion, chopped
1 small clove garlic, minced

Wash:

1 c. dry black-eyed peas

Add the peas to the ghee with:

6 c. water
1 bay leaf
1 whole organic stalk of celery, broken in a couple of pieces

Bring to a boil, cover, and reduce heat to medium. Cook until done. Add:

Salt and pepper to taste

Serve.

HAPPY NEW YEAR'S TO YOU!, especially down Texas way.

MASHED POTATOES

Preparation time: 45 minutes   Serves: 3 - 4
SATTVIC*

Boil in a covered saucepan until soft, about 30 minutes:
> **4 large Yukon Gold potatoes, or other tasty potato**
> **1 bay leaf**
> **Boiling water to cover the potatoes**

Drain (saving the water for some good soup or *kichadi*, yes?) (or your houseplants?) (or...?). Put the potatoes into a large mixing bowl. Mash with a potato masher or a sturdy fork. Add:
> **2 Tbsps. ghee or olive oil**
> **2 oz. fresh basil, minced (a large bunch)**
> **1/2 tsp. salt**
> **Enough freshly ground black pepper to make you sneeze**

Stir well. Heat in a small saucepan until it just begins to boil:
> **Up to 1 1/2 c. fresh raw milk, cow's or soy***

and stir in to the potatoes gradually, fluffing with your fork as you stir. Continue to add milk until you have the consistency you like. Serve HOT.

*With cow's milk: SATTVIC, 0 Vata,- Pitta, + Kapha

*With soy milk: SATTVIC, 0 Vata, - Pitta, - Kapha (Some people with *Vata* imbalance could have a difficulty with the soy milk-potato combination. Cow's milk is more calming for *Vata* energy than soy milk by a considerable margin, if you can tolerate it.)

**If you are following a strict rotation diet, use cow's milk or perhaps walnut milk for A ROTATION DAY 1 DISH.

CALABACITAS

Preparation time: 20 - 30 minutes   Serves: 4
SATTVIC, 0 Vata, - Pitta, 0 Kapha

This is our version of a Southwestern favorite. Wash:
> **4 small fresh squash: *calabacitas*, zucchinis, or what have you**

Chop the squash into cubes or slices. Then cut the corn off:
> **2 - 3 ears of fresh corn**

Prepare:
> **2 Tbsps. red onion, finely chopped**
> **1 garlic, minced**

Simmer the squash, onion and garlic in:
> **2 - 3 Tbsps. ghee or olive oil**

until tender, about 5 minutes. Then stir in the corn and:
> **2 tsps. fresh oregano, finely chopped**
> **Salt and freshly ground black pepper**

Simmer 5 - 10 minutes more. Serve. Good with SANTA FE PINTO BEANS and PLAIN *BAS-MATI* RICE.

Rajasic Variation: Add 2-3 fresh tomatoes, chopped and a pinch of red chili (Chimayo red chili is good) when you add the corn and oregano.

RAJASIC, + Vata, + Pitta, - Kapha

Variation: CALABACITAS STEW: Prepare as above and add 2 c. vegetable stock with the tomatoes and corn and herbs. Simmer for another 1/2 hour or more. Makes a good late summer, early fall soup.

RAJASIC, 0 Vata, + Pitta, - Kapha

FENUGREEK SPROUTS

Preparation time: 5 minutes   Serves: 2
SATTVIC, - Vata, ++ Pitta, - Kapha   ✿ ⅋ ❄

Rinse:
> **1 c. fresh fenugreek sprouts**

Warm in a skillet over low heat:
> **1 - 2 tsps. ghee**
> **1/4 tsp. black mustard seeds**

When the mustard seeds begin to pop, add the fenugreek sprouts. Stir until they begin to "wilt", a minute or two. Serve.

ABOUT FENUGREEK

While fenugreek sprouts are warming and a good way to scrape ama from the intestinal tract, they are best avoided by anyone with high Pitta, inflammation of the gut, or in pregnancy. With these precautions in mind, fenugreek sprouts are a good medicinal food after delivery, in diabetes, in indigestion related to low digestive fire, and to strengthen a sluggish liver or general debility. Calming to Kapha and Vata, they are aggravating to Pitta.

This traditional way of preparing fenugreek sprouts was suggested to me by Dr. Shalmali Joshi. Fenugreek sprouts can also be served steamed or raw, a little at a time.

STEAMED TURNIPS WITH HONEY LEMON SAUCE

Preparation time: 20 minutes   Serves: 4
SATTVIC, --Vata, slightly + Pitta, + Kapha   ૨૦ ❄

Wash well and slice in thin rounds:
4 - 6 medium turnips

Put them in a steamer, cover and steam until soft, about twenty minutes. While the turnips are steaming, make up:
HONEY LEMON SAUCE, p. 213

When the turnips are done, spoon them into a serving dish, drizzle the sauce over them, toss and serve. This is a good way to prepare turnips for an otherwise hostile or say ambivalent audience. I've even known kids to enjoy them this way.

BEETS WITH MAPLE SYRUP GLAZE

Preparation time: 20 minutes or less   Serves: 4
SATTVIC, --Vata, 0 Pitta, mildly + Kapha*   ૨૦ ❄

Wash and thin-slice:
6 medium beets (about 3 c. sliced)

Steam them until tender, 15 minutes or more. Whisk together in a small bowl:
1 Tbsp. ghee
2 Tbsps. maple syrup

When the beets are done, put them in a serving bowl and pour the glaze over them. Serve.

* Plain steamed beets are calming to Kapha; it is the sweetener and fat which make this dish imbalancing for earthy Kapha.

Variation: For a ROTATION DAY 2 DISH, omit the ghee.

SATTVIC, - Vata, 0 Pitta, 0 Kapha

**POLARITY PURIFYING DIET DISH

NOT RISOTTO

Preparation time: 30 - 40 minutes
Serves: 4
SATTVIC, - Vata, - Pitta, 0 Kapha

❀ ✳ ଛ ❄

Warm in a medium saucepan over low heat:
1 1/2 Tbsps. olive oil

Stir into the oil and saute until tender:
2 Tbsps. red onion, finely chopped

Then stir in:
1 c. uncooked white basmati (or Texmati) rice

As soon as it is well-coated with oil, pour into the rice:
1/2 c. white grape juice

Cook over medium heat until the juice has been absorbed into the rice, stirring fairly constantly. Then stir in, about 1/2 cup at a time:
3 c. vegetable stock (see VEGETARIAN SOUP STOCK, p. 113)

Leave the rice uncovered, stirring it as it cooks. Keep adding stock until the rice is tender, which can take 20 - 30 minutes. Just before serving, stir together:
1/12 tsp. saffron
1 more tsp. vegetable stock

Remove the rice from the heat. Stir the saffron into it. Salt, if necessary.

> *One simple way to begin to reconnect with the Earth is to give thanks before we eat, imagining the food in our bowls as it once was, growing from the Earth. In this giving thanks we begin to re-acknowledge our interconnections with nature on a level deeper than the intellectual one.*

IVY'S COCONUT-SESAME RICE

Preparation time: Serves: 4
SATTVIC, - Vata, - Pitta, + Kapha   ✿ ✳ ⠦ ❄

Rinse and drain:
>   **1 c. *basmati* rice**

In a medium saucepan, heat:
>   **2 Tbsps. ghee**

Add rice and stir, coating all the grains with ghee. Add:
>   **2 c. water**
>   **1 tsp. salt**

Bring the pot to a boil, then reduce heat to simmer and cover. Cook over medium-low heat until done, about 15 minutes for white *basmati* or Texmati, 45 - 50 minutes for brown *basmati*. When rice is done, remove from heat.

In separate saucepan, heat an additional:
>   **2 Tbsps. ghee**

Add:
>   **1/4 c. sesame seeds**
>   **1/4 c. unsweetened desiccated coconut**

Continuously stir the seeds and coconut in the ghee until they darken slightly. Pour immediately into cooked rice and toss until mixed. Garnish with:
>   **Fresh chopped cilantro leaves**

Comments: This recipe comes from Ivy Blank, co-director of Ayurveda at Spirit Rest, Pagosa Springs, Colorado. It is an excellent way to calm *Vata* and *Pitta*.

QUINOA CILANTRO

Preparation time: 30 minutes   Serves: 4
SATTVIC, 0 Vata, - Pitta, - Kapha   ✳ ⠦

Rinse well:
>   **1 c. dry quinoa**

This is not only to remove dirt, but to get off the naturally soapy residue on the grain, which can cause stomach upsets. Bring the quinoa to a boil in a saucepan with:
>   **2 c. water**

Cover, reduce heat to low, and cook until done, about twenty minutes. In a blender, blend until smooth on high speed, less than a minute:

> 1/2 c. fresh cilantro leaves, chopped
> 1 Tbsp. fresh ginger root, grated
> 2 Tbsps. cold-pressed sesame oil
> 1 tsp. Sucanat or fructose
> 1 Tbsp. water

Put the cilantro dressing in a large skillet over medium heat with:

> 1/2 c. grated carrot
> 1 c. mizuna, amaranth greens or spinach, finely chopped
> 1/2 c. fresh green beans, snow peas or zucchini, diced

Stir, stir, stir until the vegetables are done, about 5 - 10 minutes. Stir in the quinoa. Salt to taste.

Comment: This also makes a good salad, slightly cooled.

WARMING MILLET

Preparation time: 40 minutes
SATTVIC, slightly + Vata, + Pitta, - Kapha

Serves: 4 - 6

Warm in a medium saucepan:

> 1 Tbsp. cold-pressed olive oil
> 1/2 tsp. mustard seeds

When the mustard seeds begin to pop, stir in:

> 1 Tbsp. onion, finely chopped

and saute until it is translucent. Add to the saute:

> 1 small carrot, thinly sliced in rounds

Stir it enough to coat it with the oil. Add:

> 1 1/2 c. dry millet
> 4 1/2 c. water

Bring to a boil. Cover, reduce heat to low and cook until the millet is tender, about 30 minutes.

PLAIN MILLET

Preparation time: 30 minutes

Serves: 4

SATTVIC, + Vata, + Pitta, - Kapha

✿ 🍃 ❄

Rinse well:

1 c. dry millet

Put it in a medium saucepan with:

3 c. water
1/8 tsp. salt

Bring to a boil over medium heat, then cover, reduce heat to low and cook until done, about 30 minutes.

* ROTATION DAY 2 DISH

See also: Middle Eastern Olive Casserole, p. 146

KASHA AND LEEKS (*KAPHA* KASHA!)

Preparation time: 20 minutes

Makes 2 cups

SATTVIC, + Vata, + Pitta, - Kapha

✿ ✳ 🍃 ❄

Wash well, then chop:

1 c. leeks

Warm in a medium saucepan:

1 1/2 Tbsps. cold-pressed sesame oil

Add the chopped leeks and saute for a minute or two on low heat. Stir in:

2/3 c. uncooked kasha (toasted buckwheat groats)

and stir until the grain is lightly coated. Add:

2 c. water
1/2 tsp. salt (less if you like)

Bring to a boil, cover and reduce heat to low. Cook until done, about 15 minutes.

*ROTATION DAY 4 DISH

Polarity Variation: Skip the sautéing step and put the leeks and uncooked kasha directly into water to cook. Add the uncooked oil at the end if you like.

SATTVIC, + Vata, + Pitta, - Kapha

**POLARITY HEALTH BUILDING DISH

PLAIN BASMATI RICE

Preparation time: 15 minutes for Texmati or white basmati,   Serves: 4
45 minutes for brown basmati
SATTVIC, - Vata, - Pitta, 0 Kapha

Rinse well:
>   **1 c. white, brown or Texmati rice**

Put in a medium-sized saucepan with:
>   **2 1/4 c. pure water**
>   **1/8 tsp. salt**

Bring to a boil, reduce heat to low and cover until cooked. Grains of rice will be tender. Serve hot, with ghee if you like.

"Nature is everything. Nature is the sun, the moon. We who used to be part of this nature - now we are destroying the same nature."

Florencio Siquiera de Cravalho, from the 1993 Bioneers Seeds of Change Conference in San Francisco.

(Seeds of Change, P.O. Box 15700, Santa Fe, N.M. 87506-5700)

GHEE

Preparation time: 15 minutes

SATTVIC, - Vata, 0 Pitta, 0 Kapha (in moderation)

Makes 2 cups

✿ ✴ ✿ ❄

In a heavy saucepan, place:
1 lb. unsalted butter, preferably organic

Turn the heat to medium, and cook uncovered for about 15 minutes. You will know the ghee is close to done when a brownish coat begins to accumulate on the bottom of the pan. At this point, begin to keep an eye on the ghee (it can burn very quickly). When it becomes very quiet and is no longer bubbling away or it begins to foam up, much more than in the early stages of the process, the ghee is done and should be removed from the heat. Let it cool, then pour it through a stainless steel mesh strainer into a glass or stainless steel container with a top. No need to refrigerate it.

Comments: While it is often said that all the impurities in the butter are collected in the sediment at the bottom of the pan of ghee, I tend to trust my skepticism and continue to support organic dairies, wherever they are in existence, despite the higher price for the product. From a biochemical standpoint, there are many synthetic pollutants in circulation on the planet now with a strong affinity for animal fat.

Thich Nhat Hanh, the internationally respected Vietnamese Buddhist teacher, wrote recently in Love in Action *(©1993, see bibliography): "Our Earth, our green beautiful Earth is in danger, and all of us know it. Yet we act as if our daily lives have nothing to do with the situation of the world." We imagine we are unimportant. Nothing could be further from the truth. It is our emissions from our cars eroding the ozone layer up there.*

It is our inappropriate consumption which feeds unscrupulous corporations. Without it, their power cannot continue to accumulate and degrade the biosphere. What we do matters. Where will you put your weight? How do you want to live? In a way that will help save the planet and its inhabitants, or in a way which will continue to destroy it?

Relishes & Sauces

KEY

"−" means calms or helps the given constitution;

"+" means aggravates or increases it;

"0" means neutral effect.

 * ROTATION DIET can be helpful for people with food
   sensitivities, see p. 323.

**POLARITY DISH refers to recipes supporting Polarity Therapy
  work, see p. 342.

✿ = Spring

✱ = Summer

❧ = Fall

❄ = Winter

YUMMY APPLE BUTTER

Preparation time: about an hour
Fresh, SATTVIC, 0 Vata, - Pitta, - Kapha

Makes 3 - 4 cups

Simmer together in a stainless steel saucepan over medium heat:

> 3 c. apple juice, organic recommended
> 3 c. apples, sliced, organic recommended (no need to peel)
> 3 dried apricots
> 1 1/2 tsps. cinnamon
> 3 cloves

Stir occasionally until the mixture has cooked down into a thick fruit puree. Then let the apple butter cool slightly and put it through a blender until smooth, a few seconds. It is ready to be served.

**POLARITY PURIFYING DIET DISH

Note: If you omit the apricots and cloves, this makes a good ROTATION DAY 1 relish.

HOT APRICOT SAUCE

Preparation time: overnight soak, plus 5 minutes
SATTVIC, 0 Vata, 0 Pitta, 0 Kapha

Makes 2 1/2 cups

Stir together in a heatproof bowl:

> 2 c. boiling water
> 1 c. unsulfured dried apricots, organic preferable

Cover and let sit, overnight preferably, or at least 1/2 hour. Pour the liquid and the fruit in the blender with:

> 3 Tbsps. to 1/4 c. maple syrup

and blend until smooth.

Very good on pancakes, waffles, crepes, and the like. And a good way to get some immune-stimulating beta-carotene.

*ROTATION DAY 2 DISH

**POLARITY HEALTH BUILDING DISH

ABOUT ORGANIC FOOD

Food free of pesticides and other toxic wastes can be hard to come by, or costly. And yet obtaining organic food, that is, produce grown and processed without chemicals, is becoming increasingly important. In the early 1990s Drs. Pankaj and Smita Naram of Bombay, both Ayurvedic specialists in fertility, did a lecture tour of the United States. In their lectures they mentioned that a major cause of infertility in the West, from their findings in examining pulses, was an excess of fire. The assumption was that some habitual parts of the Western lifestyle create too much pitta for healthy fertility.

Toxins, in general, increase fire. And now it is being reported more specifically in the national news media that PCBs (poly-chlorinated biphenols), DDE (a breakdown product of the persistent pesticide DDT) and other chlorinated compounds are being implicated in a drastic drop in fertility. Sperm counts in American men, as well as those in men of twenty other countries, have dropped an average of 50% since 1938. Some of the many chemicals we have used in manufacturing and agriculture have a biochemical makeup similar to the female hormone estrogen. And these compounds seem to be wreaking havoc in both women and men, in terms of fertility, normal sexual development and overall health.

While foods rich in animal fat and high on the food chain, such as meat, fish, cheeses, full-fat milk, and butter, usually have the worst levels of contaminants, some foods commonly eaten in a "healthy" vegetarian diet have levels which are cause for serious concern. These include foods eaten a lot as healthy snacks, especially by children, for example, apples, apple juice, raisins, and peanuts and peanut butter. I would buy none of these unless they were available in a certified organic form.

If you cannot readily obtain quality organic produce in your area, it is worth considering growing your own. Then you will be assured both of the way the produce has been grown, with non-harm to the earth, and a wider choice of safe foods you prefer. For people unable or uninterested in doing this, you can check out local food co-operatives, farmers' markets and friendly organic gardeners in your neighborhood. Perhaps a gardening neighbor would be willing to exchange vegetables with you for barter. David Steinman has included an excellent listing of organic food producers in his book, Diet for a Poisoned Planet.

While the costs of organic produce often look steep, we are just beginning to see the hidden costs of chemical agriculture, a price heart-breaking to see.

MANGO SAUCE

To be made when ripe mangoes are available.
Preparation time: 15 minutes   Makes 1 cup
SATTVIC, - Vata, - Pitta, - Kapha   ✿ ✳ 🐚 ❄

Wash, peel and chop:
> **2 large fresh ripe mangos**

Chop them finely, or you can puree them until smooth in the blender. Add:
> **1 Tbsp. fresh lemon juice, or to taste**

Ready to serve, alone or as a sauce in crepes or as a fruit dip.

BOB'S APPLESAUCE

Preparation time: 30 minutes to 1 hour   Makes 3 cups
SATTVIC, 0 Vata, - Pitta, - Kapha   ✿ ✳ 🐚 ❄

Wash, slice and core:
> **8-10 apples, organic preferred**

Put them in a large saucepan with:
> **1 1/2 c. fresh apple juice, organic preferred**
> **1/2 tsp. cinnamon**
> **1/4 tsp. nutmeg**

Simmer until soft and dissolving into the juice. If you like a smooth applesauce, it can be
blended at this point. Serve warm (best for *Vata*) or cool.

BLACK CHERRY SYRUP

Preparation time: 2 minutes   Makes 3/4 cup
RAJASIC, - Vata, - Pitta, + Kapha   ✿ ✳ 🐚 ❄

Stir together:
> **1/4 c. unsweetened black cherry concentrate**
> **1/2 c. maple syrup**

Drizzle over pancakes, waffles and other such things.

*ROTATION DAY 2 DISH

**POLARITY HEALTH BUILDING DISH

Comments: We came up with this as a quick and mineral-packed alternative to the flashy chemi-
cal-laden fruit syrups. It is kid-grade, that is, adults may wish to dilute its sweetness with extra water.

FRESH GINGER PEACH SAUCE

Preparation time: 5 - 10 minutes   Serves: 4
SATTVIC, - Vata, 0 Pitta, 0 Kapha

Finely chop:
>   **4 ripe peaches, organic preferred**

Grate:
>   **1/2 tsp. fresh ginger root, with juice**

Stir these two ingredients together with:
>   **1 Tbsp. maple syrup**

mashing the fruit as you go. Serve fresh.

*ROTATION DAY 2 DISH

A GOOD APPLE RHUBARB SAUCE

Preparation time: 30 - 45 minutes   Serves: 4 - 6
SATTVIC BORDERING ON RAJASIC, 0 Vata, 0 Pitta, 0 Kapha

Put in a heavy saucepan and cook over medium heat until soft:
>   **3 lbs. of apples, sliced, organic preferred**
>   **1 lb. of fresh rhubarb, cut in 1/2.- 1" slices**
>   **1 c. fresh apple juice, organic if possible**

Stir in:
>   **1 Tbsp. of cinnamon**
>   **1/8 tsp. ground cloves**
>   **1/2 c. date sugar or Sucanat (1/5 c. sweetener/cup of cooked sauce)**

Serve, hot or cold.

Comments: The problem with rhubarb is, it is sour and *rajasic* in nature. So it has a long-term heating effect on the gut, and is aggravating to *Kapha* and *Pitta*. If this were a straight rhubarb butter made with rhubarb, water and spices, it would be considered *rajasic* for certain. Because the rhubarb is combined here with *sattvic* apple, the effect of the rhubarb is mediated somewhat.

Variation: For a POLARITY PURIFYING DIET DISH, use honey or fructose as the sweetener.

SATTVIC BORDERING ON RAJASIC, 0 Vata, 0 Pitta, 0 Kapha

HONEY-LEMON SAUCE

Preparation time: 5 minutes or less   Serves: 4
SATTVIC, -Vata, 0 Pitta, + Kapha   ✿ ✳ ⁊ ❄

Stir together:

> **3 Tbsps. ghee**
> **1 Tbsp. raw honey**
> **1 tsp. fresh lemon juice**

Very good over root vegetables like turnips, rutabagas and beets or starchy veggies like sweet potato. This uncooked sauce can be stirred into the hot vegetables just before serving.

Variation: 1 Tbsp. ghee, 2 tsps. raw honey, 1 tsp. fresh lemon juice for a version which is lower in fat and a bit more tart.

SATTVIC, - Vata, 0 Pitta, 0 Kapha

ALMOND GINGER SAUCE

Preparation time: 5 minutes   Serves: 3 - 4
SATTVIC, - Vata, mildly + Pitta, + Kapha   ✿ ✳ ⁊ ❄

Mash together with a fork:

> **1 Tbsp. fresh ginger root, finely grated**
> **1/4 c. raw almond butter**

Add:

> **1 Tbsp. Braggs Liquid Aminos**
> **1/2 tsp. maple syrup**
> **Hot water to desired consistency, 1/4 c. or more**

Mix well. Don't heat. This is very good over sauteed millet (in olive oil with turmeric and veggies).

*For a ROTATION DAY 2 DISH, skip the Braggs Liquid Aminos. If you like, 1/8 tsp. of salt can be used instead.

**POLARITY HEALTH BUILDING DISH

Comment: If you are on an allergy rotation, a good simple "Day 2" meal can be made with Almond Ginger Sauce over Plain Millet, served with steamed spinach.

CREAMED SPINACH SAUCE

Preparation time: 15 minutes   Serves: 2
SATTVIC, 0 Vata, 0 Pitta, - Kapha   ✳ 🐍

Wash well:
> **1 medium zucchini**
> **1/2 bunch fresh spinach**

Chop the zucchini into small cubes and the spinach coarsely. Saute the vegetables over low heat in a skillet with:
> **1 - 2 Tbsps. extra-virgin olive oil**

Blend:
> **1/3 c. toasted pumpkin seeds**
> **1/4 tsp. salt**
> **1 c. water**

Pour the pumpkin seed sauce over the veggies in the skillet and let warm on low for 2 - 3 minutes. Salt to taste. Spoon over: PLAIN MILLET, p. 204.

*ROTATION DAY 2 DISH

CREAMY GREEN SAUCE

Preparation time: 15 minutes max   Makes 1 1/2 cups
SATTVIC, - Vata, mildly + Pitta, 0 Kapha   ❀ 🐍 ❄

Wash and chop:
> **3 c. fresh arugula**

Saute the arugula with:
> **1 tsp. cold-pressed sesame oil**
> **1 small clove garlic, minced**

Stir constantly until done, a minute or two. In a blender, liquify:
> **2 tsps. raw sesame tahini**
> **3/4 tsp. fresh lemon juice**
> **1 c. water**

Add the sautéed arugula and blend until chopped.

Good over STUFFED CABBAGE LEAVES, p. 125.

*ROTATION DAY 4 DISH

TOWARD A SUSTAINABLE AYURVEDA

What do I mean, a "sustainable" Ayurveda? Isn't five thousand years proof enough of its sustainability? Most certainly. And yet I use the word "sustainable" here in a different way, as it is being used now in the sense of "sustainable agriculture", an agriculture which supports and maintains itself locally. In traditional Ayurveda, it is considered advantageous to use plants grown locally in one's area for healing, rather than always relying on imported herbs and foods from other regions. In fact, the original meaning of the word Charak, the Ayurvedic classic, translates as "they who walked all over the world".

Some present day Ayurvedic physicians are beginning to offer the alternative of local herbs, when appropriate. And yet there has been little advocacy to date for the creation of local approaches to Ayurvedic diet. This seems an inevitable and healthy movement to me, as interest in Ayurveda grows. There are many places in the world where mung beans and rice, the staples of the East Indian Ayurvedic diet, will not grow, yet other healing and nourishing plants will. As Dr. Shalmali Joshi has said, "Ayurveda is universal, it can be used by all peoples. Its principles do not change from culture to culture . . .(and yet) the foods and herbs used in an Ayurvedic program can vary from area to area, they need to, that's fine, healthy. Ayurveda is not limited to India and Indian foods. It is a universal medicine."

The challenge for those of us interested in creating a sustainable Ayurveda is to work to clarify the properties of plants in our regions. We need to be honest with ourselves and act as bridges between holders of indigenous and local knowledge, and Ayurvedic knowledge, working with trusted practitioners on all sides whenever possible. In my area here in the southwestern United States, the herb epazote may provide a good substitute for the Indian herb hing. Tepary beans may have many of the properties of mung beans. A lot of this remains to be seen. And yet we will have different resources, depending on whether we live in upstate New York, Hamburg, Kenya, Tokyo, Peru, China, or Australia. This is an exciting area to explore, especially when done with discrimination.

Okay, the following recipe is a compromise. We love mayonnaise with our artichokes and are as yet unwilling to give it up. (Why give it up? Due to its ingredients and the way it sits in the refrigerator, mayonnaise has a heating post-digestive effect on the gut, something we personally do not need.) Combining it with cooling cilantro leaves helps, giving a more immediately cooling effect. However, in the long run, I suspect its post-digestive effect is the same as before (i.e., heating). So I would recommend indulging in this most sporadically, if at all, if you are on a therapeutic regime.

CILANTRO MAYONNAISE

Preparation time: 5 minutes   Serves: 4
RAJASIC-TAMASIC (depending on how long your mayo has   ♣ ✳ ࿔
been adorning your fridge)*

Pulse blend together in a blender:
> **1/2 c. fresh cilantro leaves, finely chopped**
> **1/2 c. mayonnaise**

Serve in a pretty bowl. Tastes good.

* The longer it has been, the more tamasic this would be, sadly.

0 Vata, + Pitta, + Kapha

MAYONNAISE (continued)

Now there is a way out of this. But it means learning how to make your own mayonnaise fresh, as you need it. For those of us so inclined, I include the following rule. It is easiest done in a blender, if you have one. Otherwise you can use an electric beater or a wire whisk in a medium-sized mixing bowl. But be forewarned, it is a lot of whisking.

FRESH MAYONNAISE

Preparation time: 20 minutes of constant attention   Makes 1 cup plus
RAJASIC (due to the egg and mustard), - Vata, + Pitta, + Kapha ♣ ✳ ࿔ ❄ (in moderation)

First off, make sure all your ingredients are *cold*. Beat well, up to four minutes at medium speed with an electric beater:
> **1 egg**

Blend in:
> **1/4 tsp. dry mustard**
> **1/4 - 1/2 tsp. salt**
> **1/2 tsp. fresh lemon juice**

Blend well at medium speed. *Slowly*, a few drops, a teaspoonful or less at a time, begin to add:

> **1 c. cold-pressed olive oil**

After you have put in about half the oil, begin to alternate it with:

> **4 Tbsps. lemon juice**

adding just a few drops of each at a time. Keep beating until the mixture resembles the creamy mayonnaise you know. Voila! Serve fresh, but of course.

Comments: So let's face it. Even made fresh, mayonnaise is not the sort of food an Ayurvedic physician would recommend for daily consumption. (With much thanks to *The Joy of Cooking*, for original recipe beginnings.) Artichokes with fresh lemon and ghee? Fresh dill leaves and ghee?

DIPPING SAUCE

Preparation time: 5 minutes   Makes 1/4 cup
SATTVIC BORDERING ON RAJASIC, - Vata, mildly + Pitta,   ✿ ✴ ⟐ ❄
mildly + Kapha

Mix together in a small bowl:

> **2 Tbsps. Bragg's Liquid Aminos**
> **1 tsp. honey or brown rice syrup**
> **1 Tbsp. grated fresh ginger root**
> **2 Tbsps. water**

Good with nori rolls.

ROTATION DAY 3 Variation: Make as above, omitting the ginger.
SATTVIC BORDERING ON RAJASIC, - Vata, - Pitta, mildly + Kapha

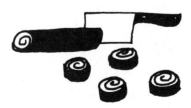

FRESH CILANTRO *SALSA*

Preparation time: 15 minutes   Serves: 2 - 4
MILDLY RAJASIC, 0 Vata, moderately + Pitta, - Kapha   ✳ ⚖

Wash well and chop finely, using all but the stems:
> **2 c. fresh cilantro, loosely packed (one large bunch)**

Wash and finely chop, leaving out the seeds if you are working with any *Pitta* at all:
> **1 large very mild fresh green New Mexico chile, about 1/4 cup chopped**
> **(or 1/2 fresh jalapeno, about 1 tsp. finely chopped)**

Put an inch or so of water in a saucepan with a steamer. Steam for 2 - 5 minutes:
> **2 Tbsps. fresh chopped onion (one small)**
> **1 clove garlic, minced**

Finely chop:
> **1 small ripe tomato**

and add it to the cilantro in a mixing bowl. Stir in the chile, the steamed onion and garlic and:
> **3 Tbsps. fresh lime or lemon juice**
> **Pinch of salt (up to 1/4 tsp.)**

It's ready to serve!

**POLARITY PURIFYING DIET DISH

Comments: This very fresh tasting *salsa*, or hot sauce, is great with tacos, tostadas, beans, and the like. It is important that the cilantro be fresh and aromatic, i.e., have a good strong smell. Cilantro is not something you buy and use three days later; it loses its potency and flavor fast. The cilantro aids digestion and calms excess fire; this *salsa* is much more calming to *Pitta* than most *salsas*. Steaming the onion and garlic makes it easier to digest, especially for *Vata*, and calms some of its pungency.

This is a variation on an old and favorite *salsa* recipe from the mother of Jésus, the friend of my friend Juan Morgan, south of Chihuahua in Mexico. I still remember with great fondness their hospitality to us one Easter many years ago. I watched Jésus's mother prepare this by the gallon for the spring *fiesta*!

FRESH TARTAR SAUCE, UNORTHODOX

Preparation time: 15 minutes   Makes 1/2 cup plus
RAJASIC, - Vata, + Pitta, + Kapha   ✳ ⚖

Mix together:
> **3 Tbsps. FRESH CILANTRO *SALSA***
> **6 Tbsps. FRESH MAYONNAISE, p. 216**

Ready to serve.

QUICK TAHINI GRAVY

Preparation time: 10 minutes

Makes 1 1/4 cups

SATTVIC, - Vata, 0 Pitta, mildly + Kapha

✳ 🍂 ❄

Put in a small saucepan:
> **4 Tbsps. raw sesame tahini**

Pour slowly into the tahini, stirring with a fork until it is a uniform consistency:
> **1 c. plain soy milk**

Heat over low heat until it is as warm and as thick as you like. Stir in:
> **1 Tbsp. Bragg's Liquid Aminos**
> **Dash of paprika (optional)**
> **Pepper to taste (optional)**

Comments: This is good over grains or vegetables, or as a good quick non-dairy sauce for macaroni, for an easy fast lunch.

Variation: For a POLARITY HEALTH BUILDING DISH: heat the soy milk and slowly stir it into the unheated sesame tahini until you have the texture you want.

SATTVIC, - Vata, 0 Pitta, mildly + Kapha

CASHEW CREAM CAULIFLOWER see p. 140

ABOUT SAME-DAY COOKING

I admit, same-day cooking takes practice, and often more time at home. It is not something to which we Americans are accustomed, with all our bottled sauces and demands to be out and about. Let the freshness be a treat, when you have the time. Make the sauces when you can; there's no need to drive yourself wild making four fresh sauces when you've got but a half-hour between work and company arriving. For example, you could make Fresh Cilantro Sauce early in the day, say to put over quick bean tacos for lunch. Then it is ready to serve as a dip with blue corn chips when guests arrive later in the day.

ABOUT PRANAYAMA

There is a bright and quirky herbalist up in the wilds of Oregon named Svevo Brooks who talks about the wonders of "Vitamin O", oxygen. And well he should! Oxygen is one of our most vital elements for life and peace of mind. I often think of "vitamin O" in conjunction with pranayama.

Pranayama *is a simple East Indian process of breathing which increases our* prana *(vital energy) and oxygen to the cells. It also helps alleviate sinus congestion, deepens breathing and helps calm the mind by controlling hyperactivity of* prana *to the brain. This last situation is quite common here in the West, contributing to general anxiety, worry, fear, paranoia, and craziness. (Not that we Westerners are a goofy bunch, mercy no.)*

The process of pranayama *is a simple straight forward one. It is important for nourishing our tissues, and not just with oxygen. Breath is a vital way to build* ojas, *our energy cushion. Clearing the respiratory passages also clears the* srotas *related to* prana *and* vata, *and so in the long term strengthens digestion and absorption as well. To do* pranayama, *get comfortable, in a relaxed position with a straight back. Take a couple of deep breaths in and out first, if you like, to settle yourself down. Blocking first your left nostril with your left middle finger, breathe slowly and gently into your right nostril. Hold for a moment at the top of the exhalation, then close your right nostril with your right middle finger and release your left hand from your left nostril. (It's a lot harder to read than to do, I promise.) Let the air naturally exhale from your left nostril. Pause for a moment, then inhale through the same left nostril again. Pause at the top of the inhalation, then close your left nostril, release your right one, and exhale out through the right nostril gently and completely. Pause at the bottom of the exhalation before you begin the next cycle of breathing. This is one complete cycle of breathing. If you want to try* pranayama *for yourself, it is best to start slowly, with ten cycles, always on an empty stomach. Early morning is a good time to do it, before meditation if you like. As you become accustomed to it,* pranayama *can be done ten to thirty times, once or twice a day as needed. The primary contraindication is that it should not be done on a full stomach. Always do* pranayama *on an empty stomach.*

Snacks

KEY

"–" means calms or helps the given constitution;

"+" means aggravates or increases it;

"0" means neutral effect.

 * ROTATION DIET can be helpful for people with food sensitivities, see p. 323.

**POLARITY DISH refers to recipes supporting Polarity Therapy work, see p. 342

❀ = Spring

✷ = Summer

🐌 = Fall

❄ = Winter

AYURVEDIC TRAIL MIX

Preparation time: 10 minutes
SATTVIC, + Vata, 0 Pitta, 0 Kapha

Makes 4 cups

Mix together in a large bowl with a spoon:

> 1 c. sunflower seeds
> 1 1/2 c. organic raisins
> 1/2 c. dried apricots, coarsely chopped
> 1/2 c. dried apples, coarsely chopped
> 1/2 c. raw walnuts, coarsely chopped
> 1/4 tsp. cinnamon
> 1/8 tsp. ground cardamom

If you can get all organic ingredients, that's great, for both the planet and you. Do the best you can.

**POLARITY HEALTH BUILDING DISH

Comments: To make this more calming for *Vata*, a handful can be soaked in hot water overnight. But it is still not a dish for *Vata* to munch regularly or in anything but small quantities! For that matter, *Kapha* would do well to munch moderately, too.

ROTATION DAY 1 COMBO: dried apples, raisins, raw walnuts or pecans, cinnamon

SATTVIC, + Vata, 0 Pitta, 0 Kapha

**POLARITY HEALTH BUILDING DISH

ROTATION DAY 2 COMBO: dried apricot or peach, dried cherries, blanched almonds, a few raw or toasted pumpkin seeds

SATTVIC, + Vata, 0 Pitta, 0 Kapha

ROTATION DAY 3 COMBO: dried pineapple, currants, raw or toasted sunflower seeds, raw filberts

SATTVIC, + Vata, 0 Pitta, slightly + Kapha

**POLARITY HEALTH BUILDING DISH, with raw sunflower seeds

ROTATION DAY 4 COMBO: dried figs, chopped dates, chopped papaya, raw or toasted cashews, shredded unsweetened coconut

SATTVIC, mildly + Vata, 0 Pitta, 0 Kapha

**POLARITY HEALTH BUILDING DISH, with raw cashews

BLANCHED ALMONDS

Method I.

Preparation time: overnight soak, plus 5 minutes
SATTVIC, - Vata, moderately + Pitta, + Kapha

Put in a small bowl:
1/2 c. raw almonds

Pour over the almonds:
1 c. warm water

Cover and let soak overnight. In the morning, rub the skins off with your fingers. This method is easiest to digest and most calming for *Vata*.

**POLARITY PURIFYING DIET DISH

Method II.

Preparation time: 15 - 20 minutes
SATTVIC, - Vata, moderately + Pitta, + Kapha

Put in a small bowl:
1/2 c. raw almonds

Pour over the almonds:
1 c. boiling water

Let soak for about 10 minutes or more. Drain off the water and rub off the skins with your fingers. The high heat alters the oil in the almonds, making it a little less digestible.

Method III.

Buy blanched almonds at the store.

SATTVIC (rare), RAJASIC, OR TAMASIC, depending on how long they've sat on the shelf. Generally the least fresh of the methods.

- Vata, moderately + Pitta, + Kapha

*ROTATION DAY 2 DISH, for all 3 methods

ROASTED ALMONDS

Preparation time: 5-10 minutes

Makes 1 cup

SATTVIC, - Vata, + Pitta, + Kapha

Heat a heavy skillet on low heat for a minute or two. Pour in:

1 c. raw blanched almonds

Roast uncovered for 5-6 minutes, stirring occasionally, until the nuts begin to have a lovely aroma or "pop" or you see small places of golden brown appear on them. Cool and serve. Nice in salads or on their own.

*ROTATION DAY 2 DISH

ROASTED SUNFLOWER SEEDS

Preparation time: 10 minutes

Makes 1 cup

SATTVIC, - Vata, 0 Pitta, 0 Kapha

Heat a heavy skillet on low heat for a minute or so. Add:

1 cup raw sunflower seeds

Roast them uncovered for 5 - 10 minutes, stirring occasionally. When they begin to turn golden brown in places, it is time to take them off the heat and let them cool. Nice touch in salads or as a topping on dishes. Also a good snack in its own right.

*ROTATION DAY 3 DISH

ROASTED PUMPKIN SEEDS

Preparation time: 10 minutes or less

Makes 1 cup

SATTVIC, - Vata, 0 Pitta, 0 Kapha

Heat a heavy skillet on low heat for a couple of minutes. Pour in:

1 cup raw pumpkin seeds

Roast them uncovered for about 10 minutes, stirring occasionally. When the seeds begin to pop, remove them from the heat. Let cool.

*ROTATION DAY 2 DISH

ROASTED NUTS

Follow the rule for ROASTED ALMONDS, with cashews, walnuts, filberts, pecans, or macadamias. Roast only so long as it takes the nuts to begin to smell lovely, aromatic, and be slightly browned.

SATTVIC, - Vata, + Pitta, + Kapha

STUFFED CELERY STICKS

Preparation time: 10 minutes   Makes 24 pieces
SATTVIC WITH SOME RAJAS, 0 Vata, 0 Pitta, 0 Kapha (in moderation)

Wash:

8 organic celery stalks

Slice off the tops and bottoms. (These are good used for soup stock later, if you like.) Cut the celery into four-inch pieces. The celery can be stuffed with:

Creamy Dill Dip, p. 228
or
Almond Ginger Sauce, p. 213
or
raw almond butter

Arrange on a colorful plate and serve.

**POLARITY HEALTH BUILDING DISH

ABOUT CHECKING IN

It is remarkable the kind of information and perspectives you can get sitting quietly, listening. There is a store of information inside you that you can find no where else, as all the great traditions have stated, repeatedly. This quiet place inside is a gateway to our higher selves and beyond. And an avenue to the unexpected.

It was shocking to me, during the Gulf War, how many people were glued to their TVs. There was a deep and genuine urge to find out what was really going on. And yet as I watched for a few minutes, I realized the television program wasn't telling me what was going on. My own mind and heart were better places to consult, to know the truth.

About Checking In (continued)

Often in our urge to understand, we turn to the TV or radio. But they are not capable of providing the kind of insight we hold within us. For that we must go inside. And endure the boredom, the silence, the nothingness until some truth arises. And it will.

We are right to want to know what is going on in our world. We just often look in the wrong places to discover this.

ANGELA'S GUACAMOLE

Preparation time: 10 minutes

RAJASIC (avocados), - Vata, moderately + Pitta, + Kapha

Makes about 1 cup

❀ ✳ ☙ ❄

In a medium-sized mixing bowl, mash with a fork:

2 large ripe avocados

Stir in:

Juice of 1/2 organic lemon
2 Tbsps. fresh cilantro leaves, coarsely chopped
4 or 5 small cherry tomatoes, finely chopped
1 clove garlic, minced (optional)
Salt to taste

Serve with chips, posole, tacos, or whatever you desire.

**POLARITY HEALTH BUILDING DISH

Variation: For a strict ROTATION DAY 1 DISH, use 2 avocados, 4-5 cherry tomatoes, 1/8 tsp. red chili pepper or 1/4 tsp. finely chopped jalapeno (optional), and 1/4 tsp. salt.

RAJASIC, 0 Vata, + Pitta, moderately + Kapha

ABOUT AVOCADOS

Avocados are considered useful for healing, despite their rajasic *quality, so long as your* agni *is good. If your digestive fire is strong, avocados are helpful, nutritive, building, moistening. If your digestive fire is weak, it can be hard to handle heavy avocado well. Avocado is a rich source of potassium and vitamin E.*

CREAMY DILL DIP

Preparation time: 5 minutes

Makes 1/2 cup

MILDLY RAJASIC, - Vata, 0 Pitta, slightly + Kapha

✳ ੭🍵

Make up one recipe:

Creamy Non-Dairy "Ricotta", p. 164

In a small mixing bowl, spoon out 1/2 cup of the creamy non-dairy ricotta, then stir in:

3 Tbsps. fresh lemon juice
1 Tbsp. extra-virgin olive oil
1 Tbsp. dried dill (or 2 tsp. finely chopped fresh)

Serve with fresh raw vegetables, such as celery, sliced cucumber or carrot wedges. (The rest of the creamy non-dairy "ricotta" can be saved to make more dip as it runs out, or to make the following Creamy Italian Dip.)

CREAMY ITALIAN DIP

Preparation time: 10 minutes

Makes 1/2 cup

RAJASIC, - Vata, + Pitta, slightly + Kapha

✳ ੭🍵

In a small saucepan with a steamer and a cup of water, steam:

1 clove of unpeeled garlic

Make up one recipe:

Creamy Non-Dairy Ricotta, p. 164

In a small mixing bowl, measure out 1/2 cup of the creamy non-dairy ricotta, then stir into it:

2 Tbsps. fresh lemon juice
1 Tbsp. extra-virgin olive oil
the steamed garlic, minced
1/8 tsp. crushed fennel seeds
1 tsp. dried oregano
1 tsp. finely chopped fresh basil, purple is pretty

Good with crackers. (The rest of the creamy non-dairy "ricotta" can be used to make up the quick Creamy Dill Dip, or saved as a base to make more dip as it is needed.)

QUICK BEAN DIP

Preparation time: 10 minutes   Makes 2 cups
SATTVIC*   ✿ ✳ ❄

In a small covered saucepan with a steamer, steam for about 5 minutes:
>   1 Tbsp. red onion, finely chopped
>   1 small clove garlic, minced

Mash in a bowl, reserving any cooking liquid:
>   2 c. well-cooked pinto beans

Stir in the onion and garlic and:
>   1 tsp. ground coriander
>   1/2 tsp. salt
>   1/2 tsp. ground cumin
>   1 Tbsp. cold-pressed sunflower oil
>   1 Tbsp. cooking liquid or water, or to desired consistency

Serve with fresh corn chips, hot tortillas for dipping, and/or FRESH CILANTRO *SALSA*, p. 218.

*Alone: + Vata, - Pitta, - Kapha

**POLARITY HEALTH BUILDING DISH

*With fresh corn chips: + Vata, + Pitta, - Kapha

*With fresh hot whole wheat tortillas: 0 Vata, - Pitta, + Kapha

*With fresh hot corn tortillas: + Vata, + Pitta, - Kapha

Variation: For a strict ROTATION DAY 3 DISH, skip the garlic and onion and add: 1/8-1/4 tsp. freshly ground pepper and 1/4 tsp. tamarind extract (optional, gives the dip a bit of zip).

SATTVIC, + Vata, - Pitta, - Kapha

LEBANESE CHICKPEAS

Preparation time: 10 minutes with precooked beans, 1 1/2 hours without   Serves: 4
RAJASIC, + Vata, - Pitta, - Kapha   ✿ ✳ 🐚 ❄

Drain:
>   **2 c. cooked garbanzos, reserving any cooking liquid**

Mash the beans with:
>   **1 - 2 Tbsps. extra-virgin olive oil**
>   **1 clove garlic, minced (omit or use 1 small clove for *Pitta*)**
>   **3 Tbsp. fresh mint, chopped**
>   **1/2 tsp. salt or less**
>   **Juice of 1/2 lemon**
>   **Cooking liquid to taste**

A potato masher works well for this, a sturdy fork will also work fine. Garnish with:
>   **Borage flowers (optional)**

Served hot, LEBANESE CHICKPEAS are good with rice and veggies. Cool, they make a nice dip with crackers. If you happen to have blue borage growing in your garden, it makes a lovely and edible garnish with the dip.

**POLARITY HEALTH BUILDING DISH

Variation: HUMMUS

Skip the mint and instead add:
>   **1 - 2 Tbsps. of raw sesame tahini**

Serve with crackers or bread.

RAJASIC, + Vata (but more calming than Lebanese Chickpeas), 0 Pitta, 0 Kapha

**POLARITY HEALTH BUILDING DISH

Note: Sesame is often used in Ayurveda to calm the *Vata*-aggravating qualities of a food, especially beans. A *Vata* preparing this recipe is likely to benefit from the maximum amount of tahini; a *Kapha* may want to use the minimum.

Variation II:

Skip the mint, add the tahini and substitute 1 - 2 Tbsps. CREAMY GARLIC SALAD DRESS-ING, P. 86 for the lemon juice. Tangy.

RAJASIC, moderately + Vata, 0 Pitta, 0 Kapha

**POLARITY HEALTH BUILDING DISH

For a good hors d'oeuvre, try **PESTO PIZZA, p. 136**, cut into small wedges.

TOASTED FENNEL SEEDS

Preparation time: 5 minutes

SATTVIC, - Vata, 0 Pitta, 0 Kapha

Makes 1/3 cup

✿ ✳ ⛄ ❄

Warm a heavy skillet over low heat for a minute or two. Put into it:

1/3 c. whole fennel seeds
1/16 - 1/8 tsp. rock salt (optional)

Stir occasionally as they toast, for about five minutes. Serve after meals as a digestive aid, each guest serving themselves from a pinch to a teaspoon at a time.

Comment: This is a traditional Ayurvedic after-meal practice. Toasting the fennel helps it enhance *agni*. The fennel itself is good for calming and strengthening the stomach's functions, and the rock salt enhances *agni*.

TAHINI ROLL-UPS

Preparation time: 5 minutes

SATTVIC, - Vata, 0 Pitta, + Kapha

Makes as many as you like

✿ ✳ ⛄ ❄

In a medium skillet, warm:

1/4 tsp. ghee or sesame oil

Put into the skillet:

1 whole wheat tortilla or *chappati* (see Rebekah's Tortillas, p. 172)

Warm it on one side, then flip it over for a minute or less. Remove it while it is still soft, not crispy. Put it on a plate or cutting board and spread with:

Raw sesame tahini

then:

Raw honey or fruit-sweetened jam

Roll it up. Ready to eat.

**POLARITY HEALTH BUILDING DIET

Variations: ALMOND BUTTER ROLL-UPS: Use raw or roasted almond butter instead of tahini.

SATTVIC, - Vata, 0 Pitta, + Kapha

ROTATION DAY 1 ROLL-UPS: Use walnut or pecan butter with apple or pear butter.

SATTVIC, 0 Vata, 0 Pitta, + Kapha

SWEET BARLEY BARS

Preparation time: 35 minutes   Makes 12 bars
SATTVIC, mildly + Vata, - Pitta, - Kapha   ✿ 🐌 ❄

Preheat oven to 425° F.

Mix together:
> 1/2 c. barley flour
> 1/2 c. rolled barley (available in bulk at some natural groceries) or rolled oats
> 1 tsp. baking powder
> 1/8 tsp. salt
> 3/4 tsp. cinnamon

Work into the dry ingredients with your hands:
> 2 Tbsps. ghee or butter

until it is pea-sized or smaller.

Then mix into the dry ingredients:
> 1/2 c. organic raisins

Mix together:
> 1 beaten egg (or Egg Replacer)*
> 1/4 c. apple concentrate (or 2 Tbsps. unsweetened apple butter and 2 Tbsps. organic apple juice)

Add the wet ingredients to the dry ones. Spoon the dough into a lightly oiled 8" square baking pan and press it into place with a fork. Bake for 20 minutes, or until a toothpick inserted into the middle comes out cleanly.

*ROTATION DAY 1 DISH. If you are using this as a rotation dish, use the Egg Replacer rather than the egg. Egg Replacer is potato-based (Day 1) and has a small amount of tapioca in it (Day 2). If you are following a very strict rotation diet and are sensitive to tapioca (rare, but possible), this would not be an appropriate recipe for you.

Comments: This is an easy snack to make, especially designed for *Kapha*. If you are working with more *Vata* or *Pitta*, more sweetener could be added if you like, or they can be served with fruit-sweetened jam and ghee. It is a simple home-made equivalent of granola bars, less sweet than the commercial varieties.

AN AYURVEDIC APPROACH TO CANDIDA

Candida, as many readers know, is a fungal infection which can become chronic in the right host. Symptoms are wide-ranging and often include fatigue, headaches, flatulence (especially toward the end of the day), depression, multiple food sensitivities, skin rashes, and/or immune weakness of varying kinds. Often a mild case will first be noticed as a "hangover"-like feeling the day after having even modest amounts of alcohol or sweets. An established case may also be indicated by a patchy irritated tongue. The Western dietary approach to Candidiasis has been a high-protein, high-vegetable, low-carbohydrate diet. It usually includes plenty of flesh foods and no sugar, and is often coupled with herbal or drug preparations which are anti-fungal in nature. Candida thrives on bread, cheese, sugar, and alcohol (or the conditions these foods create in our guts), so these items are avoided.

The Ayurvedic approach to Candida which I have used in the last several years is quite different in certain respects. It is entirely vegetarian, and there is no restriction on complex carbohydrates. I am grateful to Dr. Sunil Joshi for his education on this. This approach is a real boon for vegetarians struggling with Candidiasis, who are often told the only way to cure themselves is with generous amounts of animal flesh.

This Ayurvedic method, as always, addresses the underlying imbalances which lead to the development of a chronic fungal infection. These can vary from person to person, and yet are usually centered in the digestion. Imbalances can include low agni *(digestive fire), overeating (which dampens and inhibits* agni*), and excess fermented foods and leftovers in the diet. Imbalances related to past medical practices, such as the use of hormones or antibiotics, are also considered. Often the colon needs cleansing, and sometimes other gastro-intestinal organs as well. The Ayurvedic physician experienced in working with this condition will recommend herbs specific to their patient's body. The focus is on re-establishing a healthy balance within the body, so that it can begin to eliminate the illness itself. As in the Western approach, patients with Candidiasis get more and more adept as identifying triggering foods and conditions, and so have the choice to avoid them, so as to speed their own recovery.*

The yeast-free Ayurvedic diet generally used with Candida is no less strict than the Western one; it simply includes different foods and works to strengthen the digestive tract more specifically. Both systems emphasize the use of fresh foods in healing this condition. The fresher your food, the better. The Ayurvedic approach can be especially helpful for people with a repeated or long-standing history of Candida.

An Ayurvedic Approach to Candida (continued)

Almost all the foods in this book are suitable for a yeast-free Candida diet, unless stated otherwise. One exception: I would beware of any concentrated sweets when freeing oneself of Candida, and so would avoid most dessert recipes even in this cookbook.

The limitations on a Candida-free diet can be exasperating, no matter what type you are doing. When your "halo" starts feeling too tight for comfort, check in with yourself. Give yourself some slack, especially in the non-edible realms. For example, maybe you've had little free time to yourself, or not enough time with friends. Maybe you're really missing a walk in the woods or some other fresh-aired place. Adjust your overall life for greater comfort, as much as you can. You've probably discovered that sugar, sweets, alcohol, and fermented foods do nothing to help you in the long run. Let yourself get savvy about what foods do feel good, both as you're eating them, and a day later.

AYURVEDIC FOODS TO HEAL A CANDIDA CONDITION

These will vary from person to person. Yet they will usually include the following:
To choose:

> Any *sattvic* foods:
> Fresh fruit in moderation, raw and cooked
> Fresh vegetables, raw and cooked
> Freshly prepared legumes and grains
> Nuts and seeds in moderation, except peanuts
> Usually, fresh boiled raw milk and fresh buttermilk
> Ghee and cold-pressed oils
> Herbs as specifically recommended by an Ayurvedic practitioner
> plus some *rajasic* foods:
> Fresh lemon juice, in moderation
> Occasionally, avocado, egg, garbanzo and kidney beans, garlic, onion.

To be avoided:

> All fermented and yeasted foods, including sourdough and yeasted bread, cheese, yogurt, vinegar, pickles, ketchup, alcohol.
> Sugar
> Concentrated sweets
> White flour (refined grain) products
> Mushrooms
> Meat
> Desserts
> Peanuts
> Leftovers
> Frozen, fried, microwaved foods

An Ayurvedic Approach to Candida (continued)

***** *Nearly all the recipes included in this cookbook are suited for a Candida elimination program,* except the desserts which are best skipped. *Any other recipe which is not recommended for this program is clearly stated at the end of the recipe.*

Note: I have found the Western food preparation, grapefruit seed extract, which is anti-fungal, to be a supportive adjunct to this general program for Candida.

Note: Dr. Shalmali Joshi, an Ayurvedic physician specializing in gynecological issues and Pancha Karma in India, recommends one teaspoon of triphala *per one cup boiled water as a vaginal douche for Candida and other yeast infections.*

ABOUT COOKING WITH AGE

We move through the doshas, Kapha *to* Pitta *to* Vata, *as we age. As young children we have more moisture and solidity;* Kapha *predominates at this time. As we mature sexually we enter our time of* Pitta, *with more fire and ambition (and often less patience!). As we move into middle and older age* Vata *becomes more prominent, we use our minds more, and often our bodies less. It is easier for our tissues to dry out and our senses to become less acute.*

Ayurveda has specific rejuvenative therapies to work with aging, rasayanas. *Here I simply want to introduce the idea that our needs change over time. We need to take measures to work with the excess mucus that can arise in childhood, before it becomes colds and bronchitis. One way to do this is to help our children's digestive fire, by not serving them an excess of cheese, frozen foods and icy drinks. We are likely to need to calm fire more between the ages of 15 and 45, following at times a more* Pitta *diet, even if our constitutions are another type. This could translate as easing up on the salsa or eggs or alcohol in our lives.* Vata *needs to be soothed most in older age, again, regardless of our personal constitutions. For the older person, even with good teeth, this means more foods with moisture, more lubrication, more soups and stews and easy to digest foods, and less crispy crunchy icy foods.*

Desserts

KEY

"–" means calms or helps the given constitution;

"+" means aggravates or increases it;

"0" means neutral effect.

 * ROTATION DIET can be helpful for people with food
   sensitivities, see p. 323.

**POLARITY DISH refers to recipes supporting Polarity Therapy
  work, see p. 342.

✿ = Spring

✳ = Summer

࿇ = Fall

❄ = Winter

PEAR MOUSSE

Preparation time: 15 minutes to make, 1 hour to cool
SATTVIC, mildly + Vata, - Pitta, - Kapha

Serves: 4 - 5
✿ ✳ ༄

Warm over medium heat in an uncovered saucepan:

2 c. fresh apple or pear juice

As the juice heats, wash, core and dice:

3 c. fresh pear (about 3 medium to large pears)

Add them to the juice with:

1 1/2 tsp. cinnamon
3 dried hibiscus flowers (optional)

Bring to a boil, then simmer uncovered over medium heat for ten minutes. Pour the mixture into a blender and blend on low heat until smooth. Add:

2 tsps. Universal pectin
3 tsps. liquid calcium solution (comes with Universal pectin)

and blend again on low heat for 3 minutes, until very creamy. Blend in:

1 1/2 Tbsp. Sucanat or fructose or apple concentrate

Pour into parfait glasses to chill.

*ROTATION DAY 1 DISH with Sucanat or apple concentrate

**POLARITY PURIFYING DIET DISH with fructose

Comments: The hibiscus flowers add extra vitamin C and a touch of astringency. Astringent taste is especially helpful for *Pitta* and *Kapha*. While hibiscus sounds exotic, it is commonly found in herb stores or the bulk herb section of natural food groceries. Or if you have one growing in your home which is unsprayed with chemicals, its flowers can be used. A nice dessert for kids and adults alike.

Variation: This can be made up as a parfait. To do this, warm an extra 1/4 c. of juice. When it is warm, pour it into a small bowl with 1/2 c. raisins, and let them soak while you make up the pear mousse. Chill the mousse for 10 - 15 minutes in the blender, then spoon it into parfait glasses in layers, alternating it with the soaked raisins and 1/4 c. chopped walnuts.

SATTVIC, mildly + Vata, 0 Pitta, 0 Kapha

APPLE MOUSSE

Preparation time: 20 minutes, plus 30 minutes to chill   Serves: 4
SATTVIC BORDERING ON RAJASIC*

✸ 🍵 ❄

Wash and dice finely:

4 apples (about 3 c.)

Put them in a saucepan with:

1/2 c. fresh organic apple juice
1/2 c. Sucanat or apple concentrate
2 tsps. cinnamon

Bring to a boil, then reduce heat to simmer. Let the fruit cook uncovered for about 5 minutes. Once it is cooked, spoon half of the fruit mixture into a blender. Puree. Leave the rest in the saucepan to cool. Add to the puree in the blender:

1 tsp. Pomona's Universal pectin
1 Tbsp. liquid calcium solution (included with pectin)

Blend on high speed for a full minute. Stir the puree into the unblended fruit in the saucepan with:

1 c. fresh plain cow's yogurt or soy yogurt

Spoon into four individual serving glasses, cover and chill until set.

* *0 Vata, mildly + Pitta, + Kapha* with fresh cow's yogurt

* *mildly + Vata, 0 Pitta, mildly + Kapha* with freshly made soy yogurt

*This can be used as a DAY 1 ROTATION DISH. If so, use cow's yogurt here.

Comments: Some dishes are more *sattvic* or *rajasic* than others. This is one of these recipes where the categories could be argued. Sucanat is *rajasic* in effect. So is yogurt, especially if it has sat for a while, as most commercial yogurts have. Bottled juices are *rajasic* in their effect, fresh is *sattvic*. So these ingredients are heating to the mind. If *sattva* is important to you, fresh yogurt and fruit juices are best in this dish and honey or maple syrup can be used as the sweetener, added with the yogurt at the end.

HONEY TAPIOCA

Preparation time: 30 minutes, plus time to cool
SATTVIC*

Serves: 4

❀ ✳ ☙ ❄

Bring to a boil in a medium saucepan or a double boiler:
> **2 1/2 c. raw fresh milk or soy milk**
> **1/2 tsp. finely chopped raw fresh ginger root, peeled**

Once you have brought the milk to a boil, let it boil for 20 seconds and then stir in:
> **5 Tbsps. granulated (quick) tapioca**
> **1/4 tsp. salt**

Reduce heat to very low and cook for ten minutes, stirring only if the mixture begins to stick. Beat:
> **2 egg yolks**

Stir them well into the cooking tapioca and simmer another four minutes. Beat until stiff:
> **2 egg whites**

Fold these into the tapioca, then stir in:
> **1 tsp. vanilla extract**
> **1/4 tsp. cinnamon**
> **1/4 tsp. cardamom**

Remove from heat and let cool for a few minutes. Stir in:
> **1/3 c. raw honey**

Mix well. Cover and cool. Serve warm or cool. This tapioca is soupy.

* - *Vata, - Pitta, mildly + Kapha with cow's milk*

* 0 *Vata, - Pitta, - Kapha with soy milk*

FRUIT TAPIOCA

Preparation time: 10 minutes, with a 2 hour soak in between   Serves: 4
SATTVIC, mildly + Vata, - Pitta, - Kapha

Combine in a saucepan:
> **1/2 c. dried organic apricots, chopped**
> **2 1/2 c. fresh organic apple juice**
> **1/3 c. small pearl tapioca**
> **1/8 tsp. salt**
> **1 tsp. cinnamon**

Cover and let sit for two hours or more. (I'll mix it together in the morning, let it sit all day in the fridge, then finish fixing it when I get home that night.) Bring to a boil over medium heat. Reduce heat to low and cook five minutes more, stirring fairly constantly. Stir in:
> **2 Tbsps. maple syrup (optional)**

Let cool (while you eat your meal) and serve.

**POLARITY HEALTH BUILDING DISH

Comments: This is a dish pretty soothing to the digestion. If you want to make it more calming for *Vata*, substitute fruit-sweetened apricot nectar for the apple juice, and serve it cool, not cold.

RAJASIC (bottled juice), - Vata, - Pitta, 0 Kapha

**POLARITY HEALTH BUILDING DISH

Variation:

ALMOND-NECTARINE TAPIOCA

Preparation time: 2 1/2 hours, plus time to cool   Serves: 4
SATTVIC, - Vata, 0 Pitta, mildly - Kapha

Bring to a boil:
> **2 1/2 c. water**

Pour it over:
> **3 Tbsps. raw almonds**

Let this sit for 15 minutes or more. Then rub the peels off the almonds and blend them together with the water in a blender at high speed until you have a smooth almond milk. If necessary, pour through a wire mesh strainer to remove any rough pieces. Pour this almond milk into a medium saucepan and add:
> **1/3 c. small pearl tapioca**
> **1/8 tsp. salt**
> **1/2 tsp. ground cardamom**

Cover and let sit as above, for 2 hours or more. Bring to a boil over medium heat after the soak, then immediately reduce heat to very low. Cook five minutes more, stirring constantly. Remove from heat and stir in:

1/4 c. maple syrup
2 c. fresh nectarines, coarsely chopped

Cool and serve.

*ROTATION DAY 2 DISH

FRESH PINEAPPLE SHORTSTOP

Preparation time: 15 minutes, plus 1/2 hour to chill   Serves: 4 - 6
SATTVIC, 0 Vata, - Pitta, 0 Kapha   ✳

Wash and prepare:
2 c. fresh sweet pineapple, finely chopped

Slice off the prickly outer peel and the hard inner core. Chop the fruit finely, scooping both the fruit and juice into a mixing bowl when done.

In a small saucepan, mix:
2 c. fresh organic apple juice
4 tsps. agar agar

Bring them to a boil. Reduce heat to low and simmer for five minutes. Stir in:
1/2 c. brown rice syrup
1/2 tsp. fresh ginger root, very finely chopped

Add the pineapple and its juice. Stir well. Spoon into 4 large or 6 smaller individual parfait glasses. Chill.

**POLARITY HEALTH BUILDING DISH

Variation: This can be used as a DAY 3 ROTATION DISH. To do so, substitute fresh unsweetened pineapple juice for the apple juice, and omit the ginger.

SATTVIC, - Vata, - Pitta, moderately + Kapha

**POLARITY HEALTH BUILDING DISH

Comments: Agar agar, derived from seaweed, is soothing and mildly laxative to the colon, like pectin. Its cousin alginate is useful for pulling heavy metals from the body; the one-celled green algae *Chlorella* is reputed to be especially good for this purpose.

DORIE'S TURKISH DELIGHT

Preparation time: 15 minutes, plus 1/2 hour to set   Makes: 36 1 1/2" squares

RAJASIC, - Vata, - Pitta, - Kapha

✿ ✳ ☙ ❄

Chop:

2 Tbsps. raw hazelnuts or blanched almonds

Put them in a small skillet over low heat to toast, about five minutes. While they are toasting, bring to a boil in a small saucepan:

2 c. apricot nectar, fruit sweetened

Chop:

5 or 6 unsulphured dried apricots

When the apricot nectar has just come to a boil, pour it in a blender with the apricots and:

1/2 tsp. almond flavor*

Blend until smooth. Add:

1 Tbsp. Pomona's Universal Pectin
1 Tbsp. liquid calcium solution (comes with pectin)

Blend for at least one minute or until thoroughly mixed. Pour into an ungreased 9"x 9" square pan and arrange the toasted nuts on top in any pattern you like. Refrigerate until firm.

Comments: This recipe from Dolores Chiappone makes a nice light dessert which is a fun one for kids to help prepare and serve.

*Almond flavor is now available in non-alcoholic forms as oil of almond preserved in other oils, like soy and vitamin E. Health food or natural groceries are good places to locate it.

Variation: COCONUT DELIGHT

Follow the same directions as above, using **2 c. coconut nectar** (Knudsen's works well), **1/4 c. shredded unsweetened coconut** and **1 Tbsp. fructose or Sucanat (optional)** in place of the fruit nectar and fruit. Nuts can be skipped. Very good for *Pitta*.

RAJASIC, - Vata, - Pitta, 0 Kapha

**POLARITY HEALTH BUILDING DISH

Variation: PAPAYA DELIGHT

Following the same directions as above, bring to a boil:

2 c. papaya nectar, fruit sweetened.

Chop:

2 (4") pieces of dried unsweetened papaya.

Reserve 1/4 cup of the chopped papaya for garnish for later. Blend the rest with the hot papaya nectar. Then blend the papaya for at least one minute with:

1 Tbsp. liquid calcium solution (comes with the Universal Pectin)
3 tsps. Universal Pectin powder.

Pour into an ungreased 9"x 9" pan. Garnish with:

1/4 c. raisins and the rest of the chopped papaya. (If it's near Halloween, pumpkin designs are fun.)

RAJASIC, - Vata, mildly + Pitta, mildly + Kapha

POLARITY HEALTH BUILDING DISH

This next quartet of fresh fruit desserts comes from Liz Halford, and I think it is best if she simply speaks for herself: "It goes without saying the fruit should be in perfect condition and ripe. I find texture and smell the best guide. So touch and sniff before you buy. In selecting these dishes color has played a major role, for example, the pinky gold of cantaloupe contrasted against the dark red raspberries (in CANTALOUPE WITH FRESH RASPBERRIES). Or the green and pinky gold stripes of alternate slices of honeydew and cantaloupe contrasted against the deeper gold of pureed mango (in MELONS WITH MANGO SAUCE). So if you have to substitute a fruit, try and find one that is an exciting rather than drab addition to the color scheme!" (Ms. Halford paints as well as cooks, as might be evident here.)

COOL NECTARINES

Preparation time: 20 minutes, plus an hour to cool   Serves: 6
SATTVIC, - Vata, - Pitta, 0 Kapha

In a wide deep pan, heat until simmering:

1/2 c. apple juice concentrate
Juice and zest (finely grated peel) of 1 orange, organic
1/2 c. water

Cut in half, removing their pits:

6 nectarines, organic preferred

Add the nectarines to the liquid, simmering them until they are soft but not mushy, about 10 - 15 minutes. Remove from heat and cool. Just before serving, sprinkle with:

1 Tbsp. orange flower water*
1/4 c. pecans, chopped

*Orange flower water can be obtained at specialty baking shops.

CANTALOUPE WITH FRESH RASPBERRIES

Preparation time: 15 minutes   Serves: 6
SATTVIC, - Vata, - Pitta, mildly + Kapha   ✳

Peel with a knife:
> **1 whole cool ripe cantaloupe**

Cut in half and remove seeds. Cut each half into six slices. Place the 12 slices upright onto:
> **1 oblong serving dish**

arranging them in a straight line. Sprinkle across the center of each slice, also in a straight line:
> **3 c. fresh ripe raspberries (2 baskets)**

Serve at once.

Comment: As Liz, the originator of this recipe, says, "If you've never heard of this combination, shame on you. It's very simple and elegant." And light on the tum.

MELONS WITH MANGO SAUCE

Preparation time: 15 minutes   Serves: 6
SATTVIC, - Vata, - Pitta, mildly + Kapha

Peel and cut into six slices each:
> **1/2 cool ripe cantaloupe**
> **1/2 cool ripe honeydew**

Place the 12 slices upright in a straight line along the serving dish.

Peel:
> **2 very ripe mangoes, cooled**

Cut the flesh off the mangos to the pit. Puree the mango in a food processor or blender until smooth. Pour in a continuous stream across the center of the melon slices in a straight line. Serve at once. "A solution to those mangoes that have lingered too long in the fruit bowl."

SPICED PEARS

Preparation time: 30 minutes

Serves: 6

SATTVIC, mildly + Vata, - Pitta, - Kapha

❀ ✳ ℰ❧ ❄

Chop up, removing the seeds as you do:

1 small lemon, organic

Puree in a blender. Add:

1/2 c. apple juice concentrate
1/2 c. water
1 tsp. ground cardamom
1 tsp. ground coriander

Blend just enough to mix. Heat the mixture in a wide shallow saucepan. While it is heating, peel:

6 ripe pears

and cut them in half. Remove the cores and place them face down in the saucepan. Cover the pan. Simmer until soft, 10 - 15 minutes. Remove the pears and put them in six individual serving bowls. Continue to cook the mixture down for another 10 minutes or so, until it is thick and syrupy. Add:

1 tsp. vanilla extract (optional)

Remove from heat. Pour the sauce over the pear halves and sprinkle with:

Fresh toasted slivered blanched almonds

Can be served at once or cooled.

HALVAH BALLS

Preparation time: 10 minutes, plus time to cool

Makes 18 - 24 balls

SATTVIC, - Vata, + Pitta, + Kapha

ℰ❧ ❄

Toast in an iron skillet over low heat:

4 Tbsps. whole sesame seeds

In a bowl, mix together with a fork:

4 Tbsps. raw sesame tahini
2 Tbsps. raw honey
1 tsp. vanilla extract

When the sesame seeds just begin to brown and smell delectable, take them off the heat and pour them in the blender. Grind. Stir the ground sesame seeds into the rest of the ingredients and form into balls about 1-inch in diameter. Cool and serve.

STUFFED FRUITS

Preparation time: 5 - 15 minutes, depending on how many you make
SATTVIC, + Vata, 0 Pitta, 0 Kapha　

Pare off the stems and slit down the middle lengthwise:
dried Calmyrna or Black Mission figs

Stuff with:
whole raw walnuts or cashews*

Arrange on a plate and serve.

* For a ROTATION DAY 4 DISH, use cashews.

Variation: For a dessert calming to *Vata*, use dried dates and stuff them with cashews.

RAJASIC, - Vata, 0 Pitta, + Kapha

*ROTATION DAY 4 DISH

**POLARITY HEALTH BUILDING DISH

CRUNCHY COCONUT COOKIES

Preparation time: 30 - 45 minutes　　　　　　　Makes 15 (3") cookies
MODERATELY RAJASIC (eggs, dates), - Vata, - Pitta, 0 Kapha

Preheat oven to 300° F. Beat until they peak:
2 egg whites

Fold gently into the beaten egg whites:
1/2 c. date sugar or fructose

Then fold in:
1 chopped date (optional)
1/4 c. dried unsweetened papaya, finely chopped
1 tsp. vanilla extract*
1/3 c. toasted cashews (optional)
2 c. unsweetened flaked coconut

Spoon onto a non-stick or well-oiled cookie sheet* and garnish with:
toasted sesame seeds

Bake for 12 - 15 minutes.

Comment: When these start smelling good, it is time to take them out. Because they are so light, they go from "done" to "burnt" very quickly - be forewarned!

*ROTATION DAY 4 DISH. For the allergy rotation program (see p. 323), use sesame oil to oil the cookie sheet and vanilla bean rather than vanilla extract. One of the nice things about this cookie is that while it tastes very good, it has no added fats or flour in it.

ABOUT CLAIMING POWER

Appropriate anger can lead to effective skillful action. Suppressed unarticulated anger can create many problems, among them binging and weight issues. I put this box next to **Crunchy Coconut Cookies** *because, in my twenty years of nutrition practice, I saw a lot of women crunching their way through situations of unacknowledged power and rightful anger.*

As my partner Gordon Bruen has said, "Our bodies are our friends, telling us to speak out, to act! The movement of our times is often toward disempowerment and despair. Taking responsibility for what we eat is a very real first step toward taking care of our planet. It is empowering, it is appropriate and fulfilling. Even revolutionary."

When I was in Kainchi in the mountains of Uttar Pradesh a number of years ago, I was staying at an ashram there. One day I decided to sit in front of a large statue of Vaishnavi Devi, a Hindu goddess, and open to whatever happened. After a few hours I was overcome with a giant and terrible rage, related to nothing in particular that I could identify. It was scary. The first conclusion in the moment was that Hindu deities were not some thing or ones with which to be played, and I skeedaddled back to my room fast, hiding, I hoped, from those powerful forces. A decade or so later I still don't know what to make of it, though my suspicion is: feminine rage is real, and it is part of the sacred. What I am also beginning to realize is, it is a resource.

DREAM COOKIES

Preparation time: 20 - 30 minutes

Makes 15 cookies.

SATTVIC, - Vata, 0 Pitta, + Kapha

Preheat oven to 300° F. Grind finely in a blender, food processor or however you like:

1 c. ground raw almonds

Mix them together with:

1/4 c. maple syrup
1/8-1/4 tsp. freshly ground cardamom
2 tsps. water

Drop the batter in half-teaspoonfuls onto a well-oiled cookie sheet. They will spread a bit. Bake for 15-20 minutes or until lightly golden brown. Let them cool for just a couple minutes, then remove carefully with a spatula to cool on a plate or wooden board.

*ROTATION DAY 2 DISH, use almond or apricot oil on the cookie sheet if you are following a strict rotation program.

Comments: This yummy cookie is based closely on a recipe by the same name from *The Allergy Self-Help Cookbook*, by Marjorie Hurt Jones, R.N. (copyright 1984, Rodale Press, Emmaus, Pa.,18049). This is a marvelous source of creative recipes for the omnivorous.

Variations: For a DAY 3 ROTATION DISH, use 1 c. ground sunflower seeds, 1/3 c. traditional YIN style brown rice syrup, 1/3 c. currants, 1/4 tsp. nutmeg, and 2 tsps. water. Proceed as above.

SATTVIC, - Vata, 0 Pitta, moderately + Kapha

For another DAY 3 ROTATION DISH, use 1 c. ground hazelnuts (filberts), 1/4-1/3 c. brown rice syrup, 1/4 tsp. mace, and 2 tsps. water. Make as above.

SATTVIC, - Vata, 0 Pitta, + Kapha

GINGERBREAD KIDS

Preparation time: about 1 hour

Makes 10-12 kids plus 18 2" round cookies

*SATTVIC BORDERING ON RAJASIC**

Preheat the oven to 350° F.

Cream together:

1/4 c. butter or ghee
1/2 c. fructose

Beat into them:

    1/2 c. blackstrap molasses

Mix together:

    1 c. rice bran or oat bran
    2 1/2 c. barley or whole wheat flour
    1 tsp. baking soda
    1/4 tsp. cloves
    1/2 tsp. cinnamon
    1/2 tsp. dry ginger
    1/2 tsp. salt

Stir the dry ingredients into the batter, alternating with:

    1/2 c. or more water

Toward the end, the dough will be very thick, and it is easiest to knead in the last bit of flour with your hands. Use extra flour if you need it to get the dough to a manageable consistency. Pat the dough into a lightly oiled cookie sheet (about 11"x 16") and with a cookie cutter, cut out large gingerbread kid shapes, or whatever shapes you like. (This last winter solstice we did elves and angels.) Carefully remove the dough between the "kids" leaving them to rest on the cookie sheet.

    Use the excess dough to make round gingerbread cookies. Rolling about a teaspoon at a time into a ball in your hands, press them gently onto a second oiled cookie sheet. Put both sheets in to bake for 10 - 12 minutes or until a toothpick inserted into their centers comes out cleanly.

* - Vata, 0 Pitta, mildly + Kapha (with rice bran and whole wheat flour)

* 0 Vata, 0 Pitta, 0 Kapha (with oat bran and barley flour)

* 0 Vata, 0 Pitta, mildly + Kapha (with oat bran and whole wheat flour)

COCONUT CREAM

Preparation time: 10 minutes to make, 1/2 hour to cool   Serves: 4 - 6
MILDLY RAJASIC (due to the canned coconut milk),
- Vata, - Pitta, moderately + Kapha

Blend in a blender on low heat for one minute or more:

    2 tsps. Universal pectin
    1/2 c. boiling water

Blend in:

    14 oz. coconut milk
    1 tsp. fresh lemon juice
    1/3 c. fructose

Garnish with:

    1/4 c. toasted coconut

Serve in small bowls or over fresh fruit, like peaches, berries, or ripe mango.

GRANNY BERGER'S MILKAKEBULKIES

(pronounced mil-ka-kuh-bul-kees)
Preparation time: spans 3 1/2 - 4 hours   Makes 2 dozen
RAJASIC, 0 Vata, 0 Pitta, + Kapha   ༄ ❄

To prepare the dough, mix together in a small bowl:
> **1 tsp. rice bran syrup**
> **1/4 c. warm water**

Dissolve into the syrup-water mixture:
> **1 Tbsp. dry baking yeast**

Cover it and set it aside to "proof", about 10 minutes. In a large bowl, mix together, with a wooden spoon:
> **1/4 c. rice bran syrup**
> **4 oz.(1/2 c.) plain fresh cow's yogurt or freshly made soy yogurt**

Beat in:
> **1 c. sifted barley or whole wheat pastry flour**

Add the yeast mixture and blend well. Add:
> **1 beaten egg**
> **2 Tbsps. very soft butter or ghee**
> **2 more cups of flour, a little bit at a time**

Blend until the dough begins to pull away from the sides of the bowl. Turn the dough onto a floured surface and knead for about 7 minutes. Shape into a ball. Place in a lightly oiled ceramic or stainless steel bowl (not plastic) and turn once to oil the top. Cover with a towel and let rise in a warm place until it is doubled in bulk, about 1 hour. (Note: barley flour will not double in bulk, so just allow it to rise for no less than an hour.)

To make the filling, mix together:
> **1/2 c. rice bran syrup**
> **1/4 c. maple syrup**
> **1/2 c. raisins**
> **1 1/4 c. walnuts, finely chopped**
> **2 tsps. cinnamon**

Melt or warm:
> **2 Tbsps. butter or ghee**

Use a little of the ghee or butter to butter 2 8" round pans. Reserve the rest to butter the dough as you make the buns. Take 1/2 cup of the filling mixture and spread it as evenly as you can over the two buttered pans.

Preheat oven to 400° F.

To make the buns (milkakebulkies), punch down the dough. Divide into two parts. On a floured surface, roll out the first part into a 12" x 12" square. Brush with:
> **the melted butter**

and sprinkle with:
> **cinnamon**

Spread 1/2 of the remaining filling mixture onto the dough. With a wet knife, cut the dough into 1" thick strips and roll each strip into a bun. (If you have never made milkakebulkies before, it is important to know they are little. There can be a temptation to make them as large as cinnamon rolls. They are not. They are only an inch high, so it is important to cut the strips only that wide.)

Repeat the same procedure with the remaining dough and filling. Place in the buttered baking pans, the milkakebulkies barely touching each other. Let the buns rise, covered with a towel, for another 45 minutes.

Remove the towel and put the milkakebulkies in the oven to bake for 20 minutes, or until slightly browned. Let cool for up to ten minutes, then turn on to wire racks to cool. If some of the filling remains in the pan, spread it back on the buns while it is still warm.

Comments: This recipe is in honor of Granny Hattie Berger, the 96-year-old matriarch of the Herling clan, who passed on this last year after many years filled with great baking, feistiness and love. Her milkakebulkies were famous for their utter delectability and allure. Some residents of Baltimore will, I fear, not recognize this atrociously healthy version from her granddaughter Michele. It is the only yeasted rule in the book, and this is about how often one would have yeast in an Ayurvedic therapeutic program, once in two hundred recipes! If you are on a yeast-free diet, this is like most other desserts, best left untasted.

Variation: 1/2 c. fresh boiled cow's milk or soy milk plus 1 tsp. fresh lemon juice can be substituted for the yogurt. Let the milk cool to a warm temperature before using.

APPLE SLICES

Preparation time: 1 hour   Serves: 12
SATTVIC, 0 Vata, - Pitta, 0 Kapha*   ✿ ଌ ❄

Preheat oven to 350° F. Wash, core and slice:
12 organic apples (9 cups)

Cook the apples in a large saucepan over medium heat with:
2 tsps. cinnamon
2 Tbsps. fresh lemon juice
3/8 c. apple concentrate (sweetener)
1 c. fresh organic apple juice

Let them simmer together for 10 - 15 minutes while you make up the crust. Mix together with a fork, in a medium-sized bowl:
1 1/2 c. barley or whole wheat flour
1/4 tsp. salt
3 Tbsps. cold-pressed sesame, walnut or almond oil
1/2 c. cold water

Add extra flour, if needed, to get the crust to hold together in a ball. Transfer the ball of dough to a lightly floured cookie sheet. Pat it out onto the sheet, folding a little up along the edge for a crust.

If you like your apples relatively firm, or French, as some say, you can turn them off and cover them now. If you like your fruit softer, let them simmer until they suit you. They do not change consistency greatly after baking. Spoon the cooked apples gently onto the crust, distributing them evenly. Spoon any excess juice over the whole. Put them in the oven to bake for 30 minutes or until the crust is lightly browned. Cut into slices and serve hot or cold.

*This recipe is most calming to *Kapha* if you use barley flour rather than whole wheat.

Variation: This can be used as a ROTATION DAY 1 DISH if you skip the lemon juice.

VERY BERRY PIE

Preparation time: 1/2 hour to prepare, 1 hour to cool

SATTVIC, - Vata, - Pitta, mildly + Kapha

Makes 1 9" pie

✳ ૐ

Make up:
ALMOND NUT CRUST, p. 257

While it is baking, mash together:
4 c. fresh strawberries (2 pints)
3/4 c. fructose

Set aside. When the crust is done, set it aside to cool a bit.

Bring to a boil in a small saucepan:
1/2 c. fresh cherry juice or cider

Pour it into a blender. Add:
2 tsps. Universal pectin

Blend well on low for a minute or more. Then blend in until well mixed:
1/3 c. coconut milk

Fold the pectin mixture into the strawberries until thoroughly mixed. Gently spoon into the pie crust. Let cool in the refrigerator.

Comment: One of our favorite sweeter desserts, for special occasions.

ONE GOOD SWEET POTATO PIE

Preparation time: 2 hours   1 9" pie

SATTVIC, - Vata, 0 Pitta, + Kapha   ➴ ❄

Filling:

Wash and put in a pot of boiling water:

> **2 medium sweet potatoes**

Bring the water back to a boil, then reduce heat to medium. Cook until the potatoes are soft, about 30 - 45 minutes. Remove the peels.

Make up the crust:

> **1 unbaked 9" pie crust, BARLEY OR WHOLE WHEAT PIE CRUST, p. 257**

Put the ball of crust in the refrigerator to chill. Preheat oven to 350° F.

To make up the filling, blend in a blender:

> **2 eggs (or Egg Replacer)**

Gradually blend in, in one-inch chunks:

> **1/2 lb. firm-style tofu**
> **the cooked sweet potato**

Now add:

> **3 Tbsps. sesame oil**
> **2/3 c. Sucanat**
> **1/3 c. brown rice syrup**
> **1 Tbsp. blackstrap molasses**
> **1 tsp. cinnamon**
> **1/2 tsp. dry ground ginger**
> **1/4 tsp. nutmeg**
> **1/4 tsp. mace**
> **1/2 tsp. salt**
> **1 tsp. vanilla extract**

Press the chilled pie crust into the pan and pour the filling in. Bake for 55 - 60 minutes or until set. YUM!

Comments: It tastes just like pumpkin pie, but without the can! I make this for holiday potlucks when my only responsibility is the dessert. Clearly, it's not the kind of goodie you whip up quickly after a long day at work. It's not difficult, it just takes a long time to make. Original inspiration for this recipe came from Carol Wiley Lorente's column on pumpkin pie in the November 1993 issue of *Vegetarian Times*, with much thanks to her.

BARLEY OR WHOLE WHEAT PIE CRUST

Preparation time: 1 hour or less, most of it unattended   Makes 1 9" crust
SATTVIC*

In a mixing bowl, stir together:
> **1 1/2 c. barley or whole wheat pastry flour**
> **1/2 tsp. salt**

Crumble into the flour with your fingers until it is pea-sized or smaller:
> **6 Tbsps. cold butter or ghee**
> **(or stir in 6 Tbsps. cold sesame or almond oil)**

Stir in with a fork:
> **4 - 6 Tbsps. cold water**

Add just enough water for the dough to hold together in a ball. Cover the bowl and put it in the refrigerator to chill for a half-hour or more. Take the crust out of the fridge and press it gently into a 9" pie pan with your fingers. For a baked pie crust, bake in preheated oven at 375° F for 15 minutes or until lightly browned. Or use unbaked, following directions for whatever pie you may be fixing.

* - *Vata, 0 Pitta, + Kapha (with whole wheat)*

* *0 Vata, 0 Pitta, + Kapha (with barley flour)*

ALMOND NUT CRUST

Preparation time: 30 minutes   Makes 1 9" crust
SATTVIC*

Preheat oven to 375° F. Mix together in a largish bowl:
> **2 Tbsps. finely ground raw almonds**
> **3 Tbsps. Sucanat**
> **1 1/4 c. barley or whole wheat flour**
> **Pinch of salt**

Crumble into the flour with your hands or a pastry cutter, until it is as coarse as rough cornmeal:
> **4 Tbsps. cold butter**

Add:
> **about 4 Tbsps. cold water**

Add enough water so that the dough makes a ball that can be pressed together. Transfer the ball of dough to an unoiled 9" pie pan and press it into place. Bake for 15 minutes. Remove from oven and let cool.

* - *Vata, 0 Pitta, mildly + Kapha (with barley flour)*

* - *Vata, 0 Pitta, + Kapha (with whole wheat flour)*

KAPHA CRUST

Preparation time: 25 minutes
SATTVIC, + Vata, - Pitta, - Kapha

Makes 1 9" crust

✿ ✳ ༖ ❄

Preheat oven to 425° F.

Mix together with a fork:
>   3/4 c. barley flour
>   1 1/2 Tbsps. sesame oil
>   1/4 c. cold water
>   1/4 tsp. salt

Add a bit more barley flour if needed to get the crust to hold together in a ball. Dust a 9" pie pan with barley flour, and dust your fingers as well. Pat the dough into place. It will be thin. Bake for 15 minutes. Or use unbaked, as directed in your recipe of choice.

Comments: The *Murrieta Hot Springs Vegetarian Cookbook* has many delicious low-fat recipes. Their recipe for Quiche Crust helped me come up with this one. It's lovely in that it has no cholesterol and a minimal amount of fat, and is quite tasty. While in quiche it is best baked alone first, I use it unbaked in fruit or pot pies, baking the crust with the filling.

Whole wheat flour can be substituted for the barley flour if you are looking for a low-fat crust for *Vata* or *Pitta (SATTVIC, - Vata, - Pitta, mildly + Kapha).*

BANANA SPICE CAKE

Preparation time: 45 minutes
SATTVIC, - Vata, 0 Pitta, + Kapha

Serves: 9-12

༖ ❄

Preheat oven to 350° F.

In a medium-sized mixing bowl, mash:
>   **2 ripe bananas**

Then beat in:
>   **1 egg**

Add:
>   **1/2 c. sesame oil**
>   **1/2 c. rice bran syrup**
>   **1/2 c. ground walnuts**
>   **1 tsp. cinnamon**
>   **1/2 tsp. ground cardamom**
>   **1/4 tsp. ground dry ginger**

Mix together, then add to the batter:

>   1 c. teff flour
>   1 c. barley flour
>   1 tsp. baking soda
>   1/2 tsp. salt
>   1 c. organic raisins

Spoon batter into a lightly oiled 9" square cake pan and bake for 30 minutes, or until a knife inserted into the center comes out cleanly. Cool and ice with HONEY NUTMEG GLAZE.

Comment: Rebecca Wood's recipe for Spicey Applesauce Cake gave me the original inspiration for this one.

Variation: 2 cups of whole wheat flour or 1 1/2 cups of oat bran can be substituted for both the 1 cup of teff flour and the 1 cup of barley flour together.

SATTVIC, - Vata, 0 Pitta, + Kapha (with whole wheat flour)
SATTVIC, mildly + Vata, 0 Pitta, mildly + Kapha (with oat bran)

HONEY NUTMEG GLAZE

Preparation time: 5 minutes, plus time to chill
SATTVIC, 0 Vata, mildly + Pitta, - Kapha

Enough to ice 1 9" cake
✿ ✳ ❧ ❄

Stir together in a small bowl:

>   3 Tbsps. raw honey
>   1 tsp. fresh boiled milk or soy milk
>   1/4 tsp. ground nutmeg

Best chilled.

CREAM CHEESE FROSTING

Preparation time: 10 minutes or less
RAJASIC, - Vata, + Pitta, + Kapha

Ices 1 10" cake
❧ ❄

Mix together in small bowl with a fork, or with an electric beater for greatest smoothness:

>   3/4 c. whipped cream cheese (6 oz.)
>   2 Tbsps. fructose or Sucanat
>   2 Tbsps. fresh lemon juice

Spread over the cake with a butter knife.

Variation: An equal amount of soy cream cheese or soy sour cream can be substituted for the cream cheese. Use only one tsp. fresh lemon juice, and the same amount of sweetener.

RAJASIC, 0 Vata, 0 Pitta, moderately + Kapha

CARROT CAKE

Preparation time: 1/2 hour plus 1 hour to bake   Serves: 10 - 12
SATTVIC*   🐌 ❄

Preheat oven to 325° F. Warm in a saucepan over medium heat for 10 minutes:

> **2 c. grated organic carrot (2 large carrots)**
> **1/2 c. dried pineapple, finely chopped**
> **1/2 c. organic currants or raisins**
> **3/4 c. brown rice syrup**
> **1 c. fresh apple juice**
> **1/2 c. water**
> **1 tsp. cinnamon**
> **1/2 tsp. allspice**
> **1/2 tsp. nutmeg**
> **1/4 tsp. cloves**
> **2 Tbsps. ghee or butter**
> **1 Tbsp. fresh lemon juice**

Let cool. Mix together:

> **2 c. whole wheat or barley flour**
> **1/2 tsp. salt**
> **1 tsp. baking soda**

Beat:

> **2 eggs**

Stir the eggs into the rest of the wet ingredients. Add the dry ingredients, and:

> **1/2 c. raw walnuts, chopped (optional)**

Pour the batter into a lightly oiled 7" x 11" baking pan, and bake until done, about 1 hour. A knife inserted into the center will come out cleanly. Serve with HONEY NUTMEG GLAZE, p. 259 or CREAM CHEESE FROSTING, p. 259.

* mildly + Vata, 0 Pitta, mildly + Kapha (with barley flour)

* 0 Vata, 0 Pitta, + Kapha (with whole wheat flour)

Variation: To make a version calming for *Vata*, use whole wheat flour and pineapple or pineapple-coconut juice.

SATTVIC, - Vata, moderately + Pitta, + Kapha

CHOLESTEROL-FREE CARROT CAKE: For a cholesterol-free version, use Egg Replacer in place of the eggs and 2 Tbsps. sesame oil in place of the ghee. Use HONEY NUTMEG GLAZE with soy milk for the topping. This is a little drier than the version above, and yet still good.

SATTVIC, moderately + Vata, 0 Pitta, 0 Kapha

ROSY BEET CAKE

Preparation time: 60 - 70 minutes, mostly unattended
SATTVIC*

Serves: 8

🫖 ❄️

Preheat oven to 325° F.

Wash and grate:
>3 medium beets (2 c. grated)

Set aside. In a mixing bowl, beat:
>1 egg

Then beat in:
>2/3 c. fresh orange juice (about 1 large orange)
>1 Tbsp. orange zest (grated organic orange peel)
>1/2 tsp. grated fresh ginger root
>1 tsp. cinnamon
>1/4 tsp. nutmeg
>1/8 tsp. allspice
>2 Tbsps. ghee (warm if you need, to blend it easily)
>1/2 c. maple syrup

Stir in the grated beets. Stir together, then fold into the wet ingredients:
>2 c. whole grain flour: whole wheat or barley
>1/2 tsp. salt
>2 tsps. baking powder

Fold into the batter:
>1/2 c. organic raisins

Lightly oil a 10-inch round pan or a muffin tin for 8 - 12 cup cakes; spoon the batter into it. Bake for 40 minutes or until a knife inserted into the middle of the cake comes out cleanly. Without icing, this makes a good not-too-sweet snack.

Or top with:
>**HONEY LEMON SAUCE, p. 213**
>**or CREAM CHEESE FROSTING, p. 259**

* - *Vata, moderately + Pitta, + Kapha (with wheat flour)*

* 0 *Vata, moderately + Pitta, 0 Kapha (with barley flour)*

TROPICAL FRUIT CAKE

Preparation time: 30 minutes, with an additional
2 hours to bake
SATTVIC, moderately + Vata, - Pitta, + Kapha

Makes 1 loaf or 12 individual cakes

❄

Preheat oven to 300° F. Put one inch of water in a shallow pan on the bottom shelf of the oven. Beat:

> **2 egg yolks**

Then beat in until light and creamy:

> **3 Tbsps. ghee or butter**
> **1/2 c. Sucanat**

Mix together:

> **1/4 c. rice bran or oat bran**
> **1/2 c. whole wheat or barley flour**
> **1/2 tsp. cinnamon**
> **1/8 tsp. cloves**
> **1/8 tsp. nutmeg**

Stir the dry ingredients into the ghee and egg, about 1/4 cup at a time, alternating with a few tablespoons of:

> **1 Tbsp. organic orange zest**
> **1/4 c. fresh orange juice**

until both the flour and juice are entirely mixed into the batter. Sprinkle a cutting board with:

> **1 - 2 Tbsps. more flour**

and flour a knife as well. On this board, with this knife, chop into 1/2" pieces:

> **2 c. dried papaya (3/4 lb.)**
> **3/4 c. dried dates (1/2 lb.)**
> **1/2 c. Calmyrna figs**
> **1/2 c. raw cashew pieces**

Mix together the fruit, nuts and flour on the board, and stir them into the batter. Beat until they are stiff and just beginning to peak:

> **2 egg whites**

Fold them into the batter. Line a loaf pan with waxed paper or oiled brown paper and spoon the batter into the pan. Or line a muffin tin with 12 individual paper baking cups and spoon the thick batter into these, a heaping tablespoon per cake. Bake on the top shelf of the oven until done, about 2 hours. Fun to make and wrap up with holiday bows for little presents.

Variation: You can use Egg Replacer instead of eggs if you like. Use the equivalent of 2 eggs, and add it at the beginning.

SATTVIC, + Vata, - Pitta, moderately + Kapha

HOLIDAY FRUIT CAKE

Preparation time: 30 minutes, plus 2 hours to bake   Makes 1 loaf or 12 individual cakes
SATTVIC, moderately + Vata, - Pitta, + Kapha   ❄

Preheat oven to 300° F. Put a shallow pan filled with about an inch of water on the bottom shelf of the oven. Beat in a mixing bowl:

2 egg yolks (or Egg Replacer equivalent for 2 eggs)

Beat into them:

1/3 c. sesame oil
1/4 c. rice bran syrup
1 tsp. blackstrap molasses
1/4 c. apricot nectar or grape juice

Mix together; then stir into the batter:

1/2 c. whole wheat or barley flour
1/4 c. rice bran or oat bran
1/8 tsp. salt
1/2 tsp. cinnamon
1/8 tsp. cloves
1/8 tsp. nutmeg

Flour a knife and a cutting board with:

1 - 2 Tbsps. more flour

Finely chop on the board:

2 Tbsps. organic orange peel

Then coarsely chop:

1 c. dried Turkish apricots
1/2 c. dried pineapple
1/2 c. raw walnuts

Add these to the batter with:

1/3 c. dried cherries (if available)
1/3 c. currants
1/3 c. organic raisins

Whip until they are stiff and just beginning to peak:

2 egg whites

Fold them gently into the batter. Line a loaf pan with waxed paper or oiled brown paper and spoon the batter into the pan. Or line a muffin tin with 12 individual paper baking cups and spoon a heaping tablespoon of batter into each one. Put on the top shelf of the oven to bake until done, about 2 hours.

Comments: We first started making these two fruitcakes for Christmas, reminiscing after my mother's and Gord's grandmother's wonderful holiday creations. We longed for their rich flavor, but wanted to come up with a fresh version. These taste like the old-fashioned fruitcakes, but without the alcohol and traditional chemical-laced fruit. If you can get organic dried fruit, it is even better. When my mom gave these the nod, I knew I was on the right track!

ABOUT SWEETENERS

Raw honey and maple syrup are popular Ayurvedic sweeteners, and are sattvic in nature. Both are appropriate in an Ayurvedic program. The two have somewhat different dynamics, and so are used to calm different doshas. Raw honey is both heating and drying, and so in small amounts is an excellent sweetener for Kapha. Its heat makes it aggravating to Pitta if used on a regular basis. Honey's sweetness and warming qualities outweigh its dryness for Vata, making it a fine sweetener for Vata as well. It is important to remember if you are using honey not to heat it, as this can create ama, toxic waste. Stirring honey into hot liquid, like a cup of tea, is just fine. Honey can also be added at the end of a dish's preparation, as long as it is not cooked afterward. Maple syrup is sweet, cool and moist. It is a good sweetener for calming Pitta (in moderation as always, yes?) as well as Vata. Its qualities increase Kapha, and so it is best used rarely by people with this dosha predominant.

Sweeteners which run a close second to honey and maple syrup for their soothing qualities and purity are bottled fruit juice concentrates, jaggery, brown rice syrup, and barley malt syrup. Other sweeteners which can be used in small amounts are Sucanat (TM), fructose, sugar cane juice, and molasses. These last sweets, with the exception of freshly pressed sugar cane juice, are rajasic in effect, and so are best used infrequently. How each of these sweets interacts with the constitutional types is given in Appendix II, Revised Food Guidelines for Basic Constitutional Types.

There are differences in opinion about white and brown sugar. Many Ayurvedic cooks and physicians avoid white sugar completely. It is considered quite rajasic, and subsequently too heating (in its long-term effect). In excess, its short-term effect is imbalancing to Vata and Kapha, and its long-term effect is aggravating to Pitta. Brown sugar is essentially made up of white sugar and so also is not used. I belong to this school of thought. However, I have known Ayurvedic physicians who do use sugar as a short-term cooling agent for Pitta. In my own experience as an American practitioner, I would not do this, as so many of the people I saw were suffering from having used sugar in excess.

Beverages

KEY

"–" means calms or helps the given constitution;

"+" means aggravates or increases it;

"0" means neutral effect.

 * ROTATION DIET can be helpful for people with food
   sensitivities, see p. 323.

**POLARITY DISH refers to recipes supporting Polarity Therapy
   work, see p. 342.

✿ = Spring

✳ = Summer

ॐ = Fall

❄ = Winter

TRIDOSHIC TEA

Preparation time: 10 - 15 minutes
SATTVIC, - Vata, - Pitta, - Kapha

Makes: 3 - 4 cups

In a stainless steel saucepan, bring to a boil:
>   **4 c. water**

Remove from heat and add:
>   **1 Tbsp. dried gotu kola**
>   **1 Tbsp. dried spearmint**
>   **1 Tbsp. rose petals**
>   **1/8 tsp. fennel seeds**

Stir, cover and let steep 10 minutes or more. Strain and serve. Can be served cool or hot.

Comment: Calming and strengthening to all the *doshas*, this tea is especially good for the mind, nerves and digestion. The gotu kola in it is very good for brightening the mind and its outlook, but the tea should not be used in excess, especially if there is a predisposition toward headache, or a currently itchy skin condition.

VATA CALMING TEA

Preparation time: 15 - 20 minutes
SATTVIC, - - Vata, moderately + Pitta, - Kapha

Makes 3 - 4 cups

Bring to a boil in a stainless steel saucepan:
>   **4 c. water**

Reduce the heat to low and add:
>   **1 tsp. whole cardamom seeds**
>   **2 cinnamon sticks**
>   **1 1/2 tsps. fresh ginger root, peeled and chopped**
>   **1 Tbsp. dried licorice root, chopped or sliced**
>   **1/8 tsp. fennel seeds**
>   **1 tsp. dried organic orange peel**
>   **1/2 tsp. whole anise seeds (optional)**
>   **1 tsp. dried powdered sarsaparilla (optional)**

Stir well. Cover the pot and simmer over low for ten minutes. Remove from heat and let the tea sit another 5 minutes. Strain. Serve unsweetened, with fresh boiled milk (optional), or sweeten to taste with honey.

Comment: This sweet, *chai*-like tea is especially good for balancing *Vata* and supporting effective digestive function.

PITTA SOOTHING TEA

Preparation time: 15 minutes   Makes 3 - 3 1/2 cups
SATTVIC, mildly + Vata, - - Pitta, 0 Kapha   ❀ ✳ 🐸 ❄

Bring to a boil in a stainless steel saucepan:
>   **4 c. water**

Remove from the heat and add:
>   **2 Tbsps. dried alfalfa leaves**
>   **3 Tbsps. dried comfrey root**
>   **1 Tbsp. spearmint**
>   **1 Tbsp. red clover**
>   **1/8 tsp. fennel seeds**
>   **1 Tbsp. dried hibiscus flowers**
>   **1 Tbsp. rose petals**

Cover and let steep for 10 minutes or more. Strain, squeezing the tea out of the herbs well. Sweeten with a little maple syrup if you like. Good hot or cool.

Comment: This is a particularly nutritive tea for *Pitta*, for overall strengthening and tonifying. It is a strong brew. If you like, you can dilute it with an additional two cups of water. Plain chamomile, or mint, make good simple teas for calming *Pitta*, when simplicity is the priority.

KAPHA INVIGORATING TEA

Preparation time: 10 - 15 minutes   Makes 3 - 4 cups
SATTVIC, - Vata, + Pitta, - - Kapha   ❀ ✳ 🐸 ❄

Bring to a boil in a stainless steel saucepan:
>   **4 c. water**

Reduce heat to low and add:
>   **1/2 tsp. dried juniper berries**
>   **1/4 tsp. black pepper**
>   **1 tsp. whole cardamom seeds**
>   **1 Tbsp. dried gotu kola**
>   **1 Tbsp. fresh ginger root, peeled and chopped**
>   **1/2 tsp. dried sage**

Cover and let simmer over low heat for 10 minutes or more. Strain and serve with a little honey if you like.

Comments: Very good for clearing the mind and stimulating circulation. Simply sniffing the tea as it is being made can have a positive effect on mental clarity. This also stimulates digestion and expectoration.

Maharishi Ayur-Ved Products International now markets a trademarked series of *Vata, Pitta* and *Kapha* Teas in tea bag form. For a simple way to balance, they can be helpful.

SIMPLE HOT GINGERED MILK

Preparation time: 5 minutes
SATTVIC, - Vata, + Pitta, - Kapha

Makes 2 cups

Bring to a boil in a small saucepan:
- **1 c. fresh raw milk**
- **1 c. water**
- **1 - 2 tsps. fresh ginger root, peeled and grated or chopped**

Reduce heat to low after 20 - 30 seconds, and let simmer for a minute or two more. Remove from heat, strain and serve, sweetened with honey or unsweetened.

Comment: This is one of the best ways to have dairy, especially just before bed. The fresh ginger stimulates digestive fire, strengthens overall digestion and acts as a gentle laxative and eliminative of excess *Kapha*. It is called *vishwabhesaj*, the universal medicine, because in this way it balances all three *doshas* (in terms of its functions). Do not be mislead into thinking that *Pitta* can have as much ginger, though, as *Vata* or *Kapha*. In excess, it can set off inflammation, especially in *Pitta*.

HOT HERBED MILK

Preparation time: 10 - 15 minutes
SATTVIC, - Vata, - Pitta, 0 Kapha

Makes 1 cup

Bring to a boil in a small saucepan:
- **1 c. raw fresh milk**

Remove from heat and stir in:
- **1/4 tsp. fennel seeds**
- **1/16 - 1/8 tsp. saffron (optional)**
- **1 tsp. rose petals, organic**

Cover and let steep, off the heat, for 10 minutes or more. Strain and serve, with sweetener or no.

Comment: Calming and relaxing, with herbs soothing and/or neutral to all *doshas*. Neither rose petals or saffron should ever be heated.

LIGHT MINT TEA

Preparation time: 5 - 10 minutes
SATTVIC, - Vata (in moderation), - Pitta, - Kapha

Makes 2 cups

❁ ✳ ⋟ ❄

Bring to a boil:
>   2 c. water

Remove from heat and stir in:
>   2 - 3 tsps. dried spearmint or peppermint, or
>   1 Tbsp. fresh, chopped

Cover and let steep for 5 minutes or more. Strain and serve, sweetened if you like. This can be served cool or hot.

DIGEST EASE TEA

Preparation time: 10 - 30 minutes
SATTVIC, - Vata, + Pitta, - Kapha

Makes 2 - 3 cups

❁ ✳ ⋟ ❄

Bring to a boil:
>   4 c. water

Toss in:
>   2" fresh ginger root, peeled and cut however you like
>   1 tsp. cumin seeds
>   1 tsp. coriander seeds
>   1 tsp. turmeric
>   A pinch of fennel (optional)

Reduce heat and simmer uncovered for 10 - 30 minutes, depending on how strong you like your flavors, and how much digestive help you need. Strain and sip after meals. Especially helpful after heavier meals or meals with legumes. Excellent for strengthening *agni*.

**POLARITY PURIFYING DIET DISH

Comments: These herbs are frequently recommended in Indian dishes to aid digestion, and give them some of their unique flavor. There are times when you may not feel like eating an Indian curry, and yet need the digestive support these herbs offer. This tea can be very helpful.

LIVER WAKE-UP!

Preparation time: 5 minutes   Makes 1 cup
SATTVIC, - Vata, + Pitta (in excess), - Kapha

Bring to a boil:
> **1 c. pure water**

Squeeze into it:
> **Juice of 1/2 fresh lemon, organic preferred**

Stir in:
> **1/4 tsp. ground turmeric**

Drink. Good Morning!

**POLARITY PURIFYING DIET DISH

It's Valentine's Day, 1994. I read in the local paper that we Americans are spending $655 million on candy this holiday. And I know that 40,000 kids died yesterday of starvation across the globe, more than 14 million children in the last year. This drives me wild. I don't like what I see. If we hope to create a future where we all can live, we cannot continue on at the standard of living we, in the West, currently maintain. It is at the expense of many sisters and brothers in other parts of the planet. And at the expense of many other races, animals and plants as well as human. We must radically simplify, and work together as a world-wide community.

When I look over the menus in Appendix IV, I am struck by this same discrepancy. Few of us in America are lucky enough to eat as well as is implied in these menus. And billions of us on the planet now don't come anywhere close to three meals a day, let alone three meals of a particular sort. In some ways the menus feel like a cruel hoax, a culinary convention bred in part out of a desire to help, to give ideas how to put all these recipes together. But on another level they only emphasize the vast gap between what is and what might be, and what is not available to so many of us today.

BASIC GINGER TEA

Preparation time: 10 - 30 minutes   Serves: 6
SATTVIC, - Vata, + Pitta, - Kapha   ✿ 🐸 ❆

Bring to a boil:

> **6 c. pure water**

Add:

> **2 tsps. grated fresh ginger root, peeled**

Cover, and simmer on low heat until it is the taste you want: 5 to 15 minutes.

**POLARITY PURIFYING DIET DISH

Comments: This is an excellent tea for supporting and enhancing *agni*, digestive fire. It can be sipped after any meal, especially if you are experimenting with adding more protein into your diet in the form of legumes. It is helpful for enhancing digestion, reducing gas and alleviating nausea.

Variations: GINGER-HIBISCUS TEA: Add a couple of sticks of cinnamon and a tablespoon of hibiscus leaves for a soothing hot drink when you've got a cold. A bit of honey to sweeten this is good.

SATTVIC, - Vata, 0 Pitta, - Kapha

**POLARITY PURIFYING DIET DISH

GINGER-AJWAN TEA: Add a pinch of *ajwan* for relief of sinusitis.

SATTVIC, - Vata, + + Pitta, -- Kapha

**POLARITY PURIFYING DIET DISH

LUNG TEA: Add a tablespoon each of wild cherry bark and osha root to the basic ginger brew, sweetened with honey on completion, for those low down winter bronchial numbers. (with a touch of homeopathic Phosphorus before?)

SATTVIC, - Vata, + Pitta, - Kapha

**POLARITY PURIFYING DIET DISH

GINGER-CORIANDER TEA: Brew one tablespoon of whole coriander seeds with the ginger, for a milder, gas-dispelling alternative.

SATTVIC, - Vata, 0 Pitta, - Kapha

ABOUT FASTING

Judicious fasting is used in Ayurveda to give the digestive tract a rest and to give the body a chance to begin to release old stored toxins.

A fast can be as simple as skipping one meal, and replacing it with a cup of DIGESTIVE CLEANSING TEA, p. 274 and/or some FRESH VEGETABLE JUICE, p. 274. The potassium-rich juice keeps up electrolytes and gives calories, while the tea cleanses and tonifies the gut. When you are fasting, take a fast from rush, stress and worry as well. Let these few hours be relaxed ones. Don't schedule a fast the same time as a major push at work or home. For women, fasting the first or second day of our menstrual periods can be a helpful way to support our bodies in their natural rhythms of cleansing.

Once one meal can be comfortably skipped, you can try fasting through two meals. More than this, it is good to have the supervision of a skilled Ayurvedic or other health care practitioner, if you are new to it. Constitutionally, Kaphas are best suited for fasts. Pittas and Vatas need to take care in planning their fasts, especially in their scheduling.

How often to fast? This varies a great deal with the individual. Dr. Sunil Joshi, who is one of India's leading authorities in Pancha Karma (the five therapeutic cleansings), recommends as often as one day out of every fourteen, or as little as once every 25 days. Children, babies and pregnant mothers should not fast, except under rare circumstances. These are times to emphasize physiological building, not cleansing.

Another way to undertake a fast for the first time is to do one meal as described, the digestive cleansing tea and the fresh vegetable juice, followed by a simple kichadi (Indian healing stew, p. 121) for lunch and dinner. Let yourself notice how your body is feeling. If it has strength and enthusiasm, let that be expressed. If it is tired or scared at the idea of skipping a meal, be gentle with yourself. Do what you can, and what is appropriate for you.

AUXILIARY SUPPORTS TO A FAST

Oil massage

Yoga

Dry brush massage

Gentle walks

Pranayama

Rest

DIGESTIVE CLEANSING TEA

Preparation time: 20 minutes   Makes 4 cups
SATTVIC, - Vata, 0 Pitta, 0 Kapha   ✿ ✳ ☙ ❄

Bring to a boil:
>   **5 cups pure water**

Add:
>   **1 Tbsp. fresh grated ginger root**
>   **1 Tbsp. turmeric**
>   **1 Tbsp. dried licorice root**

Cover and reduce heat to simmer. Cook for 10 - 15 minutes. Strain and drink.

**POLARITY PURIFYING DIET DISH

Comments: This tea was originally recommended to me by Dr. Sunil Joshi of Nagpur for days of fasting. It is especially helpful for the person with an inflamed and congested gut. The ginger is used to break down waste, *ama*, the tumeric to purify the blood, and the licorice to calm inflammation. It would generally not be used where there is inflammation without *ama*, as the ginger could adversely increase heat.

FRESH VEGETABLE JUICE

Preparation time: 20 minutes, including time to clean the juicer   Makes: 2 cups
SATTVIC, - Vata, + Pitta (in excess), - Kapha   ✿ ✳ ☙

You need a vegetable juicer to make this recipe.

Wash:
>   **6 carrots, organic**
>   **1 stalk celery, organic**
>   **1/2 lb. raw spinach (1/2 bunch)**

Put the vegetables through the juicer, followed by:
>   **1/2 - 1 c. pure water**

Comment: This is a remarkably rich source of minerals and vitamins, especially good for many types of joint pain when used on a regular basis.

For the *Pitta* looking for good fresh vegetable combinations, it is wise to use much less carrot, and more Romaine lettuce, cucumber, and/or fresh fennel (finocchio), if the juice is to be drunk on a regular basis. More water can also be used to dilute the juice, up to half and half, though the nutrient quantity will be proportionally lower.

CHAI

Preparation time: 15 minutes or more
*SATTVIC**

Makes 6 cups

✿ ☙ ❄

Pour into a large saucepan:

3 cups fresh raw cow's milk or soy milk
3 c. pure water

Bring to a boil, uncovered. Add:

1 cinnamon stick
Seeds from 5 cardamom pods
1/8 tsp. whole black peppercorns
1/8 tsp. fennel seeds
1 tsp. to 1 Tbsp. fresh grated ginger root, peeled

Cover and let simmer on low until the flavor is to your liking, 15 minutes to an hour or so. Serve hot, sweetened with:

raw honey

* - *Vata, 0 Pitta, moderately + Kapha (with cow's milk and 1 tsp. ginger)*
* - *Vata, + Pitta, mildly + Kapha (with cow's milk and 1 Tbsp. ginger)*
* 0 *Vata, 0 Pitta, 0 Kapha (with soy milk and 2 tsps. ginger)*

Comment: This traditional Indian drink is a great follow-up for a company meal. And easy to prepare.

RESTORATIVE ALMOND DRINK

Preparation time: overnight soak, plus 10 minutes
SATTVIC, - Vata, - Pitta, + Kapha

Serves: 1

✿ ✵ ☙ ❄

Soak together overnight:

8 raw almonds
1 c. pure water

In the morning, reserve half the water and drain off the rest. Rub the skins off the almonds. In a small saucepan, bring to a boil:

3/4 c. raw milk

Pour the milk in the blender with the almonds and the 1/2 c. water and:

1 Tbsp. rose petals
1/32 tsp. saffron
1/8 tsp. ground cardamom (optional)
1/2 tsp. raw honey

Blend until smooth. Drink.

Comment: This variation on a traditional *rasayana* grounds *Vata*, soothes irritated *Pitta* and tonifies the nerves.

QUICK HOT CIDER

Preparation time: 10 - 15 minutes

Serves: 6

SATTVIC, 0 Vata, - Pitta, - Kapha

Warm in a large saucepan:

    3 c. fresh apple cider
    2 c. pure water
    2 cinnamon sticks
    1 clove

Serve hot.

Variation: HOT CHERRY CIDER: Use cherry cider (available bottled by the quart in natural foods groceries) with 3 cloves, or with 1/4 tsp. cardamom and 1/4 tsp cinnamon.

RAJASIC (the bottled cider), - Vata, 0 Pitta, - Kapha

HOT CAROB DRINK

Preparation time: 5 - 10 minutes

Makes 3 cups

SATTVIC, 0 Vata, - Pitta, - Kapha

Bring to a boil in a small saucepan:

    1 1/2 c. soy milk
    1 1/2 c. water

Remove from heat immediately and blend with:

    2 Tbsps. raw carob powder
    1 Tbsp. raw honey
    1 Tbsp. Dacopa (TM) (optional)

Serve hot.

*ROTATION DAY 3 DRINK

**POLARITY HEALTH BUILDING DISH

Variation: Fresh raw cow's milk can be substituted for the soy milk. Boil 20 seconds or more.

SATTVIC, - Vata, - Pitta, + Kapha

Comments: This makes a soothing drink on a cold winter night. Dacopa is simply dried dahlia root which is available commercially as an instant coffee substitute, like Postum, Caffix, or Bambu.

ALMOND MILK

Preparation time: 10 minutes, plus 2 hour soak or more   Makes: 2 cups
SATTVIC, - Vata, 0 Pitta, mildly + Kapha

❀ ✳ 🐚 ❄

Bring to a boil:

    2 c. pure water

Remove it from the heat, allow it to cool slightly, then pour it over:

    3 Tbsps. raw almonds, organic preferred

Let the almonds soak at least 15 minutes, or preferably 2 - 8 hours. Soaking them overnight is an easy way to do this.

    Rub the peels off the almonds, and put them with the soaking water in the blender. Grind at low speed for a few seconds, then on high speed until smooth. Put through a stainless steel strainer for smoothest consistency.

Sweeten with:

    1 Tbsp. maple syrup (optional)

This can be used as the basis for smoothies, soups, or in baked goods.

*ROTATION DAY 2 DRINK

NUT MILKS

Preparation time: 10 minutes, sometimes with a soak before hand   Makes 1 cup
SATTVIC, - Vata, + Pitta and Kapha (in excess)

❀ ✳ 🐚 ❄

Nut milks are easy to make, if you have a blender. Simply grind, dry, in the blender, to a fine powder:

    1 1/2 Tbsps. raw nuts - walnuts, cashews, almonds, or pecans for example

Add:

    1 c. hot water

Liquify at high speed in the blender until smooth. This nut milk can be used unsweetened in soups, sauces and baked goods. It can be seasoned with herbs, a little miso, or Bragg's Liquid Aminos. Or it can be sweetened with:

    1 tsp. raw honey (for *Vata* or *Kapha*)
    or maple syrup (for *Pitta* or *Vata*)

HOT SESAME MILK

Preparation time: 5 minutes   Serves: 1
SATTVIC, - Vata, + Pitta and Kapha (in excess)   ✿ ✳ 🍵 ❄

Put on to warm:
>   **1 c. water**

Spoon into a mug:
>   **1 teaspoon raw sesame tahini**
>   **1/2 tsp. raw honey (optional)**

When the water is hot but not boiling, pour into your mug and stir with a teaspoon. The drink can be flavored with:
>   **1/8 tsp. vanilla extract**

Good drink for sipping late at night on a chilly evening.

*ROTATION DAY 4 variation: Sweeten with date sugar or fructose rather than honey, and use a bit of vanilla bean rather than the extract.

IZA'S TROPICAL SMOOTHIE

Preparation time: 5 minutes   1 cup or more
SATTVIC, - Vata, 0 Pitta, 0 Kapha   ✿ ✳ 🍵 ❄

Blend together until smooth:
>   **1/2 ripe banana, organic preferred**
>   **Juice of 1 large orange, ditto**
>   **1/2 ripe pear, ditto**
>   **1/2 - 1 c. organic fruit juice**

Drink.

**POLARITY PURIFYING DIET DISH

Comments: I was specifically and most tersely instructed to record this secret recipe and its title by my 4 3/4-year-old chief cooking assistant, Iza Helen Rose. It makes an excellent medium for washing down noxious substances, such as Ayurvedic herbs and other arcane combinations.

PEACH SMOOTHIE

Preparation time: 5 minutes

Makes 1 cup

SATTVIC, - Vata, 0 Pitta, gently + Kapha

Grind well into a fine powder in the blender:

2 Tbsps. blanched almonds

Add, first at low speed, a little at a time, then blending at high speed ("liquify") in the blender:

1/2 c. water

Add, again first at low speed, then at high speed (giving your blender "breaks", especially if it is aging):

2 very ripe peaches, sliced

1 Tbsp. maple syrup

Serve room temperature or cool. A lovely peachy color.

*ROTATION DAY 2 DISH

Comments: Smoothies can be easily made in the blender or food processor. All you need is a liquid medium, like fresh fruit juice, fresh milk or nut milks, combined with your favorite ripe fruits, then blended until smooth. (This must be where smoothies got their name). Spices can also be added to taste, and for added digestive benefit. For "Ayurvedic smoothies", simply remember to keep your ingredients room temperature or cool, not freezing, and your combinations relatively simple. If your digestive fire is good, fruits can be mixed. If it is not, it is best to use one fruit at a time. Single fruits provide the least challenge on digestion. Iza's Tropical Smoothie is one of my favorites.

PART THREE

APPENDIX I:
Assessing Your Constitution

Each constitutional type has certain traits. You can assess yourself by filling out the questionnaire below. Place a check next to the choice which best describes you; occasionally more than one choice may need to be made. Next to any check put a "1" if this line is sometimes true for you, a "2" if it is generally or often true of you. (If you have a seriously hard time making up your mind on responses, put an extra "5" points in the *Vata* column!) Relax and be as truthful with yourself as you can be.

Vata

___ Thin, and usually have been; you also may be unusually tall or short

___ Thin as a child

___ Light bones and/or prominent joints

___ You have a hard time gaining weight

___ Small, active, dark eyes

___ Dry skin, chaps easily, especially in winter

___ Dark complexion relative to the rest of your family, tan easily

___ Dark, rough, dry, wiry, or kinky hair

___ You prefer a warm climate, sunshine, and moisture

___ Your appetite is variable. You can get very hungry, but may find that your "eyes were bigger than your stomach"

Pitta

___ Medium, well-proportioned frame

___ Medium build as child

___ Medium bone structure

___ You can gain or lose weight relatively easily, if you put your mind to it

___ Penetrating light green, grey, amber, or blue eyes

___ Oily skin and hair

___ Fair skin which sunburns easily, relative to the rest of your family

___ Fine, light, oily hair, blond, red or early grey

___ You prefer cool well-ventilated places and fresh air

___ Irritable if you miss a meal or can't eat when you are hungry; good appetite

Kapha

___ Tend to be ample in build

___ Plump or a little chunky as a child

___ Heavy bone structure

___ You gain weight easily, have a hard time losing it

___ Large attractive eyes with thick eyelashes

___ Thick skin, cool, well-lubricated

___ You tan slowly but usually evenly; your skin stays cool longer than most

___ Thick wavy hair, a little oily, dark or light

___ Any climate is fine, as long as it is not too humid or damp

___ You like to eat, your appetite is fine, but you can skip meals without physical problems if you have to (not that you like to)

Vata

___ Bowel movements can be irregular, hard, dry, or constipated

___ Digestion is sometimes good, sometimes not. Gas often occurs

___ You enjoy spontaneity more than routine

___ You are a creative thinker. You usually need to write ideas down to best remember them

___ Your mind is always active, constantly thinking of new plans and concerns

___ Your memory can be flighty

___ You like to stay physically active, or may have restless quirks like tapping your fingers or rocking a leg back and forth

___ It is easy for you to do things quickly

___ You feel more mentally relaxed when you're exercising

___ You can change your mind easily

___ Inwardly, you tend toward fear or anxiety under stress

___ You often dream, but it is rare for you to remember your dreams

___ You have changeable moods and ideas

Pitta

___ Easy and regular bowel movements, if anything, soft, oily, loose stools at least once or twice a day

___ Usually good digestion

___ You enjoy organizing and like routine, especially if you create it

___ You are a good initiator and leader; you have to take care not to be critical or impatient with yourself or others

___ You have a sharp mind

___ Your memory is usually pretty good

___ You enjoy physical activities, especially competitive ones

___ You are usually efficient and want to set your own pace

___ Exercise or creative activities help keep emotions from going out of control for you

___ You have opinions and are an articulate speaker

___ Inwardly you tend toward anger, frustration or irritability under stress

___ It is relatively easy for you to remember your dreams; you often dream in color

___ You can be forceful about expressing your ideas and feelings

Kapha

___ Regular daily bowel movements, steady, thick, heavy

___ Digestion fine, sometimes a little slow

___ You work well with routine and prefer it over a spontaneous approach

___ You are good at keeping an organization or project running smoothly; it is easy for you to be relatively calm and patient

___ It is relatively easy for you to quiet your mind; it always has been

___ Your memory is good to excellent

___ You love leisurely activities most

___ You like to take your time doings things

___ Exercise keeps your weight down in a way diet alone won't

___ You change opinions and ideas slowly

___ You tend to avoid difficult or stressful situations rather than confront them

___ You generally only remember dreams if they are especially intense or significant

___ Your moods tend to be more steady and reliable; you reveal them gradually or slowly

___ You like to snack, nibble

___ If you are ill, it is more likely to be a nervous disorder, sharp pain or indigestion

___ You are a light sleeper; insomnia can sometimes be a problem

___ When you have money, it is easy for you to share it and spend it

___ Your sexual interest comes and goes; your fantasy life is active

___ Brittle or ridged nails

___ Cold hands and feet, little perspiration

___ Thin, fast, variable pulse, hands cold

___ You are sometimes thirsty, sometimes not.

14
19

___ You gravitate toward high protein foods like beans, eggs, chicken or fish

___ If you are ill, fevers, rashes or inflammation are likely conditions

___ You usually sleep well

___ You are more likely to spend money on special items or those you need to advance yourself professionally

___ You have a ready sexual interest and drive

___ Flexible nails, but pretty strong

___ Good circulation, perspire easily

___ Strong full pulse, hands warm

___ You are often thirsty

37
16

___ You love fatty foods, bread, starch

___ If you are ill, excess fluid retention or mucus are likely conditions

___ You are generally a sound, heavy sleeper

___ Money is easy to save for you; you value quality in purchases

___ You have a steady sexual interest and drive

___ Strong thick nails

___ Moderate perspiration

___ Steady slow rhythmic pulse, hands cool

___ You are rarely thirsty

Sage (green?)
11

Sara
27

Add up your points in each column. The constitution or (constitutions) with the most points generally indicates your primary *prakruti*. If you have marked two constitutions nearly as often, you may have a dual *dosha*: *Vata-Pitta, Pitta-Kapha,* etc. Rarely, all three will be relatively equal, in which case a *Tridoshic* or *Vata-Pitta-Kapha* type results.

If you checked aspects in a *dosha* different from your constitution as a whole, this may indicate an imbalance in that *dosha*. For example, if you checked primarily *Vata* aspects, but also marked off "usually thirsty" and "prefer cool well-ventilated places" and "irritable if you miss a meal" in the *Pitta* column, and all of these last traits have developed in the last few years, this could indicate that while you are primarily a *Vata* constitutional type (*prakruti*), you may have a current imbalance in *Pitta* (your *vikruti*). See text for more information on this.

(Assessing Your Constitution is based on the questionnaire, "Discovering Your Constitution", from *The Ayurvedic Cookbook*, Morningstar with Desai, Lotus Press, 1990.)

APPENDIX II: Revised Food Guidelines for Basic Constitutional Types

NOTE: This table provides general guidelines related to how foods affect the three *doshas*. Specific adjustments will inevitably need to be made, depending on the season, time of day, individual strength of digestive fire, food allergies, and so on. It is meant to be a general guide to enable you to become more familiar with your own food needs.

▲ Aggravates *Dosha*
▼ Balances *Dosha*

FRUITS

	VATA		PITTA		KAPHA
	CHOOSE ▼	AVOID ▲	AVOID ▲	CHOOSE ▼	AVOID ▲	CHOOSE ▼
	Sweet fruits	Dried fruits	Sour Fruits	Sweet Fruits	Sour & Very Sweet Fruits	Apples
	Apricots	Apples, raw	Apples, sour	Apples, sweet	Avocado	Apricots
	Avocado	Cranberries	Apricots, sour	Apricots, sweet	Banana	Berries
	Banana	Frozen fruits	Berries, sour	Avocado*	Coconut	Cherries
	All berries	Fruit with sugar	Banana	Berries, sweet	Dates	Cranberries
	Cherries	Pears, raw	Cherries, sour	Coconut	Figs, fresh	Figs, dried
	Coconut	Persimmon	Cranberries	Dates	Grapefruit	Mango, ripe
	Dates	Pomegranate	Fruit with sugar	Most dried fruit, soaked	Grapes*	Peaches
	Figs, fresh	Prunes	Frozen fruit	Figs	Kiwi*	Pear
	Grapefruit	Quince, raw	Grapefruit	Grapes, sweet	Lemon*	Persimmon
	Grapes	Watermelon	Grapes, green	Mango, ripe	Lime**	Pomegranate
	Kiwi		Kiwi**	Melons	Melons	Prunes
	Lemons		Lemons*	Oranges, sweet	Oranges	Quince
	Limes		Limes**	Pear	Papaya	Raisins
	Mango, ripe		Oranges, sour	Persimmon	Pineapple	Strawberries*
	Melons, sweet		Papaya	Pineapple, sweet*	Plums	
	Oranges		Peaches**	Plums, sweet	Rhubarb	
	Papaya		Pineapple, sour			

NOTE: Fruits and fruit juices are best consumed by themselves for all *doshas*.

* These foods are OK in moderation
** These foods are OK occasionally

	VATA		PITTA		KAPHA	
	AVOID ▲	CHOOSE ▼	AVOID ▲	CHOOSE ▼	AVOID ▲	CHOOSE ▼
FRUITS (cont.)		Peaches Pineapple Plums Raisins, soaked Rhubarb Soursop Strawberries	Plums, sour Rhubarb Soursop Strawberries**	Pomegranate Prunes Quince, sweet Raisins Watermelon	Soursop Watermelon	
VEGETABLES	Frozen, dried or microwaved vegetables Raw vegetables in excess* Arugula* Beet greens* Broccoli** Brussels sprouts Burdock root Cabbage Cauliflower Celery Celtuce** Chicory	Cooked Vegetables, fresh Acorn Squash Artichoke Asparagus Bean Sprouts Beets Butternut Squash Carrots Cress* Cucumber Daikon Radish* Fennel Fenugreek Greens* Garlic, cooked* Green Beans, well-cooked	Pungent Vegetables Pickled Vegetables Arugula* Beets Carrots* Cress* Daikon Radish** Eggplant Fenugreek Greens Garlic Horseradish Green Olives Kohlrabi* Leeks, cooked** Mustard Greens Onions, raw Onions, cooked*	Sweet, Bitter or Astringent Vegetables Acorn Squash Artichoke Asparagus Bean sprouts Bell Pepper* Broccoli Brussels Sprouts Burdock Root Butternut Squash Cabbage Cauliflower Celery Celtuce Chicory Chinese Cabbage	Sweet, Juicy or Heavy Vegetables Pickled Vegetables Acorn Squash Butternut Squash Cucumber Fennel* Olives, black or green Parsnip** Potatoes, sweet Rutabaga Spaghetti Squash* Tomatoes Winter Squash	Raw, Pungent, Bitter, or Astringent Vegetables Artichoke* Arugula Asparagus Bean sprouts Beets Beet Greens Bell Pepper* Broccoli Brussels Sprouts Burdock Root Cabbage Carrots Cauliflower Celery

Celtuce
Chicory
Chinese Cabbage
Collard Greens
Fresh Corn
Daikon Radish
Dandelion Greens
Eggplant*
Endive
Escarole
Fenugreek Greens
Garlic
Green Beans
Guy Lon
Horseradish
Jeru. Artichoke
Jicama
Kale
Kohlrabi
Leafy Greens of
   all kinds
Leeks
Lettuce
Mache
Mizuna
Mushrooms**
Okra
Onions*

Chinese
   Cabbage**
Collards
Fresh corn**
Eggplant
Endive
Escarole
Dandelion Greens
Guy Lon**
Jeru. artichoke*
Jicama*
Kale*
Kohlrabi
Leafy Greens*
Lettuce*
Mizuna
Mushrooms
Onions, raw
Pac Choy
Parsley*
Peas**
Peppers
Potatoes, white
Purslane
Radicchio
Snow Peas*
Spaghetti Squash**
Spinach*

Horseradish**
Leeks, cooked
Mache*
Mung sprouts,
   cooked
Mustard greens*
Okra, cooked
Olives, black &
   green
Onion, cooked
Parsnip
Potato, sweet
Pumpkin*
Radish
Rutabaga
Scallopini Squash
Shallots, cooked
Summer Squash
Watercress
Winter Squash
Yel.Crkneck Squash
Zucchini

Peppers, hot
Pumpkin**
Radish
Shallots
Spinach**
Tomatoes
Turnip Greens**
Watercress*

Collard Greens
Fresh Corn
Cucumber
Dandelion Greens
Endive
Escarole
Fennel
Green Beans
Guy Lon
Jeru. Artichoke
Jicama
Kale
Leafy Greens
Lettuce
Mache
Mizuna*
Mushrooms**
Okra
Olives, black*
Pac Choy
Parsley
Parsnip
Peas
Potatoes, sweet
Potatoes, white
Purslane
Radicchio
Rutabaga

* These foods are OK in moderation
** These foods are OK occasionally

VEGETABLES
(cont.)

VATA

AVOID ▲	CHOOSE ▼	AVOID ▲
Sprouts*		
Swiss Chard*		
Tah Tsai		
Tomatoes		
Turnips		
Turnip greens		

PITTA

CHOOSE ▼	AVOID ▲
Scallopini Squash	
Sprouts of all kinds	
Snow Peas	
Summer Squash	
Swiss Chard	
Tah Tsai	
Winter Squash	
Yel Crkneck Squash	
Zucchini	

KAPHA

CHOOSE ▼
Pac Choy
Parsley
Peas
Peppers
Potatoes, white
Purslane
Radicchio
Radish
Scallopini Squash
Shallots
Snow Peas
Spinach
Sprouts of all kinds
Summer Squash
Swiss Chard
Tah Tsai
Turnips*
Turnip Greens
Watercress
Yel. Crkneck Squash
Zucchini*

GRAINS	Cold, dry, puffed cereals Frozen or microwaved products Barley** Buckwheat Corn Granola Millet Oats, dry Oat Bran Popcorn Quinoa* Rice Cakes** Rye Wheat Bran, in excess	Amaranth* Oats, cooked All Rice Teff* Wheat Wild Rice	Amaranth** Buckwheat Corn Millet Oats, dry Oat Bran* Oat Granola Popcorn* Quinoa* Rice, brown** Rye Teff* Wild Rice**	Barley Oats, cooked Rice, basmati Rice cakes Rice, white Wheat Wheat Bran Wheat Granola	Oats, cooked Rice, brown Rice, white Wild Rice Wheat	Amaranth Barley Buckwheat Corn Granola, low-fat Millet Oats, dry Oat Bran Popcorn Quinoa Rice, basmati, small amount with peppercorn or clove Rice Cakes* Rye Teff* Wheat Bran**
ANIMAL FOODS	Beef** Lamb Pork Rabbit Venison	Chicken or Turkey, white meat Duck & Duck Eggs Eggs Freshwater Fish Seafood	Beef Egg Yolk Duck Lamb Pork Most Seafood Venison	Chicken or Turkey, white meat Egg White* Freshwater Fish* Rabbit Shrimp**	Barley Oats, cooked Rice, basmati Rice cakes Rice, white Wheat Wheat Bran Wheat Granola	Chicken or Turkey, dark meat Eggs, not fried or scrambled with fat Rabbit

* These foods are OK in moderation
** These foods are OK occasionally

	VATA		PITTA		KAPHA	
LEGUMES	AVOID ▲	CHOOSE ▼	AVOID ▲	CHOOSE ▼	AVOID ▲	CHOOSE ▼
	Black Beans	In moderation, soaked and well-cooked:	Black Lentils	Aduki Beans	Black Lentils	Pre-sprouting any of these is especially good:
	Black-Eyed Peas	Aduki Beans	Red Lentils	Black Beans	Mung Beans*	Aduki Beans
	Chana Dal	Black Lentils	Soy Cheese**	Black-Eyed Peas	Kidney Beans	Black Beans
	Garbanzos	Mung Beans	Soy Margarine	Chana Dal	Common Lentils	Black-Eyed Peas
	Khala Chana	Red Lentils	Soy Yogurt	Garbanzos	Soy Beans**	Chana Dal
	Kidney Beans	Soy Cheese**	Tur Dal	Khala Chana	Cold Soy Milk	Garbanzos
	Common Lentils	Soy Milk, liquid*	Urud Dal*	Kidney Beans	Soy Cheese	Lima Beans
	Lima Beans	Soy Yogurt**		Common Lentils	Soy Flour	Khala Chana
	Navy Beans	Tepary Beans		Lima Beans	Soy Margarine	Navy Beans
	Pinto Beans	Tofu*		Mung Beans	Soy Powder	Pinto Beans
	Soy Beans	Tur Dal		Navy Beans	Soy Yogurt	Red Lentils
	Soy Flour	Urud Dal		Pinto Beans	Tempeh	Soy Milk, warmed*
	Soy Margarine**			Soy Beans	Cold Tofu	Split Peas
	Soy Powder			Soy Products:	Urud Dal	Tepary Beans
	Split Peas			Soy Flour*		Tofu, hot*
	Tempeh			Soy Milk, liquid		Tur Dal
	White Beans			Soy Powder**		White Beans
				Split Peas		
				Tempeh		
				Tepary Beans		
				Tofu		
				White Beans		

NUTS Peanuts	In moderation: Almonds, Black Walnuts, Brazil Nuts, Cashews, Coconut, English Walnuts, Filberts or Hazelnuts, Macadamia Nuts, Pecans, Pine Nuts, Pistachios**	Black Walnuts**, Brazil Nuts, Cashews, English Walnuts**, Filberts, Macadamia Nuts, Peanuts, Pecans**, Pine Nuts, Pistachios	Almonds, well-soaked**, Coconut	Black Walnuts, Brazil Nuts, Cashews, Coconut, English Walnuts, Filberts, Macadamia Nuts, Peanuts, Pecans, Pine Nuts, Pistachios	Almonds, well-soaked**
SEEDS Psyllium**	Chia, Flax, Pumpkin, Sesame, Sunflower	Chia**, Flax**, Sesame**	Psyllium, Pumpkin*, Sunflower	Psyllium, Sesame**	Chia, Flax*, Pumpkin*, Sunflower*
SWEETENERS White Sugar	Barley Malt Syrup, Brown Rice Syrup, Fructose, Most Fruit Juice Concentrates, Raw Honey, Jaggery, Maple Syrup, Molasses, Sucanat, Sugar Cane Juice	Raw Honey*, Jaggery, Molasses, White Sugar**	Barley Malt Syrup, Brown Rice Syrup, Maple Syrup, Fruit Juice Concentrates, Fructose*, Sucanat*, Sugar Cane Juice	Barley Malt Syrup, Brown Rice Syrup, Fructose, Jaggery, Maple Syrup**, Molasses, Sucanat, Sugar Cane Juice, White Sugar	Raw Honey, Fruit Juice Concentrates, esp. Apple and Pear

* These foods are OK in moderation
** These foods are OK occasionally

CONDIMENTS

	VATA		PITTA		KAPHA
AVOID ▲	CHOOSE ▼	AVOID ▲	CHOOSE ▼	AVOID ▲	CHOOSE ▼
Chili Pepper	Black Pepper	Black Sesame Seeds	Black Pepper*	Black Sesame Seeds**	Black Pepper
Ginger, dry	Black Sesame Seeds	Chili Peppers	Coconut	Coconut	Chili Pepper
Ketchup	Coconut	Daikon Radish*	Coriander Leaves	Dulse, in mod. if well-rinsed**	Coriander Leaves
Onion, raw	Coriander Leaves*	Garlic	Dulse, well-rinsed	Hijiki**	Daikon Radish
Sprouts*	Grated Cheese**	Ginger, dry	Ghee	Grated Cheese	Garlic
	Daikon Radish	Gomasio**	Ginger, fresh**	Kelp	Ghee*
	Dulse	Grated Cheese	Hijiki, well-rinsed	Ketchup	Ginger, fresh and dry
	Garlic	Horseradish	Kombu	Kombu*	Horseradish
	Ghee	Kelp	Lettuce	Lemon	Lettuce
	Ginger, fresh	Ketchup	Mint Leaves	Lime	Mint Leaves
	Gomasio	Lemon	Sprouts	Lime Pickle	Mustard
	Hijiki	Lime	Yogurt, fresh, diluted**	Mango Chutney	Onions
	Horseradish*	Lime Pickle		Mango Pickles	Radishes
	Kelp	Mango Chutney**		Mayonnaise	Sprouts
	Kombu	Mango Pickle		Papaya Chutney	
	Lemon	Mayonnaise		Pickles	
	Lettuce*	Mustard		Salt	
	Lime	Onions, esp. raw		Seaweeds, well-rinsed**	
	Lime Pickle*	Papaya Chutney		Sesame Seeds**	
	Mango Chutney*	Pickles		Soy Sauce	
	Mango Pickle*	Radishes		Tamari	
	Mayonnaise	Salt, in excess		Yogurt	
	Mint Leaves*	Seaweed, uninsed, in excess			
	Mustard				

SPICES

Onion, cooked
Papaya Chutney*
Pickles*
Radish
Salt
Seaweeds
Sesame Seeds
Soy Sauce*
Tamari*
Yogurt, fresh

Sesame Seeds**
Soy Sauce
Tamari**
Yogurt, undiluted

Neem Leaves*

Ajwan
Allspice
Amchoor
Anise
Asafoetida
Basil
Bay Leaf
Black Pepper
Caraway
Cardamom
Cayenne*
Cinnamon
Cloves
Coriander
Cumin
Dill
Fennel

Ajwan
Allspice
Almond Extract*
Amchoor
Anise
Asafoetida*
Basil*
Bay Leaf
Caraway
Cayenne
Cloves
Fenugreek
Garlic, esp. raw
Ginger, esp. dry
Horseradish
Mace
Marjoram

Fresh Basil Leaves*
Black Pepper*
Cardamom*
Cinnamon*
Coriander
Cumin
Dill
Fennel
Mint
Neem Leaves
Orange Peel*
Parsley*
Peppermint
Rose Water
Saffron
Spearmint
Turmeric

Almond Extract*
Amchoor
Tamarind

Ajwan
Allspice
Anise
Asafoetida
Basil
Bay Leaf
Black Pepper
Caraway
Cardamom
Cayenne
Cinnamon
Cloves
Coriander
Cumin
Dill
Fennel*
Fenugreek

* These foods are OK in moderation
** These foods are OK occasionally

SPICES
(CONT.)

	VATA		PITTA		KAPHA
AVOID ▲	CHOOSE ▼	AVOID ▲	CHOOSE ▼	AVOID ▲	CHOOSE ▼
	Fenugreek*	Mustard Seeds	Vanilla*		Garlic
	Garlic	Nutmeg	Wintergreen		Ginger, fresh and dry
	Ginger	Onion, esp. raw			Horseradish
	Horseradish*	Oregano*			Mace
	Mace	Paprika			Marjoram
	Marjoram	Pippali*			Mint
	Mint	Poppy Seeds*			Mustard Seeds
	Mustard Seeds	Rosemary			Neem Leaves
	Nutmeg	Sage			Nutmeg
	Onion, cooked	Savory			Onion
	Orange Peel	Star Anise			Orange Peel
	Oregano	Tamarind			Oregano
	Paprika	Tarragon*			Paprika
	Parsley*	Thyme*			Parsley
	Peppermint*				Peppermint
	Pippali				Pippali
	Poppy Seeds				Poppy Seeds
	Rosemary				Rosemary
	Rose Water				Rose Water
	Saffron				Saffron
	Sage				Sage
	Savory				Savory
	Spearmint				Spearmint
	Star Anise				Star Anise
	Tamarind				

		Tarragon Thyme Turmeric Vanilla Wintergreen				Tarragon Thyme Turmeric Vanilla* Wintergreen
DAIRY	Any Dairy Which is Not Fresh Cow's Milk, powdered Goat Milk, liquid** Goat Milk, powdered Hard Cheeses** Ice Cream Sour Cream	All Fresh Dairy OK in moderation: Butter* Fresh Buttermilk Fresh Raw Cow's Milk Freshly Made Paneer* Freshly Made Soft Cheeses* Freshly Made Yogurt Ghee	Any Dairy Which is Not Fresh Salted Butter Buttermilk Feta Cheese Hard Cheeses Ice Cream Sour Cream Yogurt, undiluted	Unsalted Butter* Cottage Cheese, fresh Freshly Made Paneer** Freshly Made Soft Cheeses** Ghee Fresh Raw Cow's Milk Fresh Raw Goat's Milk Freshly Made Yogurt, diluted 1:2-3 pts. with water	All Dairy Which is Not Fresh Butter Cheeses of All Kinds Buttermilk Cow's Milk Ice Cream Sour Cream Yogurt, undiluted	Fresh Goat's Milk Ghee* Freshly Made Yogurt, diluted 1:4 pts. or more with water
OILS	Deep Fried Foods Rancid Oils	Any Fresh Cold-Pressed Oils, especially Sesame	Deep Fried Foods Rancid Oils And in excess: Almond Apricot Corn	In Moderation, Any of the Following, Cold-pressed: Avocado* Coconut Olive	Apricot Avocado Coconut Olive* Safflower Sesame*	Any of the Following, Cold-Pressed, in Small Amounts: Almond Corn Sunflower

* These foods are OK in moderation

** These foods are OK occasionally

	VATA		PITTA		KAPHA	
	AVOID ▲	CHOOSE ▼	AVOID ▲	CHOOSE ▼	AVOID ▲	CHOOSE ▼
OILS (CONT.)		Safflower**	Sunflower Sesame* Soy Walnut	Soy Walnut		

BEVERAGES	Alcohol*
	Apple Juice
	Caffeine
	Carob**
	Carbonated Drinks
	Coffee
	Cold Dairy Drinks
	Cranberry Juice
	Icy Cold Drinks
	Pear Juice
	Pomegranate Juice
	Pungent Teas**
	Prune Juice**
	Tomato Juice
	V-8 Juice
	
	Herb Teas:
	Alfalfa**
	Barley
	Blackberry
		Aloe Vera Juice*
		Apricot Juice
		Banana Shakes or
		  Smoothies
		Berry Juice
		Carrot Juice
		Carrot-Vegetable
		  Combinations
		Carrot-Ginger Juice
		Cherry Juice
		Chocolate*
		Coconut Milk
		Hot Fresh Dairy
		  Drinks
		Grain Beverages
		Grape Juice
		Grapefruit Juice
		Lemonade
		Mango Juice
		Miso Broth*
			Alcohol
			Banana Drinks
			Berry Juice, sour
			Carbonated Drinks
			Cherry Juice, sour
			Coffee
			Sour Juices, Teas,
			  Drinks
			Pungent Teas
			Caffeine
			Carrot Juice, in excess
			Carrot-Ginger Juice
			Chocolate
			Cranberry Juice
			Grapefruit Juice
			Salted Drinks
			Ice Cold Drinks
			Lemonade
			Orange Juice*
			Miso Broth**
				Aloe Vera Juice*
				Apple Juice
				Apricot Juice
				Berry Juice, sweet
				Carob
				Cherry Juice, sweet
				Coconut Milk
				Cool Fresh Dairy
				  Drinks
				Goat Milk
				Grain Beverages
				Grape Juice
				Mango Juice
				Peach Nectar
				Pear Juice
				Pomegranate Juice
				Prune Juice
				Soy Milk
				Low-Salt Vegetable
				  Bouillons
				  like Bernard Jensen's
					Banana Drinks
					Carbonated Drinks
					Cold Dairy Drinks
					Icy Cold Drinks
					Sour Juices, Drinks
					  & Teas
					Alcohol, in excess
					Coconut Milk
					Chocolate
					Grapefruit Juice
					Highly Salted
					  Drinks, such as
					  canned or com-
					  mercial bouillons
					Lemonade
					Miso Broth**
					Orange Juice
					Papaya Juice
					Soy Milk, cold
					Tomato Juice
						Aloe Vera Juice*
						Apple Juice
						Apricot Juice
						Berry Juice
						Caffeine**
						Carob
						Carrot Juice
						Carrot-Ginger Juice
						Other Carrot Juice
						  Combinations
						Cherry Juice, unless
						  sour
						Cranberry Juice
						Coffee**
						Hot Spiced Goat
						  Milk
						Grain Beverages
						Grape Juice*
						Mango Juice*
						Peach Nectar

Borage
Burdock
Chrysanthemum*
Cornsilk
Dandelion
Hibiscus*
Hops**
Jasmine**
Mormon Tea
Nettle**
Passion Flower*
Red Clover*
Strawberry*
Violet*

NOTE: All of the above beverages are best made fresh. Fresh is preferable to bottled, and bottled is preferable to frozen, in the juices and drinks.

Wintergreen*
Yarrow
Yerba Mate

Hot Spiced Milks
Orange Juice
Papaya Juice
Peach Nectar
Pineapple Juice
Sour Juices & Teas
Soy Milk, hot & well-spiced*
Vegetable Bouillons**

Herb Teas:
Ajwan
Bansha, with milk & sweetener
Basil
Catnip
Chamomile
Cinnamon
Cloves
Comfrey
Elder Flowers
Eucalyptus
Fennel
Fenugreek
Ginger, fresh

Papaya Juice
Tomato Juice
V-8 Juice

Herb Teas:
Ajwan
Basil**
Cinnamon**
Cloves
Eucalyptus
Fenugreek
Ginger*
Ginseng
Hawthorne
Hyssop
Juniper Berries
Mormon Tea
Osha
Pennyroyal
Red Zinger
Rose hips**
Sage
Sassafras
Wild Ginger
Yerba Mate

Herb Teas:
Alfalfa
Bansha*
Blackberry
Barley
Borage
Burdock
Catnip
Chamomile
Chicory
Chrysanthemum
Comfrey
Corn silk
Dandelion
Elder Flower*
Fennel
Hibiscus
Hops
Jasmine
Lavender
Lemon Balm
Lemon Grass
Licorice
Lotus
Marshmallow

V-8 Juice

Herb Teas:
Comfrey*
Licorice
Lotus**
Marshmallow
Oat Straw*
Red Zinger
Rose hips**

Pear Juice
Pomegranate Juice
Pungent Teas
Prune Juice
Soy Milk, well-spiced & warm
Low-Salt Vegetable Bouillons, like Bernard Jensen's Mineral Broth & Seasoning

Herb Teas:
Ajwan
Alfalfa
Bansha
Barley
Basil
Blackberry
Borage
Burdock
Catnip
Chamomile
Chrysanthemum
Cinnamon
Cloves
Corn silk
Dandelion

* These foods are OK in moderation
** These foods are OK occasionally

BEVERAGES
(cont.)

VATA

AVOID ▲

CHOOSE ▼
Ginseng*
Hawthorne
Hyssop
Juniper Berries
Lavender
Lemon Balm
Lemon Grass
Licorice
Lotus
Marshmallow
Oat Straw
Orange Peel
Osha
Pennyroyal
Peppermint
Raspberry*
Red Zinger
Rose Flowers
Rose Hips
Saffron
Sage
Sarsaparilla
Sassafras
Spearmint
Wild Ginger

PITTA

AVOID ▲

CHOOSE ▼
Nettle
Oat Straw
Orange Peel*
Passion Flower
Peppermint
Raspberry
Red Clover
Rose Flowers
Saffron
Sarsaparilla
Spearmint
Strawberry
Violet
Wintergreen
Yarrow

KAPHA

AVOID ▲
NOTE: Dilute Fruit Juices 1:1 with water for Kapha and drink in moderation.

CHOOSE ▼
Elder Flowers
Eucalyptus
Fennel*
Fenugreek
Ginger, fresh & dry
Ginseng
Hawthorne
Hibiscus
Hops
Hyssop
Jasmine
Juniper Berries
Lavender
Lemon Balm
Lemon Grass
Mormon Tea
Nettle
Orange Peel
Osha
Passion Flower
Pennyroyal
Peppermint
Raspberry
Red Clover
Rose Flowers

				Saffron
				Sage
				Sarsaparilla*
				Sassafras
				Spearmint
				Strawberry Leaves
				Violet
				Wild Ginger
				Wintergreen
				Yarrow
				Yerba Mate
			Chlorella	Chlorella
				Spirulina and other blue-green algae
OTHER	Chlorella*	Spirulina and other blue-green algae*	Spirulina and other blue-green algae**	

* These foods are OK in moderation
** These foods are OK occasionally

Revised Food Guidelines for Basic Constitutional Types is based on Enlarged Food Guidelines for Basic Constitutional Types, from *The Ayurvedic Cookbook*, Morningstar with Desai, Lotus Press, 1990.

APPENDIX III:
Some Work On Your Own

This is a process I have used with my classes and clients over the last couple of decades. It is simple, and yet you can learn a lot from it. It usually takes an hour or less; you will need a piece of paper and something with which to write.

Take a moment to relax and center yourself. When you are ready, look back on the last day to five days of eating without judgement. As much as possible, simply review how and what you have been eating, without praise, blame, criticism, or comment. Just look. When you feel ready, write down everything you can remember of what you have eaten, in the last day or up to the last five days.* If you like, you can also jot down how you felt, physically and emotionally. The main focus, though, is on what you ate and how you ate it. When you have finished this dietary recall, you can do a self-assessment with it, if you want. These are questions I often ask:

1) Can you tell what tastes predominate here? Do you go more for sweet foods, or sour foods, for example? Spicy foods or bland foods?

2) Are there particular textures you tend to eat a lot? Are you more attracted to crunchy foods, smooth foods, crispy foods, mushy foods? What do you see as you look at your own dietary record?

3) Can you notice any temperatures predominating? Are you more likely to go for hot foods or cold foods? Raw foods or cooked ones?

(I use these first three areas of questioning to get clearer about what a person genuinely prefers. It also gives indicators as to whether your food choices habitually balance your constitution, or chronically aggravate it. This information creates a foundation for further work. I would then continue with the following:)

4) Do you see any challenges, areas you would like to work with more?

Can you state the challenge as an observation, in a neutral way, like "I really tend to eat a fair amount late at night, when I am alone." The observation or challenge may bring up feelings. It is okay to acknowledge them, notice you have deep feelings about this. Or maybe the challenge will bring up no feeling at all, you may be pretty numbed out to this one, or have no apparent feelings about it. That's okay to notice, too.

Alternative approach: *If memory is a challenge for you, you may want to do this process in a slightly different way. Decide how long you want to track your eating, and write down, after each meal or snack, everything you eat and drink for one day to five days. Again, as much as possible, do this without judging yourself or what or how you are eating. When you have finished taking your record, you can address the questions above as described.*

5) Is there any way you would like to meet this challenge or issue, any thing you'd like to do differently? If so, I would suggest that any changes you plan be small ones, that you are relatively certain you can do. You can always make more changes later. It is more important that you learn to trust your own ability to change, rather than plan sweeping and ideal conditions that may be difficult or impossible to meet all at once.

An example related to the late-night eating described above might be, "When I start to feel that way, the first thing I will do is make myself a cup of hot tea and sit down." Or, "When this thought comes up, the first thing I do is take myself for a walk in the night air, noticing sensations like how the air feels on my skin, whatever smells are on the air, sounds, other sensations." Whatever you come up with, let it be a small commitment that feels right for you now, that you can realistically carry out. Give it a limit as to how long you would like to try it, a week, a month, whatever. Again, committing to short periods of time is fine. If you like what you are doing, you can always re-commit for another period of time. It is more important that you give yourself a manageable amount of time, so that you can really experience this change.

6) If there are a number of challenges or potential changes that come up and you want to begin work on them now, pick one to start. You can always save your self-assessment paper so that you can work with the others later, as you are ready for them. If you find that you are not ready to make any changes right now, notice that too.

7) Take time to review your dietary recall one more time and note down any strengths you see, acknowledge these. It could be that you took time one day to fix fresh food, or to eat in a relaxed way. Or you may have shared food with others, or eaten appropriately for your needs in some or all of those five days. Whatever strengths you see, let yourself acknowledge them. If you can find no strengths in your dietary record, let yourself notice that too.

Discussion: In Ayurveda, what someone eats is a big part of their well-being and healing. The person who is eating holds the largest role in their own healing. Becoming familiar with your own style and tastes is the first step in supporting the positive things you are doing with yourself, and giving yourself the chance to change actions or attitudes that are not working for you. We have all inherited and gathered buckets of judgements that we carry with us in this journey, that want to jump in and comment on our actions, behaviors, feelings, and thoughts. In this particular exercise or process, I am asking you to set your buckets of judgement aside for a moment, as much as you can, so that you can see and hear without so much of the white noise and static that they bring. However much you do this is okay.

If you find yourself discovering key trends in preferring one taste or texture or temperature of food over another, you may want to go back and review the material about these presented earlier in this book, for additional perspectives.

APPENDIX IV:

TRIDOSHIC MENUS

SPRING DAY

BREAKFAST

A Breakfast Rice, Ginger-Coriander Tea

LUNCH

Sprouted Mung Soup or Poor Woman's Creamy Asparagus Soup with Hot Tortillas: Whole Wheat for Vata and *Pitta*, Corn for *Kapha*, Mixed Baby Greens with Tarragon Parsley Salad Dressing

SNACK

Ginger-Pear Muffins, *Tridoshic* Tea

DINNER

Fresh Spinach-Cucumber Salad with Tarragon Honey Mustard Dressing, Quinoa-Asparagus Pilaf, Steamed Artichokes

DESSERT
(optional)

Dorie's Turkish Delight, *Chai*

SUMMER DAY

BREAKFAST

Selection of Fresh Fruits: Apricots, Berries, Sweet Cherries, Purple Grapes or A *Tridoshic* Fruit Bowl or Fresh Fruit Bowl with Pitta Soothing Tea or *Tridoshic* Tea, Banana Peach Muffins (if very hungry)

LUNCH

Light Cucumber Gazpacho, Wild Rice Salad, Light Mint Tea

SNACK

Coconut Fruit Smoothie or Assortment of Fresh Fruits: Berries, Ripe Mango, Melons

DINNER

Raspberry Kiwi Jelled Salad, Paella, Fresh Grated Carrots with Spearmint and Lime, Soothing *Pitta* Tea

DESSERT
(optional)

Crunchy Coconut Cookies

FALL DAY

BREAKFAST

Hot Quinoa or Teff, Digest Ease Tea

LUNCH

A Kichadi, with fresh vegetables of the season, like leafy greens and winter squash, Zucchini Salad, *Tridoshic* Tea

SNACK

Hot *Chai*

DINNER

Cup of Hearty Vegetable Soup, Savory Pot Pie, Choice of Hot Teas

DESSERT
(optional)

Fresh Pineapple Shortstop

WINTER DAY

BREAKFAST

Tasty Scrambled Tofu, *Tridoshic* Tea

LUNCH

Ama-Reducing *Dal*, (easy on the garlic), Quinoa-Cilantro Salad, Fresh Tossed Sprouts and Greens (optional)

SNACK

Roasted Nuts or Warm Applesauce, Quick Hot Cider

DINNER

Vegetarian Stroganoff, Beets with Maple Syrup Glaze (optional), Small Tossed Salad with Creamy Pesto Dressing (optional), Hot Teas

DESSERT
(optional)

Gingerbread Kids

QUICK DAY

BREAKFAST

Selection of Fresh Fruit: Apricots, Purple Grapes, Ripe Mango, Berries, Selection of Cold Cereals: Rice, Whole Wheat, Oat, Corn, Cow's milk and Goat or Soy milk

LUNCH

Cream of Broccoli Soup, Hot *Chappatis* or Rebekah's Tortillas, Fresh Sprouts and Toasted Sunflower Seeds

SNACK

Choice of Fresh Fruit: Apples, Sweet Oranges, Bananas

DINNER

Pasta with Light Basil Sauce, (offer choice of corn or wheat pasta), Summer Squash Salad, Hot Teas

DESSERT
(optional)

Apricot Tapioca (made in the morning)

WEEKEND DAY

BRUNCH

Crepes with Assorted Fillings or Pancakes made with Oat or Barley Flour, see p. 54, with Maple Syrup, Raw Honey, and/or Hot Apricot Sauce

SNACK

Stuffed Celery Sticks or Assorted Fresh Fruit: Apples, Oranges, Pears, Bananas

SUPPER

Salad Bar Supreme, Nice Burger, Pasta Salad (optional), Fruit Smoothies or Water

DESSERT
(optional)

Apple Slices

Vata-CALMING MENUS

SPRING DAY

BREAKFAST

Rice Almond Breakfast Cereal, *Vata* Calming Tea

LUNCH

Nori Rolls and Dipping Sauce, Fresh Baby Greens with Tarragon Honey Mustard Dressing, Basic Ginger Tea

SNACK

Blanched Almonds or Fresh Fruit or Vegetable Juice

DINNER

Butter Pecan Pasta, Favorite Snow Peas, Digest Ease Tea

DESSERT
(optional)

Dream Cookies

SUMMER DAY

BREAKFAST

A *Vata* Fruit Bowl, A Breakfast Rice (if very hungry), *Vata* Calming Tea

LUNCH

Fresh Baby Zuke Salad, Cilantro Quiche, Whole Wheat Crackers (optional)

SNACK

Iza's Tropical Smoothie or Fresh Fruit: Apricot, Banana, Grapes, or Plum or Other *Vata* Fruit in Season

DINNER

My Favorite Cajun Gumbo, Sweet Potato Biscuits, Simple Salad with Creamy Garlic Dressing, *Vata* Calming Tea

DESSERT
(optional)

Coconut Delight

FALL DAY

BREAKFAST

Hot Bearmush, Simple Hot Gingered Milk

LUNCH

Ama-Reducing *Dal* with Carrot and Zucchini, Plain Basmati Rice with ghee, Warm Milk or Tea

SNACK

Banana

DINNER

Thai Stir-Fry, Plain Basmati Rice, Mashed Sweet Potatoes, *Chai* or *Vata* Calming Tea

DESSERT
(optional)

Halvah Balls

WINTER DAY

BREAKFAST

Tasty Oatmeal, Simple Hot Gingered Milk or *Chai*

LUNCH

A *Kichadi* or Sweet Potato Soup
LUNCH (cont.)

Rebekah's Tortillas, Fresh Spinach-Cucumber Salad (optional)

SNACK

Hot Cherry Cider or Roasted Nuts or Seeds

DINNER

Dorie's Molé Enchiladas, Green Beans with Roasted Almonds, Plain Brown Basmati Rice (if very hungry), Basic Ginger Tea

DESSERT
(optional)

Banana Spice Cake or One Good Sweet Potato Pie

QUICK DAY

BREAKFAST

Restoring Almond Drink, Healthy Instant Hot Oatmeal

LUNCH

Fruit Yogurt, Tahini Roll-ups, Water or Herbal Tea

SNACK

Fresh Fruit: Banana, Orange, or Grapes

DINNER

Ivy's Soup Orientale, *Vata* Calming Tea, Hot Chappatis with Ghee

DESSERT
(optional)

Stuffed Fruits: Dates with Cashews

WEEKEND DAY

BRUNCH

Your Choice of Pancakes with Blueberries, Whole Wheat Crepes, or Cilantro Quiche, *Chai*

SNACK

Angela's Guacamole and Whole Wheat Crackers or Fresh Fruit or Vegetable Juice

SUPPER

Pasta with Pesto Sauce, Digest Ease Tea, Zucchini Salad

DESSERT
(optional)

Papaya Delight

SOME VARIATIONS

BREAKFAST

Hot Quinoa or Scrambled Eggs and Veggies or Breakfast Tacos or Cinnamon Rolls with Hot Milk

LUNCHES

See Lunches, p. 62 - 63

DINNER (ENTREES)

Wild Rice Salad or Paella or Quinoa-Asparagus Pilaf or Bean Threads with Snow Peas or Savory Vegetable Pot Pie or Vegetarian Stroganoff or Homemade Egg Noodles with Light Basil Sauce or Simplest Pasta

ON THE ROAD (WHEN TRAVELLING)

Note: In general, *Vatas* do best focussing on warm, moist, cooked foods; and taking it easy on raw, light, crispy, dry foods, especially while travelling.

BREAKFAST

Fresh Fruits: apricots, berries, cherries, kiwi, mango, papaya, peach, pineapple, plum, strawberries or Oatmeal or Cream of Wheat Hot Tea (bring your own tea bags) or Poached, Soft-Boiled, or Scrambled Eggs with Whole Wheat Toast, Tortillas, or Muffins or Pancakes, French Toast, or Waffles (bring your digestive herbs!)

LUNCH

Hot Vegetable Soup and Bread or Cottage cheese, pasta salad, small lettuce salad

SNACKS

Fresh Fruits or Fruit Juices calming to *Vata* (avoid apple, pear, cranberry) or Nuts and seeds or Yogurt and/or Warm Drinks (bring a thermos of your favorite, especially good if you are flying)

DINNER

Pasta with cream sauce, cooked vegetables or Indian cuisine with mild curries and rice or Asian meals with rice and vegetables or Custards, quiches, cream soups and such

Pitta-CALMING MENUS

SPRING DAY

BREAKFAST

A *Pitta* Fruit Bowl and/or Ginger-Pear Muffins or Whole Wheat Tortillas or A Breakfast Rice and Hot Herbed Milk

LUNCH

Pasta Primavera, Mixed Baby Greens with Creamy Pesto Dressing, Water or *Pitta* Soothing Tea

SNACK

Fresh Fruit: Apple or Berries or Dried Fruit: Figs or Raisins

DINNER

Quinoa-Asparagus Pilaf, Simple Adukis, Fresh Chinese Cabbage Slaw, *Pitta* Soothing Tea

DESSERT
(optional)

Pear Mousse

SUMMER DAY

BREAKFAST

Fresh Fruit Bowl, Puffed Rice with Cow's or Soy Milk, *Pitta* Soothing Tea

LUNCH

Light Cucumber Gazpacho, Quinoa-Cilantro Salad, Lebanese Chickpeas (if very hungry), Cool Water or Light Mint Tea

SNACK

Fresh Melon

DINNER

Sopa de Elote (Corn Soup), Fresh Baby Zuke Salad, Favorite Italian Bean Salad (if very hungry)

DESSERT
(optional)

Coconut Delight

FALL DAY

BREAKFAST

Hot Bearmush, Mild Ginger-Coriander Tea, light on the ginger

LUNCH

Ama-Reducing *Dal* (without garlic), Summer Squash Salad, Plain Basmati Rice (if very hungry), *Pitta* Soothing Tea

SNACK

Bean Threads with Snow Peas, Steamed Swiss Chard, Bancha or Herb Tea

DESSERT
(optional)

Fresh Pineapple Shortstop or Tropical Fruit Cake

WINTER DAY

BREAKFAST

Tasty Oatmeal, *Chai*

LUNCH

Hearty Vegetable Soup, Butterfly Biscuits or Rebekah's Tortillas or *Chappatis*, Herbal Tea

SNACK

Ayurvedic Trail Mix

DINNER

Savory Vegetable Pot Pie, Steamed Broccoli or Brussels Sprouts, *Pitta* Soothing Tea

DESSERT
(optional)

Dream Cookies, Quick Hot Cider or *Chai* (serve an hour or more after dinner)

QUICK DAY

BREAKFAST

Fruit Smoothie and Whole Wheat Tortillas or Chappatis (with ghee) and/or Rice or Whole Wheat Cold Cereal with Cow's, Goat, Soy, or Rice Milk

LUNCH

Cream of Broccoli Soup with Hot Whole Wheat Tortillas or Stuffed Avocado with Black Beans and Cilantro, *Pitta* Soothing Tea

SNACK

Fresh Fruit: Apple, Pear, Melon or Fresh Vegetables: Celery, Jicama, Peas or Other *Pitta-Calming* Produce

DINNER

Fettucini and Broccoli with Creamy Oregano Sauce Fresh Sprouts, *Pitta* Soothing Tea

DESSERT
(optional)

Stuffed Fruits: Calmyrna Figs with Walnuts

WEEKEND DAY

BRUNCH

Apple Cakes or Tasty Scrambled Tofu with Cinnamon Rolls or Pancakes with Yummy Apple Butter and Maple Syrup, Hot Milk or Tea or Chai

SNACK

Hummus and Whole Wheat or Rice Crackers (easy on the garlic)

SUPPER

Salad Bar Supreme, Cilantro Quiche or Baked Pinquito Beans, Wild Rice Salad

DESSERT
(optional)

(served several hours after dinner) Cantaloupe with Fresh Raspberries

VARIATIONS

BREAKFAST

A *Tridoshic* Fruit Bowl or A *Kapha* Fruit Bowl or Hot Quinoa or Apple Delight Scone with Hot Herbed Milk or Hot Blue Cornmeal with Raisins

LUNCH

See Lunches, p. 62 - 63

DINNER (ENTREES)

Equinox Soup or Paella or A *Kichadi* or Nice Burger or Vegetarian Stroganoff or Pasta with Light Basil Sauce

ON THE ROAD (WHEN TRAVELLING)

BREAKFAST

Oatmeal or Cream of Wheat or Rice or Whole Wheat Cold Cereals with Milk or Whole Wheat Tortillas, Toast, or English Muffin or Pancakes or Waffles with Maple Syrup

LUNCH

Nori Rolls or Hummus and Crackers or Bean Dip and Tortillas or Broccoli-Stuffed Baked Potato or Almond Butter Roll-ups (take ingredients with you) or Salad Bars with Vegetables, Beans, Cottage Cheese

DINNER

Bean Burrito and Salad or Pasta with Cream Sauce, Salad, Rolls or Asian Cuisine: Tofu, Rice, and Vegetables

KAPHA-CALMING MENUS

SPRING DAY

BREAKFAST

A *Kapha* Fruit Bowl or Mock Boston Brown Bread (Muffins) (if very hungry), Strong Ginger Tea

LUNCH

Fresh Chinese Cabbage Slaw, Poor Woman's Asparagus Soup, Rye Crackers (optional), Digest Ease Tea

SNACK
(optional)

Apple or Pear

DINNER

Ama-Reducing *Dal* or Thai Stir Fry with Plain Barley or Kasha

DESSERT*
(optional)

A Fresh Fruit Calming to *Kapha*

SUMMER DAY

BREAKFAST

Fresh Fruit Bowl (easy on the melons) or A *Pitta* Fruit Bowl, *Kapha* Invigorating Tea

LUNCH

Rainbow Summer Salad or Large Tossed Salad with Tarragon Parsley Salad Dressing or Creamy Pesto Dressing, Cilantro Quiche, Digest Ease Tea

SNACKS
(optional)

Berries or Other *Kapha* Fruits in Season

DINNER

Fresh Carrot Aspic, Quinoa-Asparagus Pilaf, *Kapha* Invigorating Tea

DESSERT*
(optional)

Dorie's Turkish Delight

FALL DAY

BREAKFAST

Hot Quinoa, Amaranth, or Teff or A Hot Soup (like Cream of Broccoli), Ginger Tea

LUNCH

Quick Black Bean Soup, Hot Corn Tortillas, Fresh Grated Carrots with Spearmint and Lime (optional)

SNACK
(optional)

Kapha Invigorating Tea

DINNER

Steamed Summer Squash or Zucchini, Soba Noodles with Garlic and Veggies, Ginger Bancha Tea

DESSERT*
(optional)

Applesauce

WINTER DAY

BREAKFAST

Cream of Rye or Hot Blue Cornmeal with Raisins, Hot Ginger Tea

LUNCH

Pasta Primavera, (with Corn Pasta) and Fresh Spinach Cucumber Salad with Tarragon Honey Mustard Dressing, Water or Herbal Tea (if thirsty)

SNACK
(optional)

Kapha Invigorating Tea

DINNER

Fresh Sprouts and Mixed Greens with Creamy Garlic Salad Dressing, A *Kichadi* (if very hungry), Digest Ease Tea

DESSERT*
(optional)

Hot Carob Drink

Note: It is strongly recommended that *Kaphas* skip desserts in general and have them primarily on special occasions, rather than on a regular basis.**

QUICK DAY

BREAKFAST

Fresh Fruit: Apple, Pear, or Berries or, Instant Healthy Dehydrated Cup of Soup

LUNCH

Summer Squash Salad and Simplest Pasta (with Corn Pasta) with Toasted Sunflower Seeds or Cream of Broccoli Soup and Bright Sunchoke Salad

SNACK
(optional)

Fresh Fruits in Season

DINNER

Sprouted Mung Salad or Hummus and Rye Crackers, Hot Spiced Tea (commercial tea bag)

WEEKEND DAY

BRUNCH

Buckwheat Cakes or Corn Cakes with Applesauce or Potato Frittata or Cilantro Quiche, Hot Herbal Tea

SNACK

Fresh Fruit: Apple, Pear, Apricots

SUPPER

Stuffed Cabbage Leaves, Hot Ginger Tea

DESSERT*
(optional)

Pear Mousse or Cholesterol-Free Carrot Cake

VARIATIONS

BREAKFAST

Kids' Cream of Millet or Crepes or Other Hot Soups

LUNCH

See Lunches, p. 62 - 63

DINNER (ENTREES)

Brand "Z" Tofu, Generic with Kasha and Leeks or Minestrone Soup or Sopa de Eloté Soup or Mild-Mannered Green Chili Stew or Equinox Soup or Baked Pinquito Beans or Simple Adukis or Polenta with Delish Tofu Spaghetti Sauce or Homemade Buckwheat Egg Noodles with Light Basil Sauce

ON THE ROAD (WHEN TRAVELLING)

BREAKFAST

Fresh Fruits: apples, pears, apricots, berries, strawberries or other *Kapha*-calming fruits or Dried Fruits: Stewed prunes, soaked raisins, or other stewed dried fruits and Hot Tea (bring your own tea bags, and a pinch of dry ginger powder per cup) or Oat Granola, Amaranth or Corn Flakes (you can bring them with you to be sure they are available for you) with Goat or Soy Milk or Soft Boiled or Poached Eggs with Rye Toast or Corn Tortillas

LUNCH

Salad Bar, Hot Vegetable Soup, and/or Cornbread or Baked Potato or Fresh Fruit and Hot Tea

DINNER

A Spicy Chinese Stir-fry or Beans, Corn Tortillas, Salad or Lighter Indian Curries (avoid fried items) or Broccoli-Stuffed Baked Potato (hold the cheese) or Beans, Rice, and Veggies, in whatever idiom

APPENDIX V:
Rotation Diets and How to Use Them

I originally wanted to include an introduction to rotation diets and some recipes (interspersed throughout the text) for the many people I know working with food or environmental sensitivities. Rotation diets are not traditionally used in Ayurveda, and yet they can be used for short periods of time when our guts or bodies feel most "off", or as a way to begin to determine what foods might genuinely be irritating us. Alternated with work with a good Ayurvedic physician, using the proper digestive herbs and cleansings, it can help serious cases. Milder cases of allergy may respond well to an Ayurvedic program without the restriction of a rotation diet.

Rotation diets were created in the West by allergists working with people with serious food sensitivities. The basic concepts behind a rotation diet are to 1) provide more variety in eating 2) eliminate eating the same foods day in and day out, a real problem with unsuspected food allergies 3) get an idea of what foods might be disturbing you 4) group foods according to their botanical families, since this is often how sensitivities can manifest.

Rotation diets are of greatest benefit to people with acquired allergies, for example, say you developed a milk sensitivity at twenty-five. Often avoiding a food such as this, then slowly rotating it back into your diet, can help you to incorporate the milk back into your life, at least for special occasions. Rotation diets are not meant to include or heal food-sensitivities with a probable genetic basis which have been with you since birth. Example: you react violently to crab meat, and have every time you have ever had it. I have not known rotation diets to help this sort of situation.

The advantages of a rotation diet are that it really does what it says, i.e., provide variety by shaking up your diet. Say you're a vegan living on fast soy products and noticing yourself getting more and more tired. This can help you check whether you might be getting too much soy, and see whether you feel better with less of it. Or for a more drastic example, a rotation diet can sometimes be the most direct way out of a badly boxed-in condition of extreme environmental or allergic sensitivity.

The disadvantage to the person on a rotation diet is that it can seem extraordinarily restrictive and frustrating, especially initially. And it is difficult to eat out when you are in the beginning stages of a strict rotation diet. Protein can be inadequate on some days of a vegetarian rotation, my primary concern as a Western-trained nutritionist. These rotations are not designed to be used for months on end. And from an Ayurvedic perspective, the food combinations and tastes available on any given day are limited.

With all this said, the following is one example of a four-day vegetarian rotation diet. There are many versions of the rotation diet, depending on what practitioner you are seeing. I am indebted to non-vegetarian rotation handouts from Dr. Jacqueline Krohn of Los Alamos, New Mexico for the basic structure of this one. The changes are my own. Again, I want to state STRONGLY that it is difficult to get a balanced diet with a vegetarian rotation. It should only be undertaken with the guidance and supervision of a skilled nutritional physician and even so, I would usually recommend it for short periods of time.

The purpose is not to stay on a rotation diet indefinitely, but to use it as a tool for healing, so that you can return to what feels like a more normal diet for you.

HOW TO USE A ROTATION DIET:

What follows is one four-day rotation diet. Basically, you begin with **DAY 1**. On **DAY 1**, you can eat *any* food listed on **DAY 1**, and no others. So for example, **DAY 1** lists eggplants, sweet peppers, tomato, and mushrooms, under **VEGETABLES**. It lists wheat under **GRAINS**. And cows' milk and cheese under **ANIMAL PRODUCTS**. So on Day 1 you might fix a homemade spaghetti sauce with eggplant, bell pepper, fresh tomatoes, and mushrooms. You could serve it over whole wheat or regular pasta, with paneer or parmesan cheese on top. What spices to use in the tomato sauce? If you are holding to a strict rotation diet, you would use only herbs and spices listed for **DAY 1**. So you might use bay leaf, basil, oregano, and thyme, for one example. Garlic, on the other hand, is listed on **DAY 4**, so in a strict rotation you would skip garlic in this Day 1 dish.

When to hold to a strict rotation? Any time you are using a rotation diet to determine allergies. Or any time you have such serious allergies that being sloppy and eating foods more often than every 4 days could cause you trouble. If your sensitivities are mild ones, you might be less strict.

So throughout **DAY 1**, you eat foods listed for Day 1. You wake up the next morning, and begin foods for **DAY 2**, and eat only foods listed for Day 2. And so on for Days 3 and 4. When you've come to the end of your first four-day rotation, you begin again with foods for Day 1, perhaps making a stir-fry with Chinese water chestnut and bamboo shoots, or a salad with fresh basil leaves and mâche. Generally, a minimum of four four-day rotations, or 16 days total, is needed to get any kind of idea of what might be bothering you.

How to tell this? Bodily responses. Say toward the end of **DAY 1**, you notice you often have more gas, sometimes even diarrhea. But only on Day 1, no others. Or you wake up on Day 2 profoundly exhausted or depressed or headachy. Any of these feedbacks you could take as an indicator that you might be reactive to a food or foods on Day 1. For another example: your sinus drip gets worse in the middle of most Day 3s - not every one, but most. You can look at how you're handling those foods for Day 3. Indigestion, congestion and mood changes can all be common allergic responses. A back or neck which goes out, or hallucinations, are far less common, but still documented responses to food sensitivities. So if you begin to suspect a particular food is giving you problems, cut it from the rotation and go through the sequence of days again without it. If you find yourself down to a seriously restricted "mono" (as in monotonous) diet, it's time to get outside help, from a skilled Ayurvedic physician, environmental ecologist, allergist, nutritionist, or nutritional physician.

For more information about food sensitivities and rotation diets, see the Bibliography, especially Robert Buist's books, Marjorie Hurt Jones's *The Allergy Self-Help Cookbook*, Patricia Kane's *Food Makes the Difference*, and Jacqueline Krohn's *The Whole Way to Allergy Relief and Prevention*. Hanna Kroeger's *Allergy Baking Recipes* include many unorthodox yet practical suggestions for the person with food allergies. For those interested in botany, I used James Smith's *Vascular Plant Families* to enhance this rotation. This last volume, with M. H. Jones's cookbook, can help you design your own rotation diets, if you like.

For some ideas about how to follow the rotation given here, a list of sample menus follows Day 4. Ayurvedic recipes suitable for this rotation have the notation ROTATION DAY DISH on the lower left side of any appropriate dish.

Note: Unlike many rotations, I have spread grains (in the Grass family) over all four days, locating the glutenous grains on Day 1, non-glutenous millet on Day 2, non-glutenous rice and teff on Day 3, and non-glutenous corn on Day 4. Buckwheat, in a separate plant family but with low-gluten content, is located on Day 4. Many people I worked with in my nutritional practice were sensitive to one or more grains of the Grass family, but not to all of them. This rotation makes it easier on most people, and can help you identify grains friendly (and unfriendly) to you. Occasionally a person will be sensitive to all grains. If this is the case, it is best to avoid them completely, and/or use them very occasionally on one of the four days of the rotation.

I have also assumed that salt, baking soda and corn-free baking powder can be used on any day. Many brands of baking powder contain cornstarch. These need to be avoided if you are corn-sensitive.

DAY 1

VEGETABLES:
Capparidaceae/Caper Family: capers
Cyperaceae/Sedge Family: **Chinese water chestnut**
Fungi: **common mushrooms**, Shiitaake mushrooms, Reishi, oyster mushrooms, truffle, all other mushrooms
Gramineae/Grass Family: **wheat grass, bamboo shoots**
Malvaceae/Mallow Family: mallow (cheeseweed), **okra**
Solanaceae/Nightshade Family: **eggplant, sweet pepper, chile pepper, potato, tomato, tomatillo**
Valerianaceae/Valerian Family: mâche

FRUITS:
Lauraceae/Laurel Family: **avocado**
Malpighiaceae/Malpighia Family: acerola
Passifloraceae/Passionflower Family: passionflower, granadilla
Punicaceae/Pomegranate Family: pomegranate
Rhamnaceae/Buckthorn Family: jujube
Rosacea/Rose Family, pomes: **apple, crabapple**, loquat, **pear**, quince
Vitaceae/Grape Family: **grapes, raisins**

GRAINS AND FLOURS:
Grass Family: **barley, oats, rye, wheat** (and their flours, brans, malts, syrups, and extracts)
Nightshade Family: potato flour and meal

NUTS AND SEEDS:
Juglandaceae/Walnut Family: Black walnut, butternut, English **walnut**, hickory nut, **pecan**
Labitae/Mint Family: chia seeds
Linaceae/Flax Family: flax seeds
Pinacea/Pine Family: **pine nuts**

ANIMAL PRODUCTS:
Bovine Family: **cow's milk, butter, ghee, cheese, yogurt, kefir**. Milk and milk products
  from buffalo, goat, sheep.

SWEETENERS:
Grass Family: **barley malt, wheat malt (often simply called "malt"),molasses, sorghum, sugar cane, Sucanat (TM)** (Grass family).
Grape family: **raisins. Any other fruits listed on Day 1**, including, for example, apple
  concentrate.

FATS AND OILS:
Bovine Family: **ghee and butter**
Juglandaceae/Walnut Family: walnut oil
Laurel Family: avocado oil
Mallow Family: cottonseed oil (would only recommend it if organic)
Onagraceae/Evening Primrose Family: evening primrose oil

CULINARY HERBS AND SPICES:
Cupressaceae/Cedar Family: **juniper berries**
Ephedraceae/Mormon Tea Family: Mormon tea
Grass Family: **lemon grass**
Laurel Family: **bay leaf, cinnamon**, filé powder, **sassafras**
Magnoliaceae: **star anise**
Mallow Family: marshmallow root, **hibiscus**
Mint Family: applemint, basil, catnip, horehound, **lavender**, lemon balm (melissa),
  marjoram, mint, oregano, peppermint, rosemary, sage, spearmint,   summer and
  winter **savory, thyme**, yerba buena
Rose Family: rose petals, wild cherry bark
Papaveraceae/Poppy Family: **poppy seed of all kinds**
Nightshade Family: **cayenne pepper, chili pepper (of all colors), paprika, pimento,
  tabasco**

MEDICINAL HERBS:
Apocynacea/Dogbone Family (Most members of this family are poisonous, use it with
  caution): bitter root, rauwolfia, vinca

DAY 1 (continued)

Asclepiadacea: milkweed, pleurisy root
Cupressaceae/Cedar Family: thuja
Combretaceae/Combretium Family: *bibhitaki, haritaki*
Gentianacea/Gentian Family: buckbean, gentian
Ginkgoaceae: ginkgo
Grass Family: citronella, oat straw, *vamsha rochana*
Laurel Family: camphor, cassia
Mallow Family: *bala*, cotton root, malva, marshmallow root
Mint Family: bugle weed, collinsonia, hyssop, motherwort, pennyroyal, self-heal, skullcap, wood betony
Mormm Tea Family: *ma huang*
Nightshade Family: *ashwaganda*
Passionflower Family: passionflower
Poppy Family: California poppy
Rhamnaceae/Buckthorn Family: cascara sagrada, New Jersey tea root (red root)
Rose Family: agrimony, wild cherry bark
Rubiaceae/Madder Family: cleavers, *manjishta,* squaw vine
Cyperaceae/Sedge Family: *musta*
Turneraceae/Turnera Family: damiana
Valerianaceae/Valerian Family: spikenard, valerian

BEVERAGES:
Juice, soup or tea from any food listed on Day 1, including milk, apple juice. Also:
Madder Family: coffee
Sterculiaceae/Sterculia Family: chocolate, cocoa, cola

OTHER:
Rose Family, pomes: **apple cider vinegar, pectin**
Fungi: **yeast and brewers's yeast**
Grape Family: **cream of tartar**
Nightshade Family: tobacco
Sterculia Famliy: gum karaya
Pomegranate Family: grenadine syrup

SOME MEAL EXAMPLES: Baked potato with ghee and fresh yogurt; spaghetti with Light Basil Sauce or Basic Rose Petal Tomato Sauce or Basic Cream Sauce; a traditional pesto sauce with whole wheat pasta; Rose Petal Pizza; Angela's Guacamole in whole wheat tortillas as burritos; Rosemary Potato Patties and Roasted Italian Vegetables.

DAY 2

VEGETABLES:
Aizoaceae/Ice Plant Family: New Zealand spinach
Amaranthaceae/Pigweed Family: vegetable amaranth
Arum Family: malanga
Cactaceae/Cactus Family: prickly pear, cholla, saguaro, other cacti
Chenopodiaceae/Goosefoot Family: **beet, chard**, lambs quarters, orach, **spinach,**
  sugar beet
Cucurbitaceae/Gourd Family: chayote, **cucumber, gherkin, pumpkin, squash of all
  kinds, zucchini**
Dioscoreaceae/Yam Family: true yam, Chinese potato
Euphorbiaceae/Spurge Family: cassava, manioc, spurge
Oleaceae/Olive Family: **olive**
Portulacacea/Purslane Family: claytonia (miner's lettuce), purslane

FRUITS:
Annonaceae/Custard Apple Family: cherimoya, custard apple, pawpaw
Gourd Family: **cantaloupe, honeydew, muskmelon, watermelon, other melons**
Ericaceae/Heath Family: bearberry, **blueberry, cranberry**, huckleberry, lingonberry,
  manzanita berries, salal, Tibetan lyonia
Musaceae/Banana Family: **banana**, plantain
Myrtaceae/Myrtle Family: **guava**
Rose Family, stone fruits: **apricot, cherry, nectarine, peach, plum, prune**, wild cherry

GRAINS AND FLOURS:
Amaranth Family: amaranth, quinoa, and their flours
Arum Family: poi
Grass Family, non-glutenous: **millet** and millet flour

NUTS AND SEEDS:
Fagaceae/Beech Family: acorn, beechnut, **chestnut**
Gourd Family: **pumpkin seed**
Lecythidaceae: **Brazil nut**
Protea/Macadamia Family: **macadamia**
Rose Family, stone fruits: **almond**

ANIMAL PRODUCTS:
Dove Family: dove and pigeon eggs
Grouse Family: ruffed grouse eggs
Turkey Family: turkey eggs

DAY 2 (continued)

SWEETENERS:
Aceraceae/Maple Family: **maple syrup**
Fruits listed for Day 2, including black cherry concentrate

FATS AND OILS:
Oleaceae/Olive Family: **olive oil**
Rose Family, stone fruit: almond oil, apricot oil (Rose family, stone fruit).
Fats from any of the foods listed for Day 2.

CULINARY HERBS AND SPICES:
Araliaceae/Ginseng Family: **American ginseng, Chinese ginseng, Korean ginseng,** eleuthro
Boraginaceae/Borage Family: borage, comfrey
Goosefoot Family: epazote
Myrtle Family: **allspice, clove, eucalyptus,** oil of bay rum
Nelumbonaceae/Lotus Family: lotus root
Olive Family: **jasmine**
Ranunculaceae/Buttercup Family: columbine (edible flower)
Rose Family, herb: burnet
Verbenaceae/Verbena Family: lemon verbena
Zingiberaceae/Ginger Family: **cardamom, ginger, turmeric**

MEDICINAL HERBS:
Berberidaceae/Barberry Family: barberry, mahonia (Oregon grape root)
Dioscoraceae/Yam Family: wild yam
Ericaceae/Heath Family: pipsissewa, uva ursi
Euphorbiaaceae/Spurge Family: *amla or amalaki,* castor oil, stillingia
Myrtle Family: cajeput, eucalyptus, tea tree oil
Podophyllaceae/Mayapple Family: American mandrake, blue cohosh, cohosh, podophyllum (American mandrake)
Ranunculaceae/Buttercup Family: black cohosh, golden seal, gold thread, peony
Santalaceae/Sandalwood Family: sandalwood
Scrophulariaceae/Figwort Family: balmony, culver's root, eyebright, mullein, rehmannia
Verbenaceae/Verbena Family: vitex

BEVERAGES:
Juice, soup and tea from any of the foods listed for Day 2, including jasmine tea, almond milk, prune juice.

OTHER:
Marantaceae/Arrowroot Family: **arrowroot starch**
Plantaginaceae/Plantain Family: psyllium seeds and husks
Spurge Family: **tapioca**

Sapotaceae/Sapote Family: chicle (the main ingredient in chewing gum)
Miscellaneous: corn-free Vitamin C crystals

SOME MEAL EXAMPLES: Large spinach salad with black olives and Rich Almond-Cucumber Dressing; millet with Almond Ginger Sauce; Middle Eastern Olive Casserole; Creamed Spinach over Millet Toast; Stuffed Butternut with Olives; Very Basic Beet Borscht.

DAY 3

VEGETABLES:
Algae: sea vegetables of all kinds
Compositae/Aster Family: **artichoke**, burdock root, dandelion, **endive, escarole**, Jerusalem artichoke, **lettuce**, radicchio, salsify
Convolvulaceae/Morning Glory Family: **jicama, sweet potato**
Leguminosae/Legume Family: **alfalfa sprouts, all beans and their sprouts, lentils, all peas, peanut, soybean**
Umbelliferae/Parsley Family: carrot, celeriac (celery root), **celery, parsley, parsnip**

FRUITS:
Bromeliaceae/Pineapple Family: **pineapple**
Ebonaceae/Ebony Family: **persimmon**
Oxalidaceae/Oxalis Family: carambola
Rosacea/Rose Family, berries: **blackberry**, boysenberry, dewberry, loganberry, **raspberry, strawberry**
Sapindaceae/Soapberry Family: litchi
Saxifragaceae/Saxifrage Family: **currant**, gooseberry

GRAINS AND FLOURS:
Aster Family: artichoke flour, sunflower seed meal
Grass Family, non-glutenous: **rice of all kinds, including wild rice**, rice flour, rice bran; teff, teff flour
Legume Family: bean flours: urud dal, garbanzo flour, lima bean flour, soy flour, peanut flour

NUTS AND SEEDS:
Aster Family: **sunflower seeds**
Betulacea/Birch Family: **filbert (hazelnut)**
Legume Family: **peanuts, soy nuts**

ANIMAL PRODUCTS:
Duck Family: duck and goose eggs

DAY 3 (continued)

SWEETENERS:
Grass Family, non-glutenous: traditional "YIN" rice syrup (Many other rice syrups contain
  barley malt.)
Legume Family: **sage honey, clover honey**
Any fruits listed on Day 3.

FATS AND OILS:
Compositae/Aster Family: **sunflower oil, safflower oil**
Legume Family: **peanut oil**
Fats from any of the foods listed for Day 3.

CULINARY HERBS AND SPICES:
Aster Family: burdock root, calendula, chamomile, chicory, chrysanthemum, dandelion
  root, some marigolds (not all are edible), tarragon **
Birch Family: **wintergreen** (oil of birch)
Legume Family: alfalfa leaf, **fenugreek**, gum tragacanth, **licorice**, red clover, tamarind
Myristicaceae/Nutmeg Family: mace, **nutmeg**
Parsley Family: **anise, asafoetida (hing), caraway, celery seed, chervil, coriander,
  cumin, dill, fennel,** lovage, **parsley,** sweet cicely
Piperaceae/Pepper Family: **black pepper, white pepper,** *pippali*
Rose Family, berries: mountain mahogany, raspberry leaves, rose hips, strawberry leaves

**NOTE: This family also counts ragweed as a member.

MEDICINAL HERBS:
Aster Family: arnica, blessed thistle, boneset, *bhringaraj*, coltsfoot, echinacea, elecam-
  pane, gravel root, grindelia, milk thistle, mugwort, wormwood, santolina, tansy, yarrow
Convolvulaceae/Morning Glory Family: *vidari-kanda*
Legume Family: astragalus, gum arabic, indigo, kudzu, senna
Parsley Family: *ajwan*, angelica (*dong quai*), *gotu kola,* osha
Pepper Family: cubebs
Rose Family: hawthorne berries

BEVERAGES:
Juice, tea or soup from any of the foods listed for Day 3. This would include
hot carob soy milk, fresh carrot juice. Also:
Compositae/Aster Family: "Dacopa" (TM) (roasted dahlia root)
Theaceae/Tea Family, Camellia sinensis: **all black or green teas,** bansha tea, kukicha tea

OTHER:
Algae: agar agar, blue-green algae, carrageen, Chlorella, dulse, Irish moss, kelp, Spirulina,
other algae
Bee Family: bee pollen, propolis

Legume Family: **carob**, guar gum, gum acacia, kudzu, tamarind

SOME MEAL EXAMPLES: Rice, beans and veggies; A Kichadi; Brand "Z" Tofu, Generic; a large lettuce salad with bean sprouts or sunflower or alfalfa sprouts, garbanzos, parsley, and grated carrot with Tarragon Parsley Salad Dressing; Nori Rolls and Dipping Sauce; Bean Threads with Snow Peas.

DAY 4

VEGETABLES:
Cruciferae/Mustard Family: arugula, **broccoli, Brussels sprouts, cabbage, cauliflower, Chinese cabbage,** collards, cress, Daikon radish, kale, kohlrabi, mizuna, mustard greens, pak choi, **radish**, rutabaga, tat sai, **turnip, watercress**
Gramineae/Grass Family: **fresh corn**
Liliaceae/Lily Family: **asparagus, chives**, day lily, **garlic, leek, onion, shallot**
Polygonaceae/Buckwheat Family: garden sorrel
Urticaceae/Nettle Family: nettle

FRUITS:
Actinidiaceae: **kiwi**
Anacardiaceae/Cashew Family: **mango**, mombin, sumac (lemonade berry, *Rhus*)
Caprifoliaceae/Honeysuckle Family: elderberry
Caricaceae/Papaya Family: **papaya**
Moraceae/Mulberry Family: bread fruit, **fig**, jack fruit, mulberry
Palmae/Palm Family: **date**
Polygonaceae/Buckwheat Family: **rhubarb**
Rutaceae/Citrus Family: **grapefruit**, kumquat, **lemon, lime**, muscat, **orange**, pummelo, **tangelo, tangerine**

GRAINS AND FLOURS:
Buckwheat Family: **buckwheat, buckwheat flour**, kasha
Grass Family, non-glutenous: **corn, cornmeal, grits, hominy, masa harina**
Moraceae/Mulberry Family: bread fruit flour

NUTS AND SEEDS:
Anacardiaceae/Cashew Family: **cashew, pistachio**
Palm Family: coconut
Pedaliaceae/Sesame Family: **sesame seed**

ANIMAL PRODUCTS:
Guinea Fowl Family: Guinea fowl eggs
Pheasant Family: **eggs from chickens**, pheasant, quail

DAY 4 (continued)

SWEETENERS:
Grass Family, non-glutenous: fructose (corn-based)
Palm Family: date sugar, jaggery

FATS AND OILS:
Cruciferae/Mustard Family: **canola oil** (rapeseed), mustard oil
Grass Family, non-glutenous: **corn oil**
Nettle Family: hemp oil (Urticaceae)
Palm Family: palm oil, African palm oil
Pedaliaceae/Sesame Family: **sesame oil**
Fats from any of the foods listed for Day 4.

CULINARY HERBS AND SPICES:
Citrus Family: **orange peel, tangerine peel**
Mustard Family: **horseradish, mustard seeds** of all kinds
Iris Family: **saffron**
Lily Family: **aloe vera, chives, garlic, onion**, sarsaparilla
Meliaceaea/Mahogany Family: *neem* leaves
Nettle Family: nettle
Orchid Family: **vanilla beans**

MEDICINAL HERBS:
Araceae/Philodendron Family (many members of this family are NOT edible): calamus
    root, skunk cabbage
Buckwheat family: bistort, *fo-ti*, yellow dock
Burseraceae/Bursera Family: *guggulu*, frankincense
Caprifoliaceae/Honeysuckle Famuly: crampbark, elder flowers
Citrus family: buchu, dittany, prickly ash, rue
Equisitaceae/Horsetail Family: horsetail, shavegrass
Filices: maidenhair fern, male fern
Grass Family: corn silk
Hamamelidaceae/Witch Hazel Family: **witch hazel**
Iris Family: blue flag
Lily Family: agave, false unicorn, *shatavari*, solomon's seal, yucca
Mustard Family: shepherd's purse
Orchid Family: lady slipper
Palm Family: saw palmetto
Pedaliacea/Pedalium Family: devil's claw
Ulmaceae/Elm Family: slippery elm
Zygophyllaceae/Caltrop Family: chaparral, *gokshura*

BEVERAGES:
Juice, soup and tea from any of the foods listed for Day 4, including coconut milk, fresh orange juice, papaya juice. Also:
Holly Family: yerba maté

OTHER:
Palm Family: betel-nut, sago palm starch

SOME MEAL EXAMPLES: Chinese vegetable stir-fry with 100% buckwheat soba noodles; soft corn tacos with scrambled eggs; Pasta Salad with buckwheat or corn pasta; Cashew Cream Cauliflower; Pasta Primavera with buckwheat or corn pasta; Stuffed Cabbage Rolls.

SOME SAMPLE ROTATION MENUS

DAY 1:

Breakfast: Tasty Oatmeal with ghee or butter, sweetened with barley malt or Sucanat; and hot milk or lemon grass tea.

Lunch: Day 1 Hearty Vegetable Soup, with red bell pepper garnish; whole wheat tortillas; water or a DAY 1 tea.

Snack: Apple.

Dinner: Baked potato with ghee and fresh yogurt; tossed salad with fresh basil leaves, cherry tomatoes and mâche, dressed with walnut oil and sun-dried tomatoes, blended.

Dessert (optional): Pear Mousse.

DAY 2:

Breakfast: Fresh Fruit Bowl with Hot Ginger Tea, sweetened with maple syrup (optional).

Lunch: Very Basic Beet Borscht with a spinach salad with toasted pumpkin seeds and dressed with olive oil. Cool water or ginseng or jasmine tea.

Snack: Banana.

Dinner: Stuffed Butternut with Olives, steamed zucchini or spinach, with Almond Milk or a hot tea from DAY 2.

Dessert (optional): Fresh blueberries and peaches.

DAY 3:

Breakfast: A Breakfast Rice with licorice tea or black tea.

Lunch: Pinto beans, rice, celery sticks.

Snack: Fresh carrot juice.

Dinner: Brand "Z" Tofu, Generic, with basmati rice and steamed artichokes.

Dessert (optional): Fresh Pineapple Shortstop.

DAY 4:

Breakfast: Saffron or fresh lemon in hot water, with Hot Blue Cornmeal.

Lunch: Cream of Broccoli Soup with hot corn tortillas or Kasha and Leeks, and water or a DAY 4 beverage.

Snack: Orange, or Calmyrna figs.

Dinner: Pasta Primavera, with Fresh Chinese Cabbage Salad and a DAY 4 tea.

Dessert (optional): Stuffed Fruit.

DAY 1:

Breakfast: Hot Bearmush with mint or hibiscus tea.

Lunch: Fresh yogurt sweetened with molasses, apple butter or applesauce; whole wheat crackers or tortillas or Liz's Scones.

Snack: Walnuts, grapes or raisins.

Dinner: Spaghetti with Basic Cream Sauce or Basic Rose Petal Tomato Sauce; with a large salad of sliced tomato, bell pepper and avocado with fresh basil, and a DAY 1 beverage.

Dessert (optional): Apple Slices.

DAY 2:

Breakfast: Kids' Cream of Millet and jasmine tea.

Lunch: Almond Ginger Sauce over hot millet or quinoa with steamed chard and ginger tea.

Snack: Apricots or peach, or macadamia or Brazil nuts.

Dinner: Fresh Baby Zuke Salad with baked acorn squash with maple syrup and a DAY 2 beverage.

Dessert (optional): Bowl of cherries or cubed melon.

DAY 3:

Breakfast: Hot Teff, and Dacopa with hot soy milk and honey.

Lunch: A *Kichadi*, and sprouts and grated carrot with Tarragon Parsley Salad Dressing.

Snack: DAY 3 Trail Mix

Dinner: Bean Threads with Snow Peas, Mashed Sweet Potato and hot raspberry leaf or other DAY 3 tea.

Dessert (optional): Dream Cookies.

DAY 4:

Breakfast: Buckwheat Cakes with Mango Sauce and Hot Sesame Milk or a DAY 4 beverage.

Lunch: Poor Woman's Asparagus Soup with Blue Cornbread.

Snack: Grapefruit, fresh orange juice or pistachios.

Dinner: Stuffed Cabbage Rolls, steamed asparagus and yerba maté tea.

Dessert (optional): Crunchy Coconut Cookies.

DAY 1:

Breakfast: Cream of Rye and hot fresh milk or walnut milk.

Lunch: Whole wheat burrito with potatoes and *paneer* and Angela's Guacamole, and a DAY 1 beverage.

Snack: Pear or pomegranate.

Dinner: Udon noodles with bamboo shoots, Chinese water chestnuts, peppers, and Shii-taake mushrooms (black Chinese mushrooms). A DAY 1 beverage.

DAY 2:

Breakfast: Hot Quinoa with a DAY 2 beverage.

Lunch: Banana Peach Muffins with almond butter, raw zucchini sticks and hot ginger tea.

Snack: Peach Smoothie

Dinner: Creamed Spinach Sauce over Plain Millet; spinach, cucumber and olive salad; a DAY 2 beverage.

Dessert (optional): Dream Cookies.

DAY 3:

Breakfast: Rice Hazelnut Breakfast Cereal with a DAY 3 tea.

Lunch: Sweet Potato Soup and rice crackers.

Snack: Toasted sunflower seeds, or celery or carrot sticks.

Dinner: Strawberry Pineapple Jelled Salad, Nori Rolls with a tossed salad of lettuce, sprouts, sprouted garbanzos (optional), carrot and celery; Tarragon Parsley Salad Dressing, and a DAY 3 beverage.

DAY 4:

Breakfast: Fresh tropical fruit salad with ripe mango, kiwi, papaya, and orange; coconut milk.

Lunch: Ivy's Soup Orientale, with a DAY 4 beverage if desired.

Snack: Dates or Calmyrna figs.

Dinner: Cashew Cream Cauliflower, with an asparagus and watercress salad with Orange-Sesame Dressing, and a DAY 4 tea.

Dessert (optional): Fresh papaya slices with lemon.

The "Let's Get Real, I live in America, and I'm not a Cook" Rotation:

DAY 1:

Breakfast: Puffed wheat, with fresh raw milk, boiled.

Lunch: Yogurt and apple butter, whole wheat crackers or tortilla, bell pepper slices.

Snack: Grape juice, or grapes or apple or pear, or a ROTATION DAY 1 ROLL-UP.

Dinner: Avocado, tomato; pasta with ghee and warm milk. (You can add some dried basil or oregano if you're feeling adventurous. If you're feeling very adventurous, try Light Basil Sauce instead. Incredibly adventurous, add Roasted Italian Vegetables on the side.)

DAY 2:

Breakfast: Puffed millet with Almond Milk. Hot ginger tea if you like.

Lunch: Have a large salad of spinach, cucumber and black olives at a decent salad bar that guarantees they don't spray their produce. Dress it with their olive oil, BYO almonds or pumpkin seeds for garnish.

Snack: DAY 2 Trail Mix and/or any of the many DAY 2 fruits.

Dinner: Steamed beets, spinach and small cubed acorn squash. Plus you learn how to make a grain, like Plain Day 2 Millet, to survive this day.

DAY 3:

Breakfast: Puffed Rice and soy milk (check brands for one suited to Day 3) or, if you're getting tired of cold cereal, fresh strawberries and pineapple, or, A Breakfast Rice.

Lunch: Sunflower butter on rice cakes, with sunflower sprouts, some lettuce, or a carrot.

Snack: DAY 3 Trail Mix.

Dinner: A *Kichadi*. -Or- if you're branching out, Brand "Z" Tofu, Generic with some carrot or celery cooked with it; and Plain Basmati Rice. Yearning for a little something sweet? maybe an hour or two later you'd feel like a handful of dried currants (like raisins, but a different botanical family) available in natural food groceries. Or check out Dream Cookies when you're ready. Very easy.

DAY 4:

Breakfast: Scrambled eggs and warm corn tortillas, or puffed corn and sesame milk. (All these puffed cereals are usually available in natural groceries, packaged inexpensively in bags, without preservatives. Look on the lower shelves, below all the distracting expensive stuff in boxes.)

Lunch: Cream of Broccoli Soup (it really is easy, try it) and sesame corn chips.

Snack: A DAY 4 fruit, like an orange or tangerine, or cashews.

Dinner: Pasta Salad with a corn pasta and steamed broccoli. Any DAY 4 beverage.

Beverages on a Rotation Diet:

Day 1: Cow's milk, kefir, yogurt *lassis*. Apple juice, pear juice, grape juice, pomegranate juice. Wheatgrass juice. Goat milk. Walnut and pecan milks. Hot spiced apple cider. Mint tea (of all kinds). Lemon grass tea, hibiscus tea. Cocoa. Coffee. Some *drakshas*. Wine, beer, or most other alcohols (on special occasions, for those with no problem with yeast. This is not an Ayurvedic inclusion!) Pure water.

Day 2: Banana, apricot, cherry, blueberry, peach, or plum smoothie. Pure juices of any of these. Cranberry juice sweetened with maple syrup. Hot ginger tea. Almond milk. Borage, comfrey, golden seal, ginseng, or lemon verbena teas. Fresh beet or spinach juices. Pure water.

Day 3: Fresh carrot juice. Carrot, celery, parsley and/or lettuce juice. Pineapple juice. Raspberry, strawberry, or persimmon juices. Plain soy milk. Plain rice milk (some amasakes). Hazelnut milk. Spirulina smoothie. Anise, boneset, chicory, chamomile, fennel teas. Hot carob. Dacopa (TM). Bancha, kukicha, and all black or green teas. Pure water.

Day 4: Fresh orange, grapefruit or other citrus juices. Lemonade sweetened with fructose. Papaya, mango juices. Coconut milk. Sesame milk. Cashew milk. *Shatavari*, horsetail, mate, lady slipper teas. Cabbage juice! (It's good for stomach ulcers, but I can't recommend its flavor!) Water with lemon. Papaya coconut smoothie. Pure water.

Pastas on a Rotation Diet:

Day 1: Regular pasta and whole wheat pastas

Day 2: Spaghetti squash as pasta

Day 3: Rice noodles, bean threads

Day 4: Corn pastas, 100% soba noodles, buckwheat egg noodles

APPENDIX VI:
Intersecting Pathways:
Ayurveda and Polarity Therapy

Polarity Therapy was developed in the first half of this century by Dr. Randolph Stone, a remarkable man with a deep interest in the healing power of the five elements and spirit's role in healing. He was strongly influenced by both Ayurvedic and Chinese medicine, as well as by Western naturopathy. He spent many years in India and ran a free clinic there whilst in his eighties.

In the last year I have been fortunate to be able to work with the Polarity Therapy Certification Program of the New Mexico Academy of Healing Arts in Santa Fe, New Mexico, teaching an introduction to Polarity Nutrition. I have been struck by the similarities, as well as the differences, between these two healing systems. Both emphasize the use of fresh, unadulterated food within a vegetarian diet. Both avoid heavy, fried, excessively processed foods. And both work with the elements to heal. While Ayurveda works with three basic constitutional types, Polarity Therapy uses four. People following a polarity therapy program will find many of the recipes in *Ayurvedic Cooking for Westerners* readily adaptable to their needs.

Recipes particularly appropriate for the Purifying Diet and the Health Building Diet are listed in the following table. They can also be found coded into the bottom of appropriate recipes. One difference between Ayurveda and Polarity Nutrition is that in polarity, one works to avoid the use of heated oils. While in Ayurveda, small amounts of warmed oils are considered beneficial for calming air, in polarity therapy heated oils are considered harder for the liver to process. Both views have value, and so occasionally I have included a version of a given recipe more specifically oriented for Polarity practice. In many cases, the same recipe is useful both for Polarity and Ayurveda.

For readers interested in more information about polarity therapy, *The Polarity Process* by Franklyn Sills (Element Books, Longmead, England, 1989) is an excellent explication of its practice and theory. The Murrieta Foundation has released a nice cookbook based on polarity principles called *Murrieta Hot Springs Vegetarian Cookbook* (by Murrieta Foundation, the Book Publishing Company, Summertown, Tennessee, 1987) which also includes many richer vegetarian gourmet dishes. For more information about polarity nutrition straight from the doctor's mouth, see Dr. Randolph Stone's *Health Building* (CRCS Publications, Sebastopol, California, 1985) and *Polarity Therapy* (CRCS Publications, Sebastopol, California, 1986). Specific references in Volume I of *Polarity Therapy* include Book I, pages 4 and 11; the Appendix to Book 1, pages 26 - 28; and Book III, pages 105 - 112.

DISHES SUITABLE FOR A POLARITY PROGRAM:

POLARITY PURIFYING DIET DISHES: include fresh and dried fruits, raw and cooked vegetables, sprouted seeds and legumes, fresh vegetable juices, Essene bread, all cold-pressed oils except corn oil, yams or sweet potatoes, avocados, honey, fructose, soaked almonds, and herbs and spices.

POLARITY PURIFYING DIET DISHES: avoid grains, unsprouted legumes, dairy products, sugar, salt, nuts, nut butters, most baked goods, potatoes, caffeine, and vinegar.

POLARITY PURIFYING DIET DISHES in this cookbook:

A Good Apple Rhubarb Sauce
A *Kapha*-Calming Fruit Bowl
A *Pitta*-Calming Fruit Bowl
A Tridoshic Fruit Bowl
A *Vata*-Calming Fruit Bowl
Basic Ginger Tea
Basic Lemon and Olive Oil Salad Dressing
Beets with Maple Syrup Glaze
Blanched Almonds (soaked)
Bright Sunchoke Salad
Broccoli and Garlic
Carrot Raisin Salad
Chinese Cabbage with Shiitaake Mushrooms
Creamy Garlic Salad Dressing
Digest Ease Tea
Digestive Cleansing Tea
Favorite Italian Bean Salad
Fresh Chinese Cabbage Slaw
Fresh Baby Zuke Salad
Fresh Grated Carrots with Spearmint and Lime
Fresh Carrot Aspic
Fresh Cilantro Salsa
Fresh Fruit Bowl
Fresh Pineapple Shortstop
Jicama-Tangerine Salad
Light Cucumber Gazpacho
Liver Wake-Up
Mashed Sweet Potatoes
Orange-Sesame Dressing
Parsnips, Peas and Carrots

Plain Simmered Cabbage
Rainbow Summer Salad
Raspberry Kiwi Jelled Salad
Roasted Sweet Corn
Sprouted Mung Soup
Steamed Vegetables, all of them
Strawberry Pineapple Jelled Salad
Summer Squash Salad
Sweet Potato Salad
Tarragon-Parsley Salad Dressing
Very Basic Beet Borscht
Yam Soup
Yummy Apple Butter
Zucchini Salad

POLARITY HEALTH BUILDING DISHES: include everything on the Purifying Diet, plus whole grains, unheated milk products, raw nuts and nut butters, potatoes, beans, nutritional yeast.

POLARITY HEALTH BUILDING DISHES: avoid cooked cheeses, heated oils and butters, roasted nuts, seeds and nut butters, baked goods with oil or butter, fried or refined foods like sugar, white flour, white rice.

POLARITY HEALTH BUILDING DISHES included in this cookbook:

A *Kichadi*
Almond Ginger Sauce
Angela's Guacamole
Ayurvedic Trail Mix
Baked Pinquito Beans
Boston Brown Bread (Muffins)
Broccoli and Garlic
Cashew Cream Cauliflower
Coconut Delight
Cream of Broccoli Soup
Cream of Rye (TM)
Creamy Non-Dairy "Ricotta"
Creamy Pesto Dressing
Equinox Soup
Favorite Italian Bean Salad
Fruit Tapioca
Gumbo Stock

Hearty Vegetable Soup
Hot Amaranth
Hot Apricot Sauce
Hot Bearmush
Hot Blue Cornmeal with Raisins
Hot Quinoa
Hummus
Kasha and Leeks
Kids' Cream of Millet
Lebanese Chickpeas
Mashed Sweet Potatoes
Mild-Mannered Green Chili Stew
Millet Almond Breakfast Cereal
Pasta Primavera
Pasta Salad
Pesto Sauce
Polenta
Quick Bean Dip
Quick Black Bean Soup
Quinoa-Asparagus Pilaf
Rolled Barley
Rotation Day 1 Combo Trail Mix
Rotation Day 3 Combo Trail Mix
Rotation Day 4 Combo Trail Mix
Salad Bar Supreme
Simmered Okra
Simple Adukis
Simplest Pasta
Split Mung Soup
Split Pea Soup
Stuffed Avocado with Black Bean and Cilantro
Stuffed Celery Sticks
Stuffed Fruits
Sweet Potato Soup
Sweet Potatoes with Apples
Tahini Gravy
Tasty Oatmeal
Vegetarian Soup Stock
Vegetarian Soup Stock II
Wild Rice Salad

APPENDIX VII:
Resources: Sources of Foods, Seeds, Info

Arrowhead Mills, Inc., P. O. Box 2059, Hereford, Texas 79045 distributes many of the healthy dry goods mentioned here, such as organic corn meal, teff flour and nutritious instant oatmeal.

Auroma International, Inc., P.O. Box 1008-ACW, Silver Lake, Wisconsin 53170; 1-414-889-8569; 1-414-889-8591 (fax), supplier of natural incense, essential oils and Ayurvedic products.

Ayurveda at Spirit Rest, P.O. Box 3537, Pagosa Springs, Colorado 81147; 1-303-264-2573, a retreat center specializing in rejuvenation and cleansing *(Pancha Karma)*.

Bernard Jensen Products, Solana Beach, California 92075, produces many fine vegetarian products, including apple concentrate and a good powdered vegetable mineral bouillon; the latter has a small amount of yeast in it.

Ecology Action, 5798 Ridgewood Road, Willits, California 95490 distributes John Jeavons' *How to Grow More Vegetables*, a raised-bed approach to growing food, as well as many other publications and seeds. Jeavons' book is now available in Hindi, Russian, Spanish, French, and German, as well as in English and Braille. The organization is working particularly in Mexico, Kenya, India, and the U.S.

Earth Island Institute, 300 Broadway, Suite 28, San Francisco, California 94133-3312; 1-415-788-3666; fax 1-415-7887324, publishes an excellent quarterly journal of international environmental news. They also sponsor a wide variety of restoration projects.

Ener-G Foods, Inc., P.O. Box 84487, Seattle, Washington 98124-5787, 1-800-331-5222, in Washington State: 1-800-325-9788, carries a good line of foods for allergic people, including Egg Replacer and Rice Bran.

Frontier (Natural) of Norway, Iowa 52318 produces an alcohol-free line of flavoring extracts, including a vanilla flavor in glycerin.

Herbalvedic Products, P.O. Box 6390, Santa Fe, New Mexico 87502 has Ayurvedic herbs and products.

Herbs Etc., 323 Aztec, Santa Fe, New Mexico 87501, 505-982-1265 offers mail-order surface for a wide variety of herbs. Their line includes a dozen common dried Ayurvedic herbs in bulk, plus American grown liquid *ashwaganda* (from Planetary Formulations) and many high-quality Western herbs in tincture or bulk.

Institute for Wholistic Education, 33719 116th Street, Box ACW, Twin Lakes, Wisconsin 53181, correspondence courses in Ayurveda.

J.L. Hudson, Seedsman, P.O. Box 1058, Redwood City, California 94064, puts out an annual Ethnobotanical Catalog of Seeds which is both extensive and informative, with seeds from around the world.

Live Food Products, Inc., Box 7, Santa Barbara, California 93102, offers Bragg (TM) Liquid Aminos, made only of purified water and soybeans. It can be a good alternative to tamari; the company states that "this product is not fermented".

Los Chileros de Nuevo Mexico, P. O. Box 6215, Santa Fe, New Mexico, 87502, 505-471-6967 has good dried green chile and other traditional products.

Lotus Brands, Inc., P.O. Box 325-ACW, Twin Lakes, Wisconsin 53181; 1-414-889-8561; 1-414-889-8591 (fax), manufacturer and importer of numerous health oriented products including essential oils, massage oils, natural body care products, Chinese herbal supplements, bulk herbs and spices, and natural incense from India.

Lotus Fulfillment Service, P.O. 33719 116th Street, Box ACW, Twin Lakes, Wisconsin 53181; 1-414-889-8501, mail order supplier of Ayurvedic herbs, spices, products, essential oils, massage oils, homeopathic items, alternative health and body care products, books, videos, etc. Widest selection of Ayurvedic items available by mail order.

Lotus Light Natural Body Care, P.O. Box 1008, Lotus Drive, Dept. ACW, Silver Lake, Wisconsin 53170; 1-414-889-8501; 1-414-889-8591 (fax), wholesale supplier of over 7000 natural health and body care products including herbs, essential oils, massage oils, homeopathy, flower remedies, spices, books and videos including a number of major Ayurvedic product lines.

Lotus Press, P.O. Box 325-ACW, Twin Lakes, Wisconsin 53181; 1-414-889-8561, publisher of alternative health literature specializing in Ayurveda, aromatherapy and alternative healing methods. Also publishes the books of Sri Aurobindo and other spiritual literature.

Maharishi Ayur-Ved Products International (MAPI), P.O. Box 514, Lancaster, Massachusetts 01523, 1-800-255-8332, offers a variety of Ayurvedic products. As this book is going to print, I see they have even just put out a line of Vata, Pitta and Kapha Teas (trademarked) in tea bag form. This group has done most of the formal research on Ayurveda in the West and is undoubtedly the best-funded organization working in the field in the West today.

Native Seeds/SEARCH, 2509 N. Campbell Ave. #325, Tucson, Arizona 85719, great non-profit organization with the aim of preserving endangered and indigenous food crops, particularly of the southwestern USA. They sell tepary beans and a variety of native foods, for cooking, as well as seeds.

Natural Sources of Long Beach, California 90813 makes a 100% black cherry concentrate, all fruit, unsweetened, bottled.

Nichols Garden Nursery, "Herbs and Rare Seeds", annual catalog, 1190 North Pacific Highway, Albany, Oregon, 97321. Good source of seed for Tulsi basil, saffron crocus bulbs and other unusual Indian and Western herbs.

Planetary Formulations, P.O. Box 533, Soquel, California 95073 produces high-quality herbal formulations, many of them Ayurvedic, from formulas by Michael Tierra.

Pomona's Universal Pectin, P.O. Box 1083, Greenfield, Massachusetts 01302 offers pectin which can be used as a thickener without sugar.

Real Goods Trading Corporation, 966 Mazzoni Street, Ukiah, California 95482, 1-800-762-7325 (for orders), FAX 707-468-0301. This respected company is on the cutting edge of alternative energy products and education, everything from solar collectors, rechargeable batteries, composting toilets, to air filters. You name it, they are likely to have it.

Ronniger's Seed Potatoes, Star Route, Moyie Springs, Idaho 83845, annual catalog. Excellent source of organic potatoes, to plant or to eat.

Seed Savers Exchange, 3076 North Winn Road, Decorah, Iowa 52101, is a non-profit organization with a $25 annual membership fee, saving seed from around the world, especially North America. Great source of heirloom food seeds.

Seeds of Change, annual catalog, P. O. Box 15700, Santa Fe, New Mexico 87506-5700. Wide selection of rare Western and Indian seeds, like milk thistle and *ashwaganda*, and they're organic.

Solar Box Cookers International, 1724 Eleventh Street, Sacramento, California 95814, 916-444-6616, FAX 447 8689, is a non-profit organization offering information about solar box cookers, including a booklet on how to build your own.

David Steinman's *Diet for a Poisoned Planet*, Ballantine Books, New York, 1990 includes an extensive list of mail-order organic food sources of all kinds.

It is well worth the time and effort to discover if your region has a cooperative warehouse. Here in the Southwest we have Tucson Cooperative Warehouse, 350 South Toole Avenue, Tucson, Arizona 85701, 602-884-9951, serving Arizona, New Mexico, West Texas, Colorado, Utah, Nevada, and Southern California. Policies for co-ops can vary, but basically they deliver food at bulk prices to smaller buying clubs throughout their regions. Organizing with your neighbors or other friends can mean a substantial savings in food items like organic mung beans and basmati rice. Often cooperative warehouses also offer items hard to find elsewhere. Supplemented with support of local farmers and merchants, working with a co-op can be a very positive move in a healthy direction.

Trace Minerals Research, P.O. Box 429, Roy, Utah 84067, offers trace mineral drops helpful for remineralizing filtered water such as "R.O." (reverse osmolarity) water or distilled water. The drops are an especially rich source of magnesium and chloride, with many assorted trace minerals.

Vegetarian Times, P.O. Box 570, Oak Park, Illinois 60303, phone (708) 848-8175. Good coverage of vegetarian issues and vegetarian cooking.

Westbrae Natural Foods, Carson, California 90746 offers many good whole-food products, including a variety of tasty corn pastas.

Wishing Well Video, P.O. Box 1008-ACW, Silver Lake, Wisconsin 53170; 1-414-889-8541; 1-414-889-8591 (fax), features video catalog of 1000+ titles with the widest selection of alternative health and new age videos available anywhere. Wholesale, retail and mail order.

Yoga International, R.R.1 Box 407, Honesdale, Pennsylvania 18431, runs fine articles on Ayurveda.

The Yogi Tea Company, 9701 West Pico Blvd. #112, Los Angeles, California 90035, phone (310) 552-3532, has a variety of products influenced by Ayurveda, including a very good Licorice Spice tea.

APPENDIX VIII:
Glossary of Terms in Sanskrit and English

Adhidaivic: pertaining to *sattva, raja* and *tama.*

Aduki beans: small reddish brown beans popular in many Asian cuisines, strengthening to the kidneys and diuretic in action. Available in Asian and natural food stores.

Agar agar: clear, dried flakes of seaweed, used to make gels. Available in natural food stores and some Asian groceries.

Agni: digestive fire. Also the sacred Hindu god of fire and the cosmic force of transformation.

Ajwan: Indian herb, wild celery seed, excellent decongestant. Warming. Available in Indian groceries.

Akasha: ether or space, the element.

Ama: internal toxic wastes, which contribute to low energy and illness. Usually *ama* is created by incomplete digestion or elimination or through improper metabolic functioning.

Amla: sour (in taste).

Anjier: light golden or white figs, Calmyrnas.

Anupana: a medium in which medicinal herbs can be taken, like ghee or hot milk.

Ap: water, the element.

Apple concentrate: bottled concentrated apple juice, a good natural sweetener, available in health-food stores and natural groceries. Calming to *Pitta* and *Kapha* (when used in moderation) and usually not very disruptive for *Vata*. Bernard Jensen Products offers a good apple concentrate.

Artav: female reproductive tissue, one of the *dhatus.*

Asafoetida: see *hing.*

Asana: yogic posture.

Ashwaganda: a tonic and restorative herb, used to calm *Vata* and strengthen the reproductive system.

Asthi: bone tissue, one of the *dhatus.*

Atharva Veda: a later one of the ancient Sanskrit texts, the *Vedas*, from which comes the bulk of information relating to the practice of Ayurvedic medicine.

Avila: cloudy.

Ayurveda: the science of life and self-healing.

Basil: a common Western herb which is a good digestive stimulant, used fresh or dried. Found in the produce and spice sections of most food stores.

Basmati (white): a light, richly scented rice, valued in Ayurveda for its ease of digestion. It is polished. Available in Indian groceries and some natural food stores. It has no fat and contains four grams of protein per 3/4 cup cooked serving. Because of its lightness and ease of digestion, I use white *basmati* a good deal in the summer.

Basti: medicated enema.

Bhasma: Ayurvedic medicine which has been ashed, such as peacock feathers or gems.

Black cherry concentrate: concentrated black cherry juice, bottled. Natural Sources produces an unsweetened variety, available in natural groceries.

Brown *basmati*: a tasty whole grain rice closer in its action to brown rice than traditional Indian white *basmati*. It cooks up in 45 - 50 minutes, compared to white *basmati's* 15 minutes. Available in natural groceries. It has four times the potassium content of white basmati and notably more B vitamins, plus a trace of calcium. Oddly, current assays indicate it has less protein than white basmati, with 3 grams per 3/4 cup cooked serving. Because it is heavier and more nutritious, I use it more than white *basmati* during the winter.

Brown rice: a nourishing whole grain, good for grounding. Because it is heavier than *basmati*, it is generally recommended only when digestive fire is good. Available in natural food stores and sometimes supermarkets now.

Brown rice flour: available in some natural food stores. It is rough, dry, heavy, and nourishing, more aggravating to *Vata* or *Pitta* than white rice flour or Indian rice flour. Its heaviness makes it unbalancing to *Kapha* as well, if used as the primary flour. Best used in small amounts with other flours.

Brown rice syrup: a usually malted sweetener, found in natural food stores. It is usually made with rice and a little barley. The "traditional yin" variety often contains only rice.

Cardamom: a sweet spice soothing to all *doshas*, with some warmth in its action. Found in the herb and spice section of most food stores.

Chala: mobile.

Chana dal: the split version of *khala Chana*, Indian chickpeas. *Chana dal* is calming to *Pitta* and *Kapha*, and can be found in Indian groceries.

Chappati: unyeasted Indian flat bread, usually made of wheat flour; can also be called *rotis* or *rotalis*.

Charak Samhita: one of the classic Ayurvedic textbooks, written around 700 B.C. It is still a chief reference text today for Ayurvedic practitioners.

Cinnamon: a common sweet, warm spice, good for stimulating digestion and appropriate for all *doshas* in moderation. Found in the spice section of food stores.

Coriander seeds: a cooling herb helpful for expelling gas and supporting digestion, especially good for *Pitta*. In its fresh leaf form coriander is known as *cilantro* or Chinese parsley. It is easily grown.

Corn pastas: spaghetti, macaroni and other noodles made entirely of corn. A good alternative to wheat pastas for *Kapha* or wheat-sensitive individuals. Westbrae makes some nice light ones.

Cumin seeds: a common and inexpensive herb which enhances digestion and calms all three *doshas*. Can be overused! (in terms of taste, in which case you may have a hard time facing it for a while).

Dal: any split bean or pea in Indian cooking. Also, the Indian soups made from split beans or peas. While effects vary from person to person, the split *dals* can be a little more drying to the body than whole soaked or sprouted beans.

Dhatus: the seven essential tissues of the body in Ayurvedic anatomy. They are also known as the "retainable structures", meaning they are always retained within the body, in order for us to be healthy. They include *rasa, rakta, mamsa, meda, asthi, majja, shukra/artav*.

Diuretic: increases urination.

Dosha: an essential biological energy or structure in Ayurvedic anatomy. There are three primary doshas, *Vata, Pitta* and *Kapha*, which sustain all life. They move cyclically on a daily basis, and act as transporters and communicators between the essential tissues (the *dhatus*) and the *malas* (bodily wastes). Their balance is a key to health. They also determine our physical constitution at birth.

Draksha: a popular Ayurvedic herbal wine made from grape juice, raisins and spices, designed to revivify the body and strengthen *agni*.

Drava: liquid.

Dual *dosha*: a Western term for someone having two *doshas* predominant in their constitution, like *Vata-Pitta, Pitta-Kapha*, or *Kapha-Vata*.

Egg Replacer: an egg substitute especially useful in baked goods, made of potato, tapioca, calcium lactate, calcium carbonate, citric acid, and carbohydrate gum. It contains no dairy, preservatives, or artificial flavorings. It is available through Ener-G Foods, Inc.

Another egg substitute is made from flax seed. To make it, grind 1 tablespoon of whole flax seeds in the blender or grinder until fine. Stir it into 1/4 cup cold water in a small saucepan, then bring to a boil. Let it boil for 3 minutes, stirring constantly. It will thicken. Remove it from the heat and let it cool a bit. One tablespoon of this mixture can be used for each egg called for in a recipe. Flax will not give the loft egg does in baked goods, but works fairly well nonetheless in pancakes, cookies and quick breads. These directions are based on recommendations given in *Allergy Baking Recipes* by Hanna Kroeger. If you are making a larger amount, use a basic proportion of 1 part flax seed to 3 parts water.

Epazote: an easily grown Mexican herb, *Chenopodium ambrosioides*, which is used in very small amounts to season beans, to reduce *Vata*. It can be used in place of *hing*, asafoetida.

Ghee: clarified butter, much valued in Ayurvedic practice. Used therapeutically to enhance the flow of fluids throughout the body.

Ginger: a spice excellent for stimulating digestive fire, especially in its fresh form. Available in the produce section of most groceries.

Ghrita: medicated ghee, made of various herbs.

Guna: one of the twenty qualities or attributes. See also *mahagunas*.

Guru: heavy.

Hing: asafoetida, a strong-smelling Indian herb, warming in action. Useful for reducing the gas-producing qualities of foods like beans. Calms *Vata*. Available in Indian groceries and some herb and natural food stores. Is often compounded with wheat or rice flour.

Jaggery: a golden brown Indian sweetener, sold in Indian groceries. It looks like clumps of moist brown sugar and tastes a little like molasses.

Jala: water, the attribute.

Kapha: earth-water dosha or constitution.

Karma: effect or action.

Kashaya: astringent (in taste).

Kathina: hard.

Katu: pungent (in taste).

Khala chana: dark brown Indian chickpeas, smaller than American garbanzos, and sometimes easier to digest. They can be found in Indian grocery stores. Garbanzos substitute for them in a recipe relatively easily.

Khara: rough.

Kichadi: a healing stew of mung beans, basmati rice, vegetables, and spices; an easy one-pot meal.

Laghu: light.

Lavana: salty (in taste).

Madhura: sweet (in taste).

Mahagunas: the three great attributes of mind: *sattva*, *rajas* and *tamas*.

Majja: nerve and marrow tissue, one of the *dhatus*.

Malas: the body's waste products: urine, feces and perspiration.

Mamsa: muscle tissue, one of the *dhatus*.

Manda: slow.

Marma: energy pressure point.

Masur dal: red lentils, found in natural food groceries or Indian and Middle Eastern groceries.

Math dal: a small brown tepary bean grown in India and found in Indian groceries, said to calm all three *doshas*.

Medas: adipose tissue, one of the *dhatus*.

Methi: fenugreek greens, easily grown. Available in summer in Indian groceries. Good for clearing *ama* from the system, but also heating.

Miso: salty fermented soybean paste, often made with a grain like rice or barley. Available in Asian and natural food groceries; might be used occasionally in an Ayurvedic program.

Mrudu: soft.

Mung: small green-colored bean grown in India, a staple of Ayurvedic cuisine. It is used whole or sprouted, in soups and stews. It can be found in Indian, Asian and natural food stores. The same bean from which bean sprouts are grown.

Mung dal: the split version of mung beans, sometimes sold as "yellow *dal*". Hulled they look like small chipped yellow split peas. Available in Indian groceries and some natural food stores.

Nasya: nasal application of herbs and oils. Calamus oil is one example, helpful for clearing long-standing sinus congestion.

Neem: leaves, *Azadirachta indica*, can sometimes be found in the refrigerator section of Indian groceries. A bitter Indian herb calming to *Pitta* and *Kapha*. Fresh it is far more potent than dried.

Ojas: our energy cushion, aura, vital life protector.

Okasatmya: diets or lifestyles which have become non-harmful to the body through their regular or habitual use.

Oregano: a common Western herb good for stimulating digestion. Mildly warming and pungent. Found in the herb and spice section of food stores.

Pancha Karma: the five cleansing practices of Ayurveda, *vamana*, *virechana*, *basti*, *nasya*, and *rakta moksha*. Said to be one of the pillars of health, along with proper diet and lifestyle.

Pancha Mahabhutas: the five great elements, ether, air, fire, water, and earth, which sustain all creation.

Paneer: also spelled *panir*, is a soft cultured cheese product you can make yourself at home. *Paneer* is best eaten occasionally, about once a month, by those with strong digestive fire. Being cool, sour and heavy, it is not recommended for people with low *agni*. It is best suited for occasional use for *Vata*. To make *paneer*, bring a quart of fresh raw milk to a boil for a half minute. As it is still foaming, remove from heat and stir in one tablespoon fresh lemon juice. Let the mixture sit for 5 to 10 minutes, then pour it into a colander lined with cheesecloth, with enough excess cloth so that it can be tied. The excess liquid contains whey and can be used in baked products. The colander can be set over a large bowl and allowed to cool and drain for another hour. Then loosely knot the cheesecloth, squeeze out the paneer well, unknot the cloth, and knead the cheese a half-dozen times. Press it with your hands into a small clean baking or bread pan. Cover and cool it in the refrigerator for 5 - 8 hours. Use immediately, makes about six ounces.

Pippali: Indian long pepper, good for stimulating digestion and rejuvenation. Indian groceries and Ayurvedic centers are places to look for it.

Pitta: fire-water *dosha* or constitution.

Prabhau: the specific action or special potency of an herb or food, beyond any general rules which might apply to it.

Prana: the vital life force in the universe.

Pranayama: a simple daily breathing process, potent in balancing energy and health.

Prakruti: primal nature; also, our biological constitution, determined at birth.

Prapaka: normal process of digestion, proceeding through different stages of transformation and releasing excess *doshas* as wastes.

Prasad: blessed food.

Prithvi: earth, the element.

Rajas: a quality of mind which evokes energy and action. The need to create.

Rajasic: a food or activity which promotes *rajas*. Some examples are pickles, cheese, garlic, peppers.

Rakta: blood tissue, one of the *dhatus*.

Rakta Moksha: ancient *Pancha Karma* practice of blood letting. Favored in *Sushruta* and not in *Charaka*.

Ram: god-hero of the Ramayana, an Indian epic.

Rasa: taste. Also feeling. Also one of the *dhatus*, related to plasma and lymph.

Rasayana: a rejuvenative food which promotes longevity. Calmyrna figs are one example.

Ricotta: a soft cheese which can be made relatively easily at home. Follow the instructions for *paneer* here in the glossary, stopping before the final squeezing and kneading step, when the cheese has been draining in the colander for an hour. Ricotta has similar nutritional dynamics to *paneer*, but is a little lighter and easier to digest, and even better for *Vata*. This recipe makes about six ounces; the ricotta should be used immediately. Make a double batch if you are using it in Creamy Oregano Pasta Sauce.

Rig Veda: most ancient scripture of India.

Rishis: Indian sages of antiquity, guiding lights of Ayurveda.

Rock salt: stimulates digestive fire, used often in Ayurvedic herbal preparations. More effective for this purpose than sea salt or other salts. Can often be found in Indian groceries, sometimes under the label "black salt".

Ruksha: dry.

Sadhana: spiritual practice.

Saffron: a lovely (and costly) yellow spice which is calming to all three *doshas*. It is usually not heated; added at the end of a dish. *Sattvic*.

Samkya: a school of philosophy which has much influenced Ayurvedic medicine.

Sandra: dense.

Sattva: a quality of mind which evokes clarity, harmony and balance. The need to wake up and imagine.

Sattvic: a food or practice which promotes *sattva*. Most fresh fruits, vegetables, grains, and beans are *sattvic*.

Sesame tahini: ground sesame seeds, best purchased as raw tahini. Rich in calcium, B vitamins and iron, warming and grounding. Especially good for *Vata*, fine in small amounts for *Pitta* and *Kapha*. I prefer the bottled varieties to the canned ones, available in Middle Eastern or natural groceries.

Shiitaake mushrooms: available fresh or dried, the classic Chinese black mushroom, in Asian or natural food stores.

Shukra: male reproductive tissue, one of the *dhatus*.

Sita: cool (in temperature or action, like the moon). Also, goddess-consort of Ram.

Slakshna: slimy.

Snigda: oily.

Soy milk: a beverage made freshly from soy beans. Can be homemade or purchased packaged. As Edensoy has aptly pointed out, "low-fat" soy milks are often a hype; they are just regular soy milks diluted with water, which you can do yourself at home. Packaged soy milks will be more *rajasic* than fresh ones.

Srota: a vital channel in Ayurvedic anatomy for the movement of energy through the body. Varies in size from minute to substantial.

Sthira: static.

Sthula: gross.

Sucanat: an organic evaporated sugar cane juice, similar in texture and flavor to brown sugar, but more pure. Pricey, but a good transition sweetener if you're just beginning to wean yourself of sugar products. It would not be used on a regular basis in a healing Ayurvedic diet; it is more appropriate for special occasions.

Sukshma: subtle.

Sushrut Samhita: one of the three great Ayurvedic classics still available today, written in about 600 B.C., with much information from a surgical perspective.

Swedana: an Ayurvedic therapy preparatory to *Pancha Karma*. Consists of sudation, the stimulation of sweating, to begin to move *ama* so that it can be removed from the body.

Tamarind: a sour tasting bean paste sold in Indian groceries.

Tamas: a quality of mind which evokes darkness, inertia, resistance, and grounding. The need to stop.

Tamasic: a food or activity which promotes *tamas*. Some examples include frozen food, microwaved food and fried food.

Tejas: the essence of cosmic fire underlying mental activity, which is transmitted through *ojas* to the digestive tract.

Tikta: bitter (in taste).

Tofu: a bland white curdled soybean product, which can be made freshly or bought in packages, usually refrigerated, in the produce or refrigerator sections of natural groceries, Asian food stores, or supermarkets. Used occasionally in American Ayurvedic cuisine.

Tor dal: a yellow Indian *dal* that looks a lot like yellow split peas. It is also known as *toovar dal* or *arhar dal*. It is quite aggravating to *Pitta* and inflammatory conditions.

Tridosha: the three *doshas* as they work together, *Vata, Pitta* and *Kapha*.

Tridoshic: substances or practices which calm all three *doshas*. Examples would include foods such as *basmati* rice, asparagus, *kichadi*, and ghee, or a practice like *Pranayama*.

Triphala: a helpful Ayurvedic herbal combination for cleansing and rejuvenation. Available in Ayurvedic centers and in some herb stores.

Tulsi basil: holy basil, much honored in India. It is easy to grow from seed, and now can sometimes be found in the potted herb section of American nurseries. It is a cousin of Italian sweet basil, but has a distinctly different flavor.

Turmeric: common brightly colored yellow spice, very helpful for purifying the blood and assisting in the digestion of proteins.

Urud dal: split and hulled, this is ivory colored. It comes from a small bean which is black on the outside when whole, known as black lentil or black gram. *Urud dal* has a distinctive aroma and is warm and grounding; it is specific for calming *Vata* when used in small amounts. Can be found in Indian groceries.

Ushna: hot (in temperature or action).

Vagbhata: authors of the third great Ayurvedic classic, *Ashtanga Hridaya* and *Ashtanga Samgraha*. This text has just recently become available in the West in English.

Vaidya: an Ayurvedic physician.

Vamana: one of the *Pancha Karma* practices, specific for eliminating excess *Kapha*. It entails therapeutic vomiting under the supervision of a physician.

Vanillas: vanilla flavor can now be obtained in an alcohol-free version. Frontier Natural produces one with glycerin, which is beginning to be available in natural foods stores.

Vata: air-ether *dosha* or constitution.

Vayu: air, the element.

Vedas: the four ancient scriptures of India.

Vikruti: the current imbalance of *doshas* within the body, leading to discomfort or illness. This needs to be dealt with first in Ayurvedic healing, before working with one's *prakruti* or constitution.

Vipak: the post-digestive effect of an herb or food after it has been completely metabolized within the body. Usually Ayurvedic practitioners work with three *vipaks*, sweet, sour and pungent. In this final transformation, the *doshas* are used by the body to nourish the *dhatus*.

Virechana: one of the *Pancha Karma* practices, especially useful for excess *Pitta dosha*. It entails purgation therapy.

Virya: the action of a food or herb and its effect on the digestive system. Usually *virya* is heating or cooling in action.

Vishada: clear.

Vishwabhesaj: the universal medicine, ginger.

Yoga of High Altitude Baking: if you live at 5,000 feet or above, you need to reduce the amount of baking powder or soda used in these recipes. Reducing one teaspoon of leavening to a scant teaspoon usually works fine. If a great reduction is needed, it is specifically stated within the given recipes. I strongly prefer aluminum-free baking powders in terms of health and safety.

Yogurt: is a cultured milk product, usually made from cow's milk. It is considered fermented. To make your own fresh yogurt, bring 3 cups of fresh raw cow's milk to a boil, boil for one-half to one minute or more, remove from heat and let it cool at room temperature. Stir in 4 ounces (1/2 cup) of yogurt with active L. acidophilus cultures; mix well with a wooden spoon. Cover the milk-yogurt mixture (in a glass bowl with a lid works well) and incubate in a warm place, near a heater, or in the stove with the pilot light on, or wrapped in a down sleeping bag. In 36-48 hours the yogurt will be ready. You can also purchase yogurt makers which provide their own containers and heating unit. Soy yogurt can be made in exactly the same way, using soy milk and commercial soy yogurt cultures, or using a cow's milk yogurt as the "starter" culture.

APPENDIX IX:
Bibliography

Ballentine, Rudolph, M. D., *Diet and Nutrition: A Holistic Approach*, The Himalayan International Institute, Honesdale, Pennsylvania, 1978. Good introduction to Western nutrition, from a physician who also understands Ayurveda.

Banchek, Linda, *Cooking for Life: Ayurvedic Recipes for Good Food and Good Health*, Harmony Books, New York, 1989. Neat book, one of the few available on Ayurvedic cooking before 1994. Good treatment of tastes; with a more traditional East Indian approach to foods.

Begley, Sharon, with Daniel Glick, "The Estrogen Complex", *Newsweek*, March 21, 1994.

Beifuss, Joel, "Killer Beef", *In These Times*, Volume 17, Number 14, May 31, 1993.

Bubel, Mike and Nancy, *Root Cellaring: Natural Cold Storage of Fruits and Vegetables*, Storey Communications, Inc., Pownal, VT.,1991. Fine book about healthy ways to store produce.

Buist, Robert, Ph.D., *Food Chemical Sensitivity: What it is and how to cope with it*, Harper and Row Publishers, Sydney, Australia, 1986. Much good information.

Buist, Robert, Ph.D., *Food Intolerance: What it is and how to cope with it*, Prism Press, Bridport, Dorset, U. K.,1984. Distributed in the U. S. by Avery Publishing Group.

Caggiano, Biba, *Northern Italian Cooking*, HP Books, Inc., Tucson, Arizona, 1981. Really delicious Italian cooking, omnivorous. Good for ideas for vegetarian offerings.

Caraka Samhita, translated by Dr. R. K. Sharma and Vaidya Bhagwan Dash, volumes I, II, and III, Chowkanbe Sanskrit Series Office, Varanasi, India, 1976. The classic Ayurvedic medical texts, essential reference for the serious practitioner.

Chopra, Deepak, M. D., *Perfect Health: The Complete Mind/Body Guide*, Harmony Books, New York, 1991. Good clear introduction to basic Ayurvedic concepts and practice, with many inspired analogies for the Western reader.

Colbin, Annemarie, *Food and Healing*, Ballantine Books, New York, 1986. Excellent treatment of how food affects body and energy.

Colbin, Annemarie, *The Book of Whole Meals*, Ballantine Books, New York, 1983. Very good vegetarian cookbook from a macrobiotic and seasonal perspective.

Coleman, Eliot, *The New Organic Grower's Four-Season Harvest*, Chelsea Green Publishing Company, Post Mills, Vermont, 1992. Inspiring book about growing fresh food and working with the seasons, wherever you are.

Dunham, Carroll and Ian Baker, with photographs by Thomas L. Kelly and foreword by the Dalai Lama, *Tibet: Reflections from the Wheel of Life*, Abbeville Press, New York, 1993.

Frawley, David, O.M.D., *Ayurvedic Healing: A Comprehensive Guide*, Passage Press, Salt Lake City, Utah, 1989. Excellent.

Frawley, David, *The Astrology of Seers: A Comprehensive Guide to Vedic Astrology*, Passage Press, Salt Lake City, Utah, 1990. The chief presentation in the West of Vedic or Hindu Astrology. I found the discussion of planetary periods especially interesting as they relate to health and changing experiences of life.

Galland, Leo, M.D. with Dian Dincin Buchman,Ph.D., *Superimmunity for Kids*, Delta, Copestone Press, Inc., now published by Dell Publishing, New York, 1988. Thorough, readable coverage of the latest Western approaches in nutrition for kids.

Garde, Dr. R. K., *Ayurveda for Health and Long Life*, D.B. Taraporevala Sons and Co. Private Ltd., Bombay, 1975. Good history and perspectives.

Glendinning, Chellis, *When Technology Wounds*, William Morrow, New York, 1990. Pioneering work.

Glenn, Camille, *The Heritage of Southern Cooking*, Workman Publishing, New York, 1986. My favorite Southern cook.

Hagler, Louise, editor of the revised edition of *The Farm Vegetarian Cookbook*, The Book Publishing Company, Summertown, Tennessee, 1978.

Heyn, Birgit, *Ayurvedic Medicine*, translated by D. Louch, Thorsons Publishing Group, Rochester, Vermont, 1987. An introduction by a German pharmacist which I have appreciated more and more with each passing year.

Jaffrey, Madhur, *World of the East Vegetarian Cooking*, Alfred A. Knopf, New York, 1989. Such a good cook.

Johari, Harish, *The Healing Cuisine: India's Art of Ayurvedic Cooking*, Healing Arts Press, Rochester, Vermont, 1994. New release.

Jones, Marjorie Hurt, R.N., *The Allergy Self-Help Cookbook: Over 325 natural foods recipes, free of wheat, milk, eggs, corn, yeast, sugar and other common food allergens*, Rodale Press, Emmaus, Pennsylvania, 1984. She is a tremendously creative cook, who also gives comprehensive coverage to rotation diets, common environmental hazards, and other health concerns.

Joshi, Dr. Shalmali, lecture and conversations, April 1994, Santa Fe, New Mexico.

Joshi, Dr. Sunil, lectures and conversations, 1992-1994, Santa Fe, New Mexico.

Kane, Patricia, Ph.D., *Food Makes the Difference: A Parent's Guide to Raising a Healthy Child*, Simon and Schuster, New York, 1985. More good info on pediatric nutrition, rotations, and food allergies.

Kroeger, Hanna, *Allergy Baking Recipes*, Johnson Publishing Company, Boulder, Colorado, 1976. Many good options in a small booklet, from a nutritional pioneer.

Krohn, Jacqueline, M.D., *The Whole Way to Allergy Relief and Prevention*, Hartley and Marks, Point Roberts, Washington, 1991.

Lad, Dr. Vasant, *Ayurveda: The Science of Self-Healing*, Lotus Press, Twin Lakes, Wisconsin, 1984. A pioneering work, the first introduction for many of us here in the West to Ayurveda, from a practicing *vaidya*. Much excellent information.

Lad, Usha and Vasant, *Ayurvedic Cooking for Self-Healing*, Ayurvedic Press, Albuquerque, New Mexico, 1994. New release.

Drs. Vasant Lad and Frawley, David, *The Yoga of Herbs: An Ayurvedic Guide to Herbal Medicine*, Lotus Press, Twin Lakes, Wisconsin, 1986. Very fine resource on Ayurvedic use of herbs in the West, filled with essential info for the Ayurvedic cook.

Madison, Deborah with Edward Espe Brown, *The Greens Cook Book: Extraordinary Vegetarian Cuisine from the Celebrated Restaurant*, Bantam Books, New York, 1987. Very lovely. Light, refined, inspired cooking.

Mander, Jerry, *In the Absence of the Sacred: The Failure of Technology and the Survival of the Indian Nations*, Sierra Club Books, San Francisco, 1991. As Peter Matthiessen says on the back cover, "An exceptionally lucid and intelligent presentation of the urgent need to change the direction of our culture before we no longer have a choice." If you want to wake up, this is the one to read.

Moore, Michael, *Medicinal Plants of the Mountain West*, Museum of New Mexico Press, Santa Fe, New Mexico, 1979.

Moore, Michael, *Medicinal Plants of the Desert and Canyon West*, Museum of New Mexico, Santa Fe, New Mexico, 1989.

Moore, Michael, *Medicinal Plants of the Pacific West*, Red Crane Books, Santa Fe, New Mexico, 1993. Fine herbalist.

The Moosewood Collective, *Sundays at Moosewood Restaurant*, Simon and Schuster Inc., New York, 1990. Wide variety of interesting approaches to vegetarian cuisine.

Morningstar, Amadea with Urmila Desai, *The Ayurvedic Cookbook: A Personalized Guide to Good Nutrition and Health*, Lotus Press, Twin Lakes, Wisconsin, 1990. A lot of good information about Ayurvedic cooking as it applies to specific foods and constitutional types. A great book with lots of delicious recipes.

The Murrieta Foundation, *Murrieta Hot Springs Vegetarian Cookbook*, Revised and Expanded, The Book Publishing Company, Summertown, Tennessee, 1987. Primary work about cooking for polarity therapy, with lots of good recipes.

Nadkarni, Dr. K. M., *Indian Materia Medica*, Volumes I and II, Popular Prakashan Private Ltd., Bombay, 1976. Extensive information on Indian herbs, from Ayurvedic, Unani, Siddha medical, and Western pharmaceutical perspectives.

"Panel: Beef No Longer Safe, Radiation Recommended", *Newsday* release to *The Santa Fe New Mexican*, July 14, 1994.

Ram Dass, *Miracle of Love: Stories about Neem Karoli Baba*, E. P. Dutton, New York, 1979.

Robertson, Laurel, and Carol Flinders and Bronwen Godfrey, *Laurel's Kitchen*, Bantam Books with Nilgiri Press, Petaluma, California, 1976. Great, sane, well-balanced vegetarian food.

Rombauer, Irma S. and Marion R. Becker, *The Joy of Cooking*, The Bobbs-Merrill Company, Inc., New York, 1952. The American classic.

Rosso, Julee and Sheila Lukins with Michael McLaughlin, *The Silver Palate Cookbook*, Workman Publishing, New York, 1982. The new American classic! Their *New Basics* cookbook is good, too.

Sachs, Melanie, *Ayurvedic Beauty Care*, Lotus Press, Twin Lakes, Wisconsin, 1994. Includes a great bodywork process for enhancing circulation.

Sands, Brinna B., *The King Arthur Flour 200th Anniversary Cookbook*, Countryman Press, Woodstock, Vermont, revised edition, 1991. "Dedicated to the pure joy of baking." If you're curious about how to make everything from graham crackers to pot pies, this is a delightful one to check out. All about wheat.

Seeds of Change, 1994 catalog, Santa Fe, New Mexico. Fine collection of writing about biodiversity and environmental restoration.

Shannon, Sara, *Diet for the Atomic Age: How to Protect Yourself from Low-Level Radiation*, Avery Publishing Group Inc., Wayne, New Jersey, 1987. My source of information about miso. Covers many other foods as well.

Sharma, Professor P.V., *Introduction to Dravaguna (Indian Pharmacology)*, Chaukhambha Orientalia, Varanasi, India, 1976. Very helpful book.

Sills, Franklyn, *The Polarity Process*, Element Books, Longmead, England, 1989. Clear, well-written description of Dr. Randolph Stone's Polarity Therapy, with a good amount of information about polarity nutrition and the five elements.

Smith, Gar, "The Trouble with Beef", *Earth Island Journal*, Volume 8, Number 2, Spring 1993.

Smith, James Payne, Jr., *Vascular Plant Families: An Introduction to the Families of Vascular Plants Native to North America and Selected Families of Ornamental or Economic Importance*, Mad River Press, Inc., Eureka, California, 1977.

Steinman, David, *Diet for a Poisoned Planet: How to Choose Safe Foods for You and Your Family*, Ballantine Books, New York, 1990. Includes specific discussions of many foods.

Stone, Randolph, D.O.,D.C., *Health Building: The Conscious Art of Living Well*, CRCS Publications, Sebastopol, California, 1985. A popular intro for lay people.

Stone, Randolph, D.O.,D.C., *Polarity Therapy*, Volumes I and II, CRCS Publications, Sebastopol, California, 1986, published posthumously.

Sushruta Samhita, Volumes I, II and III, translated by K. L. Bhishagratna, Chowkhamba Sanskrit Series Office, Varanasi, 1981. Classic Ayurvedic medical texts, with a strong focus on surgery.

Svoboda, Dr. Robert E., *Ayurveda: Life, Health and Longevity*, Arkana, Penguin Books, 1992. Lots of good information and clear perspectives.

Svoboda, Dr. Robert E., *Prakruti: Your Ayurvedic Constitution*, Geocom, Albuquerque, New Mexico, 1988. Beautifully written, clear book on this topic.

TALONS, Environ-Mental Eco-Action Newsrap, Peter Cummings, editor, Route 4, Box 79 C, Santa Fe, New Mexico, 87501.

Tiwari, Maya, *Ayurveda, A Life of Balance: The Complete Guide to Ayurvedic Nutrition and Body Types with Recipes*, Healing Arts Press, Rochester, Vermont, 1995. New release.

Vegetarian Times, monthly issues, editorial offices at P.O. Box 570, Oak Park, Illinois, 60303. Good source of information about vegetarian issues and vegetarian cooking.

Walker, N.W.,D.Sc., *Fresh Vegetable and Fruit Juices*, Norwalk Press, Prescott, Arizona, 1970.

Wood, Rebecca, *Quinoa the Supergrain: Ancient Food for Today*, Japan Publications, Inc., distributed through Harper and Row, New York, 1989.

INDEX

H

SHIVARATRI, 1994

When Shiva comes dancing with heavy feet
through your life
laughing and singing and tearing off your blankets
leaving you naked and afraid
remember if you can he is your friend.
He is waking you up - or trying to.
When he smears ashes on your forehead and screams in your face
if you can, remember he is your Friend.
And when he comes slapping his thighs stealing your fruit
scratching his ass and
dancing dancing
in his hairy monkey god form
remember if you can
Shiva is your friend.

Jai Jai Shiva Ki Jay

Sources of Supply:

The following companies have an extensive selection of useful products and a long track-record of fulfillment. They have natural body care, aromatherapy, flower essences, crystals and tumbled stones, homeopathy, herbal products, vitamins and supplements, videos, books, audio tapes, candles, incense and bulk herbs, teas, massage tools and products and numerous alternative health items across a wide range of categories.

WHOLESALE:

Wholesale suppliers sell to stores and practitioners, not to individual consumers buying for their own personal use. Individual consumers should contact the RETAIL supplier listed below. Wholesale accounts should contact with business name, resale number or practitioner license in order to obtain a wholesale catalog and set up an account.

Lotus Light Enterprises, Inc.

P O Box 1008 ACW
Silver Lake, WI 53170 USA
414 889 8501 (phone)
414 889 8591 (fax)
800 548 3824 (toll free order line)

RETAIL:

Retail suppliers provide products by mail order direct to consumers for their personal use. Stores or practitioners should contact the wholesale supplier listed above.

Internatural

33719 116th Street ACW
Twin Lakes, WI 53181 USA
800 643 4221 (toll free order line)
414 889 8581 office phone
WEB SITE: www.internatural.com

Web site includes an extensive annotated catalog of more than 7000 products that can be ordered "on line" for your convenience 24 hours a day, 7 days a week.